Poor Women and Children in the European Past

Women and children have always featured prominently among the critically disadvantaged. They have been the persistently dominant clientele of welfare agencies. This original collection provides a comparative survey of the poverty experienced by women and children in the European past by testing the applicability of the concept of the poverty life cycle. Among the issues raised in the editors' perceptive and wide-ranging introduction are the distinctive nature of women's poverty over the life cycle, the relationship between family and demographic systems and the level of poverty, and the relative generosity of public and private charity provided by a range of European societies.

The chronological and geographical coverage of the work is uniquely broad. It extends from the middle ages to the early twentieth century, with chapters on Denmark, England, France, Iceland, Italy, Ireland and Spain, demonstrating wide differences in the systems of charity. In southern Europe relief was usually filtered through large institutions such as orphanages and hospitals, whereas in north-western Europe there was a greater emphasis on out-relief. Nevertheless in all societies, children, women who never married and widows required the particular attention of the relief agencies. Even so, few in any society were totally dependent on official charity. They survived by a combination of meagre earnings and formal and informal support networks. Equally, it was unusual for the poor in the past to depend entirely on the support of either their families or the state. This finding has serious implications for policy making in the twentieth century.

Poor Women and Children in the European Past will be of significant interest to historians of medieval, early modern and industrial Europe, sociologists and social scientists. The book provides an invaluable guide to the construction of welfare systems past and present and the fate of those women and children who were disadvantaged by demographic circumstances, economic pressures and social prejudice.

John Henderson is Senior Research Fellow of the Wellcome Unit for the History of Medicine and Fellow of Wolfson College, both in the University of Cambridge. His publications include *Piety and Charity in Late Medieval Florence* (1994). **Richard Wall** is Senior Researcher in the Faculty of History in the University of Cambridge and of the Cambridge Group for the History of Population and Social Structure. He is the co-editor of many books, including *The Upheaval of War: Family, Work and Welfare in Europe, 1914–1918* (1988).

Poor Women and Children in the European Past

Edited by
John Henderson and Richard Wall

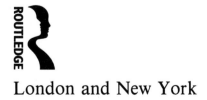

London and New York

First published 1994
by Routledge
11 New Fetter Lane, London EC4P 4EE

Simultaneously published in the USA and Canada
by Routledge
29 West 35th Street, New York, NY 10001

Typeset in Times by
Pat and Anne Murphy, Highcliffe-on-Sea, Dorset

Printed and bound in Great Britain by
TJ Press (Padstow) Ltd, Padstow, Cornwall

British Library Cataloguing in Publication Data
A catalogue record for this book is available from the
British Library.

Library of Congress Cataloging in Publication Data
Poor women and children in the European past/edited by
  John Henderson and Richard Wall.
    p. cm.
  Includes bibliographical references and index.
  1. Poor women – Europe – History. 2. Poor children –
  Europe – History. 3. Child welfare – Europe – History.
  I. Henderson, John   II. Wall, Richard
HV4084.A3P66 1994
305.5′69′094–dc20   93-47314

ISBN 0–415–07716–8

Contents

Figures and tables

Contributors

Joanna Bourke, Department of History, Birkbeck College, London.

Elaine Clark, Department of Social Sciences, University of Michigan-Dearborn, Michigan.

Philip Gavitt, Department of History, St Louis University, St Louis, Missouri.

Gísli Ágúst Gunnlaugsson, Institute of History, University of Iceland.

Loftur Guttormsson, Department of History and Sociology, University College of Education, Iceland.

John Henderson, Wellcome Unit for the History of Medicine, Cambridge University, Cambridge.

Volker Hunecke, Institut für Geschichtswissenschaft, Technische Universität Berlin, Berlin.

Hans Chr. Johansen, Historisk Institut, Odense Universitet, Odense.

Antoine Marchini, Université de Nice – URA, 1346, CNRS, Aix-en-Provence.

Sonya O. Rose, Department of History, University of Michigan, Ann Arbor, Michigan.

Thomas Sokoll, Arbeitsbereich Ältere Geschichte, Fern Universität, Hagen.

Eugenio Sonnino, Dipartimento di Scienze Demografiche, Università degli Studi di Roma 'La Sapienza', Rome.

Lola Valverde, Departamento de Historia Contemporanea, Universidad del Pais Vasco, Spain.

David E. Vassberg, Department of History and Philosophy, University of Texas, Pan American, Texas.

Pier Paolo Viazzo, Istituto degli Innocenti, Florence.

Richard Wall, ESRC Cambridge Group for the History of Population and Social Structure, Cambridge.

Introduction

John Henderson and Richard Wall

This collection of essays considers the impact of poverty on the lives of women and children in a variety of European societies from the middle ages to the late nineteenth century. Despite the diversity of populations surveyed and the length of time, the effect of poverty on women and children has remained a popular theme of the polemics of social and religious reformers over the whole period and is still a burning issue today. However, when assessing the impact of these ideas on social policy it is necessary to consider them both within the wider context of shifting attitudes towards the poor in general and in relation to different economic and demographic regimes. This will enable us to begin to sort out how far the records of poor relief agencies, one of our main sources of information about the poor, identify all persons in need, or simply those who met certain limited requirements of moral and social respectability.

Changing views about which groups of society were more or less deserving of charity have often made it difficult to compare the typology of poverty from one period to another. Historians have therefore followed a number of paths, principal among which have been various attempts at measuring the extent or depth of poverty in different societies. In this introduction we shall review the variety of ways in which poverty may be defined before moving on to consider the extent of the variation in poverty over the course of the life cycle of the individual, the relationship between the extent of poverty and the nature of the family system, the question of whether there is a distinct life cycle profile to female poverty, and, finally, the division of responsibility between the family and the community in the provision of care to the needy.

I   THE CALCULATION OF THE PROPORTION OF THE POPULATION IN POVERTY

Both absolutist and relativist definitions of poverty can be found in the literature dealing with the circumstances of the 'poor'.[1] Poverty may be measured in an absolute sense by establishing a standard poverty line that can be applied to different populations, as in the calculation of the proportion of the population unable to satisfy their basic requirement in terms of food. People may also be classed as poor if they behave in a way that we associate with being poor. Typically, they may spend a high proportion of their budget on food or minimize their expenditure on luxuries. Alternatively, a relativist definition of poverty may be adopted by setting some arbitrary poverty line such as the selection of a given percentage at the lower end of the income distribution (5, 10, 20 or even 30 per cent cut-offs would be possible) as constituting 'the poor'. A third option is to favour a cultural definition of poverty. On this basis, people are poor if they either feel themselves to be poor or are viewed by others as poor. Definitions of poverty which originate with authorities charged with supporting the needy are also 'cultural' to the extent that they reflect the decisions of these authorities about who they felt was worthy of support.

No single definition can be considered totally satisfactory. Taking first the absolutist definition, it can be shown that even the calculation of how much food a given family requires is fraught with difficulty as needs change with age and the nature of daily activities as, for example, when people enter or leave the workforce, or simply move between occupations demanding a greater or lesser degree of physical effort.[2] Furthermore, the absolutist definition of poverty relies on optimistic assumptions about the ability of consumers to locate and select the 'essential' items of food appropriate to their level of income. The absolutist definition also renders difficult comparisons of the incidence of poverty at different points in time as economic growth raises living standards and renders obsolete earlier definitions of poverty, at least in terms of contemporary perceptions.[3]

However, extending the absolutist definition to incorporate non-essential consumption does not really resolve these issues, while giving rise to a number of further problems. For example, what counts as luxury expenditure in one population at one point in time may not count as such in another. Similarly, just as improvements in the standard of living render obsolete the attempts to define poverty in terms of the proportion of the population lacking the basic means of subsistence, so do they create difficulties for definitions of poverty based on a high percentage of the family budget being devoted to the purchase of food. Only the poorest families, for example, in Seebohm Rowntree's survey of late nineteenth-century York were devoting close to 60 per cent of all their expenditure to the purchase of food.[4] High enough, one might think, yet the family budgets collected by Sir Frederick Eden in Bedfordshire and Cumberland in the late eighteenth century typically show more than two-thirds of all expenditure, sometimes more than 80 per cent of expenditure, being devoted to food.[5] This experience was shared by the poorer levels of society throughout late medieval and early modern Europe.[6] Few, indeed, of the labourers in Rowntree's survey would be considered poor according to a definition of poverty derived from the proportion of expenditure that the poor of late eighteenth-century England had to devote to the purchase of food.

Use of income and/or wealth distributions to measure relative poverty also runs into difficulties. Apart from the arbitrary nature of the decision as to whether the poorest 5 or 30 per cent are to be deemed 'poor', there is the problem that the percentage poor has to apply across all populations and time periods regardless of any material difference in the standard of living of the respective populations. An alternative approach is to hold constant a given standard of living and to calculate for different populations the proportion of their populations that are 'in poverty', but this again rests on the assumption that a definition of poverty applicable to one population can be transferred unmodified to another. There is a real danger, for example, of failing to detect an increase in 'perceived' poverty resulting from a growing disparity between the living standards of rich and poor in the society in question if living standards in a particular population improve and (relying on this definition of poverty) poverty therefore appears to decrease.

One method which has been adopted to measure the level of poverty is to examine fiscal records. For the later middle ages this is usually a matter of taking those classified by the authorities as *miserabili*, or those exempt as too poor to pay tax. Estimates vary from 30 to 50 per cent of the population in late medieval and early modern Europe.[7] While these sources may provide us with a rough and ready guide to the size of the poorer strata of society, this method has a number of disadvantages. One problem is that these records usually excluded anybody without a fixed place of residence, so that in an urban society where the population was often highly mobile the numerous people who lived on the fringes of society, such as beggars or even recent immigrants, would automatically have been excluded from the calculations. Perhaps a more grave exclusion is that fiscal surveys inevitably only reflected conditions at the time and place they were taken and therefore it is difficult to compare effectively one survey with another. Thus one survey might have been conducted when the economy was relatively prosperous and standards of living were high and another might have been during a depression or in a city recovering from the effects of a severe epidemic.

Shifting the perspective to consider perceptions of poverty, whether self-identification by the poor or the attitudes of the wealthy, choosing in other words a 'cultural' definition of poverty, may bring us a better understanding of what it was like to be poor. However, it has to be remembered that perceptions vary and may conflict with each other in certain cases. Often, such perceptions may relate individual experiences or, if applied more generally, be based on premises that we may feel reflect prejudice and ignorance rather than knowledge. Officially approved poverty lines suffer also from a further problem. Any arbitrary boundary between 'poor' and 'non-poor' can be expected both to leave a number of people above the poverty line whose standard of living is somewhat worse than that of a number who are classed as poor, and to correlate only imperfectly with contemporary views as to who in the society was 'really' poor. Regulations governing who is and who is not to be considered poor can be expected to be more generous in some places and times than in others, encompassing a broader or narrower spectrum of the population. For example, in the transition from the late medieval to the early modern poor relief systems there was an increased distinction drawn between the worthy and the unworthy poor.[8] As a rule regulations will be 'sticky' — less susceptible to change than are the circumstances of the poor which they are intended to alleviate.

One way out of the impasse created by conflicting definitions of poverty, each unsatisfactory when used in isolation, is to define poverty in all three ways and accept that absolutist, relativist and cultural definitions will result in the identification of different sections of the population as being 'poor'. The major loss with such an approach is the comparative perspective, for it makes for a complicated answer to straightforward questions, such as whether there is less poverty in one community than in another or whether poverty over time has diminished. There is, however, a major gain through applying a series of definitions of poverty: the abandonment of a simple dichotomy between poor and non-poor in favour of an emphasis on the various forms that poverty could assume in particular communities.

II   MEASUREMENT OF THE POVERTY LIFE CYCLE

Just as there are differing ways of measuring poverty, a variety of approaches have been adopted in order to measure the variation in the level of poverty over the course of the life cycle. Rowntree's now classic depiction of the poverty life cycle follows the experience of the individual with recurrent periods of poverty soon after birth, early in married life and again (and this time permanently) in old age.[9] It is sometimes assumed, quite erroneously, that such a pathway through life would hold for all at risk of falling into poverty, at least for all in the population of York at the end of the nineteenth century, regardless of gender, marital status, rank of birth or family circumstances. Such inferences do not follow. Potentially misleading comparisons can be made between Rowntree's poverty life cycle and a life cycle of poverty that is based on the experience of families and households, grouped according to the age of the family head. For adults in late middle age, the vast majority of whom would be heading households, the two measures might indicate approximately comparable proportions as 'poor', but quite large differences might appear during early adulthood and possibly during extreme old age, depending on how many individuals at these ages have households of their own.

Yet although Rowntree chose to illustrate the variation in poverty over the life cycle of the individual and not over the life time of the family, he did not view the individual in isolation. On the contrary, Rowntree's idea was that poverty varied with age not only because an individual could earn more at some ages than at others but because family circumstances also varied with age. An individual was less likely to be in poverty in late middle age because adult children were contributing to the household budget: poverty was more likely in old age because by then all the children had left the parental home. It is easy to see that the precise timing of the escape from poverty would depend critically on how soon children were able to enter the labour market and how quickly their earnings would rise towards adult levels. Also significant is the pace of departure from the parental home and whether children continued to make contributions to the parental budget following their departure.

Considerable variation in the nature of the poverty life cycle is to be anticipated then between one community and another and also between one economic sector and another, depending on the demand for labour. Variation in the incidence of poverty among the individuals of the same age belonging to different families is also likely according to whether parents had married early or late, their pattern of child-bearing, the gender of their children and how many of them survived through to working age. In addition, however, it has not always been fully appreciated that implicit in Rowntree's portrayal of the poverty life cycle is another assumption, namely, that all family members do indeed put all their earnings, or at least the largest part of them, into a common pool. The validity of the assumption, to our knowledge, has never been adequately tested, although some limited information is available on the pooling of incomes by family members who co-reside, and on the contributions from members of the family living elsewhere. For example, in a study of wage-earning families in New York in the first decade of the twentieth century, Louise Bollard Moore found that after the age of 18, sons would no longer hand over all their earnings to their parents.[10] For England, Booth noted at the end of the nineteenth century that some elderly parents received remittances from their unmarried children even when they had left the parental home.[11] Rowntree also made separate calculations of the income of the working-class families on the basis that daughters in service passed either their money wages or their total wages to their parents.[12] Should the elderly receive some assistance from non-resident children, poverty in old age would be less intense, and should some or all children not hand over most of their earnings to their parents, later middle age would be a less prosperous period in the life of an individual than is implied by Rowntree's sketch of the poverty life cycle.

The birth order of the children, even if the parents do not selectively invest in a particular child as their chosen heir, may also affect the child's well-being. For example, later born children will benefit if their older siblings do pass a major proportion of their earnings to their parents. An attempt to measure the effect of the presence of older siblings on the proportion of household income that can be assigned to a given child has been carried out based on a census of 1790 which provides information on the earnings of the inhabitants of Corfe Castle, Dorset, in the south-west of England. The assumptions used to translate earnings per head into income per head are fully set out by Wall in Chapter 15 below and require no further discussion here. In this exercise, the mother's age was used as a proxy measure of the probability of the presence of earning siblings, and it was discovered that the income of a child was higher when the mother was older than 45. The effect, however, was insignificant for children aged 1–4 (income 12–14d. per week when the mother was aged between 20 and 44, 15d. if the mother was over 45), but somewhat more marked for children aged 5–9 (income 12–13d. per week when their mothers were aged 20–44, 20d. if the mother was over 45).

The intensity of poverty at particular moments in the life cycle will also vary according to the level of expenditure required to support people of different ages. Most obviously, a child under the age of 4 will cost less to feed and clothe than, say, a child aged 12. Similarly, a family with three children aged between 5 and 14 will have a higher cost to face than a family with only two. Establishing what these extra costs might be has proved a considerably more complex task, since what parents actually spend on their children at different ages could be more a reflection of their general poverty than of the needs of their children, thereby introducing a dangerous circularity into the argument. Attempts to circumvent this problem have involved estimating the costs of children by measuring how much the presence of children in particular families depresses expenditure on items such as the consumption of tobacco and alcohol and adult clothing, compared with the amounts 'standard' childless couples expend.[13] This line of reasoning is not totally convincing. In the first place it has proved difficult to collect the necessary data (alcohol and tobacco consumption being under-reported in surveys while expenditure on clothing occurs only intermittently, requiring continuous monitoring of family budgets). Second, and more significantly, it has not been established whether the pattern of expenditure even on items that do not directly involve children is curtailed or simply modified because of the presence of a child in the family. For example, should families with young children spend less on entertainment, travel and drink than 'standard' childless families, this may be the result of their reduced mobility rather than of a reduced standard of living.

Apparently more 'independent' of expenditure patterns are the estimates that have been made of the dietary requirements of different age groups. A number of these schemes, contemporary or near-contemporary with Rowntree's work on poverty, including the estimates which Rowntree himself published, are summarized in Table 1.1, each being expressed as a certain proportion of what was thought to be necessary to sustain an adult male. Some problems, however, are fairly obvious. For example, large differences can occur between estimates and insufficient attention may be paid to the different dietary requirements of the two genders during childhood. A more serious underlying weakness is that Engel, one of the pioneers of this method of measuring nutritional requirements at a given age, derived his estimates from Quetelet's measurements of the height and weight of children and adolescents. Since the pace of growth during childhood and adolescence is largely determined by the nutritional status of the population, it would appear that the danger of circularity of argument is not avoided. Estimates of nutritional needs are derived from data that largely reflect nutritional intake. Another quite different problem is that nutritional needs will vary with the level and type of physical activity. Early employment of children, particularly if it involves fairly arduous physical labour, may not all be pure 'gain' either for the individual or for his or her family, if the result is that food consumption is increased.

Table 1.1 Index of dietary requirements by age and sex (calorific requirement of adult males = 100)

	Foley[1]	*Atwater*[2]	*United States Bureau of Labor*[3]	*Rowntree*[4]	*Engel*[5]
Father	100	100	100	100	100
Mother	60–80	80	90	80	86
Child 11–14	60	70–80	90	60	70
Child 7–10	—	50–60	75	50	57
Child 4–6	40	40	40	40	42
Child <3	20	30	30	30	37

Notes:
[1] Derived from David Davies, *Case of Labourers in Husbandry*, 1975, p. 161.
[2] United States Department of Agriculture, *Farmers' Bulletin*, 142, p. 33.
[3] Eighteenth Annual Report, 1903, p. 19.
[4] B.S. Rowntree, *Poverty: A Study of Town Life*, 1901, p. 229.
[5] F. Engel, *Die Lebenskosten Belgische Arbeiterfamilien*, 1895, and cf. his earlier study of budgets of Eden, Le Play and Ducéptiaux published in *Zeitschrift des Statischen Bureau des Königlichen Sächischter Ministeriums des Innerns*, 1857.

Source: Robert Coit Chapin, *The Standard of Living Among Workingmen's Families in New York City*, 1909, pp. 9, 15.

In practice it has proved necessary, in the absence of detailed information for most historical populations on the earnings and dietary requirements of different individuals, to estimate the degree of variation in the producer–consumer ratios over the course of the life of a household by using a set of simplifying assumptions. Christer Lundh has completed just such an exercise for households from one parish in southern Sweden between the mid-seventeenth and the mid-nineteenth centuries,[14] concluding that cottars had to wait nineteen years and that tenant farmers had to wait twenty-eight years on average to better the standard of living they had achieved on marriage. Although some of this advantage was later lost there is no indication that those farmers of Scania who survived into old age were particularly poor. Older cottars were much more prosperous on average than were cottars who were between six and thirteen years into their marriage. Both cottars and farmers appear to have escaped the descent into permanent and intense poverty which Rowntree identified in the urban working-class population of York at the end of the nineteenth century. Lundh's calculations suggest that the standard of living of these Scanian farmers reached its lowest point between five and sixteen years following their marriage when they were on average 13 per cent poorer than in their first year of marriage. By contrast, the living standards of the cottars declined more dramatically after five years of marriage to a level more than 20 per cent below the living standards achieved on marriage.

III POVERTY LEVELS AND THE EUROPEAN FAMILY SYSTEMS

Lundh's findings are also important because they indicate that a social group such as the farmers who could employ servants in periods of labour shortage and negotiate retirement contracts were not altogether able to avoid a decline in their standard of living during the early years of their marriage. It has been argued by Peter Laslett that life cycle poverty was particularly a feature of the nuclear family regime of north-west Europe where the practice of setting up an independent household on marriage coupled with live-in domestic and farm service left widows, the elderly and those who never married residentially isolated and in need of the support of the community through charity, official or unofficial, or, in England, the Poor Law.[15] Lundh provides a partial confirmation of Laslett's position as life cycle poverty was more intense for the cottars where parents and married children did not co-reside than for the farmers who did.

In the present volume the issue of the relationship between the incidence of poverty and the nature of the family system is taken up most directly by Paolo Viazzo. He argues that early marrying, high-fertility populations as found generally, though not universally, in southern Europe carried a considerably greater risk of poverty than did the later marrying, low-fertility populations of north-western Europe. This was because so many children died before they could contribute to the wealth of society and because of the higher dependency burden. Another critical question, also addressed by Viazzo, is whether the poor of southern Europe might have received a greater measure of support from their families, including non-resident relatives, than was the case in northern Europe. The evidence of this volume appears rather against this proposition as John Henderson, Eugenio Sonnino, Volker Hunecke, Lola Valverde and Philip Gavitt have each documented instances of substantial institutional support to the poor in a variety of forms and for a range of southern European populations from the fourteenth to the nineteenth centuries. The families of the poor had clearly been either unable or unwilling to provide this support.[16] In some instances there may have been no family. Yet it needs to be borne in mind that most of these contributions focus on children who were abandoned and that despite the visible presence of foundling hospitals in most of the large cities of southern Europe, and the amount of attention historians have given them, child abandonment remained very much a minority phenomenon even in Italy, as is made clear in section IV below.

There is, however, a further factor to consider. It has been suggested by Peter Laslett that when, as in north-west Europe, separate households were formed on marriage, more assistance may have been received from kin outside the household than would be the case in areas where more complex households prevailed, and some, at least, of the close kin actually co-resided.[17] One, admittedly limited, attempt to test this proposition, based on experiences of the inhabitants of a commune in Emilia-Romagna in the nineteenth century, found that, contrary to expectation, members of complex households had as many, if not more, kin resident in the same community as did members of simple family households.[18]

For the present the impact of the family system on the level of support the poor could derive from the families has to be considered unresolved and a different approach adopted. This involves an assessment of the value of the relief which state, church and private charity offered the poor within the context of a variety of family systems, and will be undertaken below in section VI. In the meantime we may conclude, with Paolo Viazzo, that even the family systems which favoured the formation of a high proportion of complex households could not entirely escape all life cycle induced poverty. Where parents were able to conclude a retirement contract with their children, other successors or even an institution,[19] or retain full control of their assets through into old age, some of the worst and permanent poverty which Rowntree identified among the old of late nineteenth-century York may have been avoided. It appears to have been much harder for such families to compensate for the inexorable rise in their costs in the years between marriage and the point when their eldest children began to make a substantial net contribution to the household economy. Stem family households, if they had for a time to carry the double burden of an elderly couple and an heir with a family of young children, may have been particularly hard hit.[20]

IV CHILDREN AND POVERTY

The topic of children's poverty relates most obviously to the question of the financial standing of their family. In some societies parents might abandon a child, at least temporarily, during a particular stage of their life cycle when their budgets were most under strain or the main breadwinner had suffered from an individual or a general economic crisis. But there is also an important moral question, how far did individual societies tolerate the rearing of illegitimate children by their own mothers?

Most of the evidence provided in this volume concerns foundlings. Three of the chapters deal with Italy and specifically with the situation in Florence, Milan and Rome. The foundling hospitals of southern Europe have in recent years become the focus of much historical interest. If one were to judge this phenomenon simply on the analysis of the earliest institutions in Italy, one might be forgiven for concluding that their importance has been exaggerated. Could one argue, for example, that the Ospedale degli Innocenti in Florence was made more famous by Brunelleschi's design than the number of children abandoned? At no point in the fifteenth century did admissions exceed 9 per cent of the annual baptismal rate and usually it was nearer 6 per cent. However, moving to the eighteenth and nineteenth centuries the picture changed dramatically: 38 per cent at the Innocenti between 1841 and 1850; 30–40 per cent in Milan; and between 10 and 30 per cent of children baptized in Paris between 1710 and 1780.[21] Yet although the impact of the abandonment of children on particular cities could be substantial, even when the institutions for the receipt of foundlings were as fully developed as in the 1840s in Tuscany, a maximum of 10 per cent of the children born in a given year would appear to have been abandoned to the care of a foundling hospital and rates of abandonment of 3 per cent of all newborn in Bologna and 6 per cent in the south of Italy were probably more typical, even in the first half of the nineteenth century.[22]

In the present volume Gavitt, Hunecke and Sonnino, although dealing with the foundlings of Florence, Milan and Rome between the fifteenth and nineteenth centuries, are nevertheless agreed that foundling hospitals were not simply dumping grounds for illegitimate children whom their parents abandoned to a rapid death as is often alleged.[23] Rather, while admitting that infant and child mortality was high, these authors assert that these institutions were regarded as one of the survival strategies of the poor. Legitimate children were frequently left in the *ruota*, or wheel, by parents who were in desperate financial straits and who hoped to reclaim their offspring when their circumstances improved. Indeed, the proportion reclaimed seems to have increased over the centuries in different parts of Europe. Within Italy the proportion of abandoned children reclaimed by their parents increased in Florence from about 6 per cent in the fifteenth century[24] to 72 per cent in the late eighteenth century, and in Rome from 19 per cent in the seventeenth to 39 per cent in the eighteenth century. Fifty-nine per cent of the children were reclaimed by their parents from the foundling hospitals of Milan in the mid-nineteenth century.[25] Recent work on eighteenth-century London has also noted instances of foundlings later reclaimed by their mothers and suggested that a major reason for the abandonment of children was not illegitimacy but the poverty of families with legitimate children.[26] But this desire to correct an historiographical misconception can go too far. The lens of the eighteenth and nineteenth centuries should not be allowed to distort our vision of the late medieval and early modern picture, as has happened more generally under the influence of Michel Foucault in the case of hospitals.[27] Recent studies of fifteenth-century Tuscany do show that the majority of abandoned children were illegitimate and that many were the result of the union between masters and their female servants or slaves.[28]

Nevertheless, if for some families in some parts of Europe child abandonment was little more than a way of getting rid of bastards, other families abandoned children as they needed, perhaps only temporarily, to reduce the number of dependants. This evidence also raises the question of the relationship between abandonment and the household and family forms of the societies at the centre of these studies. Whether we are discussing fifteenth- or eighteenth-century Florence, eighteenth- or nineteenth-century Milan or Rome, or eighteenth-century London, we are dealing with some of the most substantial cities of their period. These were cities, moreover, in which the households of the poor, at least as reflected in tax records and censuses, tended to be small and nucleated, where there was very high immigration and therefore the possibility of support from relatives was limited for families with larger than average numbers of children or where one or more adults was sick or unemployed.

The question which also arises at this point is how representative were these cities which experienced high rates of abandonment and catered for this phenomenon through the establishment of foundling hospitals? Lola Valverde's chapter is particularly relevant here as one of the few studies of southern Europe to examine the relationship between illegitimacy and abandonment in a rural environment.[29] She shows that in the sixteenth century in the Basque Country despite the high rate of illegitimacy there was a very low rate of abandonment. The explanation for this phenomenon is linked to both the household composition of the region and the prevailing moral climate. In this period there was a large number of extended and multiple family households which provided an environment suitable for the raising of children who in an urban environment would have been abandoned.

However, an association of low rates of abandonment with rural residence and extended family households should not be formulated into a rule over space and time. Much depends on geographical location. The area studied by Valverde was far from a foundling hospital. Even in the Basque region by the eighteenth century there was an increase in the rate of abandonment, as households became more nucleated. The same phenomenon appears to have been true in Tuscany, where the *mezzadria*, or sharecropping, system of farming was traditionally associated with a more complex household system. But again there are complicating factors. Florence had a very close relationship with its hinterland, or *contado*, so that many hospital patients, including the foundlings, came from the countryside, and possibly, as in early modern Emilia Romagna, landowners discouraged families from supporting too many 'unproductive consumers' in the form of children.[30]

But these differences do not simply stem from differences in rural/urban household composition or even the area's geographical location, but also more generally from the moral norms of individual societies. In the early modern Basque Country, for example, illegitimacy appears to have been acceptable to the local inhabitants and hence there was no stigma attached to the practice of keeping bastards at home. Much depended also on the position of the father. Many of these illegitimate children were the product of a union between a priest and his concubine, or of a mistress and a man who was sufficiently wealthy to afford to employ a servant. In both cases, apparently at least until the eighteenth century, this practice was sanctioned by society, which is portrayed as succumbing late to the influence of the Counter-Reformation.

More generally, as Hunecke argues, whether the presence of illegitimate children in the mother's household was accepted, or whether they were abandoned, was also governed to a large degree by two important factors: the legal provision for these offspring and attitudes towards unmarried mothers. Thus in the early modern Basque region the father was obliged to pay the mother for the maintenance of his children, but abandonment began to increase in the eighteenth century when these laws disappeared. The second point brings us on to the second main theme of this volume, the fate of poor women in the European past.

V POVERTY AND THE FEMALE LIFE CYCLE

One of the major omissions from Rowntree's sketch of the poverty life cycle was the failure to note that women and men might experience poverty at different points in their life cycle. The differences in the male and female experiences of poverty over the life cycle are highlighted by Richard Wall in Chapter 15 based on data on the earnings of the poorer inhabitants of Corfe Castle in the south-west of England in 1790. Within this particular population it appeared that women were a little younger than men when they first experienced poverty as adults. This was the inevitable consequence of their being younger on first marriage than their partners and is likely to hold true for most other societies, even those with a greater likelihood of parent and married children co-residing. In Corfe Castle it was also the case that women suffered the more abrupt decline into poverty in old age, a consequence on this occasion of the greater possibility that they would become widowed and see their living standards deteriorate more markedly with widowhood. Male earnings in this parish in many cases outstripped female earnings by a factor of seven to one and nearly always by a factor of three to one, and a widow on her own or with all her resident children under 18, after which age sons could anticipate receiving adult wages, would find it impossible to approach the standard of living that had been available throughout her married life. A considerable difference inevitably appeared between the income of women who were still married (or had remarried) and the income of women who had been widowed. It also follows that marriage was an economic necessity for a woman without property or assets of her own to support her standard of living, whereas marriage for men involved a decline in income as they came to share their higher earnings with a growing number of dependants.[31]

How far these findings for one English parish in the late eighteenth century may be of general applicability has yet to be determined. Irregular or relatively low earnings for males, particularly if women could earn relatively well, might cause women to view marriage less favourably.[32] On the other hand, it is evident that whenever there was a gross disparity in male and female earning power both widows and unmarried women who lived on their own and supported themselves from their own earnings were likely to be in poverty, although not necessarily in quite the straitened circumstances of the inhabitants of Corfe Castle, in which community the earnings differential between men and women appears to have been particularly high. Where such women were incorporated into, or remained within, more complex households, which was not the case in Corfe Castle, much of this poverty would have been alleviated. This assumes, of course, that the resources of these households were distributed according to need and not according to the income-generating power of the particular household member. On this point there is very little direct evidence, although when the resources of the household were stretched it is likely that few household members felt they had been fairly treated, as witnessed by the disputes that could break out when an unproductive farm was burdened by a retirement contract drawn up by the parents of the current head.[33] The old, the widowed and never-married who resided in complex households may therefore have been aware of their marginal position, even if their standard of living was higher than it would have been had they lived on their own.

At least in theory much of the poverty that affected so many women who never married or who were widowed could also have been alleviated by generous contributions from state and private charities. Most such agencies do indeed seem to have considered women as particularly deserving of support, except perhaps in the case of unmarried mothers, but it is doubtful whether that support ever went so far as to compensate entirely for the differential earning power of men and women.[34] Hans Chr. Johansen establishes below in Chapter 9 that poor relief provided to an unmarried woman in Denmark in the late eighteenth century represented between 6 and 26 per cent of the income of an unskilled labourer. Taking account of the likely differences in the size of their respective households (and assuming the single woman lived alone and that the labourer supported a household of four persons) it can be estimated that the support of the Poor Law would have yielded between 16 and 68 per cent of the labourer's net income.[35] The range of values reflect the fact that Poor Law allowances in Denmark increased in line with the age of the recipient. This would have helped alleviate some of the most intense poverty likely to be encountered over the course of the life cycle without, as we have seen, raising the standard of living of those women even to that of the poorest male worker whose own earnings often proved insufficient to maintain his family.[36]

In broad terms the situation in England would appear to have been similar. According to the evidence for Corfe Castle in 1790, an 'average' payment from the Poor Law of 2s. per week would double what most poor women could earn on their own but would give them no more than 28 per cent of the income of the poorly paid labourer, or about half allowing for the differences in family size.[37] As in Denmark, it was customary for payments to be varied according to need, in general rising with advancing age so that the worst effects of the poverty life cycle were alleviated, though without fully compensating women for the reduced income that resulted from the absence of an adult male.[38]

Two particularly vulnerable groups were unmarried mothers and widows. Leaving aside Lola Valverde's claim that in the Basque Country concubines were often an accepted part of local society, all contributors to this volume dealing with adult female poverty stress the vulnerability of women where children were born out of wedlock. As Clark and Johansen show, this was as true of the late medieval English countryside as of eighteenth-century Denmark. For the problem, as we have seen, stemmed not just from lack of funds, but also from the fact that they and their progeny were stigmatized as immoral and therefore less worthy of the support of society than legitimate children. Even without the stigma of unwanted illegitimate children, single women posed a moral and financial burden. Historians and anthropologists of southern Europe have long emphasized the importance of honour in Mediterranean countries, where women by themselves were seen as a potential threat to the moral fabric of society as possible temptresses of single and married men.[39]

Apart from this moral dimension, single women could often expect little financial security, particularly if they were at the botton of the social pile. One of the most important factors determining their vulnerability was the sex ratio of their community and the pool of potential husbands. In late medieval Florence, for example, although the sex ratio was quite favourable towards women (118), the wide age gap between spouses at first marriage (about twelve years) meant that the pool of eligible males for women aged 16 to 18 had shrunk considerably once men had reached the age of 30, their mean age at marriage.[40] The problem for females was also exacerbated by the very low rate of remarriage for women. Only at times of crisis did the age gap between spouses fall. Henderson, for example, has suggested in Chapter 7 that following the epidemics of the mid- to late fourteenth century, increased male immigration from the *contado* may have led to a larger number of rural men seeking Florentine wives.

Also in more modern north European societies, such as in Scandinavia and Ireland, where very different social, demographic and economic regimes prevailed, single women were financially disadvantaged. In eighteenth-century Denmark, as Johansen shows, the very high mobility of the urban populations explains why so many never-married women were on relief and had no family to support them. In rural areas farmers' daughters who did not marry fared somewhat better for many lived with relatives or even set up their own independent households. But country life did not necessarily guarantee security for the never-married, as can be seen in nineteenth-century Ireland. As in Italy, a woman was vulnerable if she or her father could not save enough money for a decent dowry.

The impact on the social and economic life of a society where a large proportion of women never married is also likely to have been considerable. In certain towns, such as early nineteenth-century Bruges, over a quarter of all women in their 50s had never married.[41] In Bruges, many of these women were lacemakers or sought different but poorly paid employment from day to day. They congregated in the poorest areas of the city, in houses where the majority of other occupants were women, widowed or unmarried, following similar trades. Within the whole of the south-east of Bruges there were only sixty adult males to every 100 females. The key positions within the city's labour force and within the social structure were of course occupied by men, but women provided the majority of the labour and through their predominance in the population dominated the social networks that underpinned the social structure.

Many of the chapters in the second half of this volume concentrate on the close connections between poverty and widowhood and offer a wide variety of evidence in terms of both financial and household status of widows. Looking first at southern Europe, the contributors that deal with Italy and Spain rightfully underline the importance of the role of the dowry as a significant aspect of the Mediterranean marriage system. The two interpretations of the position of women in general and widows in particular, however, do differ in their emphasis. Women in late medieval Florence have recently been represented as the victims of a male-dominated system. Even if in principle the dowry gave the widow some financial protection, it has been suggested that many poorer women did not necessarily benefit: some husbands squandered the dowries and some families failed to return the dowries to the widows. Alternatively the widow's own family could decide to retain the capital to reinvest to help the marriage of a younger sibling. The picture of women in sixteenth-century Castile as depicted by Vassberg is considerably more positive. Despite their legal and economic subservience to men, Castilian women played an important role in society, were recognized as household heads, controlled their own property, ran their own businesses and paid taxes. These two perspectives may stem from differences in the position of women in urban Italy and rural Spain, but they may also reflect differences in historiographical approaches. Thus studies of Florence have until recently[42] tended to emphasize the negative aspects of the position of women, legally, socially and economically.

This caveat to the negative view of the position of women in late medieval and early modern society does not detract from the basic conclusion of many studies throughout Europe, namely that widows always appeared in tax records as among the very poorest members of society.[43] As a corollary of this, widows also figured prominently as clients of welfare organizations, especially as they have been seen from well before the time of the Canonists as not just among the most vulnerable, but also as respectable members of society.[44] This was, as we have seen, in contrast to unmarried mothers, who were regarded as immoral and therefore less worthy of support. These distinctions between respectable and immoral were as true of the northern European studies in this volume, whether of early modern England, an eighteenth-century Danish city, a rural area in Iceland or nineteenth-century Ireland, as those of the Mediterranean.[45]

Despite the grim statistics which point to a close correlation between widowhood and poverty, we must beware of assuming that all widows lived in isolation. It is possible that over-reliance on tax records and, to a lesser extent, earnings, has distorted our vision of the living arrangements of the elderly. As we argued above in section III, while an elderly widow may technically have lived alone, it is possible that she may have lived in close proximity to her children, with whom she may have entered into a relationship of mutual benefit, receiving aid in cash or kind in exchange for help in their households.

VI FAMILY AND HOUSEHOLD STRUCTURES AND FORMAL SYSTEMS OF RELIEF

It is at this point that we return to one of the underlying themes of this volume, namely the relationship between family care and community care. Clearly there are many variables which affect how formal and informal systems of support intermesh, but one of the most important factors was the residence patterns of the poor.

We have already touched on the household structure of the poor in relation to abandonment. In their studies of Florence, Milan and Rome each of our authors has assumed a close connection between abandonment and household size. They argue that the smaller nuclear family households of the poor provided fewer possibilities for supporting extra mouths, an argument which is underlined by their contention – particularly from the seventeenth century onwards – that there was less association between abandonment and illegitimacy than has been believed in the past.

Small household size is also employed as the reason for the lack of support provided for widows in cities as far apart as late medieval Florence, seventeenth-century London and eighteenth-century Odense in Denmark.[46] Indeed, much of the more recent work which has been undertaken on the lower levels of society in early modern England has emphasized that the poor could not expect to be supported by their kin, but rather had to rely upon the community.[47] However, another more recent point of view is represented by the contribution of Sokoll. He argues that we must beware of assuming automatically that all widows suffered from residential isolation. He maintains that undue emphasis has been placed on one type of fiscal record, whereas the combination of more than one source, such as listings of inhabitants with 'pauper censuses', can reveal connections between households which had previously not been expected. On the basis of this evidence he shows that in late eighteenth- and early nineteenth-century Essex pauper households were no less complex than those of the rest of the population. Indeed, many of the widows in the market town of Braintree in 1821 tended to retain the headship of their households and live with their daughters. A similar pattern was also found by Sonya Rose in her study of two nineteenth-century industrial villages in Nottinghamshire. But she also emphasized that widows helped themselves through finding employment, especially in the textile industry of Arnold.

The difference between these two views of the pauper household – either nuclear or complex – may, as Sokoll has argued, stem from only a partial examination of fiscal records. However, a more comprehensive analysis needs to be undertaken of larger, urban communities than either of these two studies presented here for Essex or Nottinghamshire. Indeed, urban historians would probably need to be further convinced before accepting this argument for centres where the turnover of population was high, as in cities as large as London, Paris or Rome, or even smaller places such as Odense in eighteenth-century Denmark.

Perhaps we need also to think in more flexible terms, as indeed did the elderly poor in order to survive, and take our analysis beyond the simple child–parent relationship. Some suggestive evidence survives, for example, for late sixteenth-century Norwich. According to the 1570 Census of the Poor, while few elderly poor were discovered living with their children, there is evidence of grandchildren living with their grandparents or even unrelated orphans in the households of the elderly poor.[48] However, it is not just a question of a rural–urban dichotomy, but also, as we have seen, of more general demographic factors. The sex ratio is, for example, a very important determinant of the potential financial position of women. In a country like nineteenth-century Iceland, which was predominantly rural, Gunnlaugsson has shown that there was a very unequal sex ratio, with limited marriage prospects for women, leaving a high proportion of women as recipients of poor relief. More generally we should not forget to take into account one of the most crucial determinants of the levels of poverty in society: the dependency ratio. This calculation, which compares the total of the working population with the rest classified as 'dependent' because of their age, less than 15 or over 60/5, has often been ignored by historians of poor relief, who tend instead to concentrate exclusively on the health of the economy.[49]

All this, of course, raises the wider question concerning the significance of differences between the various institutional arrangements for relief over time and place. Perhaps one of the most striking differences between relief provided in northern and southern Europe, particularly in the late medieval and early modern periods, was the greater predominance of larger charitable institutions in Mediterranean Europe. Obviously this had much to do with precocious urban development in cities in the south. But this argument cannot be extended much beyond the sixteenth century when economic and demographic developments shifted north of the Alps. It was indeed in the sixteenth century that the differences between the poor relief systems of two of the main countries under consideration in this volume, England and Italy, began to be most apparent. Despite avowed English admiration for Italian models in charity and health care, Tudor regimes established few substantial institutions. Instead there emerged out of the ashes of the dissolved fraternities a remarkably coherent, nationwide system of out-relief, based on the parish. In contrast to many continental societies, in England the system was enshrined in law and financed by a tax on property at the parish level.[50]

An allied issue concerns differences throughout Europe in the scale of payments made to the poor in the form of out-relief aid to those poor who formed their own households and did not reside in an institution. It has been suggested by Jeremy Boulton that the degree of generosity involved in such payments may be measured in one of three ways. The first involves the calculation of the proportion of minimum subsistence needs met by the average amount of relief received by a pauper; the second a comparison of the relief given with the amounts paid against the full costs of board and lodging; and the third a comparison of the value of relief given per pauper with the earnings of lowest paid workers.[51] Using these measures, Boulton then concluded that the pensions paid to elderly paupers in late sixteenth-century London would have covered no more than between 35 and 58 per cent of the minimum subsistence needs of a childless and non-working widow, changing little in value over the course of the seventeenth century, and that in the early eighteenth century pensions provided less than two-thirds of what the same parish authorities paid when they boarded out a pauper.[52] Judged in relation to the prevailing wage rates of building labourers, pauper pensions offered about 20 per cent of the wages of a labourer in 1621, 10 per cent in 1644 and about 12–13 per cent thereafter. Taking account of the different average sizes of pauper and labouring households, Boulton calculated that these pensions were worth about 30 per cent of the labourers' weekly wage in 1607 and about 27 per cent in 1707, not far from the 33 per cent of working-class income which Hunt estimated pensions provided in 1837.[53]

Poor relief in London, therefore, can only have contributed a proportion of the resources that the poor needed for survival. Nor was the situation in London at all unusual in this respect. In 1790 in the parish of Corfe Castle in the south-west of England the poor used their meagre earnings to supplement a more generous contribution from the Poor Law of some 28 per cent of the earnings of a labourer from the same parish,[54] or about half taking account of the differences in family size. A century later a wider ranging survey of the rural poor by Charles Booth revealed that it was still the norm for the poor to derive their income from more than one source. According to Booth, under a quarter of the persons who were assisted by the Poor Law had no other sources of income. Of the remainder, a third received assistance from relatives, a further third were helped by other charitable agencies and 10 per cent were still earning or had savings or other assets that could generate a little income.[55]

Similar modest assistance from the state was accorded the poor in other countries in the north-west of Europe. Johansen suggests below in Chapter 9 that poor women in rural areas of Denmark at the end of the eighteenth century, who were treated less generously than those who lived in towns, received only a third of the minimum amount required for their subsistence. This is right at the lower end of the level of payments which Boulton suggested was achieved in London at the start of the seventeenth century. On the other hand, the amount of poor relief provided in Denmark measured in relation to the income of an unskilled labourer, ignoring differences in household size, ranged from less than a third of London payments to a level well above, and less than in rural Corfe Castle at the end of the eighteenth century. In the Netherlands and in Flanders poor relief in the early nineteenth century could also provide no more than a modest supplement to other sources of income. In Haarlem poor relief represented just 6 per cent of the earnings of an unskilled labourer, in Nijmegen 14 per cent, in Ghent between 2 and 20 per cent and in Antwerp less than 6 per cent.[56]

A number of these payments are again less than Boulton considers were provided in London in the seventeenth century and this has implications for the relationship that Peter Laslett has attempted to trace between the prevalence of nuclear family households and the provision of support to the disadvantaged both from non-resident members of their family and from the community in general through formal systems of poor relief (see above section III). In the first place it is evident that in those areas of north-west Europe for which information is currently available total dependence on formal relief was the exception rather than the rule. The poor must therefore have found other sources of income or endured a standard of living that could only end in premature death.[57] Second, however, as the amounts given out in poor relief were considerably more generous in some areas than others, there can be no clear and direct correlation between the custom of establishing an independent household on marriage, which held generally across north-west Europe, and the recognition of a common threshold of need beyond which assistance from the community was guaranteed.

While historians of poor relief have suggested that formal relief systems in north-west Europe enabled some households to retain their independence, there was clearly no uniformity; while in some areas relief was the main, but rarely the sole, source of income, in others it served as a minor source. If it is difficult to generalize about levels of relief across north-west Europe, even within a single country such as England where a uniform model was enshrined in law, how much more problematic it becomes to compare these systems with those further south. This has not, of course, prevented historians from making such comparisons, in which traditionally at least the Catholic south has suffered in comparison with the Protestant north.[58] Even if the validity of the religious divide in poor relief has now been exploded, there still remains a strong lobby which tends to see the amount of assistance provided by relief agencies further south as negligible. In Hufton's classic study of the poor in eighteenth-century France, formal relief is roundly declared as ubiquitously inadequate, regardless of the range of channels through which relief might be funnelled to the poor.[59] Yet it is possible that the low level of relief was a temporary phenomenon associated with the 'crisis of traditional charity' in the period.[60] Two centuries earlier the largest charitable organization in Lyon, the Aumône, was distributing a 12 lb loaf of wheat bread per week to individual applicants.[61]

The difficulties about making these comparisons are manifold, not least because many historians of poor relief fight shy of calculating the value of alms in terms of the budget of a recipient or the wages of a labourer, and furthermore because few studies discuss how long relief was given to individuals. Another problem which arises in comparing welfare systems north and south of the Alps in the early modern period, was the greater prominence given to the provision of dowries to impoverished, respectable girls in Catholic Europe. Already in fourteenth-century Florence provision of dowries was a major preoccupation of the city's leading charity. Prior to the Black Death contributions of only 10s. were given by the company of Orsanmichele towards dowries, equivalent to two days' work for labourers. After the plague these subsidies were increased to £24, sufficient to maintain a family of four for two months, or equivalent to fifty days' wages for an unskilled labourer. Later, in sixteenth-century Rome, dowries of 50 *scudi* were provided, equivalent to 100 days' work for a master builder.[62]

These few examples of the value of relief payments in north and south Europe can do little more than point in the direction of future research and of the necessity to adopt a more nuanced approach to comparisons across time and space, in particular to compare like with like and total systems of relief in individual cities rather than to isolate individual institutions. However, even with this extraordinary diversity of welfare, particular developments have been seen as common across early modern Europe. Thus the reorganization of poor relief systems in many urban centres from the 1520s onwards shared a move towards greater rationalization and centralization and a more systematic control of the poor, whose treatment was predicated on the distinction between the deserving and the undeserving.[63]

However, even if we consider the objectives which underlay these systems of poor relief, the ability of the authorities to mould behaviour as they would have liked is much more limited than would appear from some of their pronouncements. The whole history of the legislation governing the English Poor Law can be seen as a series of initiatives at regulation and reform which failed once the reality of coping with large numbers of poor people became apparent.[64] Such pressures could even transform the role of an institution as they did in the case of the Pia Casa in Florence over the first half of the nineteenth century. In the face of population growth and limited resources the Pia Casa lost its earlier function as an institution aimed at the rehabilitation of adults and evolved into an institution primarily concerned with the care of orphans, abandoned children and the elderly.[65]

Nevertheless, policies being pursued by Poor Law authorities could have a major impact on the lives of the poor. In some cases the authorities might even intervene directly to reconstruct the family life of the poor. For example, in the parish of Ardleigh in the late eighteenth century it is known that the officials responsible for the relief of the poor occasionally arranged for a younger widow to live with an elder one. With both dependent on the the Poor Law, the authorities by such an arrangement saved on housing costs while ensuring that a degree of care was provided when needed.[66] When there were no substantial savings to be made, as Tom Sokoll points out in Chapter 10, there was no necessity for the Poor Law officials to intervene, nor did they. Another example of interaction between the poor and relief-giving bodies can be found in the contribution to this volume by Eugenio Sonnino on the female orphans of Rome. The families of the poor clearly could not afford to ignore the policies and practices of the various charitable foundations, but equally those who were responsible for these various institutions had to accommodate themselves to the needs of the poor, accepting, for example, that poor families might reclaim their daughters once they were of an age to fulfil a useful role within the household economy.

VII POVERTY AND ITS CAUSES

Given the diversity of the populations surveyed and the length of the time period it is not surprising that the contributors to the present volume sometimes express different opinions as to the extent, intensity and causes of the poverty that afflicted women and children in the European past. David Vassberg and Joanna Bourke, for example, take a relatively optimistic view of the opportunities available at least to some of the poor. Vassberg stresses the economic freedom exercised by widows in rural Castile in the sixteenth century, while Bourke argues that women in rural Ireland in the late nineteenth century saw in marriage and housekeeping a means to avoid the drudgery and poverty which farm work had brought to previous generations of Irish women. Both Vassberg and Bourke rely implicitly on a relative rather than an absolute definition of poverty, a distinction that was discussed above. For Vassberg the appropriate comparison lies with the restrictions placed on independent economic activity of married women, and for Bourke with the low status of those women who found paid labour in a declining market for female labour. Yet, of necessity the majority of contributors have assumed as their definition of poverty that of the society they selected to study, as represented by the lists of recipients of the support provided to the poor by civil, ecclesiastical and private agencies. It has proved easier, in other words, to identify the number and type of persons considered as poor by different societies than to measure the scale and nature of poverty. In turn this has led to somewhat different emphases when seeking to explain the causes of poverty.

A number of the contributors to the present volume stress the importance of demographic factors in explaining both the incidence of poverty in general and of women and children in particular. Hans Chr. Johansen, for example, establishes that the unmarried women resident in Danish towns of the eighteenth century rarely had any relatives available to help. Being female, failing to marry or becoming widowed are viewed by Gísli Gunnlaugsson and Loftur Guttormsson as more significant than ecological factors as harbingers of poverty in their account of poverty in nineteenth-century Iceland. Antoine Marchini concludes that the cause of much female poverty in Corsica was the loss of social and legal rights when women were widowed. On the other hand, a very different relationship between the incidence of poverty and the form of the household is depicted in the contribution of Sonya Rose on poverty in Nottinghamshire mining and framework-knitting communities during the latter part of the nineteenth century. In the mining community some of the harsher aspects of life cycle poverty were alleviated as married children were able, in many cases, to incorporate their recently widowed mothers into their own households. That such a reconstruction of the child's household was possible is attributed by Sonya Rose to the fact that the miners had a standard of living which made it practical to provide such support. Economic factors, although operating to intensify rather than to alleviate poverty, also receive attention from other contributors to this volume. Volker Hunecke argues that the abandonment of children in eighteenth- and nineteenth-century Milan was the result of their mothers needing to find work. According to Elaine Clark, it was poverty, and in particular the inability to manage land that had passed to them from their husbands, which forced many women landholders in medieval England to remarry, although, as Eugenio Sonnino documents in the case of seventeenth- and eighteenth-century Rome, because widows were poorer than widowers and more likely to be burdened with young children, they were generally less likely than widowers to remarry.

Cultural influences could also intervene either to widen or narrow the extent of poverty, even to render difficult the remarriage of widows when such a course might have been to their economic benefit. Revisions to the legal code induced by cultural change rather than increased poverty are adjudged responsible by Lola Valverde for the rise in the numbers of children abandoned in the Basque Country between 1550 and 1800. Philip Gavitt also argues that it was a cultural change from the fifteenth to the sixteenth centuries that led to inheritance strategies replacing poverty as the dominant motive for the abandonment of children in Florence.[67] In neither case, however, is it likely that cultural changes proceeded entirely independently of economic changes which increased the cost to women and indeed to couples of retaining their children at home.[68]

It is of course true that any attempt to isolate the demographic, economic and socio-cultural determinants of poverty is bound to be artificial as all such factors inevitably intertwine. Nevertheless, the attempt to disentangle the varied threads does provide valuable insights into the nature of poverty both for a given individual and for society at large, and the strength of these insights is particularly evident when, as in the present volume, the focus is on the variation in the incidence of poverty over the life cycle.

NOTES

1 G.C. Fiegehen, P.S. Lansley and A.D. Smith, *Poverty and Progress in Britain 1953–1973*, Cambridge: Cambridge University Press 1977, pp. 7–18.

2 A.B. Atkins, *The Economics of Inequality*, Oxford: Clarendon Press 1975, p. 87.

3 Despite the acknowledgement of the difficulties associated with the concept of absolute poverty, we take a rather more positive view of the utility of the concept than Paul Slack, *Poverty and Policy in Tudor and Stuart England*, Harlow: Longman 1988, pp. 2–5.

4 B.S. Rowntree, *Poverty: A Study of Town Life*, London: Nelson edition n.d., p. 279.

5 F.M. Eden, *The State of the Poor*, vol. III, London: J. Davis 1747, reprinted London: Frank Cass 1966, appendix XII, pp. CCCXXIX–CCCXI.

6 See below, John Henderson, Chapter 7, Table 7.1 on fourteenth-century Italy; and on sixteenth-century Antwerp, W.P. Blockmans and W. Prevenier, 'Poverty in Flanders and Brabant from the fourteenth to the mid-sixteenth century: Sources and problems', *Acta Historiae Neerlandicae: Studies on the History of the Netherlands*, 10, 1978, pp. 20–4. C.M. Cipolla, *Before the Industrial Revolution. European Society and Economy, 1000–1700*, London: Methuen 1978, pp. 27–37; and C. Lis and H. Soly, *Poverty and Capitalism in Pre-Industrial Europe*, Brighton: Harvester Press 1982 edn, pp. 177–86.

7 See, in general, B. Pullan, 'Poveri, mendicanti e vagabondi (secoli xiv–xvii), in C. Vivanti and R. Romano (eds), *Storia d'Italia. Annali* i: *Dal feudalismo al capitalismo*, Turin: Einaudi 1978, pp. 977–8; Slack, *Poverty and Policy*, pp. 40–3.

8 B. Pullan, 'Support and redeem: Charity and poor relief in Italian cities from the fourteenth century to the seventeenth century', in J. Henderson (ed.), *Charity and the Poor in Medieval and Renaissance Europe*, in *Continuity and Change*, 3: 2, 1988, pp. 177–208; Slack, *Poverty and Policy*, pp. 22–7; R. Jütte, 'Poor relief and social discipline in sixteenth-century Europe', *European Studies Review*, 11, 1981, pp. 25–52.

9 Rowntree, *Poverty*, p. 171.

10 See Louise Bollard Moore, *Wages Earners Budgets. A Study of the Standards and Cost of Living in New York City*, New York: Henry Holt & Co. 1907, p. 87.

11 Charles Booth, *The Aged Poor in England and Wales*, London: Macmillan 1894, reprinted New York: Garland Publishing Inc. 1980, pp. 182–3, 314–15.

12 Rowntree, *Poverty*, p. 454.

13 See Fiegehen, Lansley and Smith, *Poverty and Progress*, pp. 92–109.

14 Christer Lundh, 'Households and families in pre-industrial Sweden', *Continuity and Change*, 10:1, 1995. Assumptions made by Lundh were that children under the age of 9 did not work and the labour contribution of children aged 9–15, women who were pregnant or breast-feeding and the elderly was half that of adult men and women. In terms of consumption, the assumption was that adult males and pregnant and breast-feeding females each constituted one consumption unit, other women, children aged 9–15 and the elderly 0.8 of a unit and children under the age of 9, 0.5 of a unit. It will be noted that these assumptions involve a considerable simplification of dietary needs as set out in Table 1.1, p. 7 and that they also differ from those used by Richard Wall in Chapter 15 to estimate intra-household inequalities.

15 Peter Laslett, 'Family, kinship and collectivity as systems of support in pre-industrial Europe: A consideration of the "nuclear-hardship" hypothesis', in Henderson (ed.), *Charity and the Poor*, pp. 153–75.

16 As regards the absence of family support see in particular the contributions of Lola Valverde, Philip Gavitt and Volker Hunecke.

17 Laslett, 'Family, kinship and collectivity'.

18 David I. Kertzer, Dennis P. Hogan and Nancy Karweit, 'Kinship beyond the household in a nineteenth-century Italian town', *Continuity and Change*, 7:1, 1922, p. 119.

19 Isabelle Chabot, 'Poverty and the widow in later medieval Florence', in Henderson (ed.), *Charity and the Poor*, p. 300.

20 As is suggested by Osamu Saito in Chapter 3 of Richard Wall and Osamu Saito (eds), *Economic and Social Aspects of the Family Life Cycle*, Cambridge: Cambridge University Press forthcoming 1995.

21 P. Gavitt, *Charity and Children in Renaissance Florence: The Ospedale degli Innocenti*, Ann Arbor, Mich.: Michigan University Press 1990, p. 21; and Hunecke's chapter below. In eighteenth-century London, foundlings accounted for 28 per cent of all children baptized in one London church, a percentage Valerie Fildes apparently considers more reliable than the 4–7 per cent recorded in a further seven London parishes. See Valerie Fildes, 'Maternal feelings reassessed: Child abandonment and neglect in London and Westminster, 1550–1800', in V. Fildes (ed.), *Women as Mothers in Pre-Industrial England*, London and New York: Routledge 1990, pp. 141, 164–5.

22 David I. Kertzer, *Sacrificed for Honor. Italian Infant Abandonment and the Politics of Reproductive Control*, Boston: Beacon Press 1993, pp. 82, 87, 89; and for all provinces of Italy, ibid.: 75.

23 The theme of both R.C. Trexler, 'Infanticide in Florence: New sources and first results', *History of Childhood Quarterly*, 1, 1974, pp. 98–116; and J. Boswell, *The Kindness of Strangers. The Abandonment of Children in Western Europe from Late Antiquity to the Renaissance*, New York: Random House 1988, part IV.

24 See Gavitt's chapter below; and L. Sandri, *L'Ospedale di S. Maria della Scala di S. Gimignano nel Quattrocento. Contributo alla storia dell'infanzia abbandonata*, Valdelsa: Società Storica della Valdelsa 1982, pp. 170–5.

25 See C. Corsini, 'Self-regulating mechanisms of traditional populations before the demographic revolution: European civilizations', in *International Proceedings of the International Population Conference for Scientific Study of Population, Mexico, 1977*, vol. 3, Liège: Ordina 1977, pp. 8–9. For Rome and Milan see the contributions to the present volume by Sonnino and Hunecke.

26 A. Wilson, 'Illegitimacy and its implications in mid-eighteenth-century London: The evidence from the Foundling Hospital', *Continuity and Change*, 4, 1989, pp. 103–64; and for an opposing view see Fildes, 'Maternal feelings reassessed', pp. 152–8.

27 See, for example, M. Foucault, *The Birth of the Clinic: An Archaeology of Medical Perception*, New York 1975, introduction, and chs 1 and 5. The 'hospital', particularly in the late medieval period, offered a wide range of services, not just medical treatment.

28 See Gavitt, *Charity and Children*; and Sandri, *L'Ospedale di S. Maria della Scala*.

29 See for other evidence on abandonment in Spain: L. Marz, *Poverty and Welfare in Habsburg Spain*, Cambridge: Cambridge University Press 1983, pp. 224–36; and A.M. Martin, *Economia, Sociedad, Pobreza en Castilla: Palencia, 1500–1814*, vol. 2, Palencia: Excma. Disputacion Provincial de Palencia 1985, pp. 625–73.

30 D. Herlihy and C. Klapisch-Zuber, *Tuscans and Their Families. A Study of the Florentine Catasto of 1427*, New Haven, Conn. and London: Yale University Press 1985, pp. 292–8; Gavitt, *Charity and Children*; Sandri, *L'Ospedale di S. Maria della Scala*; C. Poni, 'Family and Podere in Emilia Romagna', *Journal of Italian Studies*, 1, 1979, pp. 201–34.

31 Cf. below Chapter 15, Table 15.5 and Figure 15.1.

32 Cf. below Chapter 15; and the argument developed by Margareta Matovic, 'The Stockholm marriage: Extra legal family formation in Stockholm, 1860–1890', *Continuity and Change*, 1:3, 1986, pp. 411–12.

33 A number of such cases and folklore recounting the tensions between older and younger generations are documented by David Gaunt in 'The property and kin relationships of retired farmers in northern and central Europe', in Richard Wall, Jean Robin and Peter Laslett (eds), *Family Forms in Historic Europe*, Cambridge: Cambridge University Press 1983, pp. 249–79. See also Richard M. Smith, 'The manorial court and the elderly tenant in medieval England', in Margaret Pelling and Richard M. Smith (eds), *Life, Death and the Elderly: Historical Perspectives*, London: Routledge 1991, pp. 41–5.

34 For an opposing view based on English evidence, see K.D.M. Snell and J. Millar, 'Lone parent families and the Welfare State: Past and present', *Continuity and Change*, 2:3, 1987, p. 408; and for the suggestion that single women even if childless may not always have been treated as sympathetically as widows, Johansen, below Chapter 9.

35 These estimates, which are those of the editors and not of Johansen, have been prepared on the same basis as those in the contribution to this volume by Richard Wall, see Chapter 15.

36 As was very obviously the case in late eighteenth-century England when many labourers burdened with large families required assistance from the Poor Law; see the contribution of Tom Sokoll, Chapter 10.

37 The average payment is that made at this time in two other Dorset parishes, see Eden, *The State of the Poor*, vol. II, pp. 147, 151. For the estimate of net income taking account of family size see below Chapter 15, Table 15.4.

38 Enhanced payments to older paupers are documented by Tim Wales, 'Poverty, poor relief and the life-cycle: Some evidence from seventeenth century Norfolk', in Richard M. Smith (ed.), *Land, Kinship and Life Cycle*, Cambridge: Cambridge University Press 1984, pp. 362–3; and implied by some of the lists of payments to paupers in Eden, *The State of the Poor*. For an opposing view see Barker-Reed as reported in Pelling and Smith (eds), *Life, Death and the Elderly*, p. 24.

39 See C. Klapisch-Zuber, *Women, Family and Ritual in Renaissance Florence*, New Haven, Conn. and London: Yale University Press 1985, chs 6, 8 and 11.

40 Herlihy and Klapisch-Zuber, *Tuscans and Their Families*, p. 132.

41 The occupational family and household patterns of south-east Bruges are detailed in R. Wall, 'The composition of households in a population of 6 men to

10 women: South-east Bruges in 1814', in Wall, Robin and Laslett (eds), *Family Forms in Historic Europe.* Adult in this study was defined as all persons aged 15 and over.

42 A rather different interpretation to that of Klapisch-Zuber, *Women, Family and Ritual in Renaissance Florence,* has been offered by E.G. Rosenthal, 'The position of women in Renaissance Florence: Neither autonomy nor subjection', in P. Denley and C. Elam (eds), *Florence and Italy. Renaissance Studies in Honour of Nicolai Rubinstein,* London: Westfield College 1988, pp. 369–81.

43 See E. Fiumi, *Demografia, movimento urbanistico e classi sociali in Prato dall età comunale ai tempi moderni,* Florence: L.S. Olschki 1968; Herlihy and Klapisch-Zuber, *Tuscans and Their Families,* p. 124; Slack, *Poverty and Policy,* pp. 75–6; R.M. Smith, 'Some issues concerning families and their property in rural England, 1250–1800', in R.M. Smith (ed.), *Land, Kinship and Life-Cycle,* Cambridge: Cambridge University Press 1984, p. 78; and the chapters by Vassberg and Gunnlauggsson below.

44 On the views of the Canonists see B. Tierney, *Medieval Poor Law. A Sketch of Canonical Theory and its Application in England,* Berkeley and Los Angeles, Calif.: University of California Press 1959. T. Wales, 'Poverty, poor relief and the life-cycle: Some evidence from seventeenth-century Norfolk', in Smith (ed.), *Land, Kinship and Life-Cycle,* pp. 357, 364–6.

45 ibid.: p. 361, Table 11.3; and see Chapters 9, 11, 12 and 14 in the present volume.

46 Slack, *Poverty and Policy,* p. 85; J. Boulton, *Neighbourhood and Society. A London Suburb in the Seventeenth Century,* Cambridge: Cambridge University Press 1987, pp. 127–8; and Johansen's contribution, Chapter 9.

47 K. Wrightson, 'Kinship in an English village: Terling, Essex, 1550–1700', in Smith (ed.), *Land, Kinship and Life-Cycle,* pp. 314–19; Smith, Some issues', pp. 79–80; and Wales, 'Poverty, poor relief', pp. 384–6.

48 M. Pelling, 'Old age, poverty and disability in early modern Norwich. Work, remarriage and other expedients', in Pelling and Smith (eds), *Life, Death and the Elderly,* pp. 86–7.

49 On dependency ratios see, E.A. Wrigley and R.S. Schofield, *The Population History of England, 1541–1871. A Reconstruction,* Cambridge: Cambridge University Press 1989, pp. 217–19; and for one of the few historians to consider this in relation to poor relief, Slack, *Poverty and Policy,* p. 44.

50 Slack, ibid.: ch. 6, outlines the system, while M.K. McIntosh, 'Local responses to the poor in late medieval and Tudor England', in Henderson (ed.), *Charity and the Poor,* pp. 209–45, discusses the relationship between the Poor Law and parish fraternities. English admiration for Italian models is discussed by Slack, *Poverty and Policy,* p. 120; S. Woolf, *The Poor in Western Europe in the Eighteenth and Nineteenth Centuries,* London: Methuen 1986, pp. 32–5. A specific example is provided by K.P. Park and J. Henderson, ' "The first hospital among Christians": The Ospedale di Santa Maria Nuova in early sixteenth-century Florence', *Medical History,* 35:2, 1991, pp. 164–88.

51 Jeremy Boulton, 'The parish pension in seventeenth-century London: An investigation of its relative generosity', unpublished paper presented at the Social History Society Conference, Roehampton, January 1993.

52 ibid.: p. 20, citing the calculations of Ian Archer. The range of values reflects the fact that richer parishes could make larger payments to the poor.

53 ibid.: p. 22. Boulton assumed, based on his work on the London suburb of Southwark in the seventeenth century, that pensioners were widowed females and that their households contained on average 1.8 persons. Households of labourers he estimated contained 3.8 persons. When paupers lived in larger and more complex households, as reported in the contributions on early and late nineteenth-century English populations to the present volume by Tom Sokoll

and Sonya Rose, then the standard of living of the pauper is even more difficult to determine, as some pooling of resources within the household, earnings from some, pension income from others, may well have occurred. For the calculations by Hunt see E.H. Hunt, 'Paupers and pensioners: Past and present', *Ageing and Society*, 9, 1990, pp. 407–30, esp. p. 423; and for a much more positive view of the contribution of the Poor Law in England to the budgets of the poor, in particular that payments represented in the 1830s anything between 60 and 90 per cent of the per capita income of the labourers, D. Thomson, 'The decline of social security: Falling state support for the elderly since early Victorian times', *Ageing and Society*, 4, 1984, esp. p. 453.

54 The procedures used to produce these estimates are detailed above in note 37, and see also Chapter 15.

55 Booth, *The Aged Poor*, summarized by R. Wall, 'Relationships between the generations in British families past and present', in C. Marsh and S. Arber (eds), *Families and Households: Division and Change*, London: Macmillan 1992, pp. 63–85.

56 The results of a number of studies are conveniently summarized by Marco van Leeuwen, 'Surviving with a little help. The importance of charity to the poor of Amsterdam in comparative perspective', *Social History*, 18:3, 1993, pp. 319–38. None of the studies, as far as is known, took any account of the differences in family size between pauper and non-pauper households.

57 E.A.M. Bulder's detailed study of the economic circumstances of the elderly in a community in the north-east of the Netherlands, Winterswijk, in the late nineteenth and early twentieth centuries also indicates that the chief resource of the elderly was the combination of income from a variety of sources, but with only a minor contribution from the Poor Law. See E.A.M. Bulder, *The Social Economies of Old Age. Strategies to Maintain Income in Later Life in the Netherlands, 1880–1940*, Rotterdam: Tinbergen Institute 1993.

58 B. Pullan, 'Catholics and the poor in early modern Europe', *Transactions of the Royal Historical Society*, ser. 5, 24, 1976, pp. 15–34.

59 O.W. Hufton, *The Poor of Eighteenth-Century France 1750–1789*, Oxford: Clarendon 1974, pp. 174–6.

60 C. Jones, *Charity and Bienfaisance. The Treatment of the Poor in the Montpellier Region, 1740–1815*, Cambridge: Cambridge University Press 1982, ch. 4, pp. 76–94; and most recently see his *The Charitable Imperative. Hospitals and Nursing in Ancien Régime and Revolutionary France*, London: Routledge 1989.

61 N.Z. Davis, *Society and Culture in Early Modern France*, London: Duckworth 1975, pp. 48–9, 285 n. 125; and J.P. Gutton, *La société et les pauvres. L'example de la Generalité de Lyon, 1534–1789*, Paris: Presses Universitaires de France 1971, p. 42.

62 On Florence see Henderson Chapter 7, below; and for a more detailed discussion see his *Piety and Charity in Late Medieval Florence*, Oxford: Clarendon Press 1994, ch. 8. For a short discussion of the value of charity in sixteenth-century Italy see C.F. Black, *Italian Confraternities in the Sixteenth Century*, Cambridge: Cambridge University Press 1989, pp. 162–7; and on Rome ibid.: p. 166.

63 See Jütte, 'Poor relief and social discipline'; and Lis and Soly, *Poverty and Capitalism*, ch. 3.

64 See Slack, *Poverty and Policy*.

65 Giovanni Gozzini, 'The poor and the life-cycle in nineteenth-century Florence, 1813–1859', *Social History*, 18:3, 1993, pp. 299–317.

66 F.H. Erith, *Ardleigh in 1796. Its Farms, Families and Local Government*, East Bergholt: Hugh Tempest Radford 1978.

67 Late fifteenth- and early sixteenth-century Florence was characterized by marked demographic expansion and rising costs of living: see Herlihy and Klapisch-Zuber, *Tuscans and Their Families*, p. 74, table 3.5; R.A. Goldthwaite, *The Building of Renaissance Florence. An Economic and Social History*, Baltimore, Md. and London: Johns Hopkins University Press 1980, ch. 1.

68 Gavitt concedes that poverty bore particularly hard on the widows, at the same time preventing their providing adequately for their children and hindering their own chance of remarriage, while Valverde accepts that broader shifts in the economy had a subsidiary role in enhancing the rate of child abandonment.

Part I
Children

1 Family structures and the early phase in the individual life cycle

A southern European perspective

Pier Paolo Viazzo

THE NORTH–SOUTH DIVIDE IN EUROPEAN DEMOGRAPHIC HISTORY

Recent work on the social and demographic history of Europe has revealed the existence of marked differences in demographic regimes, marriage patterns and family structures across European regions. As is well known, the way was opened twenty-five years ago by John Hajnal, who was able to locate a major demographic boundary running roughly from Leningrad to Trieste.[1] To the east of this line, marriage appeared to have been early and universal for perhaps four centuries, whereas western Europe had been characterized by the late age of marriage for both sexes and by a high proportion of people never marrying. Further research has subsequently identified a second major 'fault line', running across western Europe from west to east. The tremendous growth of interest in the study of household composition stimulated by the work of Peter Laslett and his associates has allowed family historians to ascertain that in north-west Europe households were small and structurally simple, whereas in many parts of southern Europe they could be much larger and far more complex in structure. Moreover, evidence has been produced to suggest that in the countries of Mediterranean Europe marriage could be rather earlier than in the north, and permanent celibacy rates much lower.[2]

Demographically, late and infrequent marriage (Malthus's 'preventive check') entails low levels of overall fertility and, more generally, a low-pressure demographic regime in which both birth and death rates are relatively moderate.[3] But differentials in nuptiality are also bound to affect household formation and, ultimately, household structure. This has led Hajnal, Laslett and other leading scholars in the field to explore more accurately the functioning of household formation systems in historic Europe and to propose a number of theoretical typologies and geographical subdivisions.[4] In particular, Hajnal has drawn attention – in another highly influential essay – to the properties of two contrasting sets of household formation rules: on the one hand, the 'simple' household formation system typically encountered in north-west Europe, characterized by relatively late marriage and by a neo-local rule prescribing that a new household had to be established at each marriage; on the other, the 'joint' system found in many parts of southern Europe, characterized by earlier marriage and by a strong tendency for married couples to start and spend part of their life together in the parental household, thereby producing high proportions of households containing two or more related married couples.[5]

These findings are of considerable relevance to economic historians. It is evident, for instance, that although the same rate of natural increase may result from both high-pressure and low-pressure demographic regimes, the latter allow a more favourable balance between population and resources. For one thing, replacement will be more efficient because the number of people who live for a short time consuming resources and then die without realizing their full potential is smaller. Moreover, the proportion of people under a certain age being a function of fertility, late-marrying populations with low fertility will have a more advantageous 'dependency ratio' of children to the working population.[6]

These results are also relevant to students of poverty and welfare. Indeed, one set of questions needing further investigation concerns the extent to which the demographic regime of a given society governed the choice of the categories of paupers to subsidize. As has been recently remarked:

> a more specific study of the sex and age structure of given populations in early modern Europe would help us to identify how far regional variations in the categories of those most at risk were mirrored in the types of people chosen as the main recipients of poor relief.[7]

But a no less important area for future study is represented by the relationships between family structures and formal systems of poor relief. That poor relief systems varied across Europe, and that a clear watershed separated the northern from the southern countries, has been well known to institutional historians for a long time. Most scholars have, of course, emphasized the contrast between Protestant north and Catholic south, and a sharp division has also been assumed to exist between, for instance, English dependence on the parish for the distribution of charity and Italian reliance on large voluntary associations.[8] The new evidence about variations in household structures now makes it necessary to reassess the significance of the help provided to the poor by charitable institutions against the alternative represented by the family as a source of informal support. A crucial question to be addressed is, indeed, whether family forms are best seen as adaptations to their institutional environments, or whether, alternatively, charitable institutions themselves developed to integrate the insufficient 'welfare potential' of particular family forms.

In view of these recent developments, there clearly seems to be a case for trying to construct a framework within which variations between places and over time can profitably be studied, and a useful starting-point is provided by what Peter Laslett has termed the nuclear-hardship hypothesis.

THE NUCLEAR-HARDSHIP HYPOTHESIS

Over the last ten years, the phrase nuclear-hardship (or 'nuclear-family hardship') has been gaining currency among family historians to refer in general to the difficulties imposed upon individuals when social rules require that they live in nuclear families and marry neo-locally. More specifically, this notion is at the core of a wide-ranging hypothesis put forward by Laslett in the attempt to explain variations in the relative weight of the various forms of support provided by the family, the kinship group and the collectivity.

In its most accomplished formulation,[9] the nuclear-hardship hypothesis consists of two main statements. The first statement is that 'joint' and other complex family forms were better equipped to shield their members from hardship than was the nuclear family. The second statement is that the more dominant simple-family households are in a society, and the more strictly neo-local rules are applied, the more important will be support from the collectivity – that is, charitable organizations such as the church, municipalities and the state. The ensuing prediction is, therefore, that in northwest Europe, where nuclear families were far more widespread than in southern Europe, the role of the collectivity can be expected to have been correspondingly greater.

Testing this hypothesis is no easy task, for one has to assess not only the extent of transfers from the collectivity, but also the significance of support coming from kin outside the household in which an individual resided. As far as England is concerned, Laslett seems to be satisfied that the available historical evidence shows that transfers through the collectivity were indeed of great importance for the paupers in pre-industrial times, and transfers through the kinship network of little consequence.[10] The hypothesis would thus appear to be confirmed for England, and possibly for other northwestern countries as well. For southern Europe, however, the validity of Laslett's hypothesis is still uncertain.

One obvious problem is that, although support systems could differ considerably from those found in northern Europe, it is nevertheless clear from the work of institutional historians that in southern European countries such as Italy, Spain or Portugal large numbers of people were potential receivers of incomes from the collectivity.[11] Moreover, it is often taken as axiomatic by anthropologists and social historians alike that in the south kinship was a more basic and pervasive principle of social organization than in the north. If this assumption is correct, one can surmise that a greater amount of wealth and provisions was transferred through kinship networks.[12] Finally, a major difficulty in generalizing about the historical functions of the household in southern Europe is that recent research has brought to light a high degree of variability in family forms, both over time and across regions and social strata. Systems of 'joint' household formations are attested in several parts of southern Europe, and clearly predominated in the sharecropping regions of central Italy. But forms of domestic organization approaching the classic 'stem-family' type are also documented, and there can be little doubt that the nuclear family prevailed in southern Italy, in southern Spain and in southern Portugal and also in many parts of northern Italy since the middle of the eighteenth century.[13] Many domestic groups in southern Europe thus shared important features of north-western household structure, and it is therefore conceivable that they may have been in a similar position with respect to reliance on transfers through the collectivity.

There are, however, problems of a different nature that have to be tackled if the nuclear-hardship hypothesis is to be more satisfactorily articulated and tested. It is my impression that, although the hypothesis is in principle intended to apply to individuals at any stage of the life cycle, the main emphasis tends nevertheless to be placed on the vulnerable condition of elderly people. In fact, both the theoretical and the empirical research spurred by the nuclear-hardship hypothesis has so far concentrated (and is likely to continue to do so in the future) on the late phase of the life cycle.[14] It is also relevant to note that one important piece of evidence supporting Laslett's contention, and suggesting that joint and other complex family structures were actually better equipped to shield their members from hardship than was the nuclear family, comes from the analysis of the household position of the elderly. Recent studies of co-residential arrangements in a number of central Italian towns and villages show that most elderly people spent their later years in large complex households.[15] This is in sharp contrast with the high proportions of elderly men and women living alone to be found in historic populations of north-west Europe.[16] We may wonder, however, whether the nuclear-hardship hypothesis still holds when we turn to individuals in the early phases of the life cycle.

HARDSHIP IN INFANCY: ORPHANS AND FOUNDLINGS

In his study of York, Rowntree drew attention to the fact that an individual passes through alternating periods of 'want and comparative plenty' and constructed a sequence of phases – a cycle of poverty – shaped by typical features of the individual life cycle: marriage, the rearing of children, the departure of children from the family unit, retirement and the death of one partner. Rowntree found that for a typical labourer in York in the 1890s the first years after marriage were a period of comparative prosperity, lasting until he had two or three children, when poverty would overtake him. 'This period of poverty', he observed,

> will last perhaps ten years, i.e. until the first child is fourteen years old and begins to earn wages. . . . While the children are earning, and before they leave home to marry, the man enjoys another period of prosperity – possibly, however, only to sink back again into poverty

when his children have married and left him and he himself is too old to work.[17]

It is relevant to remark that Laslett has maintained that, although they had not developed a formal representation of a 'cycle of poverty', the village officials who were in charge of poor relief in England had been fully aware – almost 400 years before Rowntree's investigation – that the life of an individual was marked by a sequence of alternating periods of want and prosperity. And an analysis of how money was distributed suggests that the life cycle squeezes in the individual's life were largely the same as those identified by Rowntree.[18]

There were of course important differences. It is particularly worth noting here that the results of Rowntree's survey indicated that during early childhood an individual was likely to be in poverty. This phase of want was due to an unfavourable ratio between producers and consumers in the household, and would last (as we have just seen) until the first child was 14 years of age and started to earn money and augment the father's wage sufficiently to raise the family above the poverty line. Now, it is well known that in pre-industrial England children typically began to leave home at about 14 years of age to become servants, whereas in Rowntree's model they stay under the parental roof for another ten years.[19] In spite of these differences, the two patterns still look similar enough,[20] the main reason being that the individual's life cycle – and the risk of descending into poverty – were shaped to a very large extent by nuclear household formation rules.

This may be a tribute to the stability of English household structure over time. But we can ask ourselves whether the quite different set of demographic and institutional circumstances obtaining in much of southern Europe produced life cycle patterns which departed significantly from the sequence of alternating periods of 'want and comparative plenty' identified by Rowntree, and, in particular, whether essentially similar arrangements were made to meet the needs of individuals experiencing life cycle hardship.

Let us consider orphans. Studies of poor relief in various countries of Europe have shown that administrators of charitable funds paid special attention to the category of victims of life cycle poverty made up of children and adolescents who had been orphaned of one or both of their parents and were too young to work. We may expect, however, differences to have existed from one country to another both in terms of the order of magnitude of the problem and in terms of provisions.

The first main point to observe is that under different demographic circumstances the number and proportion of orphans – or, from a somewhat different angle, the average individual's chances of being orphaned by a certain age – are bound to vary quite considerably. The amount of variability can be determined both through the use of simulation techniques and through empirical investigation. This, however, only gives us information about the availability of kin (in this case, parents in the first place). Such information needs to be integrated with data on the household position of orphans. The English evidence reveals a dominant, quite typical household pattern in which widowed mothers lived in nuclear family households with their unmarried children.[21] This pattern is likely to be less frequent in areas with joint family organization, where young orphans (and their mothers or fathers) can be expected to belong to larger and structurally more complex residential units.[22] Also, more information is badly needed on the 'fate' of orphans in life-course perspective. It is known, for instance, that in north-west Europe the prospect of leaving home started to become tangible at about age 10 and was very common. In southern countries, on the other hand, leaving home to work in service was less common. It would be very interesting to establish whether orphans displayed differential patterns of mobility, either in terms of a stronger propensity to abandon the household where they had found shelter in infancy or in terms of age at leaving home.[23] Even more basically, it would be important to arrive at better estimates of how many orphans remained in their households (and, more generally, in their villages and in the countryside) and how many were sent to orphanages in neighbouring towns or, indeed, were abandoned in their first days or weeks of life.

In fact, when one focuses on the first stage of the individual life cycle, perhaps the most striking difference between northern and southern Europe is the much higher risk that a child born in France, Italy, Spain or Portugal had of being relinquished to a foundling hospital. Estimates of the number and proportion of abandoned children in the European past are not easy, especially before 1800. But there can be no doubt that abandonment was far more widespread in the southern countries.[24]

The existence of these marked differences – which were not only 'quantitative', so to speak, but also administrative, for in the northern countries responsibility for the care of foundlings lay with the parish in which abandoned children were discovered – was a puzzle for many generations of scholars, travellers and administrators. Most present-day writers would still trace these differences to the religious divide between Catholic and Protestant countries. But the fact that foundling hospitals were already much more firmly established in the southern countries than in the rest of Europe well before the Reformation has led several scholars to look for deeper cultural or structural explanations: thus, it has been observed that foundling hospitals generally flourished in societies with a widely diffused custom of sending children away to wet-nurses, and also, in a rather different vein, that a relationship seems to have existed (even in southern Europe) between the growth of large centralized foundling hospitals and a structural weakness of the parish.[25]

What has been lacking so far has been a sharper focus on the relationships between child abandonment and family forms as well as a sustained effort to link this practice to the main features of the various demographic systems – and, indeed, to specify its role within these systems. Yet, a link had actually been suggested by Malthus himself. As we have seen, the neo-Malthusian line of historical–demographic investigation inaugurated by Hajnal's work on European marriage patterns has demonstrated that the northern countries characteristically displayed a low-pressure demographic regime pivoted upon restricted nuptiality. By contrast, in the southern countries both nuptiality and, consequently, fertility were higher. In order to keep a balance, higher mortality rates were therefore needed. And 'if a person', Malthus wrote, 'wished to check population, and were not solicitous about the means, he could not propose a more effectual measure than the establishment of a sufficient number of foundling hospitals'.[26]

This may be a scornful remark by an admittedly unsympathetic contemporary observer. But it contains a theoretical core which is strongly reminiscent of arguments advanced by a number of later scholars, most notably by Carlo Corsini in his studies of child abandonment in Tuscany. Before considering these arguments, however, it is necessary to touch upon some features of household organization in central Italy which are attracting growing attention from family historians, and also to reveal a few ambiguities which are still lingering in the literature on child abandonment and allied topics.

The first point concerns the relationships between labour requirements, household structure and fertility. When we examine the literature on the central Italian rural family, we find that the joint family is unanimously regarded as the only form of domestic organization suited to cope successfully with the highly specific labour requirements of the dominant sharecropping economy. Moreover, it is generally agreed that the sharecropping families of central Italy tended to be highly fertile, and it is pointed out that 'high-fertility strategies' were perfectly understandable if one considers that in the long run they assured not only the reproduction of the family labour force, but also the possibility of taking over larger farms. A recent study demonstrates, in fact, that the fertility of sharecropping families remained higher than that of other social and occupational categories in the same areas well into the twentieth century.[27] The case of central Italy would therefore seem to conform to Kingsley Davis's notion of the joint family as one of the 'institutional patterns' favouring high fertility,[28] the causal chain being schematically as follows:

sharecropping → joint family → high nuptiality → high fertility

Yet, the same literature also indicates that the central Italian sharecroppers were far from being a peasant population operating in a flexible Chayanovian environment, in which the amount of cultivated land would expand and contract in synchrony with variations in the size of the family labour force. In reality, the long-term reproductive strategies of the sharecropping families were potentially in conflict with the shorter-term interests of the landowners, who paid (we are told) 'close attention to the size of their sharecropping households . . . and became alarmed if the number of unproductive consumers – children – became too great'.[29] When the land-lord was visiting the farm, we are also told, the sharecroppers were some-times forced to hide the children in cupboards, in order not to be evicted. In such conditions of strong dependency and high vulnerability for the whole family, hiding a child may have been just one step removed from being forced to resort to sterner measures, including abandonment.

Indeed, it seems no accident that Tuscany, the classic area of share-cropping, was also one of the Italian regions where abandonment of children was commonest.[30] It would be tempting to conclude that a system which was good for the elderly, was far less benign for infants and young children. The issue is blurred, however, by the fact that foundling hospitals were primarily designed for illegitimate children and that it is still widely assumed that foundlings and abandoned children were overwhelmingly bastards. Before going on, it is therefore necessary to consider this point.

QUESTIONS OF ILLEGITIMACY

The prominence recently acquired by nuptiality as a focus of inquiry in historical demography is bound to confer a new importance on the study of illegitimacy.[31] However, apart from a number of works on areas of southern Europe traditionally characterized by very low levels of nuptiality, like northern Portugal, the Pyrenees or the Alpine region,[32] the study of illegitimacy has so far mainly remained a 'northern' concern.[33] A surpris-ingly rigid historiographical divide has thus emerged between a specialized literature on bastardy essentially restricted to northern and central Europe and an equally specialized literature on child abandonment in France and in the Mediterranean countries. Until very recently, few attempts have been made to overcome this divide. If students of foundlings have generally been slow to react to the stimuli provided by the new historical and comparative research on illegitimacy, students of illegitimacy have for their part almost ignored abandonment, both as a substantive and as a methodological issue.

This lack of communication has produced some odd results. In particu-lar, it is striking to see that the assumption that high nuptiality was a dis-tinctive feature of southern European demography still tends to coexist in many quarters with the other assumption that the vast majority of found-lings were illegitimate. Yet, it should not be forgotten that nuptiality and illegitimacy are linked by a number of formal relations, the most obvious and important one being that the higher the levels of nuptiality, the lower the 'potential' for illegitimate fertility. As foundlings in southern Europe were obviously very numerous, there is clearly a contradiction here, some-times rather unsatisfactorily solved by resorting to the argument that links illegitimacy and child abandonment to the specific circumstances, and 'degeneracy', of urban life.

A spate of recent studies shows, however, that things are changing on both sides of the divide. The current debate on the extent of illegitimacy in

England is, in this respect, especially relevant and instructive. A few years ago, Laslett had claimed that in England illegitimacy levels had not been significantly higher in the towns than in the countryside and, in particular, that they appeared to have been surprisingly low in London.[34] This argument has now been challenged by Adrian Wilson on the basis of a detailed analysis of the records of the London Foundling Hospital in the 'General Reception' period (1756–60). Wilson's conclusion is that, at least in the mid-eighteenth century, the London foundlings (who had been explicitly excluded by Laslett in his counts of illegitimate births) were very numerous and, as contemporaries believed, illegitimate. The received view of the extent of illegitimacy in London should therefore be overturned, along with all its wide implications.[35] But Wilson's argument has been, in its turn, challenged by Valerie Fildes, who has provided counter-evidence suggesting that in fact foundlings were mostly legitimate. According to Fildes, parish registers demonstrate that, while illegitimacy may have been one reason for relinquishing a child, two equally or, probably, more common reasons were widowhood during or soon after pregnancy and desertion by the husband, both resulting in the mother's poverty and inability to support the child.[36] The question must be considered to be still open. But if Fildes is correct, then we will be forced to conclude that the collectivity, even in England, was not always efficient or provident enough to preserve children hit by life cycle hardship from abandonment and increased death chances.

On the 'southern' side of the historiographical divide, important changes are also detectable, perhaps the most significant one being a tendency to question the accepted view that southern European foundlings were mostly illegitimate. The very important book by Hunecke on foundlings in Milan is indicative of such a swing of the pendulum.[37] Hasty generalizations might, of course, prove dangerous, for the results achieved by other lines of research in family history indicate that we must be prepared to recognize variability. In socially and demographically illegitimacy-prone regions like northern Portugal, for instance, we should hardly expect to find the same patterns of child abandonment as in southern Portugal or in central Italy.[38] And in central Italy itself, contrasts could be very marked indeed.[39] On the whole, however, the evidence surveyed by Hunecke leaves no doubt that in many areas of Europe, and particularly in the nineteenth century, among foundlings bastards were definitely outnumbered by legitimate children.

Of course, the fact that abandoned children were far from being all illegitimate had been evident to administrators of foundling hospitals and other contemporary observers. One of the reasons why the 'wheel' (the revolving box where infants could be anonymously abandoned) was eventually banned in the second half of the nineteenth century was precisely that it allowed a great and probably growing number of legitimate children to be 'smuggled' into hospitals originally designed only or predominantly for the care of children born out of wedlock. Strangely enough, in the course of the twentieth century this crucial point was progressively lost sight of by social and institutional historians. Thanks to the recent upsurge of interest in this important topic in family history, it has now been reasserted by several studies, most impressively by Hunecke's own work on Milan. But very similar conclusions had already been reached over ten years ago by Corsini in his pioneering studies of abandonment in Florence and Tuscany,[40] to which we have now to turn.

CHILD ABANDONMENT AS A MECHANISM OF DEMOGRAPHIC REGULATION: THE TUSCAN EVIDENCE

Estimating the proportion of legitimate children out of all children admitted to a foundling hospital may prove a very hazardous task. The records of the London Foundling Hospital, for instance, only provide indirect evidence. This has forced Wilson[41] to resort to a laborious statistical exercise taking into account variables such as the age of abandonment as well as seasonal variations and year-to-year fluctuations in the numbers of foundlings. In other cases, however, the estimating procedure may be far more straight-forward, because of the availability of various kinds of direct evidence, and the margins of error will be much more limited.

One such case is provided by the Spedale degli Innocenti of Florence, which was by far the largest of the many foundling hospitals and 'reception homes' of Tuscany, with an average annual intake of about 500 infants in the seventeenth and early eighteenth centuries growing to over 1,000 in the late eighteenth century and no less than 1,500 towards the middle of the nineteenth. The point to be noticed here is that the rules governing admission changed considerably over time. In the last quarter of the eighteenth century the policy of this foundling hospital was to admit needy children indiscriminately, regardless of whether they were illegitimate or not. Apart from those children who were left in the 'wheel', their status is thus openly stated in the records: in the years 1792–4, no less than 71.8 per cent of all children admitted to the hospital were legitimate, 10.9 per cent were illegitimate and only 17.3 per cent of unknown parents.[42]

A proportion of legitimate children exceeding 70 per cent was clearly felt by the authorities to be too high. In 1794 stricter regulations were issued, which limited admission to illegitimate children and to those legitimate children whose families were in conditions of extreme indigence or whose mothers were unable to breast-feed them. Generally speaking, restrictive measures of this kind resulted not so much in a marked decline in the number of foundlings as in a steep rise of the number of infants introduced into the hospital through the 'wheel' – and the Innocenti Hospital, as we have seen, was no exception, for the number of abandoned children actually increased in the course of the nineteenth century. This obviously makes the task of estimating the relative weight of legitimate and illegitimate children rather more complicated. But it should be noticed that even when the status of foundlings is not openly stated in the records, the archives of the

Innocenti Hospital and of many other Italian foundling homes preserve other kinds of evidence which may assist the historian: for instance, the legitimacy of abandoned children could become apparent when they were reclaimed by their parents, as was very frequently the case. Thus, methods judiciously relying on both direct and indirect evidence are usually more than adequate to produce reliable estimates. Indeed, for the Innocenti Hospital in the first half of the nineteenth century, Corsini was able to estimate 'legitimacy rates' hovering between a conservative 40 per cent in some periods to approximately 70 per cent around the middle of the century – values which are quite close, incidentally, to the estimates proposed for Milan and for other Italian localities in the same period.[43]

Having established the general proportion of legitimate children among the Florence foundlings, the next and highly innovative step in Corsini's investigation involved linking records from the foundling hospital to the detailed evidence supplied by his family reconstitution studies of two rural Tuscan communities, Fiesole and San Godenzo. By so doing, he was able to place the practice of child abandonment within the general context of the demography of these two communities and, more specifically, to assess the weight of abandonment within the reproductive histories of those families which decided to relinquish one or more children. Corsini's findings indicate that in these families child abandonment operated, alongside mortality, as a mechanism to attain what must be taken to have been their targeted surviving family size, and that abandonment was actually rather more 'effective' (by a ratio of 1.5:1) than infant mortality. The soundness of Malthus's suggestion is thus vindicated. By paraphrasing his sentence, we might say that if a couple wished to control the number of their offspring, and were not soliticitous about the means, they could not resort to a more effectual measure than the abandonment of one or more children to a foundling hospital. And there seems to be little doubt that the availability of foundling hospitals could powerfully affect a couple's decisions and decisively shape their course of action.[44]

One crucial point remains to be considered, namely the social background of abandoning parents. The data collected by Corsini cannot be regarded as fully representative of the Tuscan case and do not allow conclusive answers. Nevertheless, they are very enlightening and highly relevant to the problems tackled in this chapter. What they indicate is that in rural communities the practice of abandonment was spread across the social and occupational board: abandoning parents included rural artisans, workers engaged in the building industry, agricultural labourers, and also – indeed rather prominently – sharecroppers. Corsini has suggested that the reasons behind abandonment could vary from one social category to another. The poorer agricultural labourers were presumably forced to relinquish their children because of sheer indigence. Couples living in sharecropping households could, on the other hand, be compelled to resort to abandonment because of the constraints imposed by sharecropping contracts. It may also be wondered whether Tuscan couples simply intended to reduce the number of children, or whether, rather, they aimed at achieving what was perceived to be a better balance in terms of age, gender and family roles. Be that as it may, what seems certain is that children of sharecroppers, presumably born into joint families, were not immune from the risk of being abandoned.[45]

ARTICULATING THE MODEL

The early modern Tuscan evidence on child abandonment shows that forms of 'joint-family hardship' are both theoretically conceivable and empirically documented, and suggests that a fuller understanding of the specific set of constraints affecting the life courses of individuals living in joint family households can make a significant contribution to the building of a more flexible and comprehensive model of the relationships between family and collectivity as systems of support. Although the extension and further articulation of the theoretical core of this model clearly represent a task for future research, a few preliminary points may nevertheless be mentioned here, however schematically.

Variability in joint family systems

The pattern of domestic organization which prevailed among the share-cropping population of the Tuscan countryside (and, indeed, of the whole of central Italy) in the late medieval and early modern periods is a classic example of joint family system and fits well with the influential definition of this family type proposed by Hajnal.[46] It should be noticed, however, that other variants of joint family organization have been found both in Europe and elsewhere. By far the best known is the 'perennial' multiple family household system of the Russian serf populations described by Peter Czap.[47] But several variants have emerged also in southern Europe.

One such variant is the joint family system recently documented for the Alpine region. The main features of this system have been described elsewhere,[48] but two relevant points need to be remembered here. The first is that in the Alps joint families, while being an adaptation to the harsh ecological imperatives of mountain environment, were none the less free from the very different but no less harsh constraints imposed on the central Italian family by sharecropping contracts. The second point is that, although this system is definitely joint and conforms to all of Hajnal's crucial criteria, nuptiality was relatively low. Indeed, marriage tended to be fairly late for both men and women, and celibacy rates could be exceedingly high.

Needless to say, low nuptiality increased the demographic potential of illegitimate fertility. It is remarkable that in many parts of the western Alps this potential appears not to have been fully realized. But there is scattered evidence of areas experiencing high levels of illegitimacy (sometimes in the form of sudden 'epidemics' of births out of wedlock), and it would seem that many of these illegitimate children were sent to foundling hospitals in the adjacent plains.[49] On balance, however, this upland system of joint family organization can be expected, at least in principle, to have provided married couples with better chances to keep their children than the stylized Tuscan system we have been outlining, because of its greater ability to control overall fertility through delayed marriage and high rates of celibacy.

Variability over time

In family history it is very often the case that exercises in model-building result in elegantly simple but essentially static pictures of the systems under study. There is even a danger that greater awareness of regional and spatial diversity, though making family historians more cautious when engaging in broad geographical generalizations, will encourage a tendency to emphasize long-term continuities and to lose sight of historical movement. Yet, a model trying to link child abandonment to family forms and nuptiality patterns will be severely limited, and in some ways positively misleading, unless variability over time is fully taken into account.

It is increasingly clear, for instance, that many misunderstandings in the debate about marriage and family patterns in the Mediterranean or southern European area have stemmed from a confusion of a medieval and possibly early modern pattern with patterns detectable later in time. The very notion of a specifically 'Mediterranean' marriage pattern is largely dependent on Herlihy and Klapisch-Zuber's characterization of nuptiality in fifteenth-century Tuscany.[50] But a number of recent studies unmistakably show that in Tuscany nuptiality declined markedly during the eighteenth and nineteenth centuries. By the middle of the nineteenth century, the Tuscan marriage pattern had lost entirely its 'Mediterranean' traits and complied very neatly with the basic criteria set by Hajnal to define his north-western European pattern.[51]

No less relevant to the problems dealt with in this chapter are the changes to the mortality of foundlings. It is often maintained that by abandoning a child to a hospital, parents were simply killing it with a good conscience, and it would be foolish to deny that infant and child mortality among foundlings was generally very high. But it would be equally wrong to overlook the fact that the mortality rates of foundlings varied very considerably over time. They appear to have reached a peak in the course of the eighteenth century, but by the middle of the nineteenth century they had dropped very substantially.[52]

This is clearly a very fundamental issue. Although it is permissible to see abandonment as a way of getting rid of surplus children, it is less clear whether parents intended to part with their children for good. As is well known, child abandonment has been taken by some family historians to be a crucial indicator of maternal, or parental, neglect.[53] Recent critics of this view have rightly remarked that the fact that identifying 'tokens' were usually attached to abandoned children testifies that many of these parents intended, or at least hoped, to be able to reclaim their children at a future date.[54] Particularly in the nineteenth century, the proportion of children reclaimed and returned to their parents in Italian cities like Florence or Milan was so high that it might be more appropriate to speak not so much of abandonment as of children temporarily entrusted to a charitable institution.[55] But the huge fluctuations observed in the mortality of foundlings over time certainly represented an all-important variable impinging on parental 'strategies of abandonment'. Surely it made a difference if parents had only a slim chance of getting back a child alive, or whether probabilities exceeded two-thirds, as was the case in nineteenth-century Milan.

Abandonment strategies in a joint family context

When dealing with strategies of abandonment, however, the crucial point is that the behaviour of married couples living in joint family households was subject to constraints which were very different from those affecting the lives of married couples heading their own nuclear family households. It has been rightly observed that the very notion of the 'developmental cycle' of the domestic unit cannot easily be applied to joint households.[56] Similarly, modelling the poverty cycle − or the risk of being abandoned − is more complex for children born into a joint family household than for children living in nuclear families.

It is usual to define 'periods of want' or 'life cycle squeezes' in terms of different stages in the life cycle of couples or individuals. But particularly when we are dealing with three-generational joint families, it is clear that focusing too exclusively on the sequence of life cycle squeezes experienced by a couple or by an individual may obscure simultaneous interrelationships to other couples or individual members of the household who are concurrently at different points in the life cycle.[57] In order to shed empirical light on the issue of abandonment strategies in a joint family context, it will be necessary to combine information from the records of foundling hospitals not only with evidence from family reconstitution studies but also with listings documenting co-residence, so as to see whether co-ordinated 'household strategies' of abandonment are detectable. This is a complicated exercise, but one which is scarcely avoidable.

CONCLUSIONS

One problem plaguing comparative research on poor relief in pre-industrial Europe is that evidence is often available for rural areas in the north and for urban areas in the south. Hypotheses concerning the relationships between household structure and the surrounding institutional environment, it has been recently suggested,[58] would serve to take research in this field away from the relatively well-studied southern European towns and into the still neglected countryside. This would help to better clarify, among other things, the links between rural and urban settings. Is it correct, for instance, to assume that the Italian town was a 'central place' that provided services (including orphanages and foundling hospitals) to an entirely dependent countryside? What about local-level welfare institutions and the welfare provided directly by the family?

In this chapter it has been argued that the nuclear-hardship hypothesis proposed by Laslett represents an important step forward in this direction and, more generally, towards the creation of a theoretical framework for the comparative study of formal and informal systems of support. However, if this hypothesis is tested in the context of a mere contraposition between northern and southern Europe, it runs the risk of being too easily refuted by simply adducing the fact that the role of the collectivity was far from being negligible in areas of southern Europe where joint families and other complex forms of household organization were widespread or even dominant.

It should not be forgotten that in southern Europe local communities were rarely homogeneous from a social and occupational point of view, and were therefore likely to exhibit more than one system of household formation. In most parts of central Italy, for instance, patrilocal residence prevailed among the sharecroppers, while day labourers and other agricultural wage-earners displayed a stronger tendency towards neo-locality. Because of its dishomogeneity, however, southern Europe can actually offer distinct advantages for controlled comparisons. The fact that nuclear and joint households often coexisted in the same communities provides quasi-experimental conditions to test the validity of the assumptions on which the nuclear-hardship hypothesis ultimately rests as well as some of its central predictions. From the vantage point adopted in this chapter, it would clearly be very interesting to establish, for example, whether children born into the nuclear family households of the Tuscan agricultural labourers had significantly higher chances of being abandoned than children born into the joint family households of the sharecroppers.

This may well turn out to be the case. But the fact that even the sons and daughters of sharecroppers were not immune from the risk of being abandoned still suggests that there might exist distinctive forms of 'joint-family hardship' resulting from the social and demographic dynamics specific to this type of domestic organization. This is a substantive and theoretical point which needs to be incorporated into a more flexible and comprehensive model of the relationships between family, kinship and the collectivity as systems of support in European history.

NOTES

1 J. Hajnal, 'European marriage patterns in perspective', in D.V. Glass and D.E.C. Eversley (eds), *Population in History*, London: Arnold 1965.

2 P. Laslett and R. Wall (eds), *Household and Family in Past Time*, Cambridge: Cambridge University Press 1972; P. Laslett, 'Characteristics of the western family considered over time', *Journal of Family History*, 2, 1977, pp. 89–115; A. Macfarlane, 'Demographic structures and cultural regions of Europe', *Cambridge Anthropology*, 6. 1980, pp. 1–17; R.M. Smith, 'The people of Tuscany and their families in the fifteenth century: Medieval or Mediterranean?', *Journal of Family History*, 6, 1981, pp. 107–28.

3 E.A. Wrigley and R.S. Schofield, *The Population History of England 1541–1871*, London: Arnold 1981, pp. 454–84.

4 J. Hajnal, 'Two kinds of pre-industrial household formation system', in R. Wall with J. Robin and P. Laslett (eds), *Family Forms in Historic Europe*, Cambridge: Cambridge University Press 1983; P. Laslett, 'Family and household as work group and kin group: Areas of traditional Europe compared', in Wall, with Robin and Laslett (eds), *Family Forms in Historic Europe*; A. Burguière, 'Pour une typologie des formes d'organisation domestique de l'Europe moderne', *Annales: économies, sociétés, civilisations*, 41, 1986, pp. 639–55; R. Rowland, 'Nupcialidade, familia, Mediterraneo', *Boletín de la Asociación de Demografia Histórica*, 5:2, 1987, pp. 128–43; M. Barbagli, 'Sistemi di formazione della famiglia in Italia', in E. Sonnino (ed.), *Popolazione, società e ambiente*, Bologna: Clueb 1990; R. Wall, 'European family and household systems', in Société Belge de Démographie, *Historiens et populations. Liber Amicorum Etienne Hélin*, Louvain-la-Neuve: Academia 1991.

5 Hajnal, 'Two kinds of pre-industrial household formation', pp. 68–72.

6 R.S. Schofield, 'The relationship between demographic structure and environment in pre-industrial Western Europe', in W. Conze (ed.), *Sozialgeschichte der Familie in der Neuzeit*, Stuttgart: Klett 1976; E.A. Wrigley, 'No death without birth: The implications of English mortality in the early modern period', in R. Porter and A. Wear (eds), *Problems and Methods in the History of Medicine*, London: Croom Helm 1987.

7 J. Henderson, 'Introduction', in his 'Charity and the poor in medieval and renaissance Europe', *Continuity and Change*, 3, 1988, p. 149.

8 See, for example, Henderson, ibid.: and B. Pullan, 'Support and redeem: Charity and poor relief in Italian cities from the fourteenth to the seventeenth century', in Henderson (ed.), *Charity and the Poor*, pp. 177–208.

9 P. Laslett, 'Family, kinship and collectivity as systems of support in pre-industrial Europe: A consideration of the nuclear-hardship hypothesis', in Henderson (ed.), *Charity and the Poor*, pp. 153–75. For an earlier formulation, see P. Laslett, 'Family and collectivity', *Sociology and Social Research*, 63, 1979, pp. 432–42.

10 See Laslett, 'Family, kinship and collectivity'; and also P. Laslett, *A Fresh Map of Life. The Emergence of the Third Age*, London: Weidenfeld & Nicolson 1989, pp. 122–39.

11 S.J. Woolf, *The Poor in Western Europe in the Eighteenth and Nineteenth Centuries*, London: Methuen 1986.

12 It should be noticed, however, that several major questions concerning the role of kinship in the European past are still far from being settled. For a recent and informative discussion of the debate on the role of kinship in England, see D. O'Hara, ' "Ruled by my friends": Aspects of marriage in the diocese of Canterbury, *c.* 1540–1570', *Continuity and Change*, 6, 1991, pp. 9–41. O'Hara argues

that the significance of kinship has been minimized and emphasizes its ideological importance in structuring social relations. However, she does not tackle the question of the role of kinship as a system of support. It is also worth noting that Laslett, 'Family, kinship and collectivity', pp. 159–60, refers to a possible paradox in the role of kinship, namely that non-co-resident kin might have been more important in securing support to needy relatives in those areas where households were less complex. A first attempt to explore this issue is D.I. Kertzer, D.P. Hogan and N. Karweit, 'Kinship beyond the household in a nineteenth-century Italian town', *Continuity and Change*, 7, 1992, pp. 103–21.

13 See Barbagli, 'Sistemi di formazione'; F. Benigno, 'The southern Italian family in the early modern period: A discussion of co-residence patterns', *Continuity and Change*, 4, pp. 165–94; Rowland, 'Nupcialidade'; P.P. Viazzo and D. Albera, 'The peasant family in northern Italy, 1750–1930: A reassessment', *Journal of Family History*, 15, 1990, pp. 461–82.

14 See, for example, J.E. Smith, 'Widowhood and ageing in traditional English society', *Ageing and Society*, 4, 1984, pp. 429–49.

15 M. Barbagli, *Sotto lo stesso tetto. Mutamenti della famiglia in Italia dal XV al XX secolo*, Bologna: Il Mulino 1984, p. 57; D.I. Kertzer, *Family Life in Central Italy, 1880–1910*, New Brunswick, NJ: Rutgers University Press 1984, p. 67. See also Laslett, 'Family, kinship and collectivity', p. 169.

16 See R. Wall, 'Leaving home and living alone: An historical perspective', *Population Studies*, 43, 1989, pp. 369–89.

17 B.S. Rowntree, *Poverty: A Study of Town Life*, London: Longmans, Green and Co. 1902, pp. 136–7.

18 Laslett, 'Family, kinship and collectivity', p. 167.

19 R. Wall, 'The age at leaving home', *Journal of Family History*, 3, 1978, pp. 181–202. The difference between the 'pre-industrial model' and Rowntree's model is probably accounted for by the severe decline in the frequency of life cycle service. But note that even in pre-industrial times, as Wall points out, significant variations could be found between the various communities.

20 Cf. R.M. Smith, 'Some issues concerning families and their property in rural England 1250–1800', in R.M. Smith (ed.), *Land, Kinship and Life-cycle*, Cambridge: Cambridge University Press 1984, pp. 73–8; and also Woolf, *The Poor in Western Europe*, pp. 14–16.

21 P. Laslett, 'Parental deprivation in the past', *Local Population Studies*, 3, 1974, pp. 11–18.

22 See, for example, R. Andorka, 'Household systems and the lives of the old in eighteenth- and nineteenth-century Hungary', in D.I. Kertzer and P. Laslett (eds), *Old Age in Past Times: The Historical Demography of Aging*, Berkeley, Calif.: University of California Press, forthcoming.

23 Very little has been done to explore this issue since the publication of the pioneering article by Laslett, 'Parental deprivation'. However, interesting findings have recently emerged from a study of an early modern English town, which suggest that apprenticeship was chiefly, or largely, a means of providing for orphans, many of whom were apprenticed within a matter of weeks of their parents' deaths. See G. Mayhew, 'Life cycle service and the family unit in early modern Rye', *Continuity and Change*, 6, 1991, pp. 216–23.

24 Hunecke has recently estimated that towards the middle of the nineteenth century approximately 120,000 infants were abandoned each year in Europe: nearly 35,000 were left at foundling homes in Italy, over 30,000 in France, 15,000 in Spain and another 15,000 in Portugal. See V. Hunecke, 'Intensità e fluttuazioni degli abbandoni dal XV al XIX secolo', in Collection de l'École Française de Rome, *Enfance abandonnée et société en Europe, XIVe–XXe siècle*, Rome: Ecole Française de Rome, 1991, pp. 36–8, and also Chapter 5.

25 B. Pullan, *Orphans and Foundlings in Early Modern Europe* (The Stenton Lecture 1988), Reading: University of Reading 1989.
26 R.T. Malthus, *An Essay on the Principle of Population*, 2nd edn, 1803, in E.A. Wrigley and D. Souden (eds), *The Works of Thomas Robert Malthus*, vol. 2, London: Pickering 1986, p. 187.
27 D.I. Kertzer and D.P. Hogan, *Family, Political Economy, and Demographic Change. The Transformations of Life in Casalecchio, Italy, 1861–1921*, Madison, Wis.: University of Wisconsin Press 1989, pp. 148–73.
28 K. Davis, 'Institutional patterns favoring high fertility in underdeveloped areas', *Eugenics Quarterly*, 2, 1955, pp. 33–9.
29 C. Poni, 'Family and *podere* in Emilia Romagna', *Journal of Italian Studies*, 1, 1979, pp. 201–34.
30 See Hunecke, 'Intensità e fluttuazioni degli abbandoni', p. 37.
31 This point is made by E.A. Wrigley, 'Marriage, fertility and population growth in eighteenth-century England', in R.B. Outhwaite (ed.), *Marriage and Society*, London: Europa Publications 1981.
32 See, for example, C.B. Brettell, *Men Who Migrate, Women Who Stay. Population and History in a Portuguese Parish*, Princeton, NJ: Princeton University Press 1986; P.P. Viazzo, 'Illegitimacy and the European marriage pattern: Comparative evidence from the Alpine area', in L. Bonfield, R.M. Smith and K. Wrightson (eds), *The World We Have Gained. Histories of Population and Social Structure*, Oxford: Blackwell 1986; B.J. O'Neill, *Social Inequality in a Portuguese Hamlet: Land, Late Marriage and Bastardy, 1870–1978*, Cambridge: Cambridge University Press 1987; and Chapter 2 by L. Valverde.
33 Cf. P. Laslett, K. Oosterveen and R.M. Smith (eds), *Bastardy and its Comparative History*, London: Arnold 1980; and M. Mitterauer, *Ledige Mütter. Zur Geschichte unehelicher Geburten in Europa*, Munich: Beck 1983.
34 P. Laslett, 'Introduction: Comparing illegitimacy over time and between cultures', in Laslett, Oosterveen and Smith (eds), *Bastardy and its Comparative History*.
35 A. Wilson, 'Illegitimacy and its implications in mid-eighteenth century London: The evidence from the Foundling Hospital', *Continuity and Change*, 4, 1989, pp. 103–64.
36 V. Fildes, 'Maternal feelings reassessed: Child abandonment and neglect in London and Westminster, 1550–1800', in V. Fildes (ed.), *Women as Mothers in pre-industrial England*, London and New York: Routledge 1990.
37 V. Hunecke, *I trovatelli di Milano. Bambini esposti e famiglie espositrici dal XVII al XIX secolo*, Bologna: Il Mulino 1989, esp. pp. 23–36. See also Hunecke, 'Intensità e fluttuazioni degli abbandoni', pp. 56–61.
38 On the contrast between northern and southern Portugal and on the relationships between demographic regimes, illegitimacy and abandonment, see R. Feijo, 'Regional distribution of foundlings and illegitimate children in Portugal (1860–1910)', paper presented to a conference on Regional Demographic Patterns in the Past, St Edmund's Hall, Oxford University, July 1985; and also C.B. Brettell and R. Feijo, 'Foundlings in nineteenth century northwestern Portugal: Public welfare and family strategies', in Collection de l'École Française de Rome, *Enfance abandonnée et société en Europe*.
39 Especially striking is the contrast between Florence and Bologna, two cities located less than 100 kilometres apart, similar in size and both serving as commercial centres for identical systems of sharecropping agriculture. Recent work by Kertzer and his associates has revealed that in the first half of the nineteenth century only 10 to 15 per cent of all children born in Bologna were abandoned and that they were mostly illegitimate. In Florence, on the other hand, in the same period up to 43 per cent of all children baptized in the city

Family structures and the life cycle 49

could be abandoned, and possibly two-thirds of them were legitimate. See D.I.
Kertzer, 'Gender ideology and infant abandonment in nineteenth-century Italy',
Journal of Interdisciplinary History, 22, 1991, pp. 1–25, who stresses that the
admission policies of the foundling homes diverged very considerably in the two
cities.

40 C.A. Corsini, 'Materiali per lo studio della famiglia in Toscana nei secoli XVII–
XIX: gli esposti', *Quaderni storici*, 11, 1976, pp. 998–1052; C.A. Corsini, 'Self-
regulating mechanisms of traditional populations before the demographic
revolution: European civilizations', in International Union for Scientific Study
of Population, *Proceedings of the International Population Conference, Mexico
1977*, vol. 3, Liège: Ordina 1977, 3, pp. 5–22.

41 Wilson, 'Illegitimacy and its implications'.

42 Corsini, 'Self-regulating mechanisms', pp. 8–9.

43 Corsini, 'Materiali per lo studio della famiglia', pp. 1006–7. On Milan, see
Hunecke, *I trovatelli di Milano*, pp. 138–42; and Chapter 5 in this volume.

44 Corsini, 'Self-regulating mechanisms', pp. 9–15.

45 Corsini, 'Materiali per lo studio della famiglia', pp. 1020–3; 'Self-regulating
mechanisms', pp. 18–22.

46 Hajnal, 'Two kinds of pre-industrial household formation', pp. 68–72.

47 P. Czap, 'The perennial multiple family household. Mishino, Russia,
1782–1858', *Journal of Family History*, 7, 1982, pp. 5–26. Cf. also P. Czap,
' "A large family: the peasant's greatest wealth": Serf households in Mishino,
Russia, 1814–1858', in Wall, with Robin and Laslett (eds), *Family Forms in
Historic Europe*, pp. 105–51; and Laslett, 'Family, kinship and collectivity',
pp. 158–9.

48 P.P. Viazzo, *Upland Communities: Environment, Population and Social Struc-
ture in the Alps since the Sixteenth Century*, Cambridge: Cambridge University
Press 1989, pp. 229–46; Viazzo and Albera, 'The peasant family in northern
Italy', pp. 465–71.

49 See, for example, P. Sibilla, *Una comunità walser delle Alpi*, Florence: Olschki
1980, pp. 105–6.

50 D. Herlihy and C. Klapisch-Zuber, *Les Toscans et leurs familles: une étude du
catasto florentin de 1427*, Paris: Presses de la Fondation Nationale de Sciences
Politiques 1978.

51 C.A. Corsini, 'Le trasformazioni demografiche e l'assetto sociale', in G. Mori
(ed.), *Prato: storia di una città*, Florence: Le Monnier 1989; Barbagli, 'Sistemi di
formazione', pp. 21–7; M. Della Pina, 'Famiglia mezzadrile e celibato: le
campagne di Prato nei secoli XVII e XVIII', in Sonnino (ed.), *Popolazione*; A.
Doveri, 'Sposi e famiglie nelle campagne pisane di fine '800. Un caso di "matrimonio mediterraneo"?', in Sonnino (ed.), *Popolazione*.

52 Infant mortality rates for foundlings exceeding the level of 800 per thousand
were by no means uncommon in the second half of the eighteenth century. By
the middle of the nineteenth century, these rates had declined in many places to
less than 500 per thousand and in Milan the infant mortality rate for foundlings
was in the region of 350 per thousand. Hunecke, *I trovatelli di Milano*,
pp. 148–58.

53 Cf., for example, L. De Mause (ed.), *The History of Childhood*, New York:
Psychohistory Press 1974; and E. Shorter, *The Making of the Modern Family*,
New York: Basic Books 1975.

54 Hunecke, *I trovatelli di Milano*, pp. 30–2; Fildes, 'Maternal feelings reassessed'.
The question is, however, very complex, as recently remarked by Hunecke himself, 'Intensità e fluttuazioni degli abbandoni', pp. 51–4; and by A.M. Maccelli,
Bambini abbandonati a Prato nel XIX secolo, in Collection de l'École Française
de Rome, *Enfance abandonnée et société en Europe*, pp. 820–1, who provides

a detailed quantitative analysis of the varying frequency of 'tokens' over time and in relation to the status (legitimate or otherwise) of abandoned children.

55   In the early 1840s the proportion of children returned to their parents was in the region of 25 per cent in Florence and nearly 40 per cent in Milan. It is worth remembering that the proportion is much higher (about two-thirds in Milan) if we consider only children surviving to age 1. Cf. Corsini, 'Materiali per lo studio della famiglia', pp. 1001–2; and Hunecke, *I trovatelli di Milano*, pp. 160–72. For a useful discussion of the reclamation of children in a number of different European settings, see Rachel Fuchs's recent contribution to L.A. Tilly, R.G. Fuchs, D.I. Kertzer and D.L. Ransel, 'Child abandonment in European history: A symposium', *Journal of Family History*, 17, 1992, pp. 8–9.

56   Czap, ' "A large family" ', pp. 135–41; D.I. Kertzer, 'The joint family household revisited: Demographic constraints and household complexity in the European past', *Journal of Family History*, 14, 1989, p. 12.

57   Cf. V.K. Oppenheimer, 'The changing nature of life-cycle squeezes', in R.W. Fogel and E. Shanas (eds), *Aging, Stability and Change in the Family*, New York: Academic Press 1981, p. 50. In Oppenheimer's definition, economic squeezes are situations in which the cost of achieving or maintaining an accustomed or desired life-style exceeds the income currently available to do so. Life cycle squeezes are those squeezes that are a product of the interaction of basic life cycle patterns associated with family and work behaviour.

58   Henderson, 'Introduction', pp. 147–9.

2 Illegitimacy and the abandonment of children in the Basque Country, 1550–1800

Lola Valverde

Historians usually try to explain why parents took the decision to abandon their children. In this chapter I will adopt the opposite approach: in other words, I will attempt to explain the reason why in the Basque Country before the eighteenth century people kept children who in other places or in other circumstances would have been abandoned.

The Basque Country lies between the river Ebro in the Iberian Peninsula and the river Adour in France. This territory of 20,664 square kilometres has no more natural frontiers than the Bay of Biscay and some parts of the above-mentioned rivers. The Basque Mountains, which are a western extension of the Pyrenees, produce two totally different environments: the northern slopes where the rivers flow into the Bay of Biscay, and the southern side, from where the rivers empty into the Mediterranean. The northern part is mountainous and wet, and little suited to the growing of corn, as practised on the wide flat fields of the south, where the climate is extremely dry. These geographical features have determined both the kind of crop and the extent of agricultural exploitation. Small farms are typical of the north as are large estates in the south. In turn this has directly influenced, over the long term, the different kind of organization and way of life of the inhabitants in each area.

There is a striking contrast between the illegitimate birth rate and the rate of abandonment. The illegitimacy rate in the Basque Country in the sixteenth and seventeenth centuries was extremely high, particularly when compared with the rates prevailing over much of rural western Europe. Nevertheless, before the middle of the eighteenth century, the number of abandoned children was so low that it can be considered a marginal phenomenon. No institution in the provinces of Guipuzcoa and Biscay took care of such children. Abandoned children from Guipuzcoa were admitted to the General Hospital in Pamplona because the diocese of Pamplona extended into this province. Abandoned children from Biscay were sent to Calahorra, which is also the capital of the bishopric, but their journey did not finish there for they were taken to the General Hospital in Saragossa until a foundling home was founded in 1794 in Calahorra. Altogether, the first set of children had to travel approximately 300 km and the second set

100 km. It is not surprising to find, therefore, that in the two parishes of the villages Asteasu and Villafranca, where between 13.4 and 22.2 per cent respectively of all the children baptized between 1560 and 1589 were recorded as illegitimate, there was no foundling baptized. The situation was the same at Motrico between 1550 and 1569 (see Tables 2.1 and 2.2). A study of the children baptized in four parishes between 1600 and 1659 also indicates that no relationship existed between the illegitimacy ratio and the rate of abandonment (see Table 2.3), although for the first time abandoned children are mentioned. At Villafranca 32.3 per cent of all children baptized between 1600 and 1619 were illegitimate.

Table 2.1 Illegitimate and abandoned children in Villafranca and Asteasu, 1560–89

Parish	Baptisms	Illegitimate children		Foundlings
		N	%	
Villafranca	698	155	22.2	0
Asteasu	760	102	13.4	0
Total	1,458	257	17.6	0

Source: AOSS: baptism registers of Villafranca and Asteasu.

Table 2.2 Illegitimate and abandoned children in Motrico, 1550–69

Parish	Baptisms	Illegitimate children		Foundlings
		N	%	
Motrico	1,076	231	21.4	0

Source: AOSS: baptism register of Motrico.

Table 2.3 Illegitimate and abandoned children in the parishes of Villafranca, Asteasu, Albacisqueta and Arrona, 1600–59

Period	Baptisms	Illegitimate		Foundlings	
		N	%	N	%
1600–9	796	174	21.8	0	0.0
1610–19	747	151	20.2	0	0.0
1620–9	640	119	18.6	1	0.1
1630–9	554	72	13.0	1	0.2
1640–9	679	107	15.7	3	0.4
1650–9	731	105	14.3	1	0.1
Total	4,147	728	17.5	6	0.1

Source: AOSS: baptism registers of Villafranca, Asteasu, Albacisqueta and Arrona.

As all these parishes were exclusively rural in character, the baptismal registers of an urban parish, Saint Vincent in the city of San Sebastian, have also been examined. However, the conclusions remain the same as only one foundling was listed between 1600 and 1609. By contrast over more or less the same period (1609–59), 4,104 foundlings were baptized at the San Lorenzo parish in Valladolid[1] and almost 10,000 children were taken in at the Casa Cuna in Seville between 1618 and 1659.[2] At La Inclusa in Madrid, as many as 55,420 babies were taken care of between 1586 and 1700. Many of them had been brought from neighbouring villages and abandoned in the streets of the city.[3] About 3,750 foundlings are reported in seventeenth-century Murcia.[4] Admittedly it is true that, Murcia apart, the afore-mentioned cities were among the largest in Spain, but it also has to be taken into account that abandonment of children was a general practice in Europe from the middle ages on, although peaking in the second half of the eighteenth century.

Consideration will now be given to the reasons for this low rate of abandonment in the Basque Country, which at first sight seems particularly surprising given the high illegitimacy ratio. Of special interest are the economic and social changes which in the second half of the eighteenth century led to a decline in illegitimacy, just when the abandonment of children began to be an almost normal practice in certain areas and circumstances.

THE SOCIAL ACCEPTANCE OF BASTARDY

If we consider the level of the illegitimacy ratio, it is not difficult to deduce that, in a society where almost a third to a quarter of the total of all children were not born within marriage, very little shame was likely to be attached to this fact. Shame did not cause young mothers to get rid of their newborn children by abandoning them. In addition, however, the wider context to bastardy needs to be examined. In the first place, in the Basque Country it almost certainly reflects the survival of customs regarding betrothal and marriage as the Catholic Reformation was much longer in taking root here than elsewhere. An exhaustive study of the reasons for this should be carried out and although this is beyond the scope of the present chapter, I would like to draw attention to the fact that the acceptance by the Basque population of canonical marriage as constituting the only valid union was a very slow process.

A very large proportion of illegitimate births in the sixteenth and seventeenth centuries were the offspring of concubinages, these being considered durable and institutionalized unions that were socially recognized and accepted. And the male partner in many of these concubinages was a priest, as indeed is the case in Guipuzcoa and Biscay before the eighteenth century. It is not possible to ascertain from the parish registers how frequently priests were involved, but the fact that an enormous number of such cases were taken before the church courts proves the importance of this matter. Admittedly, some moralists and historians have insisted that the priests who were indicted represented only a small minority of the priesthood and that the majority of priests, who were not mentioned, led chaste lives according to the rules of the church.

My view, by contrast, is just the opposite of this: namely, that the cases that found their way into the court represent the tip of an enormous iceberg. According to the 'Estado de la población de Asteasu',[5] of the thirteen priests who lived or had lived in the village with their concubines and their children, only two were taken to the court in Pamplona. The first was Don Tristan de Lizarraga in 1628, on the grounds that he cohabited with Maria Pérez de Igola by whom he had had three children.[6] And in the same year he was involved in another trial, accused of being a drunkard. In 1680, the accused was Don Jerónimo de Beroiz, who also lived with his concubine and his three children, all born of a different mother.[7] Six years after the trial, his situation had not changed. In the 'Estado' he appears as the occupant of the parish house, together with his concubine and the three children. The timing of this case from Asteasu is significant; it is on the threshold of the eighteenth century, a century after the reforms of the Council of Trent are supposed to have eliminated such practices.

Others besides priests contracted irregular unions, however, and an analysis of entries in the baptism register of Motrico between 1550 and 1568 throws some light on the motivations for forming such unions (see Table 2.4). A little more than half the illegitimate births in Motrico in these years were the consequence of the union between a man and his 'criada', literally

Table 2.4 Baptisms in the parish of Motrico, 1550–68

Period	Baptisms	Illegitimate		Illegitimate offspring of concubines		Percentage of all illegitimate
		N	%	N	%	
1550–68	1,076	223	20.7	115	10.7	51.5

Source: AOSS: baptism register no. 1, Motrico.

his servant. In this context, however, the word is used to indicate concubine. Most of these women had a dual role in that they were at the same time their master's mistress and looked after him and his household. The double meaning of this word is clearly expressed in the text of a treatise on morality published at the beginning of the eighteenth century, in which men were placed under the obligation to dismiss their concubine, even if there was a risk that they would not find another *criada* to care for them.[8] Several of those *criadas* at Motrico had more than one child by the same man, and the ambivalence of the word is emphasized when it emerges from an examination of the baptism register that some of the women were servants, *criadas*, of another man, or that they had another job. For example, there is the baptism in November 1552 of a child of 'Joan Mz. de Iturriça y Egurrola and Juana, his own servant, who was also servant in the house of Mr. Juanes de Hubillas'. Some days later, another child was baptized, of 'Joan de Arrançamendia and Maria Martiz, his servant, a woman who was resident in the mill of Caarche'.[9] Sometimes these women married the men they were living with, and became 'their wife'. In nine cases, the words '*su criada*' (his servant) have at some point been deleted and the words '*su muger*' (his wife) written above.[10]

This situation, which is comparable to that in western Europe at the end of the middle ages, seems to have persisted to an extraordinary extent in the Basque Country. In 1644 the 'Fueros' of Biscay, a digest of laws and customs of the Basque Country, revealed in the text of one of its laws that concubinage was still an accepted practice. A man declared publicly that a woman was his concubine and as a form of public affirmation had made for her several headdresses: 'and afterwards they themselves induced their friends to recognise their concubines and have made for them women's headdresses, according to the habits of the country'.[11]

As Claude Grimmer states, in France concubinage coexisted in the sixteenth century with legal marriage, and illegitimacy was a phenomenon found mostly among the aristocracy, as less than 1 per cent of the lower classes had bastard children.[12] In the Basque Country we see that this coexistence persisted into the eighteenth century, and that illegitimacy, which in sixteenth-century France was largely confined to aristocrats, was found at all levels of society.

THE PREVAILING PROPERTY SYSTEM IN THE BASQUE COUNTRY

Throughout almost the entire country the small size of the farms forced families to choose only one heir. The result was a high proportion of extended as well as multiple households, that is households containing both a core family (married couple with or without children or a lone parent) plus additional relatives. Unfortunately this is one of the least examined aspects of Basque social structure, so no hard evidence is available. However, the overall picture is clear enough. According to the census of Floridablanca (1786), 31.7 per cent of households in the Larraun valley had a complex structure and 59.1 per cent were nuclear, but if we compare the structure of the households of owners with those who were only tenant farmers it emerges that 51.3 per cent of the former were complex in character as against 16.5 per cent of the latter. In the nearby Basaburua Menor valley, 53 per cent of the households of owners were complex and 13 per cent of those of the tenants.[13] The average size of the household also varied. In Larraun the households of owners contained on average 6.8 members as against 6.2

for those in the Basaburua Menor and 5.4 in the village of Vera. The average size of households of tenant farmers was 4 in Larraun, 3.8 in Basaburua Menor and 4.2 in Vera.[14] Another study suggests that, on average, there were close to six persons per household in the Basque Country at the beginning of the eighteenth century.[15]

All these circumstances helped lower the number of abandoned children. A bastard child could be raised and integrated more easily within a large family group. Nuclear families had fewer resources to carry out this task and were more exposed to criticism. As the young mother might well have to seek employment, she had little possibility of giving her child more than a minimal amount of care. By contrast, there were more people available in a complex household on whom she could rely, such as grandparents, if they were still alive, or an uncle and aunt and/or their children, or other unmarried relatives.[16] For the purposes of illustration, data have been drawn from the eighteenth century when child abandonment was a frequent practice. Already, too, there were signs that fewer farms were owner-occupied. More and more land became concentrated in ever fewer hands and previous landowners became tenants on land they had once owned.

It is possible to chart the development of the patterns of landownership in thirteen Biscay parishes. In 1704 there were 829 owners and 526 tenants (60.4 and 38.8 per cent of the total). A hundred years later, in 1810, the number of owners had fallen to 791 and the tenants had risen to 1,387 (36.0 and 63.1 per cent respectively).[17] The proportions had virtually reversed. It is true that the absolute figures do not indicate a spectacular decrease in the number of landowners. More striking is the increase of tenants, and in the present context it is the latter trend which is of interest as it is known that the households of tenants were likely to be smaller and less complex in structure.

It seems likely therefore that the frequency of complex households in the wet mountain areas of the Basque Country was one of the factors that helps explain the rarity with which children were abandoned in the sixteenth and seventeenth centuries, just as in the eighteenth century the decrease in the number of such households accounts for the fact that many more young mothers had to abandon their children.

THE ABSENCE OF ALTERNATIVE CARE FACILITIES

Another explanation for the small number of foundlings in the Basque Country before the eighteenth century could simply be the lack of institutions dedicated to the care of foundlings. At the beginning of this chapter reference was made to the fact that foundlings from Guipuzcoa and Biscay had to be taken to Pamplona and Saragossa. In the French Basque Country, where the social and economic conditions were broadly similar, it was also the case that no establishments for this purpose existed before the nineteenth century. The presence of homes for foundlings had been considered by many commentators of the time likely to encourage the abandonment of children. Cabarrús, for example, expressed the position thus: 'We will always see the number of poor increase in proportion to the institutions founded to help them.'[18] When at the beginning of the nineteenth century, the province of Guipuzcoa decided to establish organizations for the care of foundlings, the provincial clergy expressed the same idea, arguing that with the creation of a home for children there was an important risk of young people rushing

> unbridled into the evil pleasures, and it is to be feared that evil, which is contagious, will spread to all classes and your Lordship will painfully see that dissoluteness, concubinage and immorality will be introduced everywhere.[19]

Yet it is evident that the creation of these institutions would not have taken place had there continued to be just a handful of foundlings in Basque society as in the seventeenth century. Nor can the absence of homes explain the rarity of child abandonment. Nevertheless it is reasonable to argue that once a population became accustomed to the presence of institutions of this kind, to which recourse could be made in case of need, the idea of abandonment as a commonplace would establish itself in the collective mind, and in turn lead some to think that the existence of these institutions did encourage the abandonment of children. The fact that government institutions took care of the children whom parents found difficult to raise surely provided one of the incentives for the enormous increase in the number of foundlings in Europe during the eighteenth and nineteenth centuries, more particularly as far as legitimate children were concerned. Even though other factors such as the nature of the property system were clearly more important, it could be argued that following the social acceptance of bastardy, by the late eighteenth century custom had now come to tolerate the abandonment of children. All these changes can also be considered as a consequence of the growing power of the state in areas that had previously been taken care of by the church, local authorities, the community or even individual inhabitants.

THE CHANGES TO THE LAW

The fourth factor, of critical importance in regard to the frequency of child abandonment, is the laws governing maintenance of children. In Castile, of which the Basque provinces formed part, medieval legal codes obliged fathers to provide for the maintenance of any of their children who were under the age of 3. If the mother herself wanted to feed and keep the child, the father had to give her, especially if she was poor, an amount of money equal to that usually paid to a wet-nurse. Once the child reached that age of 3, if the mother so wanted, the father was obliged to assume custody of his child and allow the child to live with him.[20] Many other European laws contained similar stipulations, as occurs, for example, in the Fuero of Navarre of the thirteenth century.[21] In fact, this remained the usual practice before the eighteenth century as is clear from an examination of many notarial deeds and court proceedings. The latter include agreements between the two parties concerning monetary compensation in cases of rape as well as the expenses incurred as a result of the birth and the need to feed the child. And in many of the cases it was determined that the child would be placed under the authority of the father. Even if the father was married to another woman, he would let his bastard child live with his own family. One such situation was documented in 1717, when Matheo de Aguirre, a resident of Albacisqueta, promised to give 120 ducats to Mariana de Mendizabal for depriving her of her virginity, and stated that they had a son 'called Juan Antonio who is living now at the mentioned Matheo de Aguirre's home', he himself being married to Cathalina de Latiegui.[22] Another case comes from 1718. Domingo de Imaz declared before the notary Arrizcorreta of Villa-franca that, after he had had sexual intercourse with Isabela de Ayesta, she had given birth to a child and that they had agreed that Domingo 'receive the child to take care of it forever, and she would not have to take charge of it'.[23] There are many documents like these in the seventeenth and at the beginning of the eighteenth centuries. But they slowly become very rare, and finally disappear completely by 1800.

Two points are especially remarkable: first, how little attachment the mothers showed to their children; and, second, the converse, the degree of responsibility taken by the father. There is, of course, a simple financial explanation for the behaviour of the mothers, who in most of the cases could not afford to take charge of their children. But, on the other hand, the reification of motherhood, which considers the link between a mother and her child as paramount and forces the mother to consider this link as more important that anything else, had clearly not emerged as a potent ideology.

Mothers who parted from their babies in this way in the eighteenth century and earlier probably did not feel any guilt as a result, nor did it turn them into bad mothers, either in their own view or in that of society as a whole. As for the fathers, very few of them denied their fatherhood. More often they contested that there had been rape, or that there had been an engagement. The child belonged to the father, who regarded the child, in a certain sense, as his property and over whom he possessed all rights. This feeling was sufficiently strong to lead him to take full responsibility for the raising of the child in his own household and to meet all the expenses that entailed. The mother was considered simply as the 'receptacle', the place where the man had 'made' the child. Even science came to support this theory of conception. Experts thought they could see, through their micro-scopes, a little man in each spermatozoon, which they called '*homunculus*'[24] who only had to grow in the womb.

In the eighteenth century, however, these laws either disappeared or if they remained in some of the codes, or were eliminated later, their appli-cation became very restricted. In case of a claim, women were asked for more and more conclusive oral, or written evidence, when they alleged the existence of an engagement, which was often very difficult to produce. A combination of circumstances discouraged women from going to the court fearing that they would not get a hearing or, even worse, that they could be convicted themselves if they were unable to prove that their accusation was well-founded. In 1817 Micaela Antonia de Irazusta was convicted in this way. She alleged rape by Juan Antonio de Garagarza but had been unable to prove this to the satisfaction of the court.[25] Finally, the new civil code which prohibited the investigation of the issue of paternity rendered unmarried mothers almost totally powerless. The historian J.-L. Flandrin has commented on this as follows: 'Young mothers, who were considered to have the sole responsibility for the conception of their children, had to cope with the financial consequences, although most of them had no economic resources',[26] and has argued that the increase in the abandonment of children in the eighteenth century was one of the direct consequences. As the father and his responsibility for the child had disappeared, abandonment of the child was the only solution open to many unmarried mothers. The foundling home was created to prevent mothers from resorting to another kind of solution, that of infanticide. In a sense the state had become a substitute for the father in that it was carrying out duties earlier performed by the father.

THE EVOLUTION OF THE PRACTICE OF ABANDONMENT

Tables 2.3, p. 52 and 2.5 indicate that the illegitimacy ratio declined slowly from the beginning of the seventeenth century. Yet in the early eighteenth century the ratio was still very high relative to the illegitimacy ratio in other rural areas of Europe. Over the same period the abandonment of children remained a rare phenomenon: 0.1 per cent for the period 1600 to 1659,

Table 2.5 Illegitimate children and foundlings in Villafranca, Asteasu, Albacisqueta and Arrona, 1660–1719

Period	Baptisms	Illegitimate		Foundlings	
		N	%	N	%
1660–9	703	63	8.9	5	0.7
1670–9	697	58	8.3	0	0.0
1680–9	847	93	10.9	2	0.2
1690–9	776	72	9.2	1	0.1
1700–9	766	63	8.2	3	0.4
1710–19	753	67	8.9	3	0.4
Total	4,542	416	9.1	14	0.3

Source: AOSS: baptism registers of Villafranca, Asteasu, Albacisqueta and Arrona.

Table 2.6 Illegitimate children and foundlings in Villafranca, Asteasu, Albacisqueta and Arrona, 1720–1829

Period	Baptisms	Illegitimate		Foundlings	
		N	%	N	%
1720–9	835	49	5.8	3	0.3
1730–9	1,003	50	5.0	0	0.0
1740–9	993	22	2.2	2	0.2
1750–9	966	24	2.5	2	0.2
1760–9	1,051	18	1.7	5	0.4
1770–9	968	11	1.1	1	0.1
1780–9	935	17	1.8	3	0.3
1790–9	1,019	21	2.0	6	0.6
1800–9	1,082	41	3.9	6	0.5
1810–19	1,165	40	3.4	15	1.3
1820–9	1,104	31	2.8	10	0.9
Total	11,121	324	2.9	53	0.5

Source: AOSS: baptism registers of Villafranca, Asteasu, Albacisqueta and Arrona.

Table 2.7 Illegitimate children and foundlings in Villafranca, Asteasu, Albacisqueta, Arrona, Legorreta, Motrico, Renteria and Saint Vincent in San Sebastian, 1770–1829

Period	Baptisms	Illegitimate		Foundlings	
		N	%	N	%
1770–9	4,484	113	2.5	84	1.8
1780–9	5,043	167	3.3	86	1.7
1790–9	4,764	135	2.8	93	1.9
1800–9	4,992	196	3.9	67	1.3
1810–19	4,358	170	3.9	152	3.5
1820–9	4,810	134	2.8	329	6.8
Total	28,451	915	3.2	811	2.8

Source: AOSS: baptism registers of Villafranca, Asteasu, Albacisqueta, Arrona, Legorreta, Motrico, Renteria and Saint Vincent in San Sebastian.

0.3 per cent for 1660–1719 and 0.4 per cent for the period 1720 to 1829 (Table 2.6) in the same four parishes.

From the end of the eighteenth century an increase in the percentage of foundlings is clearly visible. For the purposes of Table 2.7, covering the period 1770–1829, baptisms from some other rural parishes and an urban one, the parish of Saint Vincent in the city of San Sebastian, have been considered in addition to those of the four original parishes. In the city parish, the abandonment of children began to be an important phenomenon, and in the nineteenth century the trend became even more marked. The increase in the percentage of foundlings in the group of selected parishes is very largely an artefact of the rate at which children were abandoned in the city. However, the abandonment of children was not just an urban phenomenon as country-dwellers also brought children to the city in order to abandon them. Records of the number of children brought from Guipuzcoa to the Inclusa of Pamplona (see Table 2.8) also suggest an increase in the percentage of children abandoned during the eighteenth century. Every foundling brought from Guipuzcoa had to be paid for in order to be accepted at the Inclusa of Pamplona, while those coming from Navarre were received without charge. The children can be identified in the register of children received and in the books detailing payments to wet-nurses. Both record series survive from 1710.

Table 2.8 Foundlings from Guipuzcoa taken in at the Inclusa in Pamplona, 1710–59

Period	Children	Period	Children
1710–19	40	1760–9	186
1720–9	49	1770–9	254
1730–9	110	1780–9	268
1740–9	93	1790–9	256
1750–9	125		

Source: AMHN: foundling registers, 1710–99.

However, a small section of the Basque Country, the most western part, belonged, just like Biscay, to the Diocese of Calahorra. Foundlings from there were brought to the same place as the babies from Biscay. Table 2.8 therefore probably underestimates the number of foundlings from Guipuzcoa. This is especially likely to be the case in the last two decades as the increasing cost of placing children in the Inclusa may have helped deter the placement of foundlings from the Basque Country. In 1784, the contribution for children from Guipuzcoa was increased from 100 to 250 *reales*, and in 1791 to 300 *reales*. Indeed, it is known that the municipal authorities of Guipuzcoa sometimes preferred to pay a nurse in the same city where the child had been found than to send the child to Pamplona and pay the fee of 300 *reales*. Of the ten foundlings baptized in Renteria between 1760 and 1789 only seven can be found in the records of the Inclusa at Pamplona, as can three of the four foundlings from Legorreta. Some of the missing children may have been nursed locally, but another possibility should also be considered: that the child may have died after baptism, before or during the journey to Pamplona.

The overall conclusion is that the slow introduction in the Basque Country of the Counter-Reformation and the dispositions of the Council of

Trent did eventually help modify sexual behaviour. Nevertheless, concubinage persisted for a long time as did the percentage of children who were illegitimate. These natural children were not abandoned as no social stigma seems to have been attached to them or to their mothers. The existing family structures allowed for an easy integration of these children, who would have lived with their parents in any case, if the offspring of a concubinage. If the young mother did not live in concubinage and was unable to marry the baby's father, she could always demand that the father take charge of the child. Given these circumstances it was unnecessary before the nineteenth century to create institutions in the Basque Country for the care of foundlings.

Throughout this long period, the Catholic Church campaigned vigorously to reduce the incidence of extra-marital sex, arguing that sexual intercourse was lawful only within marriage. The result was that the view of sex as sin began to be accepted more widely. In the Basque Country, however, this development was delayed because it was only in the eighteenth century that the Counter-Reformation had any impact. Only then did the behaviour of the Basque clergy start to change. During this century disputes concerned with irregular unions of priests, formerly so frequent, gradually disappeared, as did the phenomenon of concubinage, while the illegitimacy ratio fell continuously and unmarried motherhood came to be considered a moral failing. The same period saw a decline in the number of complex households and, in addition, fathers ceased to have a duty to maintain their natural children. Young unmarried mothers were therefore left totally responsible for their children which helps to explain the increase in the number of foundlings in the Basque Country. Other factors, such as the greater incidence of poverty at the end of the *ancien régime* should be added to these specific causes, as should the increased willingness of the Basque population to follow the dictates of the church. Nevertheless, even in the nineteenth century the Basque Country exhibited certain differences in its attitude to foundlings, as when after 1804 the authorities of the Guipuzcoa province organized a care-taking service, distributing the foundlings among nurses, without creating a specific institution (which was only founded in 1903). In Biscay foundlings were treated in the traditional way with the creation of the Inclusa of Bilbao in September 1806.

NOTES

Abbreviations

AGG   Archivo General de Guipuzcoa: general files of Guipuzcoa
AMAMZ   Archivo Municipal de Amezqueta: municipal files of Amezqueta
AMHN   Archivo de la Maternidad del Hospital de Navarra: maternity files at the hospital of Navarre
AOP   Archivo del Obispado de Pamplona: bishopric files at Pamplona
AOSS   Archivo del Obispado de San Sebastian: bishopric files at San Sebastian

1 According to data provided by T. Egido, 'Aportación al estudio de la demografía española: los niños expósitos de Valladolid (siglos XVI−XVIII)', *Actas de las primeras jornadas de metodología aplicada de las ciencias históricas*, 3, Santiago de Compostela 1975, p. 337.
2 According to data provided by L.C. Alvarez Santaló, *Marginación social y mentalidad en Andalucia Occidental: Expósitos en Sevilla (1613−1810)*, Seville: Consejeria de Cultura de la Junta de Andalucia 1980.
3 C. Larquié, 'La mise en nourrice des enfants madrilènes au XVII siècle', *Revue d'histoire moderne et contemporaine*, 32, 1985, pp. 127, 131.
4 F. Chacón, R. Fresneda Collado and R. Elgarrista Domeque, 'Aproximación al estudio de la entidad familiar: el abandono y la adopción de expósitos en Murcia (1601−1721)', in Collection de l'École Française de Rome, *Enfance abandonnée et société en Europe, XIVe−XXe siècle*, Rome: Ecole Française de Rome 1991.
5 M.R. Ayerbe Iribar, 'Estado de la población y casas y caseríos de Asteasu en 1686', *Boletin de la Real Sociedad Bascongada de Amigos del Pais*, XXXIX: books no. 1 and 2, San Sebastián 1983, pp. 231−56.
6 AOP, Ollo c/ 654, nos 3 and 8.
7 AOP, Ollo c/ 929, no. 2.
8 F. Larraga, *Promptuario de la teología-moral*, 3rd edn, Pamplona 1799, pp. 687.
9 AOSS, baptism register of Motrico, book no. 1.
10 ibid.
11 *Privilegios, franquezas y libertades de los cavalleros hijosdalgo del Senorio de Vizcaya*, 1644, Título doze, ley IIII. The reference to headdresses requires some explanation. Unmarried women would not usually cover their hair but married women or widows wore 'headdresses'. The law of the 'Fueros de Vizcaya', mentioned here, indicates that mistresses were accorded a status equivalent to that of married women. The headdresses of the Basque women caused astonishment among travellers, for example, to Christoph Weiditz, *Das Trachtenbuch des Christoph Weiditz von seinen Reisen nach Spanien und den Niederlanden 1529−1532*, Leipzig: Walter de Gruyter & Co. 1927. Most of the authors were conscious of the phallic symbolism. The top of the widows' headdresses hung down 'pour marquer que le masle leur deffault', according to Pierre de Lancre in his book *Tableau de l'inconstance des mauvais anges et démons*, Paris 1612. Montaigne expressed the same idea in his *Essais*: 'Les femmes mariées icy prez, en forgent, de leur couvrechez, une figure sur leur front pour se glorifier de la jouïsance qu'elles en ont: en venant à estre veusves, se couchent en arrière, et esepvelissent soubs leur coeffure.' Gabriel de Minuit wrote in 1587 'Femmes de Bayonne portant un membre viril sur la coiffure de leur teste.' And so on. . . . Unmarried women had their head almost completely shaved. In 1600 the Bishop of Pamplona refused to allow women to come into the church with headdresses because he considered they were indecent and scandalous, inappropriate for decent women. The habit of phallic headdresses as well as the shaving of the hair of young women disappeared at the end of the seventeenth century.
12 C. Grimmer, *La femme et le bâtard*, Paris: Presse de la Rennaissance 1983, pp. 134, 169.
13 F. Mikelarena Peña, 'Transformaciones económicas y demográficas en el norte de Navarra en los siglos XVI y XVII', *Evolución demográfica bajo los Austrias* III, Alicante: Il Congreso de la Asociación de Demografía Histórica 1991, pp. 115−25.
14 ibid.
15 A.R. Ortega Berruguete, 'Matrimonio, fecundidad y familia en el Pais Vasco a finales de la Edad Moderna', *Boletin de la Asociación de Demografía Histórica*, 7:1, 1989, p. 67.

16 Eugenio Sonnino in his contribution to this volume (Chapter 4) also points out the larger capacity of complex households to provide familial support for needy relatives even in difficult circumstances.

17 E. Fernández de Pinedo, *Crecimiento económico y transformaciones sociales del Pais Vasco, 1100–1850*. Madrid: Siglo XXI de Espana Editores, SA 1974, p. 264.

18 F. de Cabarrús, *Memoria sobre los Montes Pios*, quoted by V. Pérez Moreda, *Las crisis de mortalidad en la España interior, siglos XVI–XIX*, Madrid 1980, p. 171.

19 AGG, first section, neg. 20, leg. 17.

20 Partidas. Cuarta Partida, título XIX, ley III: 'en cuya guarda del padre o de la madre deuen ser los fijos para nodrescer, e criarlos'.

21 Fuero General de Navarra, 4° book, title IV, ch. 1.

22 AGG, 2972.

23 AGG, 2972.

24 L.A. Landa, 'The Shandean Homunculus: The background of Sterne's "Little Gentleman"', in C. Camden (ed.), *Restoration and Eighteenth Century Literature: Essay in Honor of A.D. McKillop*. Chicago, Ill.: University of Chicago Press 1963, pp. 49–68.

25 AMAMZ, 44.

26 J.-L. Flandrin, *Le sexe et l'occident*, Paris: Editions du Seuil 1981, p. 291.

3 'Perche non avea chi la ghovernasse'

Cultural values, family resources and abandonment in the Florence of Lorenzo de' Medici, 1467–85*

Philip Gavitt

Precisely because the majority of studies of abandonment to institutions have focused on the period after 1600, these studies have formed a consensus of sorts around the important findings of Carlo Corsini that families employed abandonment as a strategy to prevent themselves from sinking irrevocably into poverty.[1] Both the overwhelming scale and pattern of abandonment during the three centuries between 1600 and 1900 pre-suppose enormous population pressure that resulted in oppressively harsh economic conditions for rural populations on the margins of subsistence. In fifteenth-century Florence, however, the records of the foundling hospital of Santa Maria degli Innocenti, which was opened in 1445, make it abundantly clear that abandonment was not exclusively, or even largely, the recourse of poverty-stricken families. Only after the sixteenth century did abandonment of children to the Innocenti less frequently involve the Florentine patriciate. Before 1600, strategies of inheritance resulted in as much abandonment to the Innocenti as strategies of survival.

Equally distinctive of the earlier period was the importance of the relationship between gender and abandonment. As John Henderson's researches on late medieval Florentine charity in general have shown, women accounted for well over a majority of the disbursement of confra-ternal charity.[2] Similarly, females made up a substantial majority of infants admitted to the Ospedale degli Innocenti between 1445 and 1485 (see Tables 3.1–3.4).[3] That women should be the focus of Florentine charity during the Renaissance and early modern period stems from the unhappy conflict between the demography of fifteenth-century Tuscany and its prevailing system of inheritance. The average age of marriage for Florentine males was close to 30 years; for females, mid-to-late teens.[4] Michelangelo's lament at the age of 37 that 'if more of life remains to me, I want to live it in peace',[5] and Alessandra Strozzi's declaration that her daughter's advanced age, 16, depressed her value in the marriage market, illustrate in concrete terms the widespread expectation that women were likely to become widows and to face the prospect of remarriage.[6]

At first glance, one would expect the system of inheritance current in Tuscany during the fifteenth and sixteenth centuries to support the position

Table 3.1   Admissions to the Ospedale degli Innocenti, 1467–85

Year	Males admitted	Females admitted	Gender unknown	Total admitted
1467	59	101	0	160
1468	78	108	2	188
1469	70	106	0	176
1470	82	79	0	161
1471	63	96	0	159
1472	65	76	7	148
1473	55	79	2	136
1474	73	79	0	152
1475	80	121	0	201
1476	92	99	0	191
1477	97	123	0	220
1478	110	169	0	279
1479	153	204	0	357
1480	125	135	0	260
1481	87	126	0	213
1482	107	103	0	210
1483	85	137	0	222
1484	104	170	0	274
1485	87	109	0	196
Total	1,672	2,220	11	3,903
Per cent	42.8	56.9	0.3	100

Source: Archive of the Hospital of the Innocenti (AOIF), Balie e Bambini G–L (XVI, 7–11), 1467–85.

of women, married or unmarried. Even at the lowest end of the socio-economic scale women had a dowry of some sort. The girls of the Innocenti in the fifteenth century, for example, by any measure at the very bottom of the social order, commanded dowries up to 200 lire, a figure that would be raised to 300 lire in the later sixteenth century.[7] In theory, in addition to guaranteeing family honour, the dowry should have served to protect a woman in the event of her husband's death. Indeed, for those wealthy families who could provide dowries more than ten times the size of the minimum provided by the Innocenti, the reversion of dowries to the males of the widow's original household did offer protection. The letters of Alessandra Strozzi, herself in this fortunate group of widows, show how her kinsmen allowed considerable latitude and provided substantial help so that she could raise sons and daughters.[8] Elaine Rosenthal has also shown that women in such families as the Giovanni and the Parenti could rely upon the support of kinship networks, and that these patrician families lavished considerable attention and protection on children left suddenly fatherless.[9] At the lower echelons of the socio-economic scale, however, a widow could not have expected her kinsmen to support her for an extended period of time, especially if she had children. However adequate dowries

Table 3.2 Admissions under 1 year to the Ospedale degli Innocenti, 1467–85

Year	Males admitted	Females admitted	Total admitted
1467	59	90	149
1468	72	99	171
1469	66	100	166
1470	80	73	153
1471	63	91	154
1472	62	63	125
1473	53	75	128
1474	67	76	143
1475	78	114	192
1476	86	92	178
1477	82	105	187
1478	93	141	234
1479	124	170	294
1480	118	126	244
1481	82	122	204
1482	101	94	195
1483	73	112	185
1484	87	126	213
1485	79	95	174
Total	1,525	1,964	3,489
Per cent	43.7	56.3	100

Source: AOIF, Balie e Bambini, G–L (XVI, 7–11), 1467–85.

might have been, relatives needed to preserve them for subsequent marriage.

Yet, should a woman with children wish to embark on a subsequent marriage, the patrilineal inheritance system that was designed to protect her, instead obstructed her both from remarrying and from providing for her children. If she remarried, the inheritance rights of children born of the first marriage automatically conflicted with those of any offspring from the second, a conflict that few prospective fathers greeted with enthusiasm and that parents often resolved by abandonment of children to foundling hospitals.[10] In cases where the mother died first, not even fathers could always count on support from those extended family networks that populate our stereotypes of Mediterranean systems of inheritance.

Among families in the *contado*, the numerical importance of wet-nurses, especially in the Mugello and Casentino (see Table 3.5), suggests that the economic status both of married and unmarried women was fragile. Once institutions such as the Innocenti permitted abandonment in larger numbers, the practice grew exponentially as women both in Florence and in the *contado* found an infinitely expanding market for their own milk.

Yet the same family strategies and economic powerlessness of these wet-nurses accounted for the high rate of mortality among children sent to

Table 3.3 Number of admissions <1 year old compared to baptisms in Florence

Year	Males admitted	Males baptized	Females admitted	Females baptized	Total admitted	Total baptized
1467	59	1,113	90	1,095	149	2,208
1468	72	1,063	99	982	171	2,045
1469	66	1,097	100	1,022	166	2,119
1470	80	1,235	73	1,080	153	2,315
1471	63	1,314	91	1,183	154	2,497
1472	62	1,238	63	1,208	125	2,446
1473	53	1,293	75	1,257	128	2,550
1474	67	1,298	76	1,235	143	2,533
1475	78	1,265	114	1,271	192	2,536
1476	86	1,313	92	1,199	178	2,512
1477	82	1,286	105	1,253	187	2,539
1478	93	1,362	141	1,302	234	2,664
1479	124	1,115	170	1,011	294	2,126
1480	118	1,118	126	1,097	244	2,215
1481	82	1,168	122	1,169	204	2,337
1482	101	1,273	94	1,139	195	2,412
1483	73	1,282	112	1,233	185	2,515
1484	87	1,215	126	1,144	213	2,359
1485	79	1,215	95	1,206	174	2,421
Total	1,525	23,263	1,964	22,086	3,489	45,349

Sources: AOIF, Balie e Bambini G–L (XVI, 7–11), 1467–85; M. Lastri, *Ricerche sull'antica e moderna popolazione della città di Firenze per mezzi dei registri del battistero di San Giovanni dal 1451 al 1774*, Florence 1775.

wet-nurses. Valerie Fildes's studies of wet-nursing have explained the demand among wealthy families for wet-nurses as a deliberate strategy to minimize lactation and therefore maximize fertility.[11] At the same time, the smaller household size of poorer families, as documented in the Catasto of 1427, led Herlihy and Klapisch-Zuber to conclude that poorer households exercised, if only through abandonment, some form of limitation on family size.[12] Certainly, in a culture that rarely fed two children with a single wet-nurse (in over 5,000 cases between 1445 and 1485 I was unable to find a single wet-nurse who held two of the Innocenti's children simultaneously at the breast), the relationship between a wet-nurse's occupation and her immediate household size was direct.[13] If a wet-nurse did not farm out her child to another nurse, the child had either died or, more frequently in the fifteenth century, had been abandoned. Since paying another nurse effaced the economic benefit of selling one's own milk, abandonment was the more likely alternative.

The most likely reason for the high rate of mortality among infants at wet-nurse was not the rigours of the journey, as has been documented for eighteenth- and nineteenth-century France,[14] nor suffocation,[15] but starvation. By the terms of most contracts, wet-nurses agreed to return the child

Table 3.4 Percentage of admissions <1 year old to baptisms in Florence by gender, 1467–85

Year	Males %	Females %	Total %
1467	5.3	8.2	6.7
1468	6.7	10.1	8.4
1469	6.0	9.8	7.9
1470	6.5	6.8	6.6
1471	4.8	7.7	6.2
1472	5.0	5.2	5.1
1473	4.1	6.0	5.0
1474	5.2	6.2	5.7
1475	6.2	9.0	7.6
1476	6.5	7.7	7.1
1477	6.4	8.4	7.4
1478	6.8	10.8	8.8
1479	11.1	16.8	13.9
1480	10.6	11.5	11.0
1481	7.0	10.4	8.7
1482	7.9	8.3	8.1
1483	5.7	9.1	7.4
1484	7.2	11.0	9.1
1485	6.5	7.9	7.2
1467–85	6.6	8.9	7.7

Sources: AOIF, Balie e Bambini G–L (XVI, 7–11), 1467–85; M. Lastri, *Ricerche sull'antica e moderna popolazione della città di Firenze per mezzi dei registri del battistero di San Giovanni dal 1451 al 1774*, Florence 1775.

to the hospital if the child fell ill or the wet-nurse became pregnant, and to notify the hospital immediately in the case of the child's death. In the case of pregnancy, however, a strong economic disincentive prevented many wet-nurses from fulfilling their obligation to notify the hospital, since in such cases the hospital demanded the child's return and payments ceased.

Moreover, if wet-nurses either perceived or harboured an anti-feminine bias, they would have been more likely to fail to return a female than a male child, which would explain the higher mortality of female infants in the fifteenth century (see Tables 3.6–3.8).[16] The wet-nurses' own family strategies also seem to have attempted to maximize fertility, given the great number of children whom wet-nurses returned to the Innocenti 'badly cared for', or 'neglected, to the point of starvation', or worse yet, 'dead of hunger'.[17]

Both in Florence and the *contado*, the numbers of '*fanciulle vedove*' (girl widows), which tended to increase in times of economic hardship, underscore both the precarious economic status of this group of women and the paradoxes inflicted by the disparity between the sexes of age at marriage.[18]

Throughout the period 1445–85, in a society for which it has been suggested that the embrace of extended family and neighbourhood networks

Table 3.5 Towns and regions with five or more children abandoned to the Innocenti or with five or more wet-nurses who served the Innocenti

Town/Region†	Children	Wet-nurses
Ancisa	1	5
Antella	1	6
Barberino Val d'Elsa	1	5
Barberino di Mugello	0	37
Borgo San Lorenzo	5	28
Brozzi	0	6
Calenzano	1	9
Campi	4	12
Carmignano	1	24
Cascia	2	42
'Casentino'	11	4
Castello	3	6
Castello S. Giovanni	2	5
Castello S. Niccolò	4	186
Certaldo	2	8
Chasale Guidi, Val di Marina	2	10
Dicomano	3	24
Empoli	12	10
Fiesole	7	12
Figline	1	12
Firenze	179	62
Firenzuola	5	26
Fronzano	0	11
Ghagliano	0	7
Ghaleata	0	5
Greve	1	12
Impruneta	3	6
La C[h]avallina	1	9
La Lastra	5	6
Lamporecchio	0	6
Manghona	0	31
Midwives in Florence	83	—
Montale	0	13
Montecatini	0	7
Montelupo	8	16
Montemagnio	0	19
Montemurlo	0	7
Monterappoli	2	6
Montespertoli	4	14
'Mugello'	26	34
Palazzuolo	1	10
Piancaldoli	0	8
Pieve di Doccia	2	5
Pistoia	6	7
Pitiano	0	6
Poggio a Caiano	0	8
Pontassieve	8	38
Ponte a Rignano	0	11
Poppi, Casentino	1	10

Town/Region†	Children	Wet-nurses
Portic[h]o	0	5
Pozzolatic[h]o	3	11
Prato	10	42
Pratolino	0	7
Pratovecchio	1	11
Quarantola	0	5
Quarrata	1	5
Ripoli	4	5
S. Casciano	7	20
S. Donato in Fronzano	0	6
S. Godenzo	1	10
S. Martino La Palma	3	5
Scarperia	7	24
Sc[h]opeto	0	5
Sesto	4	13
Settimo	2	8
Signa	4	6
Terranuova	4	7
Ti[n]gnano	2	6
Tizzano	0	10
'Val d'Arno'	11	10
'Val di Pesa'	3	8
Vicchio, Mugello	3	51
Villore	0	18
Vinci	2	18
Vitigliano	0	6
Vitolino	0	8
Totals*	470	1,181

Notes: † Region indicated by quotation marks.
* Totals are not in any sense comparable to one another, since parents, unlike wet-nurses, were not required to state their town or region.

Source: AOIF, Balie e Bambini G–L (XVI, 7–11), 1467–85.

would protect children from abandonment and isolation, one finds instead that our functionalist view of patrilineage and extended family has important limitations. Clearly, the organization of familial systems in Renaissance Florence failed to cover circumstances that were far from rare. In addition, the view of children consigned impersonally to permanent oblivion in early modern foundling hospitals, a view articulated in Boswell's *The Kindness of Strangers*, requires some revision in the light of evidence from the Innocenti, where some 6 per cent of children were returned to their families.[19] Moreover, almost all notes left by abandoning parents expressed the hope that circumstances might permit them to reclaim their child. Indeed, the multiplicity of countersigns left with the hospital shows that parents viewed the abandonment of children as a temporary measure. Even

Table 3.6 Comparison of infant mortality rates by gender, 1467–85, per thousand infant admissions

Year	Male	Female
1467	755.1	788.2
1468	597.0	705.3
1469	600.0	640.5
1470	671.2	608.7
1471	509.1	674.7
1472	477.3	557.7
1473	500.0	727.3
1474	666.7	768.1
1475	577.5	600.0
1476	626.7	735.6
1477	680.6	652.2
1478	790.1	769.2
1479	805.3	886.8
1480	644.9	728.1
1481	577.5	669.7
1482	546.5	658.2
1483	701.5	828.3
1484	813.3	822.4
1485	808.2	847.1
Average, 1467–85	649.9	719.4

Source: AOIF, Balie e Bambini G–L (XVI, 7–11), 1467–85.

where abandonment was permanent, mothers and fathers sometimes monitored carefully the progress of their abandoned children, as well as providing dowries for their abandoned daughters. That the rate of return was not higher reflects infant mortality rates that, after 1460, hovered around 50 per cent, and in years of plague and famine reached 70 per cent. Moreover, only twice in the years 1445–85 did the percentage of children abandoned to those baptized at San Giovanni rise above 10 per cent, as compared to 30 and even 40 per cent for the eighteenth and nineteenth centuries.[20]

Our knowledge of the motivations for abandonment comes from both indirect and direct sources. Indirect sources include patterns of admissions and mortality, as well as of the provenance of both children and wet-nurses. Fortunately, the richness of the archives of the Innocenti also permits the examination of direct testimony in the form of notes and depositions of parents and others who brought children to the foundling hospital, and upon which I will rely for the discussion first of motives, followed by the economic and gender issues mentioned above.

Between 1467 and 1485 the hospital of the Innocenti admitted 3,903 children, of whom approximately 89 per cent were less than a year old on admission (see Table 3.9). Of the 3,489 children less than a year old admitted, 56.3 per cent were female, and this can be compared to baptisms

Table 3.7 Percentage of neonatal (<1 month old) to infant (<1 year old) admissions, by gender, 1467–85

Year	Male %	Female %
1467	81.4	82.2
1468	84.7	79.8
1469	90.9	90.0
1470	92.5	90.4
1471	93.7	89.0
1472	88.7	85.7
1473	86.8	84.0
1474	94.0	89.5
1475	87.2	78.9
1476	88.4	81.5
1477	79.3	83.8
1478	80.6	76.6
1479	79.0	69.4
1480	89.0	88.1
1481	92.7	90.2
1482	88.1	84.0
1483	87.7	85.7
1484	77.0	75.4
1485	87.3	92.6
Average	86.7	84.0

Source: AOIF, Balie e Bambini G–L (XVI, 7–11), 1467–85.

at San Giovanni, where females made up 48.7 per cent of children baptized (see Table 3.3, p. 68). Only in 1470 and in 1482 did the number of males exceed the number of females admitted: in 1470, males made up 53.3 per cent of baptisms at San Giovanni (the average for the period was 51.3 per cent). Similarly, in 1482, males accounted for 52.8 per cent of all baptisms. In both those years, in other words, unusual and temporary surges in the number of male babies born in Florence explain the admission to the Innocenti of more males than females. Yet even in those two unusual years, the ratio of girls abandoned to those born remained higher than the equivalent ratio for boys (see Table 3.4, p. 69).

This predominance of females has led a number of historians to suggest that Florentines during the Renaissance reserved their affection for male children. These historians have connected abandonment of females to other phenomena such as the age-based undercounting of females in the Catasto of 1427,[21] and the practice of committing young patrician girls to convents at a very early age.[22] Although the importance and interrelationships of these phenomena are incontestable, it is less clear that they have anything to do with affection, or the lack of affection, towards female children. Rather, the abandonment of children was increasingly connected, among the patriciate, and over the course of the late fifteenth and early sixteenth

Table 3.8 Average age in days at admission for children admitted <1 month old whose exact age at admission is known

Cohort	Male	Female
1467	4.9 (n = 20)	6.2 (n = 25)
1468	5.9 (n = 16)	5.9 (n = 21)
1469	6.3 (n = 11)	5.1 (n = 16)
1470	7.8 (n = 9)	5.1 (n = 8)
1471	4.4 (n = 7)	9.2 (n = 9)
1472	6.4 (n = 4)	7.8 (n = 4)
1473	5.9 (n = 7)	6.8 (n = 9)
1474	4.9 (n = 8)	10.3 (n = 3)
1475	7.1 (n = 9)	7.4 (n = 17)
1476	3.6 (n = 9)	9.9 (n = 7)
1477	6.0 (n = 6)	11.5 (n = 4)
1478	6.6 (n = 8)	8.9 (n = 15)
1479	4.7 (n = 9)	5.4 (n = 8)
1480	2.1 (n = 7)	9.4 (n = 5)
1481	8.0 (n = 1)	7.5 (n = 2)
1482	6.5 (n = 4)	10.8 (n = 5)
1483	23.0 (n = 2)	13.5 (n = 1)
1484	3.6 (n = 22)	3.0 (n = 22)
1485	1.5 (n = 29)	2.8 (n = 44)
Mean	6.26 (n = 188)	7.71 (n = 225)

Source: AOIF, Balie e Bambini G–L (XVI, 7–11), 1467–85.

centuries, to strategies of inheritance, and among families of lesser social status and wealth, to strategies of survival.

Moreover, it is extremely misleading to undertake a sociological analysis of motivation on the basis of gender alone. The situation at the Innocenti is greatly complicated by the problem that approximately half of children admitted there between 1445 and 1466 were the offspring of liaisons between slaves or servants and their *padroni*. In the period 1467–85, of 268 mothers described (of a sample of 2,200 records), 107 (39.9 per cent) were either *schiava*, *serva* or *fante* (Table 3.10). Christiane Klapisch-Zuber has noted the special vulnerability of female domestic slaves and servants to the sexual advances of their masters and masters' sons. Sexual attacks on female slaves, in particular, fell not into the category of violations of female honour, but of damage to property.[23] Indeed, contemporaries themselves perceived the connection between the unforeseen number of admissions to the Innocenti and the city's population of slaves and servants. In 1448, the silk guild complained that

> great is the number of tiny infant foundlings now abandoned there. At wet-nurse are 260 or more, and this increases daily, due, we believe, to the presence of a larger than usual number of slaves and servants in the city.[24]

Table 3.9 Admissions <1 year old compared to all admissions, 1467−85

Year	Admitted <1 year old	Total admitted	Percentage <1 year old
1467	149	160	93.1
1468	171	188	91.0
1469	166	176	94.3
1470	153	161	95.0
1471	154	159	96.9
1472	125	148	84.5
1473	128	136	94.1
1474	143	152	94.1
1475	192	201	95.5
1476	178	191	93.2
1477	187	220	85.0
1478	234	279	83.9
1479	294	357	82.3
1480	244	260	93.8
1481	204	213	95.8
1482	195	210	92.9
1483	185	222	83.3
1484	213	274	77.7
1485	174	196	88.8

Source: AOIF, Balie e Bambini G−L (XVI, 7−11), 1467−85.

When in 1456 the guild presented a petition to the Signoria asking for a subsidy of 10 per cent of prisoners' fines and certain taxes on the importation of raw materials into the city, the final petition omitted a number of proposals discussed in several previous drafts. One proposal suggested a tax of 1 florin to be levied on every person who bought or hired a slave or servant, a tax to be paid directly to the treasurer of the hospital. In addition, those *padroni* who had impregnated their servants or slaves would have to reimburse the Innocenti for the cost of raising the child. As the proposed legislation expressed it:

> Given that the majority of children abandoned to this hospital are born of persons of low estate and servants who care not for their honour, it is requested that any person who places, hires, or brings into the city, environs, or countryside of Florence any slave or servant . . . should pay and be required to pay for each head to the treasurer of the hospital of the Innocenti one large florin within eight days from when she was hired.[25]

Thus, in a striking example of Freudian projection, the petitioners, themselves the social group most likely to burden the Innocenti with unwanted children, ascribed to their slaves and servants a lack of care for their own honour. If the proposal reveals the psychology of the *ceti dirigenti*, its omission from the final version of the petition suggests the political

Table 3.10 Motives for abandonment of foundlings to the Innocenti and parental occupations and descriptions

Motives mentioning mothers only		268
Mother placed as wet-nurse	33	
Injury or illness of mother	36	
Death of mother	28	
Mother a slave or servant	107	
Youth of mother	28	
Poverty of mother	6	
Widowhood and/or remarriage	14	
Other (occupational or descriptive)	16	
Motives mentioning fathers only		118
Father absent, out of town, or whereabouts unknown	18	
Death of father	19	
Poverty of father	6	
Occupational/descriptive*	75	
Motives mentioning father and mother		48
Illness of father and mother	3	
Poverty	10	
Death of both parents	10	
Mother ill, father dead or absent	5	
Mother ill, father alive	1	
Mother dead, father alive	2	
Father dead, mother alive	3	
Father dead, mother remarried	1	
Father alive, mother remarried	1	
Mother placed out to wet-nurse, father absent or dead	2	
Mother placed out to wet-nurse, father alive and present	2	
Illegitimacy	5	
Other	3	
Motives mentioning children		26
Handicaps	6	
Illness or prematurity	20	
Motives of honour and shame		7
Poverty		8
Other descriptions and miscellaneous		19
Total motives		494

Note: Sample of the years 1472–80 and 1482 includes only those children with declared motives and descriptions.
* See Table 3.11

Source: AOIF, Balie e Bambini G–L (XVI, 7–11), 1467–85.

impossibility of making the patriciate openly accountable for its sexual behaviour.

Further research will have to reveal whether the gender disparities that hold for hospital admissions to the Innocenti also hold true for the children of slaves and servants. None the less, the argument that the Innocenti was a hospital built by the élite for the problems of the élite carries conviction only from the perspective of the élite. Certainly for slaves and servants themselves, abandonment of their children was a key to economic survival, despite at least one instance in which the tie between mother and child was so powerful that a slave escaped to the *contado* to 'steal' her child from the wet-nurse.[26] A similar bond between mother and child must have been present when the bearers of an infant girl wrote to the officials of the Innocenti: 'Do not show the said little girl to anyone except the bearer of the said note written in your [sic] handwriting. And if any person or slave or other ask, tell them she is dead.'[27]

Among families who were not slaves and servants, the absence of the mother was most likely to precipitate the sort of crisis that would lead to abandonment. Of the 268 mothers described in the sample from the *Balie e Bambini*, thirty-six were ill and in the hospital, while another twenty-eight had recently died, ten of them in childbirth. Thus approximately one-quarter of the children admitted to the Innocenti were abandoned there because of the mother's temporary or permanent indisposition, not surprising in the case of infants who required nursing. Moreover, bearers and notes almost never cited the illness of the father as the sole cause of abandonment, but only in conjunction with difficult circumstances for the mother, such as having to take care of several children, remarrying or putting herself out to wet-nurse. Thus a father in 1468 abandoned his son to the Innocenti:

The said boy was brought on Thursday 5 May at 20 hours and was placed on the font. Mona Andreuola, wife of Niccolò di Bartolo brought him from his house. He was born in the early days of March 1467 [equals 1468 modern]. She brought a note that said 'In the name of God, Zanobi Benedetto son of Niccolò di Bartolo di Niccolò doublet-maker. The mother is dead and she left five children.'[28]

In another case, the mother's illness presented insurmountable problems for the father:

Monday the 9th of April 1470 at 13 hours or so a girl was placed on the font. A peasant from Quinto brought her; he said that she was his daughter and that his wife was ill in the hospital so he brought the daughter here because he had no way to get her to a wet-nurse. The said peasant who brought her is named Antonio called 'Picchiane' who seems poor, and has few possessions. The said girl appears on sight to be 6 months old.[29]

These circumstances were the most likely to result in the return of a child to his parents. Thus the father of a certain Corrado was a *paltoniere*, 'one of those who goes about begging'. Notwithstanding the father's dire poverty, 'the prior returned the said boy to the father'. Yet four days later someone abandoned Corrado a second time to the Innocenti, yet reclaimed him a second time in the summer of the following year.[30] Similarly:

> Arrigo di Piero, a German, brought a male child and said that he was the legitimate son of Mona Andrea his wife. He said he brought him here because his wife was sick, and when she is cured he would like him back and [he said] he would repay the hospital for all the expenses made for the child.[31]

Bearers also cited a mother's remarriage as the primary motive for abandonment, suggesting that in such cases the support of extended family was either non-existent or unavailable:

> Friday morning 9 June at 10 hours or so a girl was placed on the font. The person who brought her said she was 3 months old and said that she was the daughter of Cerolo di Giovanni . . . from the Vicariate of Firenzuola. He said that the father was dead and the mother remarried, and [that] she [had] left several abandoned children. The one who brought her said his name was Giovanni di Polo, a neighbour.[32]

A girl of 14 months was abandoned at the hospital of San Gallo:

> Thursday 2 February a girl of 14 months or so was placed on the font at the hospital of San Gallo. The person who brought her said she was the daughter of someone from Borgo San Lorenzo who is dead. Her mother remarried and [he brought the child to the hospital] because she has no one who can take care of her.[33]

This offers a particularly striking example of the ineffectiveness of the extended family as protector of children, implying as it does that this remarrying mother had no family members on whom she could rely. This lack of extended family was sometimes poignant, as in the case of Ventura Disavventura, abandoned because her mother 'has neither father, mother, nor husband. She [the child's mother] is 18 or 19 years old'.[34]

Those who brought children to the Innocenti were much less likely to leave a description of the father. Of 494 descriptions (see Table 3.10, p. 76), only 118 refer to the father alone, and these descriptions are more likely to give the father's occupation (see Table 3.11) than to reveal other details about his circumstances. If the illness of fathers rarely precipitated a family crisis by itself, none the less the death of a father was cited in nineteen out of the 118 (16.1 per cent) descriptions. In eleven cases, the father was described as a 'person of means', or simply 'a citizen', while in another eighteen cases the father 'is absent' or 'out of town'. Another twelve fathers were described as '*tessitori*', eight as '*lavoratori*' (both categories, weavers

Table 3.11 Occupations and descriptions of fathers who abandoned children to the Innocenti

Occupation	No. in sample
Baker	1
Banker in Rome	1
Barber	1
Barber from Bologna	1
Barber from Pitiano	1
Butcher	2
Captain for the King of Spain	1
Citizen	1
Cleaner	2
Cloth-cutter	1
Cloth-merchant	1
Craftsman for the Medici	1
Doublet-maker	1
Dyer	1
Foreigner	2
Friar	1
Garment worker	4
Hosier	3
Household servant	2
Labourer	8
Miller	1
Notary for the Mercanzia	1
Olive-oil seller	1
Page for the Parte Guelfa	1
Peasant	2
Person of means	10
Priest	4
Producer of squirrel fur garments	1
Servant	2
Servant for the Otto di Guardia	1
Serving in the galleys	2
'Sir'	1
Spice merchant	1
Stays at Or San Michele	1
Tailor	2
Weaver	2
Weaver of fine cloths	4
Weaver of silk	2
Total occupations in sample	75

Source: AOIF, Balie e Bambini G−L (XVI, 7−11), 1467−85.

and labourers, imply working poverty) and five as '*povero*' or '*povero vergognoso*'. In general, approximately 30 per cent of fathers came from occupational levels that might not have permitted the support of large families, although in most cases the depositions do not explicitly state that the father's occupation is linked to the abandonment.

Even more rare (forty-eight cases) were those instances in which father and mother were mentioned together. Of these, poverty and the death of both parents were the motives cited most often. Each was mentioned as a factor on ten occasions. Finally, of the twenty-six reasons given having to do with children, fifteen described the child's illness as a reason for abandonment, and twelve described the child as '*leggitimo*' or '*leggitima*', terms that hospital officials used to denote children who were abandoned for reasons of economic or other personal hardship within a recognized marriage. Another eight bearers mentioned poverty as a motive, but only seven referred to '*scandalo*' or the '*honore della città e di nostra casa*' or '*buon rispetto*'.[35] Various handicaps also made up only a small proportion of reasons for abandonment: one child was deaf and mute, another was 'blind and crazy' and a 5-year-old was described as having 'few brains'. His persistent crying on the *loggia* finally moved the door-keepers to bring him inside.[36] These and similar cases where parents brought the child on the point of death, so that 'he is not able to survive', may have shielded parents from the brutal reality of the child's last moments.[37]

Parents' fears of their own violence also prompted the abandonment of children. Thus two peasant women brought a child to the hospital for protection: '[She is the daughter, they said] of one of Francesco Ghuiducci's slaves. They took her [away from the mother] and sent her here because she did not like the child and they were afraid lest she smother it.'[38] Another parent wrote to the hospital:

> In the name of God amen. I record that on Thursday evening, 27 April 1468 a poor girl who lacks any subsidy of this world was sent [to you] so as not to have to throw her away or place her in a ditch.[39]

This parent invoked economic necessity, pleading with the hospital that her child should 'not be treated worse than any other, and should be sent to a good wet-nurse',[40] so that eventually she could be reclaimed.

At first glance, the list of stated motives among descriptions of abandoning mothers gives wet-nursing secondary importance to slavery and servitude. Of the 268 descriptions given, only thirty-three mention wet-nursing as a primary motivation for abandonment. It is only when one examines the provenance of children abandoned to the Innocenti that the importance of wet-nursing emerges, and even then a smaller proportion of children than wet-nurses appears to have come from the Mugello or the Casentino, traditionally the source of the Innocenti's nurses. Of 642 place-names identified for the years 1472 to 1480, and 1482, Florence was listed

179 times (27.9 per cent), the Mugello fifty-two times and communities in the Casentino only seventeen times.

This evidence is somewhat misleading, however, once it is compared with the number of wet-nurse brokers and midwives who brought children to the Innocenti so that their clients could sell their milk. The most enterprising of these midwives, a certain Mona Vanna 'che sta nel chastellaccio',[41] accounts for sixty-one of the 642 children in the sample whose provenance is known. When her name is added to 'Mona Taddea che raccette le donne grosse', Mona Iachopa 'che leva fanciulle' and Mona Paghola 'che aconcie le balie',[42] and ten other women of similar description, one finds that pregnant women who sought out these midwives account for eighty-three children, second only to Florence as a description of origin. Unfortunately, it is impossible to tell how many of these clients were urban and how many came from the *contado*. None the less, it seems a reasonable hypothesis that Mona Vanna and her competitors ministered to the prospective wet-nurses from the Mugello and the Casentino whose origins are not otherwise represented. Finally, the importance of these midwives as brokers clearly contradicts Christiane Klapisch-Zuber's argument that wet-nursing was men's business. Her major example, Piero Puro, is unrepresentative, since he was not only a *balio*, but also the Ospedale degli Innocenti's procurer.[43]

The salary of wet-nurses, ranging from 50 to 60 *soldi* per month, hardly sufficed to support one child, and the number of 'widowed girls', though increasing in the period 1467–85, still made up a small proportion of wet-nurses. Much more frequent in the accounts, indeed, nearly universal, was the notation that the wet-nurse's salary should be paid to a third party, implying that repayment of a family debt was not an unusual motive for a married woman to sell her milk.[44]

Yet the high concentration of wet-nurses in a single *podesteria* in the Casentino, Castello San Niccolò (see Table 3.5, pp. 70–1), suggests that a micro-economy of wet-nursing flourished in the *quattrocento*,[45] especially given that a majority of these wet-nurses came from two parishes, Sant' Angelo and San Pancrazio in Cetica. When wet-nurses sang their carnival songs in street processions, the lyrics took particular note of nurses' origins in the Casentino.[46] In the sample covering the years 1472–80 and 1482, hospital officials sent children to nurse in Castello San Niccolò 186 times, more than twice as often as either of its nearest rivals, Florence, mentioned sixty-two times, and Vicchio di Mugello, mentioned fifty-one times (see Table 3.5, pp. 70–1).

The economic pressures endured by these wet-nurses and their families come through clearly in their notes to the Innocenti:

Friday the 25th of March 1468 at about 12 hours the said boy was placed on the font with a note that said 'On the 25th day of March 1468: This boy is legitimate and he has the name Benedetto from the *popolo* of Cierrata. He is [the son] of Mona Appolonia di Deo di Martino [who] lives near Marradi. He was born on the 19th of March 1467 [equals 1468 modern]. He has a mother [who] has four children left without a father, and to be able to bring up the others she has placed herself out as a wet-nurse. He is recommended to you. Write him down because if possible she wants to return for him. It is the wars that have undone her.'[47]

Yet the same economic hardship that drove women to abandon their own children also severely affected the care the foundlings of the Innocenti received. Most commonly, wet-nurses failed to report the deaths of children under their care, continuing to collect payments from the hospital, and often failed to report their own pregnancies, a more pernicious form of abuse because it caused the Innocenti's foundlings to starve slowly to death.

The case of Lucha di San Miniato, abandoned to the Innocenti in October 1467, is a straightforward and classic case of overpayment. After the hospital fed this infant for a month and a half, the hospital gave him to Mona Cecca, wife of Lorenzo di Falco, a labourer in the parish of San Martino a Pagliorono in the *podesteria* of Vicchio di Mugello. Lucha, the infant, died a month after going to wet-nurse. The hospital continued paying Mona Cecca, however, for another full year. Then:

> On 23 January 1468 [equals 1469 modern] the aforesaid Lorenzo, called 'Falco', was arrested. By vote of the [silk guild] consuls they sent him to the Stinche [the Florentine debtors' prison] with this [proviso]: that he sign an agreement [to repay] all that for which he is debtor, and that before he is released he must have five black beans [i.e., affirmative votes] of the consuls.[48]

Altogether Mona Cecca received 25 lire of overpayments, and 'although the said boy was dead we kept on paying said Lorenzo husband of said wet-nurse, and gave him clothes for the boy and other things'.[49] Common as this sort of fraud was, however, the silk guild preferred to prosecute by making an egregious example of one case rather than by pursuing fraud consistently.

Even more deadly than fraud was the unannounced pregnancy of wet-nurses. In 1474, Dora Tommasa, abandoned at the age of 10 months, went to wet-nurse in San Godenzo:

> The wet-nurse brought her back the said day starved and dead from hunger, so badly taken care of that she could not be worse. Our women who saw the wet-nurse say that she did not have a drop of milk. She should not be paid anything.[50]

Other, more subtle frauds might escape detection, at least longer than outright starvation. Although officially the first record of artificial feeding in the west after antiquity was in 1577, when Grand Duke Francesco visited the Innocenti to try out new methods of artificial feeding heard about in Spain,[51] the real innovators were the wet-nurses of the Innocenti over a century earlier. In 1468, a 6-month-old girl was brought to the *pila* of the

Innocenti and immediately sent to wet-nurse. Eight months later, the wet-nurse 'brought back the said girl on the 25 September 1468. She is in bad condition. She brought back her things. I have heard that the said wet-nurse was pregnant and fed her [the child] cow's milk'.[52] Similarly, hospital officials sought the return of a boy, Pagholo Bonifazio, given to wet-nurse in Castelfranco di Sotto: 'we were given to understand by a person worthy of faith that because the wet-nurse was pregnant she was feeding him from a goat'.[53]

When abandoning parents wrote notes to the officials of the Innocenti, they made the distinction between the milk of pregnant women, *latte prengno*, and the milk of a good wet-nurse, *latte frescho*. As one solicitous parent wrote: 'Take either this one or that as you please, that she may be a good wet-nurse and her milk fresh, and that she take good care of him, and that the hospital observe [her] well.'[54] In another case, where the child's father agreed to subsidize the wet-nurse, the Innocenti set her pay at 55 rather than 50 *soldi* per month 'because the milk is fresh'.[55] By contrast, when the hospital sent a child to wet-nurse in Empoli:

> I was told that he is very ill. I want him to be brought back. Money is not to be paid. On 8 January 1470 [equals 1471 modern] a friend of the hospital told us she died of neglect and that the [wet-nurse] gave him 'pregnant' milk for several months.[56]

Even more poignant are the cases in which former foundlings of the Innocenti became caught up in the cycle of poverty and abandonment:

> Thursday 20 October 1468 the said baby was borne by one of our girls who got married [and then] for reasons of poverty came to give birth here in the hospital. And so it will make sense to give her to wet-nurse and feed her as with the other abandoned children.[57]

Often, as in the case of a certain Lionarda in 1477, this cycle was repeated even more viciously. As her plight makes clear, the lack of institutional and structural supports for women who were neither wealthy nor under the protection of male kinsmen served as the foundation of the charitable system in which the Innocenti had such an important role:

> Thursday 25 September 1477 at about 11 hours, a baptized girl, who on sight seemed to be about 12 months old, was placed on the font. Her maternal grandmother brought her and said that she was the daughter of Lionarda her daughter [and alumna of the hospital], and that the said Lionarda is going to be remarried. And she [the maternal grandmother] left her here. She did not want to keep her because she did not have any way to do it and because she did not know how and so she brought her [here].[58]

Here, then, is a cycle of poverty and charitable assistance spanning three generations, in which neither mother nor grandmother had the financial resources nor, in the case of the grandmother, the requisite skills to be able to avoid abandoning the child. One can easily imagine the cycle of poverty and abandonment continuing for another generation, in this case frustrated only by the death of the child at wet-nurse less than a year later.[59]

If in the middle of the fifteenth century hospital officials perceived their most intractable problem to be the number of slaves and servants whose children were abandoned to the Innocenti, by the mid-sixteenth century both reality and perception had changed. These changes in perception undoubtedly sprang from a massive increment in scale. Until 1475, admissions to the hospital of the Innocenti rarely rose above 200 per year, and only in 1479 did admissions exceed 300 annually (see Tables 3.1 and 3.2, pp. 66, 67). In the decade of the 1530s, according to the hospital's own statistics, 5,499 children were abandoned (Table 3.12).[60] In the famine year of 1539, the hospital received nearly 1,000 children, who suffered an infant mortality rate of 70 to 90 per cent.[61]

Table 3.12   Admissions to the Ospedale degli Innocenti, 1530–9

Year	Admissions
1530	549
1531	500
1532	556
1533	520
1534	462
1535	491
1536	427
1537	468
1538	565
1539	961
Total	5,499

Source: G. Bruscoli, *Lo Spedale di Santa Maria degli Innocenti dalla sua fondazione ai nostri giorni*, Florence 1900, pp. 268–70.

Vincenzio Borghini, appointed superintendent in 1552 by Cosimo I, ascribed the willingness of parents to abandon in the sixteenth century to 'the evils of the times and of men'.[62] By the former, Borghini meant genuine economic hardship. By the latter, Borghini referred to greedy relatives of an orphaned child, noting that while outside the hospital such a child could rely on the protection of the Magistrato dei Pupilli, once relatives abandoned the child to the Innocenti, the hospital's horrifying mortality rates usually left the child's estate to be devoured.[63]

Even if Borghini exaggerated the numerical importance of orphans and the crowds of greedy relatives, he was still not far from the heart of the matter. By the sixteenth century, even wealthy Florentine families suffered an inheritance crisis, in which testators increasingly attached strict *fidei-commissi* on the alienation and transfer of property as a means to preserve their patrimony through patrilineal inheritance. Under such an increasingly inflexible system, children of the wrong number or gender threatened the integrity of the family holding.[64] The work of Samuel Cohn on Siena, for example, calls the sixteenth century 'the great age of selfishness', in so far as testators turned from strategies for the afterlife focused on salvation and towards strategies that focused on earthly immortality through family and property.[65] It is not surprising that where patrilineal inheritance was the most rigid, the south of Europe, both abandonment and institutions modelled on the Innocenti flourished.[66]

As a consequence, the gender issues that were already pressing in the fifteenth century became overwhelming in the sixteenth. During the fifteenth century, children of both sexes who survived placement to the hospital could hope for some sort of adoption or apprenticeship.[67] By the sixteenth century, only boys could hope for apprenticeship, and even then not until the ages of 10 to 14. The hospital occasionally succeeded in marrying off girls, but by the third quarter of the sixteenth century getting girls out of the hospital at all became extremely difficult. Borghini's statistics from 1579 show that of 1,220 staff and children in the hospital, 968 were females, 733 of whom were of marriageable age or older. Indeed, a substantial proportion, 223, were women over the age of 40.[68] Around the time of Borghini's death in 1580, there is some evidence that hospital officials simply turned a large number of girls out of the hospital,[69] while other female wards of the Innocenti found more permanent accommodation in the widows' home of Orbatello.[70]

Evidence from both the fifteenth and the sixteenth centuries suggests the prevalence of an inheritance system dramatically at odds with demographic reality. As this inheritance system became more rigid, more fossilized, in the sixteenth century, charitable institutions had to respond by vastly expanding both the scale and the variety of services offered. Cosimo de' Medici's reform of hospitals and convents[71] (the two were already linked as symptoms of a common problem) attempted to address a crisis that amplified the dissonance between the ideals of extended family and lineage and the realities of quotidian life. Interest in noble families and lineages, of which Borghini's weighty tome on the Florentine nobility offers a striking example,[72] increased in proportion to the extended family's decreasing effectiveness in providing for its female members and second and third sons. As a result of the ineffectiveness of these family strategies an elaborate and extensive market for milk prospered, inextricably linking until the nineteenth century strategies of survival to strategies of inheritance.

86   *Philip Gavitt*

NOTES

* The Italian phrase, a recurrent complaint of parents who abandoned children, means 'because she has no one to take care of her'. This study was made possible by generous grants from the National Endowment for the Humanities, the Leopold Schepp Foundation, and the Harvard University Center for Renaissance Studies (Villa I Tatti). I also wish to thank the Department of History at the University of Tennessee, Knoxville, for granting a leave of absence in 1990–1. For a survey of the early history of the Ospedale degli Innocenti, see P. Gavitt, *Charity and Children in Renaissance Florence: The Ospedale degli Innocenti, 1410–1536*, Ann Arbor, Mich.: University of Michigan Press 1990. In my research for the book, data on admissions and mortality, taken from the first six volumes of the Innocenti archive's series, *Balie e Bambini*, were available only for the years up to 1466, because a previous archivist incorrectly assured the archive's patrons that the five subsequent volumes, covering the years 1467–85, were copies of the first five. Since then, however, the good offices of Professor Pier Paolo Viazzo, Dr Franco Sartini and Dr Annamaria Macelli have made it possible to pursue researches in infant mortality up to 1485. At that point, a genuine gap in the data exists for the years 1486 to 1529, when the series begins again and continues uninterruptedly until the mid-twentieth century.

1 C. Corsini, 'Materiali per lo studio della famiglia: gli esposti', *Quaderni storici*, 33, 1976, pp. 998–1051.

2 J. Henderson, in Chapter 7 of this volume, places the figure for the mid-fourteenth century at close to 80 per cent, and at the close of the fifteenth century at 70 per cent. See his *Piety and Charity in Late Medieval Florence*, Oxford: Clarendon Press 1994, ch. 9. At the Innocenti during the fifteenth century, female infants accounted for approximately 57 per cent of admissions. See also I. Chabot, 'Widowhood and poverty in late medieval Florence', *Continuity and Change*, 3, 1988, pp. 291–311; and T. Kuehn, 'Some ambiguities of female inheritance ideology in the Renaissance', *Continuity and Change*, 2, 1987, pp. 11–36.

3 AOIF (Archivio dell'Ospedale degli Innocenti di Firenze), Balie e Bambini A–L (XVI, 1–11), 1445–85. During these years female children constituted 57 per cent of admissions to the Innocenti.

4 D. Herlihy and C. Klapisch-Zuber, *Tuscans and Their Families: A Study of the Florentine Catasto of 1427*, New Haven, Conn. and London: Yale University Press 1985, pp. 204–11.

5 E.H. Ramsden (ed.), *The Letters of Michelangelo*, vol. 1, Stanford, Calif.: Stanford University Press 1963, p. 69: letter from Michelangelo Buonarotti to Buonarotta Simoni in Florence, 5 June 1512. I wish to thank Professor James Beck for this reference. Five years later, at the age of 42, Michelangelo described himself as 'an old man, [so] it doesn't seem to me worthwhile wasting so much time in order to save the pope two or three hundred ducats' (ibid: p. 106, letter to Domenico Buoninsegni, 2 May 1517).

6 For Alessandra Strozzi's estimation of her daughter's position in the marriage market, see C. Guasti (ed.), *Lettere di una gentildonna fiorentina*, Florence: Sansoni 1877, pp. 4–5, letter of 24 August 1477.

7 On dowries in general, see J. Kirshner, 'Pursuing honor while avoiding sin: the Monte delle Doti in Renaissance Florence', *Studi senesi*, 89, 1977, pp. 178–258. See also J. Kirshner and A. Molho, 'The dowry fund and the marriage market in *Quattrocento* Florence', *Journal of Modern History*, 50, 1978, pp. 403–38. For a historical survey of dowries in southern Europe, see D.O. Hughes, 'From brideprice to dowry in Mediterranean Europe', *Journal of Family History*, 3, 1978, pp. 262–96. For Venice, see S. Chojnacki, 'Dowries and kinsmen in early

Renaissance Venice', *Journal of Interdisciplinary History*, 5, 1975, pp. 571–600. On dowries at the Innocenti, see ASF (Archivio di Stato di Firenze), Provvisioni Registri, 142, fols 380v–382r, 30 December 1451, and for the sixteenth century, AOIF, Suppliche e Sovrani Rescritti (VI,2), fol. 22v, n.d., where the hospital's superintendent proposed the increase, and AOIF Suppliche e Sovrani Rescritti (VI,1), fol. 443v, 14 February 1571 [equals 1572 modern].

8 See Guasti, *Lettere*, p. 9, Alessandra Strozzi's letter of 18 August 1447, and pp. 43–4, her letter of 17 December 1450, for examples.

9 E. Rosenthal, 'The position of women in Renaissance Florence: Neither autonomy nor subjection', in P. Denley and C. Elam (eds), *Florence and Italy. Renaissance Studies in Honour of Nicolai Rubinstein*, London: Westfield College, Committee for Medieval Studies 1988, pp. 369–81.

10 AOIF, Balie e Bambini H (XVI,8), fol. 2r, 19 June 1472:

Venerdì mattina adì 19 giungnio ci fu rechato dallo spedale nostro di San Gallo una fanciulla che in vista mostrava anni due disono che ve sera a ore 1 1/2 di notte fu posta appie della porta della chiesolina . . . era male in punto. Questo dì 20 di giungno ci fu Mona Ermellina donna di Pagholo Borgherini e disse che lla detta fanciulla era sua figliuola e cche sara rimaritata a detto Paghol e cche la voleva allevarle perche è [la?] zia della fanciulla non la volevano e che la voleva elle chosidetto di se ne le porto fecce fede Mona Maddalena donna di Nicholò di Domenicho lavoratore di Tomaxo di ser Bonozo che la detta fanciulla era sua.

Friday morning 19 June 1472 a child was brought to us from our hospital of San Gallo; [she] seemed [to be] two years old and they say that at half-past one at night she was put in front of the door of the little church . . . she was very ill. Today, 20 June, Mona Ermellina, wife of Pagholo Borgherini, [came] to us and she said that the girl was her daughter and that she [Mona Ermellina] was remarried to Pagholo and that she wanted to bring her up because the girl's aunt did not want her and that she wanted to bring her up and . . . to confirm that she was saying the truth she brought a witness, Mona Maddalena wife of Nicholò di Domenicho, the labourer of Tomaxo di ser Bonozo, to testify the girl was her daughter.

Although in this case the mother took back her child, it is clear that when the relatives refused to take her, the mother's recourse was to the Innocenti. Christiane Klapisch-Zuber has documented the problems of remarriage in 'Maternité, veuvage et dot à Florence', *Annales: économies, sociétés, civilisations*, 38, 1983, pp. 1097–109. She has also established the important connection between patrilineal systems of inheritance and the precarious position of the woman alone, although her examples come from wealthier families. Needless to say, those women with insufficient dowries or insufficiently supportive kin must have found their situation even more desperate, especially in the face of an often unresponsive legal system. See Chabot, 'Widowhood', p. 295.

11 V. Fildes, *Breasts, Bottles and Babies: A History of Infant Feeding*, Edinburgh: University of Edinburgh Press 1986, pp. 98–133.

12 Herlihy and Klapisch-Zuber, *Tuscans and Their Families*, pp. 147, 286–7.

13 C. Klapisch-Zuber, 'Blood parents and milk parents: Wet-nursing in Florence 1300–1530', in her *Women, Family, and Ritual in Renaissance Italy*, Chicago, Ill.: University of Chicago Press 1985, p. 137, also notes the unwillingness among Florentines to nurse more than one child at a time.

14 J.-P. Bardet, 'Enfants abandonnés et assistés à Rouen', in Société de Démographie Historique (ed.), *Sur la population française au XVIIIe et au XIXe*

siècles: hommage à Marcel Reinhard, Paris: Société de Démographie Historique 1973, p. 31.

15 R. Trexler, 'Infanticide in Florence: New sources and first results', *History of Childhood Quarterly*, 1, 1973, pp. 98–116, and many others have attributed to suffocation the high death rate among children sent to nurse. In the sources, however, deaths attributed to suffocation by the wet-nurse are extremely rare. Of approximately 6,400 children abandoned at the Innocenti between 1445 and 1485, only thirteen were described as '*affoghato*' or '*trovato morto al lato della balia*'. Of the thirteen, nine were boys, a figure disproportionately high if one assumes malice on the part of the nurse, especially in a society as allegedly anti-feminine as that of Renaissance Florence. Moreover, twelve of the thirteen 'suffocated' infants were less than 6 months old. The proportions involved and the age and gender of the victims strongly suggest Sudden Infant Death Syndrome, a hypothesis I hope to support even more strongly in a forthcoming article. In her study of Florentine books of the dead, Ann Carmichael notes the same distribution by age and gender among the deaths attributed to suffocation, although her dismissal of SIDS as a cause is rather curious. See her *Plague and the Poor in Renaissance Florence*, Cambridge: Cambridge University Press 1986, pp. 51–3.

16 Trexler, 'Infanticide in Florence', p. 101. Although I disagree with Trexler's conclusions concerning infanticide, it is clear from both his and my researches that the infant mortality rate for females abandoned to the hospital was higher than that for males (see Table 3.6, p. 72). This disparity is all the more striking because under normal circumstances girls are less likely to die during the crucial first weeks of life. The average age at admission is also slightly higher for girls than for boys between 1467 and 1485, which suggests that being admitted at a younger, more vulnerable age cannot be cited to explain higher female mortality (see Tables 3.7 and 3.8, pp. 73 and 74). For a fuller discussion of these issues, see Gavitt, *Charity and Children*, pp. 216–17. Higher female infant mortality was not true for society at large, at least not in the eighteenth century, for which some of the best data are available. See M. Breschi, 'L'evoluzione della mortalità infantile', in C. Corsini (ed.), *Vita, morte e miracoli di gente comune: Appunti per una storia della popolazione della Toscana fra XIV e XX secolo*, Florence: La Casa Usher 1988, pp. 98–9. Nor has it been documented, so far as I know, for any other foundling hospital after the fifteenth century.

17 Gavitt, *Charity and Children*, pp. 232–6.

18 Thus when Orbatello is described as a 'widows' asylum', it cannot be assumed that it was a home for *old* women. See R. Trexler, 'A widows' asylum of the Renaissance: The Orbatello of Florence', in P. Stearns (ed.), *Old Age in Pre-industrial Society*, New York: Holmes & Meier 1982, pp. 119–49.

19 J. Boswell, *The Kindness of Strangers: The Abandonment of Children in the West from Late Antiquity to the Renaissance*, New York: Pantheon Books 1988, *passim*; Gavitt, *Charity and Children*, p. 204.

20 Gavitt, *Charity and Children*, p. 21.

21 A. Molho, 'Deception and marriage strategy in Renaissance Florence: The case of women's ages', *Renaissance Quarterly*, 41, 1988, pp. 193–4.

22 R. Trexler, 'Le célibat à la fin du moyen-age: les religieuses de Florence', *Annales: économies, sociétés, civilisations*, 27, 1972, pp. 1329–50. Donald Queller, however, in a paper read at the 1991 Pacific Coast Branch meeting of the American Historical Association, and soon to appear in *Renaissance Quarterly*, notes that at least some fathers in early fifteenth-century Venetian wills clearly gave their daughters the choice between marriage and the religious life. In most cases, fathers faced the problem that dowries for convents cost nearly as much as dowries for marriage. Moreover, the demographic weakness of

fifteenth-century Italian families made marriage the much more sensible choice for lineages hoping to increase their power and influence.

23 C. Klapisch-Zuber, 'Women servants in Florence during the fourteenth and fifteenth centuries', in B. Hanawalt (ed.), *Women and Work in Preindustrial Europe*, Bloomington, Ind.: Indiana University Press 1986, pp. 69–73.
24 Gavitt, *Charity and Children*, p. 76. ASF, Provvisioni registri, 139, fol. 46v, 29 April 1448. On Tuscan servants and slaves, see I. Origo, 'The domestic enemy: Eastern slaves in Tuscany in the fourteenth and fifteenth centuries', *Speculum*, 30, 1955, pp. 321–66.
25 These drafts are preserved in AOIF, Filza d'Archivio (LXII,9), fol. 600r ff.:

> Prima che conciosa cosa che la magiore parte di fanciulli che si danno a questo spedale sono nati di persone mechaniche e serve le quali non churono loro honore s'adimanda che per l'avenire qualunche persona . . . mettere o condurre o fare venire nella città contado o directo di Firenze alchuna schiava o serva o altra qualunche creatura . . . paghi e paghare sia tenuto et debba per ciaschuna testa al camarlingo del decto spedale degli Innocenti fl. 1 largo fra 8 dì [di] poi l'avesse condotta.

26 Gavitt, *Charity and Children*, p. 202.
27 AOIF, Balie e Bambini H (XVI,8), fol. 99r, 18 December 1473: 'Non manifestate detta fanciulla se già non vi recha detta poliza che sia di vostra mano et se persona o schiava o altra dimanda dite sia morta.'
28 AOIF, Balie e Bambini G (XVI,7), fol. 116r, 5 May 1468:

> Giovedì adì 5 di maggio 1468 a ore 20 fu rechato e messo in pila detto fanciullo rechòllo Mona Andreula donna di Nicchòlo di Bartolo rechòllo di chaxa sua naqque circa dì primi di marzo 1467 [equals 1468 modern]. Rechò una poliza che dicea al nome di dio Zanobi e Benedetto figliuolo di Nicchòlo di Bartolo di Nicchòlo farsettaio. E morta la madre e [h]a lasciata 5 figliuoli.

29 AOIF, Balie e Bambini G (XVI, 7), fol. 209r, 9 April 1470:

> Lunedì adì 9 d'aprile 1470 a ore 13 o circha fu messa in pila una fanciulla rechòlla uno chontadino da Quinto che disse era sua figliuola e che la moglie era all'ospedale malata e pero ci e la rechava [per]che non avea modo a darla a balia e detto chontadino che la rechò a nome Antonio detto Picchiane che pare povero e l'a ppocho. Mostra in vista detta fanciulla mesi 6.

30 AOIF, Balie e Bambini H (XVI,8), fol. 79r, 19 July 1473.
31 AOIF, Balie e Bambini G (XVI,7), fol. 320v, 20 August 1470:

> Lunedì adì xx d'aghosto 1470 fu rechato un fanciullo maschio rechòllo Arrigho di Piero tedescho disse era suo figliuolo leggitimo nato di Mona Andrea sua donna e disse lo rechava qui perche la moglie era malata e che quando fusse ghuarita lo rivoleva e che satisfarebbe la chaxa delle spese si facessino in lui.

32 AOIF, Balie e Bambini H (XVI,8), fol. 220r, 9 June 1475:

> Venerdì mattina adì 9 di giugno a ore 10 in circa fu rechato e messo in pila una fanciulla che chi lla rechò disse aveva tre mesi e disse ch'era figliuola di Cerolo di Giovanni da Rapezo vichariato di Firenzuola e disse che'l padre era morto e che la madre si rimaritò e rimase parecchi fanciulli abbandonati e rechòlo uno che disse aveva nome Giovanni di Polo suo vicino.

33 AOIF, Balie e Bambini G (XVI,7), fol. 183v, 2 February 1468 (equals 1469 modern):

> Giovedi adì ii di febraio fu messo nella pila di San Ghallo una fanciulla di mesi xiiii o circha e chi la rechò disse era figliuola d'uno da Borgho a San Lorenzo ch'era morto e che la madre s'era rimaritata e perche non avea chi la ghovernasse.

34 AOIF, Balie e Bambini G (XVI,7), fol. 85r, 12 January 1467 (equals 1468 modern): 'nonn [h]a ne padrene madre ne marito. Era d'età di 18–19 anni'.

35 See, for example, AOIF, Balie e Bambini G (XVI,7), fol. 235r, for mention of *'scandalo'*. On legal issues concerning illegitimacy, see T. Kuehn, 'Reading between the patrilines: Leon Battista Alberti's *Della Famiglia* in light of his illegitimacy', *I Tatti Studies*, 1, 1985, pp. 161–87.

36 'Sordo e muto', AOIF, Balie e Bambini G (XVI,7), fol. 104r, 11 March 1467 (equals 1468 modern); 'cieco e pazzo'; H (XVI,8), fol. 296r, 12 March 1475 (equals 1476 modern): 'poco cervello', I (XVI,9), fol. 32r, 29 January 1476 (equals 1477 modern).

37 In the late fourteenth and early fifteenth centuries the beauty of childhood deathbed scenes was a frequent *topos* in family diaries and letters. See C. Guasti (ed.), *Lettere di un notaio a un mercante*, vol. 1, Florence: Le Monnier 1880, p. 247, Ser Lapo Mazzei to Franceso Datini, 31 July 1400; Giovanni di Pagolo Morelli's *Ricordi*, translated into English by Richard Trexler, 'In search of father: The experience of abandonment in the recollections of Giovanni di Pagolo Morelli', *History of Childhood Quarterly*, 3, 1975, pp. 225–51; for Alessandra Macinghi Strozzi see Guasti's edition of her *Lettere*, pp. 196–7, Alessandra to Filippo degli Strozzi, 13 September 1459. Yet Herlihy and Klapisch-Zuber, in *Tuscans and their Families*, p. 147, suggest that the practice of wet-nursing may have shielded some parents from the direct experience of infant death. In any case, the emergence of this *topos* precisely at the time of the first appearance of *putti* in Renaissance art (Jacopo della Quercia's decoration for the tomb of Ilaria del Carretto in Lucca) reflects an issue of strong psychological importance for early fifteenth-century Tuscans. See C. Seymour, *Jacopo della Quercia, Sculptor*, New Haven, Conn.: Yale University Press 1973, p. 34.

38 AOIF, Balie e Bambini G (XVI,7), fol. 407r, 1 April 1472:

> Mercholedi adì 8 d'Aprile 1472 a ore 18 o circha fu messa in pila uno fanciullo rechòla 2 chontadine che dissono [lacuna] di una serva di Francesco Ghuiducci e che l'aveano tolta e mandata qui perche essa non è in suo sent[imento?] e che anno paura non l'affoghasse.

39 AOIF, Balie e Bambini G (XVI,7), fol. 155v, 27 April 1468:

> Al nome di dio amen. Richordo chome nel 1468 adì 27 d'aprile in giovedì sera si manda chosì una povera fanciulla la quale mancha d'ogni sussidio di questo mondo. Cioè, per non avere gittarla via neanche abiametterla nella fossa.

40 ibid.

41 That is, who lives in the Via del Castellaccio. The Via del Castellacio still exists in Florence within easy walking distance from the Ospedale degli Innocenti. See, among many other references, AOIF, Balie e Bambini H (XVI,8), fol. 14r, 9 September 1472.

42 That is, Mona Taddea 'who accepts pregnant women', Mona Iachopa 'who raises up children' (probably literally, as a midwife) and Mona Paghola, 'who arranges for wet-nurses'.

43 Klapisch-Zuber, 'Blood parents', p. 163. See also Gavitt, *Charity and Children*, p. 239.

44 In a seminar held at the Istituto degli Innocenti in Florence in May 1991, Tomoko Takahashi also pointed out that the vast majority of wet-nurses served

the Innocenti only once, which would also support the hypothesis that such work was undertaken as a temporary second income.

45 Gavitt, *Charity and Children*, pp. 228–9.
46 C. Singleton (ed.), *Canti carnascialeschi del Rinascimento*, Bari: Laterza 1936, nos 29, 39 and 94; Klapisch-Zuber, 'Blood parents', p. 137.
47 AOIF, Balie e Bambini G (XVI,7), fol. 198v, 25 March 1468:

> Venerdì adì xxv di marzo 1468 a ore circha 12 fu rechato e messo in pila detta fanciullo con una poliza dice adì 25 di marzo 1468 questo fanciullo è leggitimo e a nome Benedetto di popolo da Cierrata e di Mona Appolonia di Deo di Martino sta presso a Marradi nacque adì 19 di marzo 1467 [equals 1468 modern]. Ha madre e 4 figliuoli rimasti sanza babbo e per potere allevare gli altri s'e posta per balia. Si e vi racchomandato e scrivetelo perche se potea lo vuole risquotere. E lle ghuerre hanno disfatto.

48 AOIF, Balie e Bambini G (XVI,7), fol. 67v, 19 October 1467, 23 January 1468 (equals 1469 modern):

> Adì 23 di gennaio 1468 fu preso sopradetto Lorenzo detto Falcho et per partito de' chonsoli lo mandorono alle Stinche chon questo: che prima n'ebba e abi achordare de tutto quello si fuse debitore chon questo che prima esche di la gli bisognia il partitto de' chonsolí chon v [5] fave nere.

49 ibid.: 'benche detto fanciullo fusse morto chontinuamente aviamo paghato a detto Lorenzo marito di detta balia . . . e datogli panni pel fanciullo et altre chose'.
50 AOIF, Balie e Bambini G (XVI,7), fol. 171r, 10 November 1474: '[La balia] rimenò lla adì detto stentata e morta di fame e tanto male tenuta che peggio non potea essere e dichono le donne nostre che vidono la balia che non avea ghoccia di latte e non si vu[o]lle darla nulla.'
51 AOIF, Giornale N (XIII,20), fol. 7v, 4 June 1577:

> Ricordo come per adventimento anchora del Ser[enissi]mo Gran Duca N[ostro] S[ignore] che verrà pochi dì sono in Siena con il R[everendissi]mo Carlo d'Austria suo parente a visitar e visitò il nostro spedale e intendendo cosa noi haveviamo gran charestia di balie disse che haveva visto in Spagna tener' vaccha da latte per darne e che ne davono a bambini per nutrimento loro.

> I record how our Lord the Most Serene Grand Duke arrived again a few days ago in Siena, with his relative the Most Reverend Carlo of Austria, and visited and saw our hospital and, perceiving that we had a great shortage of wet-nurses, he said that he saw in Spain that they kept cows for milk to give to them and that they gave the milk to nourish the children.

52 AOIF, Balie e Bambini G (XVI,7), fol. 98r, 19 February 1467 (equals 1468 modern): 'Riarechò el detta fanciulla adì 25 di settembre 1468. E male in punto e arechò le sue chose. La detta balia ora inteso che era grossa e davale e latte delle vacche.'
53 AOIF, Balie e Bambini G (XVI,7), fol. 398r, 26 January 1471 (equals 1472 modern): 'fu fatto noto da persona dengnia de fede poppava una chapra perche la balia è grossa'.
54 AOIF, Balie e Bambini G (XVI,7), fol. 89r, 23 January 1467 (equals 1468 modern): 'togliate per balia o di questo o d'un altro chome a voi piacie che buona balia el latte suo è frescho e terrallo bene oserva bene lo spedale'.
55 AOIF, Balie e Bambini G (XVI,7), fol. 247v, 23 September 1469: 'perche e latte è frescho'.

56 AOIF, Balie e Bambini G (XVI,7), fol. 268v, 16 January 1470 (equals 1471 modern):

> e mi stato detto che sta molto male. Voglio che la [sic] rechi. E non si dia danaio. . . . Adì 8 di gennaio 1470 [equals 1471 modern] ci fu detto da uno amicho della chaxa morì per chattivo governo e che gli diede latte prengnio parecchi mesi.

57 AOIF, Balie e Bambini G (XVI,7), fol. 161r, 20 October 1468:

> Giovedì insino adì xx d'ottobre 1468 si naque in chasa detta fanciulla d'una nostra fanciulla di chasa la quale è maritata e per povertà venne a partorire qui in chasa e chosì se la chonverrà dare a balia e notrichalla chome gli altri abandonati.

58 AOIF, Balie e Bambini I (XVI,9), fol. 71v, 25 September 1477:

> Giovedì adì 25 di settembre 1477 a ore xi o circha fu messo im pila una fanciulla battezata che in vista mostrava mesi xii. Rechòlla l'avola materna e disse era figiuola della Lionarda sua figliuola e nostra fanciulla di chaxa e che detta Lionarda sara rimaritata. E lasciatole detta fanciulla e che non la voleva tenere [per]che non avea il modo e [per]che non sapea farne e però la rechava.

59 Cf. the somewhat analogous situation described for nineteenth-century Stockholm by M. Matovic, 'The Stockholm marriage: Extra-legal family formation in Stockholm 1860–1890', *Continuity and Change*, 1, 1986, pp. 385–413.
60 AOIF, Filza d'Archivio (LXXII,12), fol. 338r, n.d.
61 AOIF, Balie e Bambini A–G (XVI,15–21), covering the years 1530–9.
62 AOIF, Suppliche e Sovrani Rescritti (VI,1), fol. 242v, 4 November 1553: 'La causa della moltiplicazione delle spese par che sia in somma la cattività de' tempi et degli huomini: perche i figliuoli esposti crescono ogni dì et le donne continuamente fanno maggior massa.' ('The cause of the increased expenses appears to be the dangerous nature of the times and of men, because the number of abandoned children increases every day and women continuously make up a larger proportion of them.')
63 AOIF, Suppliche e Sovrani Rescritti (VI,1), fol. 442v, 14 February 1571 (equals 1572 modern):

> E si truovo certi maligni che se qualche creatura loro attenente in età da poter mandarìa qui, rimane abandonata che habbia qualcosa: per torgli la roba c'e la mandono segretamente che pur talvolta si scuopre: et questo caso meriterebbe che si facesse provisione, che è un vero assassinase[sic]: et poco fa, certi verso Bibbiena, essendo morto il padre d'un[a] puttina che haveva certi beni, la mandorono qui.

> And one finds certain bad people who if they have some children with possessions who are of the right age to send here they abandon these creatures in order to steal their goods and [even though] they send them to us secretly we sometimes discover nevertheless: and this case merits a provision because it is virtually equivalent to assassination; and recently certain people near Bibbiena following the death of the father of a little girl who had some possessions sent her here to us.

64 Nor was this decreasing flexibility unique to Tuscany. For other areas, see J.P. Cooper, 'Patterns of inheritance and settlement by great landowners from the fifteenth to the eighteenth centuries', in J. Goody, J. Thirsk and E.P. Thompson (eds), *Family and Inheritance: Rural Society in Western Europe, 1200–1800*, Cambridge: Cambridge University Press 1976, pp. 192–327; and R.B. Litchfield, 'Demographic characteristics of Florentine families', *Journal of Economic History*, 29, 1969, pp. 191–205.

65 S.K. Cohn, *Death and Property in Siena, 1200–1800*, Baltimore, Md.: Johns Hopkins University Press 1988, pp. 97–127.

66 What I suggest here, in other words, challenges the 'nuclear-hardship' hypothesis by proposing that as often as not, the extended family networks of southern Europe did not afford adequate protection and sustenance to their members. See P. Laslett, 'Family, kinship and collectivity as systems of support in pre-industrial Europe: A consideration of the "nuclear-hardship" hypothesis', *Continuity and Change*, 3, 1988, pp. 153–75.

67 Gavitt, *Charity and Children*, pp. 243–59.

68 AOIF, Filza d'Archivio (LXII,30), fol. 491r–v, 18 June 1579.

69 ASF, Manoscritti, 129, vol. 4, the *Memorie Fiorentine* of Francesco Settimanni, fol. 182v, 21 August 1579:

> si pubblicò per Firenze la rovina dello spedale degli Innocenti, dov'erano in custodia 1600 poverelli dell'uno e dell'altro sesso, avendone il Gran Duca levato tutti li danari ch'erano stati adunati dalla buona amministrazione di Luca di Tommaso Alamanni priore di detto spedale a cui era succeduto D. Vincenzio Borghini monaco benedettino della badia di Firenze, uomo letterato, ma gran dissipatore.

> the ruin of the Ospedale degli Innocenti, where there were 1,600 poor children of both sexes, was known throughout Florence, the Granduke having taken all the money that was collected through the good administration of Luca di Tommaso Alamanni, Prior of the aforesaid hospital, who was succeeded by Don Vincenzio Borghini, the Benedictine monk of the Badia of Florence, a learned man, but a great spender.

In his entry on fol. 212r–v marking Borghini's death on 15 August 1580, Settimanni wrote that Borghini, on the advice of Senator Carlo Pitti, had sent most of the Innocenti's boys to the galleys, and dismissed hundreds of young girls, 'le quali per necessità divennero meretrici'.

70 Trexler, 'A widows' asylum', pp. 139–42. When, in 1580, the silk guild set up a commission of nine to investigate the disordered finances of the Innocenti, one of its recommendations was to send surplus girls, with a dowry of clothes and of 30 *scudi*, to the Orbatello. See AOIF, Suppliche e Sovrani Rescritti (VI,1), fol. 564r, 21 October 1580: 'dando a ciascuno di loro li panni come di sopra s'è detto: et di più scudi xxx. Et debbisi porger loro ogni possibile aiuto, a fine che venghino accomodate di habitatione nel convento di Orbatello di questa città' ('giving to each of them clothes plus 30 *scudi*. And they must be given every possible help in order to find accommodation in the convent of the Orbatello of this city').

71 A. D'Addario, *Aspetti della controriforma a Firenze*, Rome: Ministero dell'Interno, Pubblicazioni degli Archivi di Stato 1972, pp. 81–91, 132–5.

72 See the treatise by Vincenzio Borghini, *Delle armi delle famiglie fiorentine*, which was published posthumously in Florence in 1585. Roughly contemporary were Paolo Mini's *Discorso della nobiltà di Firenze e dei fiorentini*, published in 1593, and Scipione Ammirato's *Delle famiglie nobili fiorentine*, published in 1615. On this literature in general, see F. Diaz, 'L'idea di una nuova "elite sociale" negli storici e trattatisti del principato', *Rivista Storica Italiana*, 92, 1980, pp. 572–87, and R.B. Litchfield, *The Emergence of a Bureaucracy*, Princeton, NJ: Princeton University Press 1986, p. 32.

4 Between the home and the hospice
The plight and fate of girl orphans in seventeenth- and eighteenth-century Rome

Eugenio Sonnino

WELFARE POLICIES IN ITALY FROM THE MIDDLE AGES TO UNIFICATION

The complex historical development of welfare in Italy, and of the policies of the various states before Italian unification in regard to poverty and begging, has been divided by historians into three phases. The characteristic of the middle ages was an ethical and social attitude that was essentially sympathetic to the plight of the poor. This was followed by an 'inward-looking' phase roughly from the late sixteenth to the end of the seventeenth century and then by a period, specific to the eighteenth century, in which charity and economic considerations intermingled.[1]

According to Bronislaw Geremek, it was in the second phase that a welfare system for the poor in Italy was reordered and reorganized, and it became necessary to found specialized institutions.[2] One of the paradoxical achievements that followed from the flourishing of charitable activities was the prohibition of begging, and the attempt to eliminate beggars altogether. In this connection, Geremek has pointed out that the policy to remove beggars and vagabonds from the Italian peninsula developed out of the Counter-Reformation programme to improve Christian life and the development of the modern state.[3] This would confirm the analysis made by Brian Pullan who saw the 'sixteenth-century programme' as 'inspired both by religious and state action, which aimed at eliminating abject poverty and at drawing outcasts into an industrious Christian society, partly by means of enclosed and specialized institutions aimed at reshaping character and values'. This was a programme whose characteristic weapon was to be 'the enclosed institution, at once protective and transforming, designed to span the gulf between idleness and industry, poverty and independence, brutish ignorance and Christian knowledge, vice and virtue, anarchy and order, *perfidy* and faith'.[4]

In the progress towards religious and political statehood which provided the context for Italy's welfare experiences in the post-medieval period, Rome occupied a unique position because of the way in which the religious and state functions were merged in the Papal government. The Counter-

Reformation model of the Christian order and *raison d'état* were very closely interconnected and led to only one solution: the need to take radical measures to regulate the problem of beggars.[5] Rome provided an ideal testing ground for this programme, as a city of great wealth and great poverty, permanently occupied by hordes of beggars whose poverty was seen both by the city as a whole and by the poor themselves as the source and the expression of every moral and social threat. The aim was clear:

> The purpose of setting up a public hospice is to ban begging for ever, and to provide spiritual and temporal succour with economy, order and method, for all the poor people of a town who would otherwise be forced to beg without such assistance.[6]

These are the first words of an anonymous pamphlet attributed to the Jesuit, A. Guevarre, as a manifesto in praise of the great Ospizio Apostolico for the poor set up by Pope Innocent XII in 1692 to revive the idea of closed almshouses. Pope Gregory XIII had briefly considered such a scheme in 1581 and the policy had been pursued even more vigorously by Sixtus V when he created the S. Sisto beggars' hospital in 1587.[7]

Guevarre propounded the notion that it was in the interests of society to establish the Ospizio Apostolico, subdividing the different categories of poor people into three institutions: adults of both sexes at the S. Sisto hospital, girls in the Papal Palace of St John Lateran and boys in the grandiose building of S. Michele a Ripa:

> It is extremely beneficial to the public, because not only is society relieved of huge numbers of vagabonds who are likely to commit a variety of misdeeds, but all those poor people who would otherwise have to beg in the streets, and all the orphans, boys and girls, who would otherwise lead an idle and wasteful life, can subsequently become good servants and good workers for the town and labourers in the countryside after they have been educated and brought up to work in these hospices.[8]

The practical implementation of the plan underlying the central policies for dealing with poverty implemented by the Popes between the late sixteenth and the end of the seventeenth centuries went through periods of success and failure, but the approach designed at the end of the seventeenth century remained in force practically until the fall of the Papal States. One specific aspect worth emphasizing is the way in which the functions of the large centralized institutions for the poor coexisted with a wide variety of other smaller institutions, particularly the confraternities, both religious and those created by the various 'national' groups or by 'arts and crafts' guilds that existed in Rome to provide mutual support and welfare. Far from competing with each other, the central and peripheral organizations devised ways of working together by setting up a complex network of activities. It is the purpose of this chapter to describe the functions and activities of some of the many orphanages that existed at the time.

CHARACTERISTICS OF THE POPULATION OF ROME 1600–1850

> Five hospices have been opened for orphans and poor children . . . and no less than 919 pupils have been taken in, free of charge, without counting those who pay for their food. For the orphans and poor girls, there are seventeen *conservatori* . . . [where] 1,294 spinsters are maintained and educated [not counting the boarders].[9]

Such is Morichini's brief description of the vast network of homes and *conservatori* for orphans of both sexes in mid-nineteenth-century Rome which concludes his analytical description of the history and features of each one. On the basis of these data and those provided by Fanucci and Piazza, together with the results of the latest research, a summary appraisal can be presented of the welfare systems available in Rome in 1601, 1698 and 1842. First, however, it is necessary to examine the growth rate of the Rome population. Table 4.1 shows the development of the population from the beginning of the seventeenth to the middle of the nineteenth century at approximately fifty-year intervals. The total population of the city is divided in terms of sex and age group according to the information provided by the 'Listae status animarum', taken by the Papal administration from the end of the sixteenth century. The information on age is derived from the note that was made of the number of persons who were 'ready for communion' and 'not ready for communion', representing roughly the numbers of persons of both sexes who were respectively over and under 13 years of age.

The increase in the population was small. However, the number of males consistently exceeded the number of females, while the four categories of the population considered here grew at different rates. No further comment on the unbalanced sex ratio will be offered except to say that this phenomenon, which has also been noted for other Italian cities which were state capitals, such as Venice and, at least in certain periods, Naples as well, was occasioned

Table 4.1 Population trends in Rome at fifty-year intervals from 1601 to 1847

		Three year moving averages			
Period	*Population*	*Ready for communion*	*Not ready for communion*	*Males*	*Females*
1601–3	101,912	82,473	19,439	57,841	44,071
1647–9	121,063	92,007	29,056	72,131	48,932
1697–9	134,547	101,980	32,567	78,338	56,209
1747–9	151,317	117,190	34,127	84,481	66,836
1797	166,280	125,933	40,347	91,872	74,408
1797–9	155,021	114,960	40,061	83,516	71,505
1847	175,883	127,700	48,183	94,835	81,048

Source: 'Listae status animarum almae urbis Romae', in Archivio Storico del Vicariato di Roma.

by the heavy migration flows of adult males to the city. By contrast with the female population, which grew in a much more regular way, the number of males in Rome was very sensitive to economic and political changes, even if only temporary in their impact. This becomes even more evident when it is recalled that when the growth in population was at its height, during the seventeenth century, the male population grew at a much faster rate than did the female population, while the opposite occurred between the end of the seventeenth and the mid-nineteenth century, when there were many economic crises and serious political upheavals and wars. The disruption to population growth which occurred after 1797 is one such episode. The creation of the Republic in 1798−9 resulted in a reduction in the male population which had been on the increase up until that point. The same applies to those who were declared to be 'ready for communion', a category in which males outnumbered females, while the check to growth was far less pronounced for the female population as a whole, and practically non-existent for boys and girls of both sexes, who are represented by the category 'not ready for communion'. It should also be noted that the numerical prevalence of males over females consistently lessened over the course of time.

Another major feature of the development that occurred over the two and a half centuries under examination here is the particularly large increase in the number of those 'not ready for communion', according to the index numbers given in Table 4.2. As a result of the different trends experienced by the various categories into which the population has been divided, throughout this long time-frame children under 13 usually accounted for between a fifth and a quarter of the total population. For every adult, indicated by the category 'ready for communion', there were between 0.24 (in 1601−3) and 0.38 (in 1847) persons 'not ready for communion', i.e., children under the age of 13. Relative to the total female population, there was one child 'not ready for communion' to every 2.3 women in 1601−3, one to every two women in 1747−9 and one to every 1.7 women in 1847. The relative growth in the number of children per woman, however, was far from regular, as the ratios of the late seventeenth century are somewhat higher than those of the middle and later years of the eighteenth century. These dynamics are consistent with the trend in the ratio of births per 1,000 women in Rome in the corresponding periods.[10]

The high mortality rate of the past ended many marriages prematurely and many children were orphaned as a result.[11] It is therefore evident that in periods when the birth rate was expanding, and the mortality rate was unchanged, the number of orphans in the population must increase. They remained orphaned for a longer or shorter time depending on their survival chances (which on average were almost certainly less than for children in general), and the speed with which their remaining parent remarried and on whether any new step-parent was prepared to welcome the offspring of the previous marriage into their household.

Table 4.2 Population of Rome, 1601–1847, ready and not ready for communion: index numbers and ratios

| Period | Population | Index number 1601–3 = 100 | | | | Not ready[1] | Ratios[2] | |
		Ready for communion	Not ready for communion	M	F		(a)	(b)
1601–3	100.0	100.0	100.0	100.0	100.0	19.1	23.6	44.1
1647–9	118.8	111.6	149.5	124.7	110.3	24.0	31.6	59.4
1697–9	130.2	123.7	167.5	135.4	127.5	24.2	31.9	57.9
1747–9	148.5	142.1	175.6	146.1	151.7	22.6	29.2	51.1
1797	163.2	152.7	207.6	158.8	168.8	24.3	32.0	54.2
1797–9	152.1	139.1	206.1	144.9	162.2	25.8	34.8	56.0
1847	172.6	154.8	247.9	164.0	183.9	27.4	37.7	59.4

Notes: [1] As a percentage of the total population.
[2] (a) Number of persons not ready for communion per 100 persons ready for communion.
(b) Number of persons not ready for communion per 100 females.

Source: 'Listae status animarum almae urbis Romae', in Archivio Storico del Vicariato di Roma.

A variety of factors therefore help determine the number of orphans of a particular age in a given area at a given time: the marriage rate, the marital fertility rate and the survival chances at different ages both of parents and children. Nuptiality, fertility and mortality – and the consequent 'production' of orphans – are also affected, as indicated earlier, by the rate of remarriage, which also responds to the nature of the 'marriage market'. However, this response varies according to the sex and age of the surviving parent and the number of surviving children: normally it was widowers, rather than the widows, who remarried, and among the widows, the younger ones, and hence the ones with fewer children, rather than the older ones. It should also be remembered that even in a society where remarriage was frequent, there could be many orphans. In the first place the interval between the dissolution of one marriage and the formation of the next could last from a few months to several years. Second, when the number of orphans is high, the burden on the surviving parent could, to a considerable extent, be relieved if it could be arranged for one or more of the children to leave the family group, a move which could also be a necessary precondition for the remarriage of a surviving parent with a few children. It is evident that where institutions existed to take in orphans, widowed parents were likely to entrust the upbringing of some of their children to them, on either a temporary or permanent basis.

In many cases, the death of one parent might scar the life experiences of orphans making it more difficult for them to form affective or social relationships, which could further downgrade them into 'second-class children' even when they were incorporated into the new household. Moreover, an orphan from a previous marriage may still have remained an orphan, even when he or she continued to live with the remarried parent. The distinctive sign of this unfortunate experience is evident in the parish registers where parish priests customarily identified the orphans of the late parent, distinguishing them from any other children born to the second marriage.

These considerations are not intended as a prelude to further analysis of the various demographic, cultural and social factors and processes that conspired in such traditional societies to emphasize the presence of orphans, presented them as socially relevant figures and guided their subsequent destiny. Certainly, such a complex analysis should be carried out as should any inquiry into the experience of widowhood, particularly for women. However, in the present chapter all that can be attempted is to highlight the complexity of these factors, and focus the discussion on a more limited analysis of the status and the fate of orphans in the city of Rome in the context of the institutions that were established to look after them and the interaction between these institutions and the orphans' families.

THE ORPHANS OF ROME

Over time, the number of these institutions and their inmates increased. The data given in the first column in Table 4.3 indicate that the number of orphans of both sexes living in the hospices and *conservatori* of Rome doubled between the beginning and end of the seventeenth century, and almost trebled by the mid-nineteenth century. The number increased more steeply than the number of those 'not ready for communion' from whom, broadly speaking, the orphans were drawn. The ratio between the two rose from 4.1 orphans cared for in the institutions for every 100 children under the age of 13 and therefore reported as 'not ready for communion' in 1601, to 4.9 in 1698 and 5.4 in 1842. This growth in the accommodation capacity of these institutions reflects the increased involvement of the government in this area of social and welfare policy and the role of these institutions was somewhat altered as a consequence. This is also shown by the growth in the number of such institutions from seven in 1601 to twelve in 1698 and twenty-two in 1842 according to Morichini, as a result of a number of mergers of old orphanages and the creation of new ones. This led to a reduction in the average size of the institutions and a growing tendency to specialize, as they harmonized their functions with their objectives and the type of persons for whom they cared.

Table 4.3 also indicates the number of foundlings received in the same years in order to provide a comprehensive picture of the population of the

Table 4.3 Children in the care of Rome institutions in 1601, 1698 and 1842

Year	Orphans in hospices and conservatori	Foundlings	Girls in foundling homes	Total	Not ready for communion
1601	780	634	476	1,890	18,882
1698	1,602	700	494	2,796	32,497
1842	2,213	843	490	3,546	40,940
	Percentage of 'Not ready for communion'				*Percentage of population*
1601	4.1	3.4	2.5	10.0	18.6
1698	4.9	2.2	1.5	8.6	24.3
1842	5.4	2.1	1.2	8.7	25.5

Sources: The data on orphans in 1601 were taken from C. Fanucci, *Trattato di tutte l'opere pie dell'Alma Città di Roma*, Rome 1601; for 1698 from C.B. Piazza, *Eusevologio romano, overo delle opere pie di Roma accresciuto et ampiato secondo lo stato presente*, Rome, 1698, but completed and estimated using more recent information supplied by R. Chiuppi on the hospices of S. Michele and S. Giovanni in Laterano; for 1842 from L. Morichini, *Degl'istituti di pubblica carità e d'istruzione primaria in Roma*, Rome 1842. For foundlings and the girls in the foundlings hospice, the data have been taken from or estimated from time series constructed by C. Schiavoni (1991). The number of the 'Not ready for communion' and of the population of Rome were taken from the 'Listae status animarum' for the years concerned.

children's institutions of Rome. Among these foundlings are included both those children taken to the Santo Spirito in Sassia hospital (newborn babies who, after a short period of care in the hospital, were fostered by wet-nurses residing out of the hospital in or around the city of Rome), and those female foundlings who, having been cared for by wet-nurses and foster families in the community, were again admitted to the hospital between the ages of 10 and 12. There the girls were put to work and given some education in a special *conservatorio*, the oldest of all such establishments, until they either married or became nuns. The treatment they received, therefore, was comparable to that meted out to their contemporaries in the *conservatori* of the orphanages. The data indicate that there was a decline in the proportion of both groups of foundlings of all children under the age of communion, in line with the ratio between foundlings and births in Rome.[12] In turn this implies that there had been a gradual increase in the proportion of orphans among all children in the care of these institutions in Rome. Thus orphans accounted for 41 per cent of the total of orphans and foundlings (both types) in 1601, 57.3 per cent in 1698 and 62.4 per cent in 1842.

THE FATE OF THE FEMALE ORPHANS OF ROME

As Morichini writes, 'The *conservatori* were established in order to save the honour of girls, to give them a Christian education and train them for domestic and household work, to prepare them to become good mothers.'[13] Similar ideas had been expressed by Piazza one and a half centuries earlier when he noted 'the many homes and *conservatori* opened and maintained by Roman piety, either to conserve the modesty and decorum of the poor maidens' – hence the name '*conservatori*' – 'or to remove them from greater threats to their virtue, the need for which continued to grow because of the numbers of threatened maidens'.[14]

The expression 'threatened maidens' refers to girls who were *threatened* with loss of virtue and honour. The regulation of Rome's *conservatori* imposed very strict age limits for the admission of young girls of between 6 and 12 years of age. Twelve was approximately the age of maturity, which, as has been observed, 'Implied the full possession, and hence the possibility of its loss, of that good, namely sexual honour, which could only be strictly guaranteed by taking vows or taking a husband.'[15] However, many girls also entered the *conservatori* at a later age, but, for them, it was necessary for a person enjoying the confidence of the institution, such as a parish priest or a benefactor, to confirm their moral worth. When the young girls were picked up from the streets, and therefore had no one to vouch for them, the severe discipline to which they were then subjected provided the most obvious explanation of their good behaviour within the institution. An appropriate illustration is provided by the history of the Conservatorio di S. Eufemia, an ancient institution created to help young girls totally without means 'who were abandoned and scattered around Rome' and which, in the eighteenth century, also opened its doors to the daughters 'of non-infamous parents' in difficulty, such as small craftsmen, traders and servants. By the end of the 1630s, 302 girls were being cared for at S. Eufemia, gradually declining to 204 by mid-century and 133 towards the end. This decline continued until the mid-eighteenth century when there were only fifty girls in the institution. This reflected the gradual reduction in the number of annual admissions from seven to eight in the early seventeenth century to six in the later seventeenth century and only two in the first half of the eighteenth century.[16] In the first half of the eighteenth century, 49 per cent of newly-admitted girls were aged between 6 and 12, and 30 per cent between 13 and 15. As far as their fate was concerned, of the girls admitted to the course over that fifty-year period, 42.7 per cent left to marry, 21.9 per cent to take vows and 26 per cent spent their whole lives in the institution, with only 9.4 per cent returning to their families.[17]

The way in which the Conservatorio di S. Eufemia operated is a good example of how an institution was left to decide for itself the future destiny of the girls in its care, substituting in full for the missing family. To marry, take the veil or stay in the *conservatorio*, in the cases of the girls who survived at S. Eufemia, were effectively the only alternatives open to these girls, all three capable of saving them from the vices and perils of this world, according to the aims of the institution.

However, not all Rome *conservatori* adopted the same policy, or at least not in such an all-embracing manner. Information is available for three of them, detailing the numbers and the characteristics of the children entering and leaving in different periods of the seventeenth and eighteenth centuries. The first, and perhaps the most famous, was Divina Provvidenza, established in 1672 to provide protection for poor orphaned and abandoned girls, or girls living in poverty or in danger.

At first this *conservatorio* was essentially a charitable and welfare institution. When the girls could prove that they needed help they were taken in, regardless of their background, origin or age, and were given different types of jobs and some education. Teachers were employed, and the girls were taught 'not only in Christian discipline and the holy fear of God, but every domestic task, not only to keep them occupied and train them in honest skills, but in order to earn the wherewithal to maintain themselves'.[18] Work and prayer lasted all day, even while the girls were carrying out domestic and other types of work, as they were intended to be 'continually occupied in prayer and spiritual occupations'. The religious zeal and the monastic discipline of Divina Provvidenza attracted the attention and financial support of the church, principally the Pope, and enabled its fame to spread throughout the city. As a result, its finances flourished. This was also due to the revenue from the sale of gloves which the girls made at various times and from a sharp increase in the demand to take in new girls. This led to a change in its rules.

From the early eighteenth century, the upper age limit for the admission of the girls, normally 15 years, was adhered to more strictly, and an attempt was made to keep them longer and to discourage their returning home after a short stay. The girls now came from a broader social spectrum, from less needy and more decent backgrounds, and fees were introduced and the families and benefactors were required to supply linen. In other words, they began to prefer young girls who were 'poor, but of a civil condition', as Morichini put it in 1842.[19] Nevertheless, in the *conservatorio* there were many different types of girls, all subject to the same rigid discipline in an institution that was half hospice and half school.[20] As time passed, fewer girls entered, and the number resident at any one time at Divina Provvidenza declined from 200 to 170 by the end of the seventeenth century, to about 150 fifty years later and 100 by 1842.

The second *conservatorio* to be considered here is that of S. Pasquale Baylon, founded in 1732 for the care of orphaned girls. It was smaller than Divina Provvidenza into which it was absorbed in 1828, and began with about twenty-five girls, rising to fifty in the mid-eighteenth century. The maintenance of girls was provided for from a combination of sources: a subsidy from their Cardinal protector, the fees paid by other benefactors and the proceeds from the girls' work, which involved the manufacture of silk ribbons. However, the financial situation of the institution was never totally assured and some of the girls were sent out daily to collect alms. Even though the discipline inside was equally severe, throughout the eighteenth century S. Pasquale Baylon was much more willing than was Divina Provvidenza to adapt to a production-oriented approach. The fact that the girls also received a wage for their work, proportionate to its quality and quantity, is particularly relevant. On the other hand, the institution never evolved into a fully-fledged work unit, retaining a traditional role which apparently was closer to that of a hospice rather than of an educational institution.

The third institution, the Conservatorio Pio, founded in 1775 by Pope Pius VI, was given a more explicitly productive role. The approach was revolutionary in its attempt to build a modern wool mill employing some male workers in a girls' *conservatorio*. The woollen cloth mill (1782–97) employed men, while in a separate building a linen, hemp and cloth mill provided work for girls whose average age on entry was as high as 16, precisely because of the working skills that were required. The spirit and the organization of the whole venture, such as the division of labour, the payment of wages, the element of vocational training and the fact that there was employment for both sexes, can be seen as signalling the transition at the end of the eighteenth century from a traditional institution into a new type based on work instead of assistance, with all the benefits as well as all the problems of an industrial-type experiment.

Between 1672 and 1750 over 1,000 girls passed through Divina Provvidenza, while S. Pasquale Baylon recorded 102 admissions between 1740 and 1760 and Conservatorio Pio, 198 between 1775 and 1797. The age of the girls and whether their parents were still alive at the moment the girls entered these institutions (Table 4.4) and their reasons for leaving (Table 4.5) are all known. Orphans accounted for a substantial proportion: 78 per cent at the Conservatorio Pio, 82 per cent of Divina Provvidenza and 93 per cent at S. Pasquale Baylon. The average age on entry was 16, 13 and 13.5 respectively, reflecting the different functions of the three institutions.

As Table 4.5 shows, entering a *conservatorio* marked a complete change in the lives of a substantial proportion of the girls. Thirty-seven point three per cent in S. Pasquale Baylon died there, 31.4 per cent left to get married, 26.4 per cent returned home and 4.9 per cent went to another institution. The distribution was quite different at Conservatorio Pio: the vast majority of girls left to return home (39 per cent), followed by those who remained for the rest of their lives (25 per cent) and those who left because of illness or to go to other institutions (21 per cent). Far fewer left to marry (12 per cent) and only a small percentage (3 per cent) took vows.

That the destinations of the inmates of the two institutions differed so greatly was in large measure a reflection of the fact that each institution fulfilled a different role in regard to the girls in its care. Nearly all the girls in S. Pasquale Baylon were orphans, almost half having lost both parents. It is very likely therefore that many of them had no home to which they could return, so that the institution became their only home, where they stayed until death. Such girls, however, may have deliberately opted to remain, since the *conservatorio* did not discourage them from leaving for marriage, as can be seen from the regime established by the institution, which gave the girls some independence through their work and some contact with the outer world. To remain in the *conservatorio* was different from choosing a religious vocation, but afforded the same degree of protection. The 37.3 per cent of the girls who remained in the *conservatorio* until they died, resided there on average for thirty-seven years and had a very high average age of death of 51 years.

The role of Conservatorio Pio meant it was less likely that a girl would opt to remain in the institution. Its production requirements did not gel easily with a purely protective function. The turnover of inmates was very high, and the average age of the inmates at death was 36, with a mean length of stay of about eighteen years. Many of the girls did not like what must have been very unhealthy work and left because their health deteriorated or were returned to their families because they were sick, with tuberculosis the most frequently mentioned malady. Comparing the two institutions, two possible and different, but equally bleak, alternatives are clearly visible: orphans living in care or working orphans.

The existence of these two patterns suggests that very different motives may underlie what are apparently similar causes for leaving the institutions. The reason why so many girls returned to their families from Divina Provvidenza in the last quarter of the seventeenth century was that the institution could provide only a temporary solution to their problems, whether in the

Table 4.4 Orphanhood status of girls at the moment of entry into three of the *conservatori* of Rome

Conservatorio (entry periods)	Number of cases	Orphans of			Non-orphans (%)	Not known (%)	Total (%)	Average age on entry
		Both (%)	Father (%)	Mother (%)				
Divina Provvidenza (1672–1750)	992	23.0	42.4	17.0	16.2	1.4	100.0	13
San Pasquale Baylon (1740–60)	102	43.4	27.1	22.4	7.1	—	100.0	13.5
Conservatorio Pio (1775–97)	198	31.0	12.0	35.0	—	22.0	100.0	16

Table 4.5 Reasons for leaving the *conservatori* in Rome

Conservatorio (entry period)	Number of cases	Marriage (%)	Death (%)	Vows (%)	Return home (%)	Other (%)	Total (%)
Divina Provvidenza*							
(1672–1700)	499	34.1	16.6	2.6	36.1	10.6[a]	100.0
(1701–50)	489	38.2	25.8	9.2	19.4	7.4[b]	100.0
San Pasquale Baylon							
(1740–60)	102	31.4	37.3	—	26.4	4.9[c]	100.0
Conservatorio Pio							
(1775–97)	198	12.0	25.0	3.0	39.0	21.0[d]	100.0

Notes:
* The year of entry is not known in four cases.
[a] 8.4 per cent were placed in service with families. No information on cause of leaving: 2.2 per cent.
[b] 2.3 per cent were placed in service with families. No information on cause of leaving: 5.1 per cent.
[c] Girls placed with other institutions.
[d] 10 per cent left due to sickness, 11 per cent to manage other conservatories or schools. Many sick girls were also among those who returned home.

form of support for their families or protection of the girls. In the case of Conservatorio Pio, the large number of girls who returned to their families was probably due to the fact that they were not suited for the work of the institution.

For the same reasons more girls died in the Conservatorio Pio. The similar frequency of death at Divina Provvidenza for girls who entered in the first half of the eighteenth century, and the even higher frequency in the case of S. Pasquale Baylon, is due to the fact that the girls spent a much greater part of their lives there. This also explains the wide gap in the frequency with which the girls left the institutions to marry: a high proportion from Divina Provvidenza and S. Pasquale Baylon, in view of their functions of acting *in loco parentis*, but a far lower proportion in the case of Conservatorio Pio, where marriage was inconsistent with the whole purpose of the institution.

In the case of Divina Provvidenza, the differences observed in the destinies of the girls who entered at the end of the seventeenth and the first half of the eighteenth centuries can be analysed in greater detail as the individual histories of the girls making up the two consecutive intakes between 1685 and 1700 and 1701 and 1750 have been reconstructed.[21]

Table 4.6 shows the changes that occurred in the 'calendar' in terms of age at admission, duration of stay and age at leaving. The average age on entry of the second group was lower by some eighteen months, the average period of stay was over four years longer and the average age on leaving, for whatever reason, was consequently two and a half years higher. This therefore increased the institution's chances of influencing the lives of the girls in the critical phase of the transition from puberty to adolescence and young adulthood.

Table 4.6 Age on entry and length of stay of the girls at Divina Provvidenza in Rome in the seventeenth and eighteenth centuries

| *Age and length (years)* | *Periods of entry* | | |
	1685–1700	*1701–50*	*1685–1750*
Average age on entry	13.6	12.1	12.7
Average length of stay	10.6	15.4	13.5
Average age on leaving	24.2	27.5	26.2

The prospects of the girls after joining the institution were affected both by the philosophy of the institution and by promptings from outside, such as the wishes of their families, marriage opportunities, the offer of work with a private family or the chances of entering a convent. However, to a certain extent the institution could also control these offers from outside, both by selecting and filtering those deemed to be most appropriate and by making it possible for the girls not to choose any of the offers by allowing them to stay in the institution. In addition, another powerful filter also operated, namely the high death rate in their age group during the periods under review.

Any examination of the events in the lives of these girls, and the choices they made, must therefore take account of both the pattern of the alternative reasons for leaving at different ages and the risks of dying in the *conservatorio*. The procedure involved the calculation of the probability of dying at a particular age, based on a total of 165 deaths. This made it possible to construct a life table for the institution, net of changes due to reasons other than death. The survival chances of the girls while they remained in the *conservatorio* during this period can be summarized in the following way. Taking 1,000 as the number of survivors at their tenth birthday ($l_{10} = 1,000$), the survival function each 10 years thereafter was as follows: $l_{20} = 896$, $l_{30} = 802$, $l_{40} = 682$, $l_{50} = 571$. These data indicate a high mortality rate, consistent with the levels in the rest of Rome and Italy. Comparisons with the model life tables[22] indicate that the values approximate to low survival levels of the 'southern' model. However, the values given do not appear to fit just one level of mortality in the model tables. Survival between the tenth and twentieth year of life was closest to level 2 — which is typical of the populations with a life expectancy at birth of 22.5 years. On the other hand, the rates of survival between the twentieth and thirtieth year of life are consistent with level 4 of the model tables (an average life expectancy of 27.5 years), and after the age of 30 with conditions half way between level 4 and level 3 (the latter with a life expectancy at birth of 25 years). Moreover, whereas in the standard tables the probability of death increases consistently after the tenth birthday, for the girls of the *conservatorio* they fall from high values to lower values between the thirteenth and twenty-third year, and only then rise steadily. This atypical pattern, however, does not negate the findings presented above, but suggests that consideration should be given to their specific significance, for this group of girls experienced markedly different conditions from their contemporaries outside the *conservatorio*. It was certainly a more protected way of life, less precarious from many points of view, above all in regard to nutrition. The transition from a broken family, with most of the girls having suffered the shock of the death of a parent, to the well-regulated life of the *conservatorio* may well have enhanced their capacity for survival during the delicate stage of adolescence. The identified mortality models (assumed to be constant over time) will therefore be used in the study of the lives of the cohorts in question.

According to this analysis, the change in the 'calendar' of the ages upon entry, leaving and the cause of leaving, interacting with the high mortality rate indicates that the situation of the inmates differed markedly in the first half of the eighteenth century from what had been the case earlier. The results are given in Table 4.7 in the form of a model which requires a few

Table 4.7 Modelling the exits of inmates from Divina Provvidenza in Rome

Average age	Survivors	Leavers	Balance	$_aq_x$	Died as inmates	Leavers per 100 survivors	Cause of leaving
Period of entry: 1685–1700			No. of cases: 275				
13.6	1,000	—	1,000	0.0553	55	—	—
18.6	945	44	901	0.0101	9	4.7	Other accommodation
19.7	892	338	554	0.0452	25	37.9	Return home
24.7	529	429	100	0.0248	2	81.1	Marriage
27.1	98	33	65			33.7	Vows
Period of entry: 1701–50			No. of cases: 459				
12.1	1,000	—	1,000	0.0856	86	—	—
19.8	914	205	709	0.0205	15	22.4	Return home
22.0	694	91	603	0.0156	9	13.1	Vows
24.1	594	410	184	0.0094	2	69.0	Marriage
24.8	182	22	160			12.1	Other accommodation

words of introduction. The girls who entered the *conservatorio* in the two periods 1685–1700 and 1701–50 had different average ages on entry and on leaving, regardless of the specific cause. In short, the assumption is that experience of each category of entrant or leaver is adequately captured in the average age corresponding to the individual event. It should also be noted that for ease of comparison both groups have been standardized at 1,000. In other words, as far as the first group is concerned, it is assumed that all the girls entered the *conservatorio* aged 13.6 years (the average age of the group upon entry) and that none of them left before the age of 18.6 years, the average age of the girls who left to take up employment with private families. However, the level of mortality experienced by this age group (the probability of death between 13.6 and 18.6 years: $q_x = 0.0553$) eliminated fifty-five girls to leave 945 survivors, forty-four of whom left to work for private families, conventionally at age 18.6. Of the remaining 901, nine more were to die before the age of 19.7, the average age of departure of the 338 girls who were returned to their families of origin. This left 554 girls to experience mortality levels applicable to older ages, and other reasons for leaving the institution (see Table 4.7, first cohort). Of course, it is recognized that these calculations represent a model of behaviour patterns and need to be tested through further research.

According to the rate of entries and exits, and the levels of mortality experienced at different ages within the *conservatorio* (assumed to have been constant over time), the group of girls who entered in the seventeenth century was prematurely and sharply reduced by the fact that they moved to other families or returned to their own families before the age of 20, on average just over six years after their entry. It was only later, when these causes for leaving in conjunction with mortality had halved the size of the initial cohort of 1,000 girls, that the institution had to concern itself with the other options: marriage or the convent. In reality, the veil was only a residual option because, on average, a move to a convent occurred only when the women were at an advanced age (on average 27 years), later than all the other possibilities, and when only 10 per cent of the original group remained.

However, the experience of the girls who entered the *conservatorio* in the first half of the eighteenth century, on average at the age of 12, was quite different. They returned to their families after a longer period in the institution and in fewer numbers, and fewer of them took employment with private families, which was deferred to the average age of 24.8 when the girls had already spent more than twelve and a half years in the *conservatorio*. Conversely, they left for a convent when much younger, on average when aged 22, when the survivors still accounted for 69.4 per cent of the initial entrants. Marriage was an option for 59.4 per cent of the original group, but affected a much smaller proportion than in the previous cohort. Of the girls who entered the *conservatorio* in the seventeenth century only 6.5 per cent were left when all solutions for leaving had been exhausted, compared with the 16 per cent who remained of the entrants of the eighteenth century once all options had been taken. Moreover, because of the different strategies at work and the lower age at entry in the first half of the eighteenth century, although 7.5 per cent of the girls who entered before 1700 died in the institution between the average age on entry and the average age of leaving (22.4), in the eighteenth century, while the average age upon leaving remained virtually the same (22.6), 11 per cent of the girls now died in the institution. In other words, by the eighteenth century the institution seems to have taken even more care to steer the destiny of the girls, encouraging them to marry or take vows or to stay in the *conservatorio*. As far as the increased numbers taking vows is concerned, this could also be viewed as an attempt on the part of the institution to offset the widespread decline in the membership of religious orders in eighteenth-century Italy.[23]

THE ORPHAN GIRLS AND THEIR FAMILIES OF ORIGIN

A further perspective on the events which affected the girls at Divina Provvidenza might explore the existence of a relationship between their range of experiences and certain features of their families of origin. For the purposes of an initial analysis the causes for the girls leaving the *conservatorio* can be compared with the survival status of their parents at the time of entry.

Table 4.8 provides the results of the test carried out on all the cases. What immediately emerges is the very high percentage (41 per cent) of girls whose parents had both been alive when they entered the institution and who in due course returned home, compared with the general average of 27.9 per cent. This same group was less likely than any of the other groups to leave for other reasons. Second, girls who had lost their mother were more likely than were others to die in the *conservatorio*.

If the causes for leaving are grouped as follows: first, marriage, second, vows and death in the *conservatorio* and, third, returning home and settling with other families, marked differences are evident depending upon the different survival conditions of the parents at the moment of entry. The first group reveals the institution's capacity to encourage the creation of new families, mainly in the case of orphans, and particularly for girls who had lost their fathers. Second, there is the group of girls who either remained with the institution or entered a convent. Such destinies were particularly the fate of girls who had lost their mothers: 32.5 per cent of these girls ended their lives in the *conservatorio* or in a convent, compared with 21.8 per cent for those whose parents were alive, 25 per cent for those who had lost their father and 27.2 per cent who had lost both parents. Lastly, returning to their families of origin or settling with other families – both solutions in which the institution did not play a major decision-making role in deciding their future – was particularly likely in the case of girls

Table 4.8 Reasons for leaving Divina Provvidenza, Rome, by survival of parents at time of entry

Reason for leaving	Orphans of			Non-orphans (%)	Not known (%)	Total (%)
	Both (%)	Father (%)	Mother (%)			
Marriage	35.6	39.1	34.9	30.4	35.8	36.2
Death	21.5	18.6	26.6	16.8	21.4	20.4
Return home	22.8	27.6	24.3	41.0	14.3	27.9
Other accommodation	10.5	3.8	1.2	5.0	21.4	5.3
Vows	5.7	6.4	5.9	5.0	–	5.8
Not known	3.9	4.5	7.1	1.8	7.1	4.4
Total	100.0	100.0	100.0	100.0	100.0	100.0

whose parents were alive (46 per cent) and to a lesser degree (25.5 per cent) those who had lost their mothers.

The examination of these figures cannot be pursued much further. However, seeing the importance of the interaction between the institution and family situations, it is important to gain a better understanding of the features of the universe from which the inmates of the *conservatorio* were drawn. Other sources that could provide details of certain typical features of their families of origin were therefore consulted. These sources were the parish registers and the *status animarum* and the other parish books, since the parish from which the girls came was almost invariably named in the records of the *conservatorio*, together with the name and surname of the parents, whether alive or dead, and the Christian names of the girls themselves.

This examination included locating the parish records relating to the families of 200 girls, or 25 per cent of the 813 girls whose home parish was known (82 per cent of the total). These 200 cases were selected on the basis of a classification of the parishes in terms of size and location in the city. It was a particularly difficult task and it was possible to trace only 103 families, of whom three had to be eliminated for lack of documentation.

These families had 5.5 members, including 3.5 children, at the latest point of observation prior to the girls entering the *conservatorio*. The average number of children is a significant indicator, and many sources refer to the fact that it was a necessary precondition for eligibility for alms, food aid and the reception of a child into a hospice for a family to have more than three children.[24] Evidently this must have represented a further test of eligibility in addition to other conditions of poverty, because, as Pullan has said referring to the case of Rome, it was not necessary to have many children to be a poor family.[25]

Among the families in question, there was a very high proportion residing in simple family households, mainly widows and widowers with children.[26] These latter account for 63 per cent of the total, much higher than the average for Rome where widows/widowers with children accounted for 11 per cent of all households, and married couples with and without children 39 per cent.[27] There is a fairly straightforward explanation for this difference. It was the simple households, not those extended to include other relatives, which were the most fragile, given that following the death of one of the parents, the survivor might well find it impossible to support the financial and organizational burden of bringing up more than three children. Such a situation was the main source of inmates to the *conservatori* and the hospices.

In 83 per cent of the family histories that have been reconstructed, the death of one of the parents was the circumstance which preceded the entry of a daughter into the *conservatorio*. However, other factors could also be involved. The break up of the household caused by a parent's death often made it impossible for the family to continue to live in the same house. The family literally disappeared from the *status animarum* on average 4.5 years prior to the entry of the girl into the *conservatorio*. This, coupled with the death of a parent, affected 30 per cent of all families, but rose to 47 per cent for those girls who had lost either their mother or both parents. The households were apparently more stable following the death of the father of the girl, since in this case 53 per cent of the families remained in the parish. Not surprisingly, a higher proportion of families where both parents had survived also remained in the parish throughout the period during which a daughter entered the *conservatorio*. Almost 60 per cent of these families are recorded in the annual *status animarum* both before and after the entry of a daughter into the *conservatorio*.

When the family lived permanently in the parish, the girls were more likely to return after a few years in the *conservatorio*. This occurred in the case of 46 per cent of these families. However, returning home did not mean simply a return to the previous situation, but to a new and perhaps more difficult one. Such was probably the case when a girl returned to her mother after her remarriage (the records state simply 'returned to their mother who has remarried' in 16 per cent of the cases of girls who had lost their father). It must have been equally difficult for the girls who returned to a widowed father or were entrusted to an uncle or a brother or sister who had already created their own family while the girl had been in the *conservatorio*.

CONCLUSION

These interactions between the families and the homes for orphans require much more detailed study than has been possible here given the small number of cases. The histories of the various *conservatori* that have been examined and the alternative destinies of the girls who remained within them for a longer or shorter period of time demonstrate that a network of relationships between families and institutions did exist, and must have been a very important phenomenon in the demographic and social history of Rome in the seventeenth and eighteenth centuries. This interaction also had important repercussions of various kinds, on such aspects as the survival of the girls concerned, the proportion of those who married, their age at marriage and their subsequent reproductive life span. These are factors that need to be examined in terms of the situations affecting members of the surrounding community.

On the other hand, another interesting result of the analysis concerns the marked difference in the fates of the girls depending upon whether they had lost their mother or their father. This is something that needs to be examined in the context of the much poorer standard of living of widows and widowers, and the different opportunities they had of contracting a new marriage, depending in part on the number and the age of their children from the previous marriage. In addition to this more systematic examination, the survey also needs to be extended to cover different populations, to towns and cities of different sizes and experiencing other political and administrative conditions.

NOTES

1 F. Giusberti, 'Per una morfologia del sistema assistenziale urbano in età moderna', *Cheiron*, 2:3, 1984, p. 51.
2 B. Geremek, *La pietà e la forca. Storia della miseria e della carità in Europa*, Bari: Laterza 1986.
3 ibid.: p. 222.
4 B. Pullan, 'The Old Catholicism, the New Catholicism and the Poor', in G. Politi, M. Rosa and F. Della Peruta (eds), *Timore e carità. I poveri nell'Italia moderna* (Annali della Biblioteca statale e libreria civica di Cremona XXVII–XXX), Cremona: Libreria del convegno editrice 1982, pp. 23, 25.
5 Geremek, *La pietà e la forca*, p. 222; see also, *Ricerche per la storia religiosa di Roma*, 3, 1979: the issue is devoted to the theme of the poor in Rome.
6 Anon. (A. Guevarre), *La mendicità proveduta nella città di Roma coll'Ospizio pubblico fondato dalla pietà e beneficienza di N.S. Innocenzo XII P.M.*, Rome 1693, p. 1.
7 C. Fanucci, *Trattato di tutte l'opere pie dell'Alma Città di Roma*, Rome 1601; C.B. Piazza, *Eusevologio romano, overo delle opere pie di Roma accresciuto et ampiato secondo lo stato presente*, 2 vols, Rome 1698; P. Simoncelli, 'Note sul sistema assistenziale a Roma nel XVI secolo', in Politi, Rosa and Della Peruta (eds), *Timore e carità*, pp. 145ff.
8 Anon. (A. Guevarre), *La mendicità proveduta*, p. 8.
9 C.L. Morichini, *Degl'istituti di pubblica carità e d'istruzione primaria in Roma*, vol. 2, Rome 1842, p. 106.
10 C. Schiavoni and E. Sonnino, 'Aspects généraux de l'évolution démographique à Rome: 1598–1824', *Annales de démographie historique*, 1982, pp. 105–8, table II.
11 A model which illustrates the characteristics of this process is proposed in S. Bertino and E. Sonnino, *Nota preliminare sullo studio di una coorte di matrimonio*, Rome: Dipartimento di Statistica, Università degli Studi di Roma 'La Sapienza', Serie A 1991, n. 32.
12 C. Schiavoni, 'Gli infanti "esposti" del Santo Spirito in Saxia di Roma tra '500 e '800', in Collection de l'École Française de Rome, *Enfance abandonnée et société en Europe, XIVe–XXe siècles*, Rome: École Française de Rome 1991.
13 Morichini, *Degl'istituti*, vol. 2, p. 71.
14 Piazza, *Eusevologio romano*, vol. 2, p. 205.
15 E. Grendi, 'Ideologia della carità e società indisciplinata: la costruzione del sistema assistenziale genovese (1470–1670)', in Politi, Rosa and Della Peruta (eds), *Timore e carità*, p. 71.
16 A. Saltafuori, *Il Conservatorio di S. Eufemia*, Rome: tesi di laurea in Lettere e Filosofia, Università degli Studi di Roma 'La Sapienza', 1987–8.
17 V. Mariantoni, *Le zitelle a Roma tra '700 e '800: S. Eufemia e S. Caterina della Rosa*, Rome: tesi di laurea in Lettere e Filosofia, Università degli Studi di Roma 'La Sapienza', 1985–6.
18 Piazza, *Eusevologio romano*, vol. 2, p. 205.
19 Morichini, *Degl'istituti*, vol. 2, p. 78.
20 Cf. F. Gemini, 'Interventi di politica sociale nel campo dell'assistenza femminile: tre conservatori romani tra Sei e Settecento', in Società Italiana di Demografia Storica, *La demografia storica delle città italiane*, Bologna: Ed. CLUEB 1982, pp. 165ff. This is also the source of data in Tables 4.4 and 4.5 (pp. 105, 106) on

the characteristics of the female inmates of S. Pasquale Baylon and Conservatorio Pio. A thorough analysis of the data on the girls at Divina Provvidenza has been undertaken by the author. Preliminary findings were published by F. Gemini and E. Sonnino, 'La condition féminine dans une structure d'assistance à Rome', *Annales de démographie historique*, 1981, pp. 235–50. The data have since been further processed and additional information extracted from the records of the parishes and conservatories. The Divina Provvidenza records are in the Accademia dei Lincei in Rome, while the data on the families of the girls were derived from the parish registers, located in the Archivio Storico del Vicariato di Roma. See also A. Groppi, *I conservatori della virtù*, Rome-Bari: Laterza 1994.

21 It may be useful to recall the nature of the data. The *conservatorio* was opened in 1672, but the earliest known register of the inmates dates from Easter 1684, when 170 girls remained of all those who had entered since 1672. The fate of these girls and those who entered after Easter 1684 to the end of 1750 is therefore known. Of the 992 girls who were present at some point during this period, 170 were there at Easter 1684, thirty more entered before December 1684, 303 between the beginning of 1685 and the end of 1700 and 489 between 1701 and 1750. The results given here only relate to the latter two cohorts. The reconstruction of the individual events took account of the age on entry and leaving, and the reason for leaving. Age on entry is known for 779 girls (298 who entered between 1685 and 1700, 481 between 1701 and 1750). The complete set of information (age and date of entry, age and date of leaving, reason for leaving) is known for only 724 of these (275 plus 449), plus a further ten girls who entered in the second period and were still resident in the *conservatorio* at an advanced age in 1795 – the final year of analysis.

22 A.J. Coale, P. Demeny and B. Vaughan, *Regional Model Life Tables and Stable Populations*, 2nd edn, New York: Academic Press 1983.

23 P. Stella, 'Strategie familiari e celibato sacro in Italia tra '600 e '700', *Salesianum*, 1979, p. 41; L. Del Panta and M. Livi Bacci, 'Le componenti naturali dell'evoluzione demografica nell'Italia del Settecento', in Società Italiana di Demografia Storica, *La popolazione italiana nel Settecento*, Bologna: Ed. CLUEB 1980, pp. 127–9.

24 I. da Villapadierna, 'L'età moderna', in V. Monachino (ed.), *La carità cristiana in Roma*, Bologna: Cappelli 1968, p. 216; Piazza, *Eusevologio romano*, vol. 2, p. 357.

25 B. Pullan, 'Poveri, mendicanti e vagabondi (secoli XIV–XVII)', in *Storia d'Italia. Dal feudalesimo al capitalismo. Annali 1*, Turin: Giulio Einaudi Editore 1978, p. 1027.

26 Simple family households comprise married couples with or without unmarried children or lone parents with unmarried children.

27 E. Sonnino, 'Typologies familiales à Rome au milieu du XVIIe siècle: premier examen général', in J.-P. Bardet, F. Lebrun and R. Le Mee (eds), *Mesurer et comprendre. Melanges offerts à Jacques Dupaquier*, Paris: PUF 1993, p. 538, tableau 4.

5 The abandonment of legitimate children in nineteenth-century Milan and the European context

Volker Hunecke

During the last twenty-five years or so the historians of childhood and family have discovered a new domain of research – the abandonment of children in Christian Europe and its colonies. There are now more than 200 studies on this subject. A brief consideration seems therefore appropriate in order to explain the need for further thought on this subject in relation to the city of Milan.

The foundling home of Milan was one of the oldest in Europe and, from its beginnings, one of the largest. There were, however, half a dozen other foundling homes which were equally old, and during the early modern period some cities (Florence, Venice, Rome, Naples and Paris) had found-ling homes where considerably more children were abandoned than in Milan, at least after the mid-seventeenth century.[1] The really noteworthy phase of the Milanese history of child abandonment begins only in the late eighteenth century and ends in the 1860s. During this period, more exactly between 1780 and 1869, over a quarter of a million children were abandoned in this city – a figure twice the size of the population of Milan in the 1820s (see Table 5.1). In relation to the size of the population and to the number of births, only very few other places in Europe saw a similar number of newborn children being abandoned to a foundling home. This raises the question as to why foundlings were so numerous in Milan in this period, which requires in turn the identification of the abandoned children and their parents. In most cases, one of the essential features of a foundling is that neither his nor her identity is known, nor that of his or her parents. This inevitably sets limits to all attempts to explain the millions of cases of child abandonment in nineteenth-century Europe. Yet in the case of Milan it has been possible, thanks to an exceptional set of sources, to reveal the identity of most abandoned children, and this is the main reason why the study of child abandonment in Milan is enormously rewarding.

Table 5.1 Admissions to the Milan foundling hospital, 1659–1900

Decade	Admissions	Per cent variation against previous decade
1660–9	4,057	
1670–9	3,715	−8.4
1680–9	3,600	−3.1
1690–9	5,315	+47.6
1700–9	5.307	−0.2
1710–19	5,094	−4.0
1720–9	4,422	−13.2
1730–9	6,220	+40.7
1740–9	7,054	+13.4
1750–9	6,866	−2.7
1760–9	6,877	+0.2
1770–9	6,812	−0.9
1780–9	9,594	+40.8
1790–9	14,642	+52.6
1800–9	14,710	+0.5
1810–19	19.020	+29.3
1820–9	19,380	+1.9
1830–9	26,147	+34.9
1840–9	30,294	+15.9
1850–9	42,378	+39.9
1860–9	50,727	+19.7
1870–9	20,510	−59.6
1880–9	15,492	−24.5
1890–9	13,910	−10.2
1659–1900	343,406	
1800–69	202,656	

Sources: Archives of the Milan Foundling Hospital, *Registro Generale*.

A EUROPE-WIDE PERSPECTIVE ON THE ABANDONMENT OF CHILDREN

Before trying to discover who all these children were and why they were abandoned, however, we must examine more closely those institutions which accepted them so readily, not only in Milan but also in several other cities. The point is of utmost importance for the following reasons. It is certainly true that the evidence from all periods and regions of Christian Europe shows isolated cases of children being abandoned by their parents.[2] However, child abandonment as a mass phenomenon (i.e., the abandonment of hundreds or even thousands of infants within one single year and at one single place) emerged only where foundling homes existed which were willing to accept the large number of foundlings. Yet little is known about where and when foundling homes were first established in Europe and how these institutions spread over the continent in subsequent centuries. Even less is known about the factors which contributed to the mushrooming of foundling homes and foundlings in large parts of Europe particularly from the mid-eighteenth century. Just as in other cities, the care of foundlings in Milan had never been a purely local affair. Rather, from its origin it was shaped by developments which took place on the larger Italian and later on the European level. If we were to neglect this wider European context, we would not be able to understand why Europe came to be divided, during the 'long' nineteenth century, between countries without, or almost without, child abandonment and those countries where altogether far more than 10 million children were abandoned.[3]

In dealing with the foundation and diffusion of foundling homes it is necessary first of all to define these establishments. Not all medieval hospitals which cared for pilgrims, the ill and impotent and abandoned children can be considered as foundling homes, any more than modern hospitals and orphanages which occasionally still care for abandoned children. Brian Pullan, the only historian who has raised this issue, defined the 'classical' foundling hospitals of early modern as well as nineteenth-century Europe as 'specialized institutions designed to permit and regulate anonymous abandonment for fear of worse evils'.[4] Such foundling hospitals were sometimes, as in Florence, Venice and Madrid, independent establishments designated for this specific task and none other; in other cases they were sub-departments of large hospitals, as in Milan before 1780, in Naples and Paris. Clearly different from this 'classical' type are those hospitals which, in the absence of specialized foundling homes, were obliged to take in foundlings, but only among other groups of needy persons, and more because of necessity than because of choice. Among the latter there were probably *all* those hospitals in Europe which had granted assistance to foundlings even before the fifteenth century, as is shown by numerous evidence on the care of foundlings in the middle ages. Medieval sources show that we are dealing either with no more than pious legends (as in the case of Milan and Rome),[5] or else the alleged foundling homes were merely hospitals which were by no means specialized in foundling care. Taken together, all credible evidence suggests that the foundling homes of the 'classical' type first emerged in the course of the fifteenth century and initially only in the larger cities of Italy: in Florence, Venice, Milan, Bologna, Rome, Brescia and perhaps also in some others.[6] Contrary to the hypothesis which maintains that already during the fourteenth century 'many large German, French, and Italian cities had established institutions specifically for abandoned children',[7] it should be emphasized that the 'classical' pattern of foundling care did not emerge more or less simultaneously in several European countries, nor in all southern European countries, nor in all Romance countries, nor in all countries which remained Catholic after the Counter-Reformation. Rather the 'classical' approach to the care of foundlings emerged initially in one country only, namely Italy, and it took generations and centuries for other countries to follow its example.

Apart from Italy, the countries which were the first to adopt the institutionalization of child abandonment by establishing large specialized foundling homes were Portugal and Spain. The beginnings of modern foundling assistance in Lisbon date from the foundation of the Santa Casa da Misericórdia in 1498, the initiative of a brotherhood which they later extended to other Portuguese cities.[8] In Spain, the emergence of large foundling homes was a process which continued over the entire sixteenth century. The earliest examples were the foundling homes of Burgos and Santiago de Compostela, established around the turn of the fifteenth century; Toledo, Segovia, Valladolid, Palencia, Seville, Madrid and others followed in their wake.[9]

A very different picture evolved in the parts of Europe north of the Alps and the Pyrenees. Here, too, there were perhaps some hospitals which, from the late twelfth century on, explicitly included assistance to abandoned children among their manifold tasks. During the late middle ages and even more in the sixteenth century, sources mention foundling homes or foundling and orphan hospitals in a considerable number of German cities, but it seems that none of them followed the Italian and Iberian policy of open admission (i.e., a more or less unrestricted admission of all children who were deposited in these institutions). The same situation as in the northern regions prevailed in France, where up to the mid-seventeenth century few abandoned children were admitted into hospitals.[10] Change occurred here only in 1670 when the Parisian foundling home, founded by St Vincent de Paul, was taken over and financed by the state. In the following century, other French cities created special facilities for abandoned children, but it seems that with the exception of Paris, the number of children began to rise to some extent only after the mid-eighteenth century.[11] It was only during the revolutionary period and under Napoleon that the French system of foundling care was systematically developed.[12] In Britain, the only serious attempt at introducing some care for abandoned children in the early modern period was the provision that Christ's Hospital in London, founded in 1552, should also assist these pitiable creatures. It certainly did so, but its main task was – and remained – to care for the education of the poor and orphaned children of the City of London.[13]

A new chapter in the history of the care of foundlings, one of enormous expansion and perfection, opened in the Enlightenment. Among the first generation of new foundling homes were those of Dublin and London, but it was only for a brief time that they played an important role in the assistance of abandoned children. The real protagonists of the new policy on foundlings, inspired by philanthropical and utilitarian motives, were Russia and the Habsburg monarchy. In these empires, some foundling homes were founded by the government, and in the second half of the nineteenth century they grew to dimensions that went far beyond even the largest establishments in the Romance countries. Even at the periphery of the

Habsburg Empire, care of the foundlings expanded considerably.[14] At the same time, philosophers of the German Enlightenment entered into a heated discussion over the question of whether foundling homes might have more advantages or more disadvantages; most of them rejected such institutions, and therefore the creation of specialized foundling homes in Germany remained restricted to an occasional initiative in, for example, the cities of Hamburg and Cassel.[15] A last strong impulse to create new foundling homes was initiated by the Napoleonic Decree of 19 January 1811 which prescribed at least one such institution for each *arrondissement*. It was in this way that they came to be established in some of the territories under French rule where they had been previously unknown.

An important insight can be derived from this chronological and geographical development. Until the mid-seventeenth century, the care of foundlings practised by specialized institutions on a large scale was confined to the Italian and Iberian peninsulas, whereas large sections of Catholic Europe adopted the 'classical' scheme of foundling care only very late or not at all. On the other hand, some Protestant cities flirted with the idea at times, most of all London, and the largest foundling homes sprang up in the two capitals of orthodox Russia. In this brief study, it is not possible further to explore the reasons why 'classical' foundling homes emerged in this particular chronological sequence and in these particular cities and not in others.[16] But it is obvious that the cities and regions where assistance to foundlings had become firmly rooted as early as the period of the Renaissance were also those with a remarkably high rate of child abandonment in the nineteenth century, such as Milan and other parts of Italy, Spain and Portugal. Yet this circumstance is not enough to explain why the abandonment of newborn children was to increase so enormously after the second half of the eighteenth century and why the geographical distribution of abandoned children was so extremely uneven. In fact, both issues depended to a large degree on the attitude towards unmarried mothers in the respective countries and on the legal provisions which regulated the maintenance of children born out of wedlock.

It is well known that in almost all of Europe the number of illegitimate births increased considerably from the mid-eighteenth century. At the same time, the lot of unmarried mothers and the issue of infanticide attracted more public attention than ever before. Numerous philanthropists and social reformers believed that the life of illegitimate children was at risk unless the community at large intervened in order to protect them. To many people, the most appropriate way to prevent infanticide appeared to be the creation of maternity hospitals, but their opinions differed widely as to what attitude to adopt both to the women who gave birth and to the children who were born in these lying-in hospitals. Those responsible for most German maternity hospitals considered it sufficient to ensure free and secret confinement for the pregnant women, but, for instance, according to the rules of the lying-in ward in Hamburg, it was expressly forbidden that the mother should leave the hospital without her child, or at least fail to take responsibility for the cost of raising the child.[17] Yet at the same time, the facility of free and secret confinement was not of great help to an unmarried mother; in fact she faced a much more serious problem of how to raise the child on her own should she retain the child in her care, and how to deal with the disgrace and discrimination encountered by a 'fallen' woman. One way out of this double calamity for unmarried mothers was the institution of the foundling home.

At least some of the foundling homes, such as that in Milan, took on the tasks of a maternity hospital from the time of their origin, caring for the illegitimate children by treating them as if they had been abandoned. The main purpose of all foundling homes had always been to render possible the abandonment of illegitimate, and therefore undesired, children. But the distinctive feature of the development during the eighteenth century was that this scheme, which formerly had been practised only on a modest scale, was now adopted by cities and states which previously had not or hardly known an institution designated for the public assistance of those children at risk of abandonment. An illuminating example of this new policy towards unmarried pregnant women is the maternity hospital at Vienna, inaugurated in 1784. According to an official announcement, it was to protect 'the mother from shame and misery' and 'at the same time to grant protection to the innocent creature' by ensuring strict secrecy for the parturient woman and by granting her the choice of either taking her child with her or letting the obstetrician take it to the foundling home. Three months later, on 20 September 1784, almost identical provisions were enacted in Milan.[18] This procedure, which had been practised in the Moscow and St Petersburg foundling and maternity hospitals from the beginning, was also adopted in other large cities of the Habsburg Empire. From the late eighteenth century it became the normal procedure in many, perhaps most, Italian foundling homes. In Spain and Portugal, too, measures were taken to safeguard the anonymity of abandoning persons.[19]

The obstacles which in the past had prevented a higher number of children from being abandoned were also removed in the region of Brussels. From 1771, child abandonment was no longer liable to punishment and at the same time the investigation of illegitimate parenthood (*recherche des parents*) was prohibited. One consequence of these measures, resulting from the pro-natalist motivations of their authors, was that the number of abandoned children in Brussels and other Belgian cities increased dramatically up until the mid-nineteenth century.[20] A similar policy was pursued in revolutionary France. A law of June/July 1793 prescribed a secret maternity hospital for each district and allowed unmarried mothers to leave their illegitimate child, considered to be an *enfant naturel de la patrie*, to a foundling home. Four months later, and not only in the Code Civil of 1804, the *recherche de la paternité*, for all practical purposes, was prohibited. In fact, the right of an unmarried pregnant woman to appeal to a court which would oblige the father of her child to contribute to the support of the child had already been undermined by a change in sentencing policy during the final decades of the *ancien régime*. When unmarried mothers were ultimately deprived of this old-established legal entitlement the state compensated them for their loss by granting them the right to abandon their child.[21]

In the nineteenth century this scheme, which was not adopted in Germany except temporarily by the extravagant Landgrave of Hesse-Cassel Frederick II,[22] was called 'the Catholic system of support for illegitimate children'. It included three essential features: first, the prohibition on the establishment of paternity, which thereby removed the obligation of the father to pay child maintenance; second, material and moral protection for unmarried mothers who, in many people's view, were entitled to 'secrecy of maternity'; and third, raising of an illegitimate child in a state-sponsored foundling home should the mother so desire. This regime differed fundamentally from the so-called 'Protestant system' which permitted the investigation of fatherhood and forced the next of kin to support the child, along a legally fixed sequence of responsibility (mother, father, mother's parents, etc.). Only in those rare cases where no member of the family could be held responsible for support did this responsibility pass to the community.

Endless were the debates among contemporaries as to which system would be the more beneficial for mothers, their childen and, last but not least, for society at large; these issues cannot be dealt with here. More important in this context is the following consideration: the institutionalization of the care of foundlings was the essential precondition that from the late eighteenth century caused millions of European parents to abandon their newborn children. This institutionalization proceeded in two stages. The first one dates from the Renaissance when specialized foundling homes in Italy, Spain and Portugal became one of the most important branches of public welfare. Already at that time in many cities, the customary abandonment of infants by needy parents came to be socially acceptable. During the second stage over the course of the eighteenth century, public assistance to foundlings received a significant stimulus when enlightened philanthropists and monarchs as well as revolutionary governments came to see foundling homes as the ideal solution for improving the situation of unwed mothers, as a curb on infanticide and as a means of generating useful subjects. In both the first and the second stage, the principal concern of those actively involved in promoting the foundling homes was probably the lives of illegitimate children, but no less important, particularly in view of the later developments in the nineteenth century, is that only rarely did the founders and administrators of foundling homes totally exclude legitimate children from admission. Even when the intention was to prohibit the admission of legitimate children effective measures were rarely taken to enforce such a policy. Most revealing in this respect are the turning cradles, most of which were installed only in the decades around 1800. Many of those responsible for the foundling homes believed the turning cradle to be the most appropriate means to ensure that the abandonment of illegitimate children would proceed under the cover of strict secrecy and thereby to protect the 'honour' of the mother. But as long as there were turning cradles and other ways of abandoning children without being recognized, married parents also took advantage. Consequently, everywhere in Europe, from the fifteenth to the nineteenth century, married parents were accused of 'abusing' the foundling homes. In fact, it was largely due to the abandonment of legitimate infants that the foundling homes became ever more crowded, the mortality of the foundlings reached a staggering height and the expenses incurred in the support of foundlings increased dramatically. These 'abusive' abandonments were the main reason why the system of 'classical' foundling assistance, invented in the first place for the protection of illegitimate children and unwed mothers, not only expanded so greatly during the nineteenth century, but plunged into a deep crisis which led inevitably to the dismantling in the late nineteenth and early twentieth centuries of the entire system for the care of foundlings.

THE ABANDONMENT OF CHILDREN IN MILAN

This historical background and larger European context may usefully guide our understanding of the reasons for the abandonment of legitimate children in nineteenth-century Milan. The origins of the modern system of foundling care in Milan reach back to the mid-fifteenth century when, along with the foundation of the Ospedale Maggiore (1456), measures were taken to ensure that foundlings received more effective assistance. The criteria of their admission were defined and laid down in an *ordinatio pro expositis* of 1529, the main rules of which remained in force until 1868. The registers in which the newly-admitted children of each year were painstakingly described are lost for the period before 1659, but we know from other evidence that already at the beginning of the sixteenth century the Milan hospital was 'almost always' responsible for the care of over 1,000 *expositi* in any one year.

There were already many complaints being voiced that parents were also abandoning legitimate children, even though they may not have been in dire poverty. In order to prevent the abandonment of legitimate children a variety of proposals was put forward at various dates between the late fifteenth and the late eighteenth centuries to assist poor parents in the rearing of their infants. But because of financial constraints, little was done in this respect, and many sources suggest that parents who were not eligible for direct support from the Ospedale Maggiore, abandoned their children anonymously. For this purpose, they could avail themselves, from 1689, of a turning cradle (*torno*). Parents who wished to abandon their children anonymously were quick to take advantage of this facility and this was one of the reasons why the number of abandoned children almost doubled during the following decade.[23]

As elsewhere in Europe, care of the foundlings in Milan entered a new phase in the late eighteenth century. Because the assistance granted by the Ospedale Maggiore to foundlings and parturient women was ever more obviously seen as inadequate, the Empress Maria Theresa ordered a new special hospital to be established for this purpose, the Pia Casa degli Esposti e delle Partorienti in S. Caterina alla Ruota, founded in 1780. At the same time, assistance for both the mothers and their children was considerably expanded and improved, and this led to a rise in the annual rate of abandonment; it continued to increase, with few and brief interruptions, up until 1867–8, when the *torno* was finally closed and further restrictive measures blocked the abandonment of legitimate babies (see Table 5.1, p. 118). In only seventy years, from 1800 to 1869, the Pia Casa admitted 202,656 children, and from mid-century on the number was over 4,000 and eventually over 5,000 per year. Measured against the size of the population, the abandonment rates were equally high in Vienna, Moscow and St Petersburg. But the comparison must also take into consideration the fact that the Vienna Landes-Findel-Anstalt was the only one in all of lower Austria and the two Russian foundling homes were the only ones in a huge empire, whereas in Lombardy, the Milan foundling home was only one in eight. In total, the other seven admitted almost as many children as the Milanese institution. During the 1840s, 60 per cent of the Milan foundlings came from the city itself and this proportion of 'native' foundlings increased even further in the two following decades. At that time, 30–40 per cent of all children born in the city were handed over to the Pia Casa; in the words of an author of that time: 'almost half of the children of our city's poor'.[24] It seems that there were only a few other cities or regions where the abandonment rate, as measured against the number of births, was as high as that of Milan.

In some cities where well-endowed foundling homes practised open admission, the high abandonment rate resulted from a high rate of illegitimate births, as, for example, in Vienna where around the middle of the century half of the newborn were born out of wedlock. A completely different situation prevailed in Milan where the proportion of illegitimate children was barely 16 per cent. Even though most of them were delivered to the Pia Casa, they were still a minority among its protégés. In Milan the clear majority, between 50 and 70 per cent, were the offspring of married parents. The only other city with a similar situation, at least temporarily, seems to have been Florence. The two special features which distinguish the case of Milan so strikingly from most other cities, namely the very high abandonment rate and the very high proportion of legitimate foundlings, can be explained through the way in which its foundling home functioned.

There was perhaps no other place where parents could so easily not only abandon their infants, but also claim them back. At Milan, virtually everybody could abandon and later recognize and reclaim the child without any danger of punishment; if a child was still alive that child was then returned to the parents. The Pia Casa encouraged parents to reclaim their children, since it refrained from asking the parents to refund the expenses incurred by the home in the care of their children. Of course, such liberalism reinforced the temptation to leave a baby to the institution, because, for those children who survived, there was a guarantee that they would be returned if wanted. In contrast to the policies pursued in Milan, from 1811 the French authorities pursued the policy of preventing abandonment by rendering recognition more difficult and reclamation virtually impossible. In fact, to a certain degree they did succeed in preventing married parents from abandoning their children.[25] Altogether it seems reasonable to argue that the more liberal was the attitude of the authorities towards abandoning parents and abandoned children, the greater the number of foundlings, particularly the legitimate ones, and the greater the desire of the parents to get them back from the institution. In the first two-thirds of the nineteenth century, Milan was probably the most liberal European city in this respect. Therefore it is a revealing example of how married parents might behave when they had the option of raising their children with the assistance of a public welfare institution.

Yet the Pia Casa's liberalism was no more than a precondition for the abandonment of large numbers of legitimate children. In order to explore and explain this phenomenon in greater depth, we must turn to the abandoning parents and particularly to the mothers. In over two-thirds of the cases they are well known, because even those parents who had delivered their child anonymously through the *torno*, often returned to the Pia Casa in order to recognize and possibly claim their child; in 1842 – the year of my sample – the proportion of the reclaimed children among the *torno* children was 58.6 per cent. Of course, children born out of wedlock were less often recognized, but the cases where a child of married parents was never recognized remained exceedingly rare, constituting only 10 per cent, possibly less than 5 per cent of all cases. Therefore we can identify most of those parents who, even though they were regularly married, abandoned the majority of their children.

WORKING MOTHERS, FAMILY POVERTY AND CHILD ABANDONMENT IN MILAN

The ten most popular occupations of these particular fathers and mothers are detailed in Table 5.2, and are indicative of their standard of living. These, as well as the less frequently encountered occupations which do not figure in the table, reflect accurately the overall composition of the working population and the state of the urban economy in the middle of the nineteenth century. There were as yet few modern factories; nonetheless, if we disregard military personnel, school and university students and those without occupation (*senza professione*), the majority of the Milan population was employed in manufacturing. The Milanese 'industries' were still predominantly organized as artisan shops and domestic industry. The result was a low productivity, wages were miserly and an extensive exploitation of the labour force prevailed. The very high proportion of people employed in the textiles and clothing industries and in the service sector was also characteristic of an old commercial, manufacturing and administrative city.

Table 5.2 The ten most frequent occupations of abandoning parents in Milan

Fathers	Per cent	Mothers	Per cent
1 Shoemakers	11.0	Seamstresses	21.1
2 Carpenters	10.9	Domestic servants	10.1
3 Weavers	7.6	Weavers	9.3
4 Tailors	5.9	Dressmakers	8.7
5 Blacksmiths	5.3	Laundresses	7.7
6 Domestic servants	2.7	Concierges (*portinaie*)	6.6
7 Masons	2.6	Embroiderers	4.4
8 Printers	2.1	Silk-throwers (*incannatrici*)	2.5
9 Hat-makers	2.0	Ironers (*stiratrici*)	2.2
10 Porters (*facchini*)	1.8	Pedlars of vegetables (*ortolane*)	1.9

Sources: V. Hunecke, *Die Findelkinder von Mailand. Kindsaussetzung und aussetzende Eltern vom 17. bis zum 19. Jahrhundert*, Stuttgart: Klett-Cotta 1987, p. 157.

The standard of living of the Milanese lower classes was extremely low. Only a few of the male workers earned 3 lire *per diem*; most of the others made only 1.5 or 2 lire. All sources agree that these wages were insufficient to support a family with children.[26] Therefore the mothers had to seek paid work, even though they usually earned only 1 lire per day. One observer commented as follows upon the parents who brought their infants and their weaned children to the first crèche which was opened in 1850:

> Among these families there is none where the father or the mother could afford to stay at home during the day. The daily abandonment of the family is inevitable, because if the parents need something to live on for themselves and their offspring, they must search for bread where it can be found. It is a proven fact that in a large manufacturing town such as Milan, a large part of the families of the workers cannot live in the home and for the home. If, then, the parents must abandon their home all day long, who will care for the small ones who need such care throughout the day?[27]

For a somewhat later period, the years around 1900, it has frequently been asserted that the female workers in Milan, just as elsewhere, 'usually' or 'often' quit their job upon marriage and were even more likely to do so following the birth of their first child. This view requires qualification, at least in respect of Milan. As late as 1903, 29.3 per cent of the women who had borne a child in this year continued to work outside the home, while women who were employed as workers and who also cared for an infant or other small children made up around 50 per cent of all female workers. The corresponding numbers for the mid-nineteenth century cannot be determined with any degree of precision, but there is no doubt that at the very least they were similar, and may well have been higher.[28]

Such mothers, upon the arrival of a child who needed to be nursed when artificial nutrition would have meant, at that period, certain and imminent death, faced a dilemma. One choice was unrealistic, namely to give up the job and to nurse the child herself, because the family could not survive without the mother's earnings. A second alternative, which came to be recommended by the early social reformers of Milan, was equally unrealistic: that the mothers should take their infants to a crèche where they could nurse them three times a day, briefly interrupting their work and otherwise pursuing it as before. This apparently ideal solution failed, just as it did in France. It failed not because the number of crèches was insufficient (in Milan they had existed since 1850), but because the mothers simply would not accept the crèches. For instance, the female tobacco factory workers openly declared that they would rather pay a wet-nurse out of their earnings. For them to bring the child to a crèche would entail a loss of wages, since they were on piece-work. Moreover, the absences for breast-feeding were incompatible with the regulations governing their employment. As late as 1903, similar conditions prevented the majority of home-workers from nursing their babies themselves. Even though they were not subjected to rigidly fixed working hours or work rules, domestic industry relied heavily on piece-work, and such workers were particularly subjected to exploitation. As early as 1850, observers had recognized that a mother employed in the domestic system was no more able to breast-feed a baby than the woman employed in the factory.

How, then, might a working mother arrange to nurse her own baby? Obviously, some of them did so. But it is not possible to ascertain their numbers, establish whether they temporarily gave up their job for this purpose, nor calculate the mortality of those babies who were nursed by their working-class mothers. Many other women placed their infant into the hands of a wet-nurse whom they paid out of their meagre earnings. But again, we know hardly anything about them, because in Milan, as opposed to Paris, there were no *bureaux des nourrices*, the archives of which would tell us about the private business of wet-nursing.[29] Yet we know much about those families who abandoned at least some of their children and who later reclaimed them. It has already been mentioned that such children represented almost half of all those born into poor families resident in the city.

Table 5.3 is based on a sample of 649 such abandoning families. Before commenting in detail on the results, two points need to be clarified. First, the number given in column A overstates the percentage of children who had not been abandoned and who were therefore nursed by their own

Table 5.3 Fate of children at risk of being abandoned by rank of birth in Milan: sample of 649 couples who abandoned at least one of their children

Birth rank	Not abandoned	Abandoned	Breast-fed by wet-nurse	Number of children at risk
	A (%)	B (%)	C (%)	D
1	58.2	35.9	6.0	588
2	48.0	45.2	6.8	586
3	43.1	52.4	4.5	582
4	34.8	62.5	2.7	554
5	29.4	68.1	2.5	524
6	31.0	66.9	2.1	480
7	27.0	69.4	3.7	434
8	27.1	71.5	1.3	376
9	20.8	77.1	2.1	327
10	24.1	74.1	1.8	274
11	25.7	72.5	1.8	218
12	21.8	77.0	1.2	165
13	21.5	78.5	0.0	121
14	21.5	74.7	3.8	79
15	23.7	74.6	1.7	59
16–22	20.8	76.0	3.1	96
Mean	34.6	62.0	3.4	

Sources: V. Hunecke, *Die Findelkinder von Mailand. Kindsaussetzung und aussetzende Eltern vom 17. bis zum 19. Jahrhundert*, Stuttgart: Klett-Cotta 1987, p. 245.

mothers. In reality, the proportion of these children was considerably lower as can be seen from column C, which indicates the percentage of children who were breast-fed by a wet-nurse. These children could only be identified when they died while staying with a wet-nurse. If it is assumed that the mortality of these sucklings was no higher than that of the foundlings, it follows that even the abandoning parents gave one out of ten children to a wet-nurse whom they paid themselves. Second, the proportion of abandoned children was even higher than the numbers in column B suggest, because nearly 5 per cent of the abandoned children could not be identified, namely some of those who had been reclaimed and restored to their families. On the basis of these two corrections we may conclude that only one out of five children, rather than one out of three, was possibly nursed by its own mother as the child was neither nursed by a wet-nurse of the Pia Casa nor by one who was paid privately by the parents.

One of the most surprising features is that so many parents had repeated recourse to the service of the Pia Casa. On average, parents delivered two out of three children to the Pia Casa in order to have them placed with wet-nurses in the Milanese countryside. However, fewer first-born children were sent to the Pia Casa and it would appear that a majority of parents had some scruples about abandoning their first and, indeed, their second-born child. On these occasions it would seem parents were more ready to pay 100 lire for a wet-nurse; to the parents this was a very large amount in view of their poverty. From the third child on, such scruples appear to have vanished, and virtually all of the higher birth rank children were abandoned.

For married parents from the city there were essentially two ways to ensure that their baby was taken in by the Pia Casa. First, they could bring the child during daytime to the admission office and request the *allattamento gratuito*, i.e., free breast-feeding by a wet-nurse of the foundling home. From the seventeenth century, the *allattamento gratuito* was granted for sixteen months, benefiting between 20 and 35 per cent of the children who were admitted. In order to claim this service, the parents had to present a poverty certificate from their priest together with another certificate which testified that the mother was 'physically' unable to nurse her child. The second option was to leave the child at night in the *torno*. In theory, this possibility was reserved for the illegitimate children whose mothers were to be spared the 'shame' of having their identity revealed. Moreover, an illegitimate child who was delivered in the *torno* had the right to be taken care of by the foundling home up until his or her fifteenth birthday. But as long as the *torno* existed, many parents 'abused' the system in that they placed their child in the *torno* even though they were legally married.

In the case of married couples from Milan, until the 1820s this 'abuse' was confined within certain limits. Prior to this period the *allattamento gratuito* was requested for almost two-thirds of the children (62.3 per cent) who were abandoned by their parents and only 37.7 per cent were placed in the *torno*. In this respect, later years brought a sudden and drastic change. From the 1830s parents abandoned nine out of ten sucklings in the *torno* and requested the *allattamento gratuito* for only one out of ten. There were two reasons for this change. As more children were abandoned, the Pia Casa was less ready to grant the *allattamento gratuito* and in 1839 reduced the period of its operation from sixteen to twelve months. The second reason why parents preferred the *torno* was the fact that the period for which the *allattamento gratuito* was granted, whether for twelve or sixteen months, no longer met the needs of the parents. They did not just need a free wet-nurse, but in addition someone who would take care of the child during the years after weaning. The *torno* was the ideal solution to this problem, because this system allowed the parents to decide for themselves the precise time when the child would return. How long they might wait is revealed by Table 5.4. Only one-third of the children were reclaimed before the age of 2, half between the ages of 2 and 10 years and the rest even later. Unless the parents waited more than five years, they could count on getting back on average at least every second child whom they had abandoned.

Of course, the customary habit of not breast-feeding their children or breast-feeding only very few of them affected the fertility of those women who abandoned their children. The age-specific marital fertility rates of such women exceeded those of Hutterite women. For example, the total

Table 5.4 Age of *torno* children at the time they were reclaimed by their parents in Milan

Year of life	Children reclaimed (irrespective of survival)		Children returned i.e., alive (per cent of reclamations)	
	Number	%	Number	%
1st	154	5.6	83	53.9[a]
2nd	794	28.6	533	67.1
3rd	574	20.7	317	55.2
4th–5th	473	17.1	242	51.2
6th–10th	327	11.8	137	41.9
11th–15th	153	5.5	43	28.1
Later	298	10.7	106[†]	35.6
Total	2,773	100.0	1,461	55.3

Note: [a] Still alive, but not returned.

Sources: V. Hunecke, *Die Findelkinder von Mailand. Kindsaussetzung und aussetzende Eltern vom 17. bis zum 19. Jahrhundert*, Stuttgart: Klett-Cotta 1987, p. 238.

marital fertility ratio for women who abandoned their children (aged 20–44) was 12.2 and on average couples whose marriages survived until the wife had reached the age of 45 produced 9.9 children. Such high fertility in conjunction with a high rate of child abandonment might suggest that the abandonment of two-thirds of this numerous progeny might be considered as a form of family planning. But such an inference has only limited validity. It is true that more younger children were abandoned and that they were usually reclaimed later than their older siblings, but there were only very few married couples who intended to abandon their children permanently. In fact, 70.1 per cent of the parents reclaimed all of their abandoned children before their fifteenth birthday (after this date they would not get them back), and just 2.8 per cent of parents did not reclaim any of their children. Given the high number of children reclaimed by their parents, there were very few among the abandoning parents who had none of their children in their household. Despite the very high infant and child mortality rate, parents who had abandoned at least some of their children on average still had 2.1 children residing with them before their fifth child was born and four co-resident children prior to the birth of their tenth child. One-quarter of all households included at some stage five and more children under the age of 15 years. But even in the nineteenth century families of such a large size were relatively rare.

Most of the wives and husbands who abandoned legitimately-born children were probably living in chronic and dire poverty which could only be alleviated through their mothers finding some employment. As soon as children were born, the problem was how to care for them without the mother having to either reduce or even totally cease her paid work. A minority of them dealt with this problem, as did so many couples in French cities, by entrusting some of their infants, preferably those born first, to a private wet-nurse. However, the majority of the Milan parents chose from the beginning the other alternative, i.e., to abandon their children to wet-nurses or foster parents employed by the Pia Casa. Such parents acted in this way because they were either unable to pay the wages of a wet-nurse, not even for only one or two of their babies, or because they preferred to use the money for other purposes. The placement of children in the Pia Casa had the additional advantage that they could be left there for any length of time, so that the number of those children who were supported at any one time in the parental household could be limited. The motives of these abandoning mothers were summarized by a medical doctor who cared for the poor and who knew these women well:

> In fact all mothers who abandoned their children, assured me that they would not leave them for ever in the Pia Casa, but that they would call them back as soon as they were able to care for them themselves and when the children would no longer require their unremitting attention; they act in this way in order to dedicate themselves fully to the work which brings them the earnings on which they live.[30]

During the first half of the nineteenth century, the possibility to abandon a legitimate child in the *torno* and consequently have that child raised at the expense of the community had become a kind of customary right of the poor. By the early years of the nineteenth century the *beneficenza del torno* had assumed a significance for the family economy of the labouring poor so that it required nearly fifty years of intense debate before the authorities dared take the decision to close the turning cradle. This measure was mitigated by the introduction of other kinds of assistance to needy mothers: among the measures were one-off payments to women in childbed, breast-feeding allowances for twelve months, more places for both breast-feeding and weaned children in the crèches. All these measures could not entirely compensate the mothers for the loss of the *torno*, even though the changes may have been revolutionary and far-reaching in their impact on the evolution of attitudes towards 'appropriate' child care. Some of the mothers were now forced to pay a wet-nurse out of their own earnings, some had no other choice than to care for the children themselves even though this may have been incompatible with their situation as workers. In fact, after the closure of the *torno* more mothers nursed their children, but this could not prevent the infant mortality in Milan remaining very high until the end of the century. The infant mortality rate began to decline only when male wages rose and fewer mothers were required to contribute to their family's survival by obtaining paid work.

NOTES

1 C. Povolo, 'Dal versante dell'illegittimità. Per una ricerca sulla storia della famiglia: infanticidio ed esposizione d'infante nel Veneto nell'età moderna', *Crimine, giustizia e società veneta in età moderna (La 'Leopoldina'*, no. 9), Milan: 1989, pp. 154, 156; C. Schiavoni, 'Gli infanti "esposti" del Santo Spirito in Saxia di Roma tra '500 e '800: numero, ricevimento, allevamento e destino', in Collection de l'École Française de Rome, *Enfance abandonnée et société en Europe, XIVe–XXe siècle*, Rome: École Française de Rome 1991, pp. 1051–3; G. Da Molin, 'Modalità dell'abbandono e caratteristiche degli esposti a Napoli nel Seicento', in Collection de l'École Française, *Enfance abandonnée*, p. 462; E. Charlot and J. Dupâquier, 'Mouvement annuel de la population de la Ville de Paris de 1670 à 1821', *Annales de démographie historique*, 1967, pp. 512–15.

2 J. Boswell, *The Kindness of Strangers. The Abandonment of Children in Western Europe from Late Antiquity to the Renaissance*, London: Allen Lane/Penguin Press 1988, *passim*.

3 V. Hunecke, 'Intensità e fluttuazioni degli abbandoni dal XV al XIX secolo', in Collection de l'École Française de Rome, *Enfance abandonnée*, pp. 37–8.

4 B. Pullan, *Orphans and Foundlings in Early Modern Europe*, Reading: University of Reading 1989, p. 7.

5 Boswell, *The Kindness of Strangers*, p. 225, n. 158; I. Walter, 'Die Sage der Gründung von Santo Spirito in Rom und das Problem des Kindesmordes', *Mélanges de l'École Française de Rome, moyen age – temps modernes*, 97, 1985, pp. 819–79.

6 P. Gavitt, *Charity and Children in Renaissance Florence. The Ospedale degli Innocenti, 1410–1536*, Ann Arbor, Mich.: University of Michigan Press 1990; V. Hunecke, 'Findelkinder und Findelhäuser in der Renaissance', *Quellen und Forschungen aus italienischen Archiven und Bibliotheken*, 72, 1992, pp. 123–53.

7 Boswell, *The Kindness of Strangers*, p. 415.

8 V. Ribeiro, *A Santa Casa da Misericórdia de Lisboa (subsídios para a sua história) 1498–1898*, Lisbon: Typographia da Academia Real das Sciencias 1902, pp. 391ff.; I. dos Guimarães Sá, 'The "Casa da roda do Porto": Reception and restitution of foundlings during the eighteenth century', in Collection de l'École Française de Rome, *Enfance abandonnée*, p. 545; C.R. Brettell and R. Feijó, 'Foundlings in nineteenth-century north-western Portugal: Public welfare and family strategies', ibid., p. 275.

9 A. Marcos Martín, 'Infancy and the life-cycle: The problem of abandonment in Spain', Tenth International Economic History Conference, Louvain, 1990. Session C40: Charity, the Poor and the Life-Cycle; idem, *Economía, sociedad, pobreza en Castilla: Palencia, 1500–1814*, 2 vols, Palencia: Deputación Provincial 1985, vol. 2, pp. 628–9; A. Eiras Roel, 'La Casa de Expósitos del Real Hospital de Santiago en el Siglo XVIII', *Boletín de la Universidad Compostelana*, 75–6, 1967–8, pp. 295ff.; L. Martz, *Poverty and Welfare in Habsburg Spain. The Example of Toledo*, Cambridge: Cambridge University Press 1983, p. 225; T. Egido, 'Aportación al estudio de la demografía española: los niños expósitos de Valladolid (siglos XVI–XVIII)', *Actas de las I jornadas de metodología aplicada de la ciencias históricas*, 3, Santiago de Compostela 1975, p. 333; L.C. Alvarez Santaló, *Marginación social y mentalidad en Andalucía Occidental: Expósitos en Sevilla (1613–1910)*, Seville: Consejeria de Cultura de la Junta de Andalucía 1980, p. 19; J. Sherwood, *Poverty in Eighteenth-Century Spain. The Women and Children of the Inclusa*, Toronto: University of Toronto Press 1988, pp. 3–4.

10 I. Robin and A. Walch, 'Géographie des enfants trouvés de Paris aux XVIIe et

134   *Volker Hunecke*

XVIIIᵉ siècles', *Histoire, économie et société*, 6, 1987, p. 344; F. Langlois, 'Les enfants abandonnés à Caen, 1661–1820', *Histoire, économie et société*, 6, 1987, pp. 307–8; C. Billot, 'Les enfants abandonnés à Chartres à la fin du moyen âge', *Annales de démographie historique*, 1975, p. 167; L. Denis, 'Notes sur les enfants trouvés à Rouen', *Revue des sociétés savantes de Haute-Normandie*, 42, 1966, p. 35.

11 J.-P. Bardet, *Rouen aux XVIIᵉ et XVIIIᵉ siècles. Les mutations d'un espace social*, 2 vols, Paris, Société d'Edition d'Enseignement Supérieur 1983, vol. 1, p. 331.

12 J.R. Potash, 'The foundling problem in France, 1800–1869. Child abandonment in Lille and Lyon', Ph.D. dissertation, Yale University 1979; R.G. Fuchs, *Abandoned Children. Foundlings and Child Welfare in Nineteenth Century France*, Albany, NY: State University of New York Press 1984; A. Taeger, 'Der Staat und die Findelkinder. Findelfürsorge und Familienpolitik im Frankreich des 19. Jahrhunderts', Ph.D. dissertation, Technische Universität Berlin 1985.

13 R.K. McClure, *Coram's Children. The London Foundling Hospital in the Eighteenth Century*, New Haven, Conn. and London: Yale University Press 1981, pp. 8–9; V. Fildes, 'Maternal feelings re-assessed: Child abandonment and neglect in London and Westminster, 1500–1800', in V. Fildes (ed.), *Women as Mothers in Pre-Industrial England. Essays in Memory of Dorothy McLaren*, London: Routledge 1990, pp. 146ff.

14 D.L. Ransel, *Mothers of Misery. Child Abandonment in Russia*, Princeton, NJ: Princeton University Press 1988; there are no historical studies on the Austrian foundling hospitals.

15 O. Ulbricht, 'The debate about foundling hospitals in Enlightenment Germany: Infanticide, illegitimacy, and infant mortality rates', *Central European History*, 18, 1985, pp. 211–56.

16 On this problem see Pullan, *Orphans and Foundlings*; and Hunecke, 'Findelkinder'.

17 O. Ulbricht, *Kindsmord und Aufklärung in Deutschland*, Munich: Oldenbourg 1990, pp. 297–307; M. Lindemann, 'Love for hire: The regulation of the wet-nursing business in eighteenth century Hamburg', *Journal of Family History*, 6, 1981, pp. 389–90; M. Lindemann, 'Maternal politics: The principles and practice of maternity care in eighteenth century Hamburg', *Journal of Family History*, 9, 1984, pp. 44–63.

18 'Nachricht über die Einrichtung des Hauptspitals in Wien (20. Juni 1784)', *Handbuch aller unter der Regierung des Kaisers Joseph II. für die K.K. Erbländer ergangener Verordnungen und Gesetze . . . vom Jahre 1784*, 2nd edn, Vienna: G. Moesle 1786, vol. 6, pp. 209–16; 'Metodo prescritto da Sua Maestà pel ricevimento delle donne gravide nello Spedale di S. Caterina alla Ruota', *Istituzione della Pia Casa degli Esposti e delle Partorienti in Santa Caterina alla Ruota*, n.p. (Milan), n.d. (1784).

19 Ransel, *Mothers of Misery*, pp. 40–1; S. Cavallo, 'Bambini abbandonati e bambini "in deposito" a Torino nel Settecento', in Collection de l'École Française de Rome, *Enfance abandonnée*, pp. 355–7; C. Grandi, 'L'abbandono degli illegittimi nel Trentino dell'Ottocento', in Collection de l'École Française de Rome, *Enfance abandonnée*, pp. 665–9; S. Raffaele, 'Il problema degli esposti in Sicilia (sec. XVIII–XIX). Normativa e risposta istituzionale: il caso di Catania', in Collection de l'École Française de Rome, *Enfance abandonnée*, p. 922; T. Bruttini, 'Legittimi e illegittimi: Aspetti istituzionali dell'assistenza all'infanzia abbandonata a Siena nell'Ottocento', *Bulletino Senese di Storia Patria*, 89, 1982, pp. 223–4; P. Unda Malcorra, 'La exposición en Vizcaya en el siglo XIX: nacimiento e problemática financiera de la Casa de Expósitos de Bilbao', in Collection de l'École Française de Rome, *Enfance abandonnée*,

p. 1154; L. Valverde, 'Legitimidad e ilegitimidad. Evolución de las modalidades de ingreso en la Inclusa de Pamplona, 1740–1934', Collection de l'École Française de Rome, *Enfance abandonnée*, pp. 1195–6; Brettell and Feijó, 'Foundlings', pp. 275–6; dos Guimarães Sá, 'The "Casa da roda do Porto" ', pp. 553–4.

20 P. Bonenfant, 'Une entreprise d'exportation d'enfants à Bruxelles au XVIIIe siècle', *Annales de la société royale d'archéologie de Bruxelles*, 35, 1930, pp. 95–120; idem, *Le problème du paupérisme en Belgique à la fin de l'ancien régime*, Brussels: Académie Royale de Belgique 1934, pp. 42 n. 2, 437 n. 2; E. Ducpétiaux, 'Du sort des enfants trouvés et abandonnés en Belgique', *Bulletin de la commission centrale de statistique*, 1, 1843, pp. 207–71; J.-P. Bougard, 'Des enfants trouvés en Belgique au début du XIXe siècle: le cas de Bruxelles de 1797 à 1826', in Collection de l'École Française de Rome, *Enfance abandonnée*, pp. 259–71.

21 M.-C. Phan, 'La séduction impunie ou la fin des actions en recherche de paternité', *Les femmes et la révolution française. Actes du colloque international 12–13–14 avril 1989 Université de Toulouse-Le Mirail*, vol. 2, Toulouse: Presses Universitaires du Mirail 1990, pp. 53–64; N. Arnaud-Duc, 'L'entretien des enfants abandonnés en Provence sous l'ancien régime', *Revue historique du droit français et étranger*, series 4, 47, 1969, pp. 56–9; J.-L. Flandrin, *Les amours paysannes. Amour et sexualité dans les campagnes de l'ancienne France (XVIe–XIXe siècle)*, Paris: Editions Gallimard/Julliard 1975, pp. 229–31, 243–6.

22 C.W. Ingrao, *The Hessian Mercenary State. Ideas, Institutions, and Reform under Frederick II, 1760–1785*, Cambridge: Cambridge University Press 1987, p. 74.

23 V. Hunecke, *Die Findelkinder von Mailand. Kindsaussetzung und aussetzende Eltern vom 17. bis zum 19. Jahrhundert*, Stuttgart: Klett-Cotta 1987, ch. 3 (Italian translation: *I Trovatelli di Milano. Bambini esposti e famiglie espositrici dal XVII al XIX secolo*, Bologna: Il Mulino 1989); F. Reggiani and E. Paradisi, 'L'esposizione infantile a Milano fra Seicento e Settecento: il ruolo dell' istituzione', in Collection de l'École Française de Rome, *Enfance abandonnée*, pp. 973–79.

24 Hunecke, *Die Findelkinder von Mailand*, p. 139.

25 Fuchs, *Abandoned Children*, pp. 236–40; Potash, 'The foundling problem in France', pp. 198–9.

26 F. Della Peruta, *Milano. Lavoro e fabbrica, 1814–1915*, Milano: Franco Angeli 1987, pp. 161–3; V. Hunecke, *Classe operaia e rivoluzione industriale a Milano 1859–1892*, Bologna: Il Mulino 1982, pp. 391–5.

27 G. Sacchi, 'Sullo stato morale ed economico del Pio Ricovero pei bambini lattanti in Milano dall'epoca della sua istituzione sino al 31 dicembre 1850. Terza memoria', *Annali universali di statistica*, 106, 1850, p. 236.

28 V. Hunecke, 'Madri e figli nelle famiglie operaie a Milano dopo l'Unità', in A. Gigli Marchetti and N. Torcellan (eds), *Donna lombarda 1860–1945*, Milan: Franco Angeli 1992, pp. 554–62.

29 G.D. Sussman, *Selling Mothers' Milk. The Wet-Nursing Business in France, 1715–1914*, Urbana, Ill.: University of Illinois Press 1982.

30 M. Rizzi, 'Su le vicende dei bambini delle madri povere assistite in istato di puerperio dal medico del Pio Istituto di Santa Corona del quartiere esterno di Porta Tosa dal mese di gennajo a tutto agosto 1851', in *Relazione compilata per cura di una Commissione stata eletta dalla Società d'Incoraggiamento delle scienze, lettere ed arti intorno alla Pia Casa degli Esposti*, Milan: Tipografia Guglielmini 1853, p. 68.

Part II
Women

6 Mothers at risk of poverty in the medieval English countryside

Elaine Clark

Until recently few historians discussed the material conditions and social constraints under which mothers supported families in the rural world.[1] By no means did peasant women always achieve independence once they headed households of their own. Although access to property afforded many widows a sense of security, intergenerational dependency remained a problem whenever women lacked the resources to meet the demands of family and work. For mothers with young children the difficulty was acute. No public agencies or government programmes aided dependent families in the medieval countryside. What poor relief there was generally involved private charity, although not even benefactors claimed that almsgiving cured the chronic infirmity and want that plagued impoverished folk. Socially-minded preachers concurred. Time and again they urged the public to help the needy, to shelter the orphaned and comfort the bereaved.[2] But how did women behave? Were widows and unmarried mothers simply the objects of charity, or did they purposefully contribute to the design of social welfare in the past?

To make the welfare of women an aspect of inquiry is to find that mothers, no less than fathers, participated in rural networks of mutual support. But my purpose is not to argue that peasant women enjoyed a rough equality with men. Nor do I wish to idealize the struggle of poor mothers to survive. Instead this chapter explores the reality of choice in mothers' lives, then argues that the decisions women made were shaped as much by childbirth, marriage and death as by customs and social norms that limited rather than enhanced female opportunities in the countryside.

CHRONOLOGY, SETTING AND SOURCES

The events in rural life most closely associated with economic hardship and want were readily apparent during the later middle ages, particularly in the generations before and after the Black Death (1348–9).[3] By the early 1300s population expansion had contributed to a climate of economic insecurity for farmers and labourers. Hard-pressed peasants remained vulnerable to land shortages and high rents as well as to the crop failures and famines that struck England between 1315 and 1322. Although rural society was under stress, life in the countryside remained basically intact until shattered by plague and epidemic disease in 1348–9. The following generations saw a progressive decline in population and a relative improvement in the ratio of land to labour. As the pressure of population on land lessened, economic disparities among the peasantry increased. This was in part the consequence of a rural land market that facilitated the accumulation of substantial holdings in the hands of a peasant aristocracy. Land-wealthy farmers prospered at the expense of less fortunate neighbours.

Amidst these changes the cultural norms which ordered family life remained much the same and emphasized the dependent status of women in the countryside. Neither the role of wife nor that of mother accorded a woman undisputed prestige. Of course, the welfare of women was not simply the result of cultural norms or complex legal forces, but evolved from the action and interaction of people living in small groups.[4] Under these circumstances the household ties and domestic concerns that circumscribed family life were certainly subject to change. Yet what touched mothers and daughters did not always affect fathers and sons in the same way. Women encountered obstacles that put them at a disadvantage. The participation of women in village land markets never matched that of men, nor did women share equally in the use of property and resources. Although the daughters in peasant households could inherit land, the claims of sons took precedence. The greater importance that property law conferred on males closely corresponded to the political realities of rural life. Throughout the countryside local government was government by men. Peasant women never held political office, never acted as jurors, never served among the village notables who enforced customary law. Manor courts welcomed women as litigants and suitors, but still remained noticeably male forums. Rural labour markets, although open to women, better rewarded men.[5] When villagers worked for pay, they encountered employers accustomed to undervaluing female labour. A well-known handbook on husbandry, written in the thirteenth century, reminded bailiffs that a woman required 'less money' than a man.[6] Given such bias, agricultural wages proved no small matter to women, especially in the early 1300s when the supply of labour far exceeded available work. During these years female rates of pay remained less than men's, although this differential decreased in the aftermath of the Black Death.[7] By the close of the fourteenth century the wages of women had improved even if not always matching those of men.

By any measure men and women seldom led exactly parallel lives. Neither social critics nor religious reformers endorsed equality as a goal. Medieval thinkers emphasized instead the balance of power characteristic of a hierarchical society and promoted the ideal of publicly-active husbands and legally dependent wives.[8] The experiences of women were correspondingly seen as denser in domestic detail than men's. Household position, rather than wages or work, shaped the possibilities and constraints inherent in women's lives. It mattered greatly where women stood in relation to men as sisters, daughters and wives. Everywhere widows and single mothers faced the problem of finding a secure place. If widows possessed a pension or property, they fared far better than unmarried mothers without ready incomes. An unwed mother was an anomaly. The need to raise and support small children required single women to fill the dual roles of nurturer and provider, to behave as both a husband and a wife.

Any discussion of women at risk of poverty certainly must take these mothers into account. For the middle ages, though, relevant facts about motherhood are elusive. They are contained mainly in literature, in local records and in the more intimate accounts of private life, such as custodial arrangements, wills and charitable bequests. The problems of dependent mothers generated no real interest among chroniclers and political commentators whose writing reflected a noticeable ambivalence about the role and status of women. This ambivalence bespoke the bias of men in centres of power and paralleled the reluctance of medieval authorities to reconcile conflicting opinions about women's place.[9] Were unmarried mothers the 'fallen' daughters of Eve or sisters to Mary, the handmaiden of God? Whatever the ambiguities in the minds of moralists, the problems of mothers and children were not entirely ignored by preachers and parish priests. Sermons, letters and manuals of pastoral care included counsel on matters of family life, albeit from the perspective of unmarried men. The stories told by the clergy reported not so much what mothers did, but what churchmen alternately admired and disliked about women's conduct.[10] The literature produced by poets and social critics also described extremes, depicting women as ennobled by motherhood or sadly burdened by the children they had.[11] Saints' lives more often idealized 'holy' mothers, while handbooks of moral advice tended to emphasize the vices rather than the virtues associated with maternity which in itself garnered approval only within marriage.[12] Churchmen censured the unwed mother, the unchaste wife and the defiant concubine of priests. When motherhood was the focus of discussion, the underlying issue frequently became sexuality. Moralists retold stories of female promiscuity, disorder and frailty to warn medieval audiences that social acceptance depended on women maintaining lawful relationships with men.

When mothers spoke for themselves, as they occasionally did in manor courts, the concerns they voiced were not so much about men but the economics of family life.[13] Recently bereaved widows told the court about children too young to labour on farms or manage paternal estates. Impoverished mothers discussed the need for support and had family agreements, pensions and sometimes wills read in court and entered into the official record. Pregnant widows asked manorial officials to find guardians to manage farms and fields until children came of age. The infirm and disabled reported problems created by overdue rents and unpaid debts.

For none was the threat of poverty, or the need for support, an idle concern. Even though mothers seldom testified about politics or matters of village governance from which they were excluded, they certainly understood how the public world intruded on the private. Seigneurial authority was unmistakable in the countryside. Powerful lords expected dependent tenants, including widows and unmarried mothers, to appear in court and answer questions about marriage, the custody of minors and the use of customary land.

The record of this testimony gives us almost our only direct evidence of women's ideas about the struggle against poverty in peasant society. Of course, these ideas can only be inferred from what women said in response to the questions and demands of manorial lords. English villagers have left us no treatises or systematic accounts that explain popular perceptions of social welfare in the past. Yet in the testimony of peasants, in their lawsuits and attendant behaviour, we can discern how villagers addressed problems of economic hardship and also responded to pressures emanating from a wider feudal world. Throughout the countryside the lords of manors had considerable power because of the rights they exercised over persons and the control they maintained over land. The very factors of unfree status and customary tenure, which ensured the seigneurial governance of land and people, prompted dependent tenants not only to appear in court but to defend their self-interests. When women testified, they moved from the peripheries of public debate and momentarily occupied the centre. In this position widows and mothers provided a sharp contrast to stereotypical images of women as the causes of discord and woe. The discussion of social welfare consequently broadened as courts heard testimony that linked the threat of insecurity not to feminine failings, but to difficulties posed by child care, marital status and traditional support laws. When we turn to these problems we see how the experiences of mothers influenced the struggle against poverty and variously reflected the persistence of inequality in village society.

DEMANDS OF CHILD CARE

The didactic literature and social advice of the later middle ages reminded readers that women differed from men in that they had so many domestic matters with which to contend.[14] Women's sphere of activity centred on the household where the life of the family, its comfort and day-to-day needs involved endless routine. Women prepared food, planted gardens, raised poultry, laundered clothes, hauled water, gathered kindling, spun wool and when necessary laboured for hire: they hoed, weeded, turned hay, bundled and harvested grain. Although wage labour afforded women the opportunity to supplement household incomes, familial demands more frequently shaped the work habits and choices of rural mothers. The nurture and supervision of small children required women to divide their time between field and housework in a way that reflected the family's needs. To achieve this balance entailed time and effort. Contemporaries saw that women laboured alongside men in fields and farms, while men shared less openly in women's work.

Everywhere the care of the young remained primarily a female task. Rural mothers, if physically able, nursed infants for several years and kept the children close at hand.[15] The practice of swaddling babies and tying them in cradles seldom freed poor women from responsibilities for the young. Once infants no longer nursed, they still had to be fed and occasionally took food which mothers first chewed then put in the children's mouth.[16] As infants grew, people never approved of leaving them alone. Walter of Bibbesworth, a thirteenth-century priest, advised mothers to make older boys and girls watch toddlers trying to walk lest they suffer harm, 'stumble or fall'.[17] Confessors, too, urged the supervision of the young but, in doing so, often reminded mothers of what the women already knew: infants and little children needed considerable care in order to thrive. Everywhere accidents and injuries posed real dangers to the young, but hardship and want no less certainly disrupted the lives of children raised in impoverished homes. Peasants without adequate resources struggled to earn a living by working for hire. As parents they had to arrange for child care or, failing this, bring little children into fields to wait until the day's work was done. The arrangement suited mothers if infants rested in cradles or cots, but older boys and girls distracted anxious parents. No one familiar with the *Ploughman's Crede* easily forgets the barefooted mother it describes at work in a field.[18] Her feet bled. She was poorly clad and had only a winnowing sheet to protect her from the weather. Three small children, ragged and cold, kept watch in the mud while she helped her husband drive a plough along icy furrows. Worn out from work, she had no strength to comfort her children when they wept.

The problems that beset impoverished mothers were problems that the renowned author, William Langland (d. 1387), saw and understood. He was a father himself and no stranger to the adversity that needy families experienced in the decades following the Black Death. Many social inequities troubled Langland when he wrote *Piers Plowman*, an allegory incorporating a wide range of contemporary thought. When asked, 'who are the poor?', he answered in much the same way as the dissident cleric, John Wycliffe (d. 1384):[19] the needy included the 'blind and the halt' as well as hapless parents without the means to support the children they had. 'I have seen enough of the world', Langland wrote, 'to know how they suffer, these folk who have many children and no resources but a craft to clothe and feed them.'[20] At greatest risk, he claimed, were mothers living alone in horrid cottages, overburdened with children and charged exorbitant 'house-hire'. What little money the women earned by spinning had to be spent on rent or on 'milk and meal' to feed children always clamouring for food. These mothers were often hungry and lonely. On 'cold, sleepless nights' they rocked cradles cramped in a corner, then rose before dawn to card and comb wool, to peel rushes, to wind yarn, to wash, scrub and mend. The women suffered in want and the lives they lived, Langland thought, were too sad for him to describe in verse.[21]

As much as he pitied poor mothers, Langland did not urge fathers to assume the tasks of early child care. If, as he believed, children were central to family life, they still were a mother's responsibility. Ideally, women fulfilled the traditional roles of nurturer and caretaker even when the care of children conflicted with the demands of the workplace. In humble households, where parents had no hired help, pregnancy and child-bearing responsibilities diminished a mother's wage-earning capacities, leading economically-vulnerable families to depend on the father's support. If he died or disappeared, uncertainty beset mother and child.[22] For a woman who owned little property and needed to earn her own way, child care posed a problem. Pregnant maids and servants had special cause to worry since they risked losing jobs due to judgemental employers. The norm was expressed by the Goodman of Paris. A man of learning, he wrote a manual of domestic advice that counselled the mistress of a household not to hire a maid dismissed elsewhere for having lost her virtue.[23] His concern to restrict employment in the interests of morality applied less to men. A man's reputation, his 'honesty' and worth were never as closely linked to sexual behaviour as a woman's, nor was a man expected to meet a child's needs.[24] The division of domestic labour was such that responsibility for the young was not equally shared – the burden fell to women.

Since the work involved in raising children was women's work, it received little recognition and scant reward.[25] Few chroniclers noticed or measured the time that mothers expended in child care. Even a collection of biographies as admirably detailed as the *Golden Legend* portrayed a decidedly masculine world. Yet the book's compiler, James of Voragine, was not uninterested in women and saw, much as Langland would, that the burdens of family life relegated poor mothers to the margins of society. His biography of the regal Elizabeth of Hungary (d. 1231) described the hardship that forced unmarried mothers to live a hand-to-mouth existence made all the more difficult by ill health and despair.[26] As a young woman Elizabeth responded to the misery she saw by founding a hospital where she nursed the poor by day and fitfully slept at night, waking as often as seven times to carry a baby to the privy and wash the child's bedding. Paupers called her mother but respected the distance that separated benefactor and supplicant. Elizabeth, after all, was hardly an ordinary mother. She pitied the destitute, but expected young and old to conform to her rules. Order and rank mattered to the saint. Her time was valuable and the poor had to await her, although she seldom suggested, as the wealthy often did, that idleness characterized the needy. True charity, she thought, required almsgivers to share the work of the poor: to spin, to sew, to clean, to cook, to supervise children. Consequently, the role of benefactor neither insulated nor prevented Elizabeth from seeing poor mothers as busy people. Without the help of a spouse, she concluded, they had trouble handling the time-consuming demands of children and work.

THE VARIED STATUS OF MOTHERS

During the middle ages advocates of the poor were admittedly generous folk, but not all were self-effacing saints. Benefactors, like social critics, occasionally spoke with a disparaging voice when discussing the status of mothers. Preachers and sermon-writers deplored the poverty that threatened widows, but expressed little if any concern for the plight of unwed mothers. Many clerics believed that infants born out of wedlock grew up to be what William Langland called society's 'wretches'.[27] For them illegitimacy was a 'curse'. It fostered suspicion since respectable people mistrusted children of uncertain parentage, seeing them as imposters likely to become 'swindlers, beggars, vagabonds, and liars'. This reaction seems harsh but Langland and like-minded thinkers were often judgemental. To penalize illegitimacy, many believed, was to uphold public morality. While an orphan elicited pity, the illegitimate child provoked alarm and was thought 'easily to slide into imitation of paternal crimes' and to corrupt the morals of the group.[28] As time passed the child became a 'rebel', an 'ingrate' and a charlatan inevitably prone to 'fault'.[29] Yet the greater fault, in the church's view, was the mother's: 'With illegitimate offspring she defiled the blood of her ancestors.'[30] Children 'blushed' for her and anxiously questioned the identity of their father. If, as John of Salisbury claimed, the unwed mother was a 'victim of lust', she was also morally culpable and brought shame upon the child she was powerless to protect from the disabilities of 'bastardy'.

Equally troubling to the medieval public was the mother of a child with birth defects. Was the unfortunate woman at fault? The question concerned benefactors of the poor as well as the clergy and drew attention to the argument that any deformity an infant suffered was a sign of parental guilt. The church had long taught that a child conceived during 'forbidden times' would have too few limbs or too many.[31] It would be physically deformed or morally impaired and no better than Cain who was conceived by Eve during a period of penitence and fast. For medieval people the story of Cain was compelling and, though often embellished, it reinforced the commonplace notion that the sins of the old were visited upon the young.[32] Some ecclesiastical commentators criticized the injustice of the assumption, but most claimed that moral laxity tainted any children born of illicit couplings, particularly the unions of concubines and priests.[33] Langland shared this belief as did the members of synods and ecclesiastical councils.

Not unexpectedly, all condemned concubinage as well as the mothers of infants conceived in unlawful relationships with prelates and priests.[34] Although the Gregorian reformers of the eleventh and twelfth centuries had forbidden clergymen to marry, concubinage remained a problem in Europe during the later middle ages.[35] Consequently, church officials in England, as elsewhere, called upon popular preachers and synodal lawmakers to identify and sternly rebuke women living as 'prestes wyves'.[36] Even the maids employed by poor rural priests risked the disapproval of reformers. Moralists cautioned the public that a clergyman's housekeeper must be 'elderly and honest' lest she scandalize the faithful and 'disturb the holy life of the priest through lechery'.[37] Should a pastor or chaplain keep a servant, and with her have offspring, he incurred sanctions, but so too did mother and child. Penalties ranged from moderate to harsh and mirrored the unequal standing of men and women in the eyes of the organized church. Errant priests risked suspension from office and, if publicly defiant, faced the anger of religious superiors. They warned subordinate clerics that sexual scandal disrupted parish life and fuelled the faithful's resentment.[38] To restore peace the clerical transgressor had to express remorse, promise to reform and abandon mistress and child. Through them, the church believed, it justly punished the errant priest.

The influence of ecclesiastical reformers was such that the mother of a priest's child often had to face ridicule and censure. To moralists she was a 'vile Jezebel', a woman they called the 'prestes mare'.[39] Her children were the 'cursed seed' of lust, the offspring of 'disobedience', the 'walking witness to paternal crime'.[40] More than other women, clerical concubines felt the force of the church's disdain. They were denounced from pulpits, banished from parishes, excluded from the sacraments, forbidden entry to churches, imperilled by excommunication and denied burial in consecrated grounds.[41] That the concubine of a priest lived as his 'hearthmate' antagonized religious reformers, believing as many did that women had no place in the lives of consecrated clerics. Not only did concubines defy canon law, they contradicted the reformers' view of the church as a world where men and women occupied mutually exclusive spheres, a world distinct in various ways from the world created by a mother, father and child. The mandate to segregate women from the company of priests threatened clerical households and certainly made concubines all the more vulnerable to desertion and neglect. Although these women were at risk of poverty, neither they nor their children received public aid. Even critics sympathetic to the poor supported the church's strategy of correcting unchaste priests by punishing concubines and excluding the women from parish life.[42] Moralists justified church policy on the grounds that a clergyman's concubine jeopardized the welfare of impoverished parishioners; she misused, if she did not actually steal, the alms and tithes that rightfully belonged to the destitute.[43] Worse still, critics complained, concubines disregarded the demands of charity and along with 'lascivious' priests fed their children with 'the substance of the poor'.[44] In doing so the clerical couple sinned, the priest no less than the concubine because he shamelessly 'wasted the possessions of Christ's poor'.[45]

POOR RELIEF AND SUPPORT LAWS

This defence of the 'patrimony of the poor' against 'false' claimants, including unworthy women and priests, had widespread support. If individual benefactors felt sorry for needy mothers, social commentators nevertheless believed that unchaste women brought hardship and suffering upon themselves.[46] Langland, too, deplored the 'shiftless poor', although more than many of his peers he noticed the variety of mothers populating the rural world. His concern for the impoverished led him to mention, if only in passing, the circumstances that compelled mothers to raise children alone.[47] Married couples separated. Husbands died. Fathers abandoned families or did not marry the mothers of children born of illicit encounters. As varied as these circumstances were, the difficulties that poor mothers confronted were sadly the same. When a marriage or illicit relationship ended, a family did not; small children continued to need nurture and material support. The best hope Langland had for mothers living in want was the kindness of neighbours: 'I tell you it would be a real charity to help cottagers so burdened with children and to comfort them along with the blind and the halt.'[48] Yet private alms and the charity of the church furnished little more than a temporary remedy. Neither represented a perfect policy since benefactors seldom saw all the poor as alike. Medieval guidelines for almsgiving were many, but commonly directed donors to help neighbours and kin impoverished 'by misfortune rather than sin'.[49] Along with prostitutes and 'shrews', unwed mothers and clerical concubines never ranked among the 'righteous' and blameless poor. Everywhere the church warned: 'if you give [alms] to sinners, you sacrifice to demons'.[50]

To prevent misplaced charity, churchmen developed an etiquette for almsgiving that drew a distinction between the 'deserving' and the 'undeserving' poor, and thus reinforced the conventional notion that economic want was the consequence of improvidence and intemperance among the poor. This point of view encouraged benefactors to ignore 'harlots' and 'scolds' in favour of the women Langland described as 'meek' and 'powerless', that is, 'widows with no means of support' and 'helpless young maidens'.[51] Neither sinned with men nor wasted the alms and gifts of food that donors had 'sweated to earn'.[52] Promiscuous women, on the other hand, led 'careless', improvident lives. The women, Langland implied, were unnatural mothers; they brought forth illegitimate offspring, allowing sadistic tramps to break the infants' bones and with these 'misshapen' children sit along highways, begging for alms.[53]

Of course, churchmen realized that mothers and infants did not need to depend solely on charity to survive. In medieval England, child support was a matter of law. Among church authorities there was a broad consensus concerning the obligations of family life and an equally firm conviction that fathers, along with mothers, had a duty to the young. During the later middle ages, as in earlier times, the church admonished both parents to protect infants from harm and ensure the physical well-being of children who as dependants and 'supplicants' needed generosity and care.[54] To ignore the welfare of the young was to violate God's law. The fourth commandment not only affirmed the honour due fathers and mothers but required them to nurture and guide sons and daughters in 'the ways of the Lord'.[55] By the later fourteenth century, clerical spokesmen reminded the public of how God punished parents guilty of neglect by unleashing pestilence and plague and 'so taking your children as you see even this day'.[56] For the faithful to gain the blessings of a better life, family relationships had to be directed towards external, unselfish ends and, in particular, towards the care of the young.

In England, as elsewhere, lawyers and judges advised the public on the church's view of family law. Should married couples separate or divorce, canon law required husbands to support children and provide alimony to wives as long as the women lived what lawyers considered orderly lives.[57] The church accorded sons and daughters a right to maintenance even if their parents' marriages were declared invalid. Support benefits also applied to illegitimate children, albeit not their mothers. As early as the 1180s the papacy acted on behalf of the offspring of adulterous couples, warning parents that the children were entitled to the necessities of life.[58] Thereafter, spokesmen for the church extended this mandate to include all children born out of wedlock. Although the children stayed in the mother's care, the father was legally obliged to contribute to their support within his means. Failure to do so put negligent men at risk of prosecution. Church courts provided mothers with a forum to bring grievances and prosecute claims.[59]

Child support and maintenance generally depended on the resources and wealth of the father. If he alleged poverty, the mother of his child had little choice but to wait until that time when the court found him to have 'more abundant fortune'.[60] Even then the payments made to mothers seldom exceeded 1–3d. weekly.[61] Equally troubling for the poor were disputed paternity cases. While the pregnancy of women was simply a matter of observation, the identity of fathers depended on accusation. A typically confused situation in which promiscuity, but not paternity, was admitted occurred in the diocese of Worcester in 1312.[62] In that year, according to the bishop's register, the rector of Alvechirch in Wych stood accused of serious wrongdoings. It was said he 'publicly kept a concubine named Emma and had children by her'. Not only did he 'set a bad example', he 'broke his word' when he failed to pay her 10 marks, two cows and 'small things'. After discussing the charges with his superior, the rector acknowledged his misdeeds at 'one time' but denied 'keeping Emma publicly'. As to children, he said, 'he was uncertain'. Discussion ended when the rector offered church officials a fine of 1 mark for 'pious uses'. Nothing more was heard about Emma and her children; apparently she decided not to pursue her case further.

Among unwed mothers the need for child support, even if pressing, had no bearing on inheritance laws. Royal courts barred claims on behalf of illegitimate children in keeping with the common law's exclusion of bastards from inheriting land.[63] When, as occasionally happened, manor courts made an exception, this exception depended upon the approval of the manor's lord for whom the welfare of 'illegitimate heirs' mattered less than the efficient farming of seigneurial estates.[64] The desire to see productive holdings in the hands of productive workers prompted lords to favour able-bodied, if illegitimately born, males as tenants rather than women and girls even if not tainted by the stigma of bastardy. Ecclesiastical authorities were equally concerned to restrict inheritance whenever it involved the lands, revenues and houses of the church. Bishops and lawmakers wanted, above all else, to prevent clerics from leaving legacies to concubines. Any clergyman 'bold' enough to defy the church risked excommunication.[65] His bequest, authorities said, represented a 'damnable presumption' and 'converted the goods of the church not to the poor', but to promiscuous women without valid claims.[66] Any bequest to a concubine consequently remained 'null and void'.

SANCTIONS

This is not to say that spokesmen for the church ignored pleas for justice on behalf of unwed mothers and children. Then, as now, the problem was one of enforcement and drew attention to the behaviour of husbands and fathers. If many men honoured their obligations at law, others either failed to aid estranged wives or refused to acknowledge illegitimate offspring.[67] Nor were problems of enforcement easily solved in villages and small towns. Although socially-minded clerics warned parishioners – in sermons and penitential counsel – against family neglect, the church lacked the machinery to appropriate the property of absent husbands and fathers. Even so, the hierarchy had the will to publicize its displeasure with recalcitrant men. Should a case of neglect scandalize the church, as when a husband 'shamelessly' abandoned his wife, officials intervened. [68] If they were ignored, the bishop called upon the priests of his diocese to 'proclaim a sentence of excommunication during Mass on Sundays and feast days so that when bells sounded and candles burned' all present knew the danger of violating God's law.

Throughout the countryside the laity was certainly mindful of the range of penalties the church imposed for adultery, fornication and the desertion of a spouse. Men and women, if promiscuous, were equally subjected to ecclesiastical discipline, to excommunication, penitential floggings and fines. All created the suspicion that illicit sexual relationships were not easily concealed, attracting as they did the concern of the organized church. For many this suspicion was confirmed when bishops sent officials into the countryside to gather information about the immorality of inhabitants, including the local priest. To secure presentments, bishops authorized parish juries, numbering twelve or more men, to make inquiries and identify any villager thought guilty of transgressing moral norms. During 1397 the Bishop of Hereford authorized visitations in 281 parishes of which forty-four simply informed him that 'all was well'.[69] As for the remaining parishes, each made, on average, four or five presentments – half involved accusations of adultery and fornication against the laity, 10 per cent denounced the sexual indiscretions of the clergy. A concern on the part of jurors to report the misbehaviour of peers also governed visitations in the dioceses of Rochester, Canterbury and Norwich.[70] It consequently appears that lay opinion, at least as it was represented by parish notables, incorporated and upheld ecclesiastical standards of morality.

These standards, although everywhere pronounced, were variously enforced in the secular world. At the insistence of powerful lords, manor courts fined the mothers, but rarely the fathers, of children born out of wedlock.[71] Manorial juries, composed of male tenants from leading village families, had the duty of informing the lord about any 'bondswoman who was unchaste of her body'.[72] When penalizing offenders, courts affirmed what the lord claimed was his right to exercise a paternal control on his manor in the interests of morality.[73] Yet, it need not be supposed that lords forced upon courts unshared standards. The morality that peasant juries chose to maintain supported and enhanced the differential treatment of women in the countryside. What troubled a lord and his court were not extramarital affairs as such, but rather the affairs of unmarried women. Under these circumstances manor courts fined females for behaviour that was largely ignored in males and thus burdened women alone with the consequences of extramarital sex.

UNWED MOTHERS

Nowhere was this double standard more apparent than in the case of unwed mothers. They had, of course, the right to bring claims for child support before church courts, but the suits necessarily involved travel and expense. Manor courts, while readily available, seldom afforded the women a sympathetic forum. This was certainly true at Cranfield (Bedfordshire), where, in 1311, Dulcia Tela asked to enter, by way of inheritance, her late father's land.[74] On the advice of the manor's tenantry, the court denied her request. Dulcia was unmarried but had a child, therefore, the court said, she must forever forfeit the property of both parents in keeping with the custom of the manor. At Horsham St Faith, a village near Norwich, local officials evicted Agnes Miller from her house in 1282 because 'she was pregnant' and had neither 'claimed freedom' nor purchased the lord's grace.[75] In 1284 the court threatened to confiscate what little property Cristina Gocelyn had unless she compensated the lord for the wrong she had done him by having an illegitimate child.[76] Even when jurors knew the identity of unmarried fathers, and named the men in court, the lord cared only to have information about the misconduct of women.[77] An identical situation prevailed on the nearby manor of Salle where the lord expected jurors to amerce mothers with children born out of wedlock. The usual fine of 2s. 8d., equivalent to an agricultural labourer's wage for eight days' hard work, was seldom paid, suggesting the problem of fining the poor.

The evidence from Horsham and Salle, although not perfectly matched, is consistently detailed over time. Between 1282 and 1288 eleven unwed mothers came to the attention of Horsham's lord. In Salle jurors identified twenty-two mothers with thirty-two illegitimate children born between 1327 and 1356. As far as their place in the rural community was concerned, the women were hardly representative. They were neither from prosperous families nor from households of middling rank. Instead the mothers numbered among the village poor. They laboured as maids, they boarded with widows, they looked for work in neighbouring villages and towns. Many experienced a prejudice strong enough to interfere with their ability to secure a livelihood. Agnes Neth and Emma Neth, soon after having babies in 1284, were declared 'suspect' by Horsham's court and expelled from the village.[78] In 1291, when Agnes Snepegate was pregnant, she fled Horsham of her own accord, but the lord ordered her arrest lest he lose the 'satisfaction' she owed him.[79] Circumstances in Salle were particularly bleak among villagers known as 'anilepiwymen'. Being unmarried and poor, they enjoyed no real stake in the village. Their parents held little if any land from the lord and engaged in day labour while occupying cottages let by better off peasants and farmers. These daughters of hired men clearly had few prospects. They were economically dependent and, like poor girls everywhere, extremely vulnerable when they had infants to support.

Historians have written about single women in premodern England, leading marginal lives and trapped in a cycle of poverty and neglect.[80] The pattern was not unknown in Salle where, by the 1350s, four families of 'anilepimen' had daughters responsible for fourteen illegitimate births. Although poor girls were certainly not the only villagers to have an illicit affair, the problems they faced were difficult to solve. Living as servants and lodgers, with babies to care for, they simply lacked the material resources to acquire a dowry and marry. Yet social custom being what it was in medieval villages, the manorial lord and his leading tenants expected peasant women to become wives. We need, then, to ask how central marriage was to the welfare and economic security of women forced by circumstance to raise children alone.

WIDOWED MOTHERS

The best evidence we have on widows comes from manors of lay and ecclesiastical lords in East Anglia as well as from the estates of the Abbots of St Albans in Buckinghamshire and Hertfordshire.[81] During the generations before and after the Black Death these courts kept careful records of the land that devolved upon women when their husbands died. Should widows remarry, the lord asserted his interest by collecting an amercement for the marriage, an entry fine for the land. Yet not only the demands of lordship, but the requirements of family and work, affected a woman's decision to marry. Much depended on the ages of her children and the actual labour a farm required. On no manor would a lord countenance his land falling into disuse or judge unimportant the labour services he was due. A manor's lord derived part of his income from rents and also expected tenants to labour on his behalf, to plant, to plough and to harvest his demesne. Any widow failing to meet seigneurial expectations jeopardized her holding and risked the distraint of her property or the confiscation of her crops.[82] Of course, the older a woman's children were, the more she could rely on them for help in performing the labour services encumbent on land. Mothers with small children had fewer options. Live-in servants required the kind of payment that only prosperous villagers could easily afford. Hard-pressed widows might place children in the homes of neighbours and kin, but legal guardians expected compensation in the form of access to land and seldom welcomed a child too young to help with domestic chores.[83]

Although the status of women as dependent wives immediately altered once husbands died, there was no mistaking the vulnerability of mothers without the resources to meet family needs. Bailiffs and reeves saw the problem first hand when they collected rents from impoverished widows or visited the cottages of peasants near death. For the dying to transfer customary land to family and kin required the approval of manorial officials since unfree land belonged to the lord and in theory reverted to him at a tenant's death. When the Prior of Norwich sent his steward and cellarer to the Norfolk village of Hindolvestone in 1401, they found that John de Brunham, though mortally ill, welcomed their counsel.[84] He wanted his holding of 5.5 acres of bondland to remain in his wife's hands, provided she did not remarry. At her death, the land was to descend to the five children they had. Because each child was under age, John worried about what the future held. Should 'poverty and want' afflict his widow, he said, she could sell her land 'at the discretion of the steward and cellarer'. For a husband and father to involve manorial officials in his widow's welfare was not unusual.[85] They had the experience to know that the smaller an inheritance was, the more pressing became the need to help the bereaved handle what a Suffolk villager called 'the fear of living alone'.[86]

Widowhood was, after all, an exceptionally complex time. Access to property afforded widows the chance to participate more fully and publicly in the business of village life, but the opportunities a woman now possessed did not change the responsibilities she incurred as a householder, tenant or executor of her late husband's estate. If he died in debt, she had to satisfy his creditors no matter how meagre her holding in land.[87] Equally difficult for a poor woman to manage was the intrusiveness of neighbours. Should they come into court and allege promiscuity or question a widow's friendships with men, she had to establish innocence or forfeit her free-bench, that is, her holding in land.[88] Courts protected the dower rights of a widow, but only as long as she remained 'pure and chaste'.[89] To speak, then, of the 'liberation' of peasant widows, as some historians do, partially obscures the complexity of the problems that mothers faced as widows.[90] Among 131 widows named as guardians in nine manor courts, 54 per cent had children younger than 7 when their husbands died.[91] Many guardians, in turn, possessed meagre tenements: 39 per cent held less than 5 acres of land, fully 57 per cent had less than 10 acres. With small children to nurture and support, single mothers obviously faced hard choices. Should they behave as husbands or wives? That many of the women purchased the lord's permission to remarry need not be taken to mean that they misunderstood the autonomy which widows had in the rural world.[92] The mothers of small children simply experienced widowhood differently from women without dependants to support. Economic insecurity all too frequently threatened the welfare of unmarried mothers, and for them a spouse represented a helpful and useful partner in managing a household, raising a family and running a farm.

CONCLUSION

If medieval commentators and social critics clung to the notion that the poor 'deserved' what they received, the testimony of women provided a different point of view. Many unmarried mothers understood and variously experienced the handicaps of circumstance and inequality that characterized rural life. Although the uneven distribution of land influenced the welfare of women as well as men, economic hardship was not simply the consequence of limited resources and income. When women hired out their labour and still experienced need, they were at risk of poverty because their wages were too low. When unwed mothers faced economic uncertainty because they had no place to live, it was prejudice and moral bias that prevented them from securing a livelihood. Marital disruption, no less than non-marital births, affected the welfare of women and intensified the problems that mothers had in supporting families without fathers. What must be kept in mind, then, are the economic risks associated with inequalities of gender. To ignore these risks, and make the male life cycle the norm, as medieval authorities often did, is not only to overlook the divergent experiences of men and women but also to misunderstand the economic needs of single mothers in the past.

NOTES

1 The discussion of family welfare and support has primarily focused on church law: see J.A. Brundage, *Law, Sex, and Christian Society in Medieval Europe*, Chicago, Ill.: University of Chicago Press 1987, pp. 245, 345, 408, 479–80,

543–4; R.H. Helmholz, 'Support orders, church courts, and the rule of *Filius Nullius*: A reassessment of the common law', *Virginia Law Review*, 63, 1977, pp. 431–48.

2   R. Morris (ed.), *Old English Homilies of the Twelfth Century*, London: N. Trübner & Co., Early English Text Society (hereafter EETS), no. 53, 1873, pp. 8–9, 156–7; W.O. Ross (ed.), *Middle English Sermons*, London: Oxford University Press, EETS, no. 209, 1940, reissued 1960, pp. 42, 151–2; T. Erbe (ed.), *Mirk's Festival: A Collection of Homilies*, London: EETS, no. 96, 1905, pp. 4, 70–1, 85, 270; M.A. Devlin (ed.), *The Sermons of Thomas Brinton, Bishop of Rochester (1373–1389)*, London: Camden Society, vol. 85, 1954, pp. 194–200.

3   For detailed discussion of economic problems and population trends in the English countryside, see C. Dyer, *Standards of Living in the Later Middle Ages*, Cambridge: Cambridge University Press 1989; J. Hatcher, *Plague, Population and the English Economy 1348–1530*, London: Macmillan 1977; P.D.A. Harvey (ed.), *The Peasant Land Market in Medieval England*, Oxford: Clarendon Press 1984; R.M. Smith (ed.), *Land, Kinship and Life-Cycle*, Cambridge: Cambridge University Press 1984.

4   See, in particular, J.M. Bennett, *Women in the Medieval English Countryside: Gender and Household in Brigstock Before the Plague*, New York: Oxford University Press 1987.

5   S. Shahar, *The Fourth Estate: A History of Women in the Middle Ages*, trans. C. Galai, London: Methuen 1983, pp. 242–3.

6   D. Oschinsky (ed.), *Walter of Henley and Other Treatises on Estate Management and Accounting*, Oxford: Clarendon Press 1971, p. 427.

7   For a fuller discussion of female wages, see Bennett, *Women*, pp. 82–4, 118–19; Dyer, *Standards of Living*, pp. 229–33; B.A. Hanawalt, *The Ties That Bound: Peasant Families in Medieval England*, New York: Oxford University Press 1986, pp. 149–51; R.H. Hilton, *The English Peasantry in the Later Middle Ages*, Oxford: Clarendon Press 1975, pp. 102–3.

8   P.H. Barnum (ed.), *Dives and Pauper*, London: EETS, no. 275,vol. 1, pt i, 1976, p. 339; Bennett, *Women*, pp. 100–4; Shahar, *The Fourth Estate*, pp. 3–11.

9   J.A. Phillips, *Eve: The History of an Idea*, San Francisco, Calif.: Harper & Row 1984, pp. 49–51, 57–72, 77, 131–47; E. Power, *Medieval Women*, Cambridge: Cambridge University Press 1975, pp. 14–16; Shahar, *The Fourth Estate*, pp. 24–5.

10   For examples, see G.R. Owst, *Literature and Pulpit in Medieval England*, Cambridge: Cambridge University Press 1933, reprinted Oxford: Basil Blackwell 1961, pp. 118–20.

11   This literature was informed by the views of the Church Fathers. For the argument that women, although weak, could achieve salvation through motherhood, see B. de Montfaucon (ed.), *Opera Johannis Chrysostomi*, vol. 11, Paris 1838, columns 662b–4a. For the opinion that children increase a mother's troubles, see Ambrose, *De Virginibus Liber Primus*, in vol. 16, J.P. Migne (ed.), *Patrologia Latina*, Paris 1845, columns 195–7.

12   C. Horstmann (ed.), *The Lives of Women Saints of our Contrie of England*, London: EETS, no. 86, 1886, pp. 110, 123, 158–9. Fourteenth-century manuals of moral advice include F.J. Furnivall (ed.), *Robert of Brunne's Handlyng Synne A.D. 1303*, London: EETS, no. 119, 1901; Dan Michel, *Ayenbite of Inwyt or Remorse of Conscience*, edited by R. Morris, London: EETS, no. 23, 1886, reprinted 1895; W.N. Francis (ed.), *The Book of Virtues and Vices*, London: EETS, no. 217, 1942; A. Brandeis (ed.), *Jacob's Well: An English Treatise on the Cleansing of Man's Conscience*, London: EETS, no. 115, 1900.

13 For cases brought by mothers in manor courts, see E. Clark, 'The custody of children in English manor courts', *Law and History Review*, 3, 1985, pp. 333–48.

14 The literature is cited by Hanawalt, *Ties That Bound*, pp. 147–55.

15 ibid.: pp. 178–9.

16 John of Trevisa's translation of Bartholomaeus Anglicus, *De Proprietatibus Rerum*, revised as *Batman uppon Bartholome*, London: 1582, book 6, p. 74, Hildesheim and New York, Georg Olms Verlag 1976.

17 *Le Traité de Walter de Bibbesworth sur la langue française*, cited by N. Orme, *From Childhood to Chivalry*, New York: Methuen 1984, p. 15. Also, see Hanawalt, *Ties That Bound*, pp. 175–7.

18 W.W. Skeat (ed.), *Pierce the Ploughman's Crede*, London: EETS, no. 30, 1867, pp. 16–17.

19 F.D. Matthew (ed.), *The English Works of John Wycliff*, London: EETS, no. 74, 1902, p. 234: 'men become poor when overcharged with feebleness, loss of chattel and with many children'.

20 D. Pearshall (ed.), *Piers Plowman by William Langland: An Edition of the C-Text*, Berkeley, Calif.: University of California Press 1979, Passus IX, lines 88–90.

21 ibid.: lines 72–85.

22 ibid.: line 176; Langland mentions pregnancy and notes that 'the woman with child who cannot work' may lawfully beg.

23 *The Goodman of Paris*, transl. E. Power, London: G. Routledge & Sons 1928, p. 208. Also see M. Bowker, *The Secular Clergy in the Diocese of Lincoln, 1495–1520*, Cambridge: Cambridge University Press 1968, p. 119 which describes a pregnant girl who begged the Chancellor not to let the woman with whom she lodged know of her condition.

24 S.D. Amussen, *An Ordered Society: Gender and Class in Early Modern England*, Oxford: Basil Blackwell 1988, pp. 99–100.

25 For the tendency of authors to devalue women's time and work, see Reginald Pecock, *The Reule of Crysten Religioun*, edited by W.C. Greet, London: EETS, no. 171, 1927, p. 321. Also, 'Ballad of a tyrannical husband', in T. Wright and J.O. Halliwell (eds), *Reliquiae Antiquae*, London: 1843, reprinted New York: AMS Press 1966, pp. 196–9.

26 *The Golden Legend of Jacobus de Voragine*, transl. G. Ryan and H. Ripperger, New York: Longmans, Green & Co. 1941, reissued 1969, pp. 680–6.

27 *Piers Plowman*, Passus X, lines 210–18, 295–6; M. Chibnall (ed.), *The Historia Pontificalis of John of Salisbury*, London: Thomas Nelson & Sons 1956, p. 14; Walter Map, *Courtiers' Trifles*, transl. R. Tupper and M.B. Ogle, New York: Macmillan 1924, p. 299.

28 Owst, *Literature and Pulpit*, pp. 467–8, for discussion of children imitating parental vices.

29 C. Swan and W. Hooper (eds), *Gesta Romanorum*, New York: Dover Publications 1959, pp. 80–1.

30 John of Salisbury, *Policraticus*, book 8, in J.B. Pike (ed.), *Frivolities of Courtiers and Footprints of Philosophers*, Minneapolis, Minn.: University of Minnesota Press 1938, p. 364.

31 *Piers Plowman*, Passus X, line 288; Francis (ed.), *The Book of Virtues and Vices*, p. 248; Michel, *Ayenbite of Inwyt*, pp. 223–4.

32 *Piers Plowman*, Passus X, lines 296–330.

33 ibid.: lines 234–42; Owst, *Literature and Pulpit*, p. 259. For a detailed discussion of priests' sons, see B. Schimmelpfennig, '*Ex Fornicatione Nati*: Studies on the position of priests' sons from the twelfth to the fourteenth century', *Studies in Medieval and Renaissance History*, II (o.s. XII), 1979, pp. 1–49.

34 'The Tale of the Priest's Concubine and how fiends carried off her dead body', in Furnivall (ed.), *Handlyng Synne*, pp. 253–6. Also see F.M. Powicke and C.R. Cheney (eds), *Councils and Synods with Other Documents Relating to the English Church*, Oxford: Clarendon Press 1964, vol. I, pp. 269, 320, 346–7, 427–8, 463, 486, 645–6, 710, 756–7; vol. II, pp. 1013–14, 1083.

35 C.N.L. Brooke, 'Gregorian reform in action: Clerical marriage in England, 1050–1200', *Cambridge Historical Journal*, 12, 1956, pp. 1–21; Schimmel-pfennig, *'Ex Fornicatione Nati'*, pp. 20–5; Brundage, *Law*, pp. 474–5.

36 Furnivall (ed.), *Handlyng Synne*, p. 252.

37 ibid.: p. 252; Bowker, *Secular Clergy*, pp. 117–18.

38 W.W. Capes, *The English Church in the Fourteenth and Fifteenth Centuries*, New York: AMS Press n.d., p. 259. Also, J. Bossy, *Christianity in the West, 1400–1700*, New York: Oxford University Press 1985, p. 66.

39 Furnivall (ed.), *Handlyng Synne*, p. 253; R.I. Moore, 'Family, community and cult on the eve of the Gregorian reform', *Transactions of the Royal Historical Society*, 5th series, 30, 1980, p. 68.

40 *Golden Legend*, p. 740; G.G. Coulton, *Five Centuries of Religion*, vol. II, Cambridge: Cambridge University Press 1927, pp. 250, 273.

41 Powicke and Cheney (eds), *Councils and Synods*, vol. I, pp. 25–6, 132; vol. II, pp. 1014–15.

42 T.F. Crane (ed.), *The Exempla of Jacques de Vitry*, London: Folklore Society 1890, p. 101, no. ccxlii.

43 For discussion of parishioners withholding tithes from priests with concubines, see P.H. Barnum (ed.), *Dives and Pauper*, London: EETS, no. 280, vol. 1, pt 2, 1980, pp. 168–9; Owst, *Literature and Pulpit*, p. 259; G.A. Williamson (ed.), *Foxe's Book of Martyrs*, London: Secker & Warburg 1965, pp. 22–3.

44 Owst, *Literature and Pulpit*, pp. 244, 258, 267.

45 W.W. Skeat (ed.), *The Vision of William concerning Piers the Plowman*, London: 1886, reprinted by Oxford University Press 1954, B. Passus IX, lines 90–1.

46 Barnum (ed.), *Dives and Pauper*, vol. 1, pt 2, p. 287.

47 For a detailed discussion of poverty, see G. Shepherd, 'Poverty in Piers Plowman', in T.H. Aston, P.R. Coss, C. Dyer and J. Thirsic (eds), *Social Relations and Ideas: Essays in Honour of R.H. Hilton*, Cambridge: Cambridge University Press 1983, pp. 169–89.

48 J.F. Goodridge (trans.), *Piers the Ploughman*, Harmondsworth: Penguin Books 1970, p. 260.

49 Francis (ed.), *The Book of Virtues and Vices*, pp. 212–3; Michel, *Ayenbite of Inwyt*, pp. 192–3; Barnum (ed.), *Dives and Pauper*, vol. 1, pt 2, p. 292; *Cursor Mundi: A Northumbrian Poem of the XIVth Century*, London: EETS, no. 68, 1878, reprinted 1966, pp. 156–9.

50 Skeat (ed.), *The Vision of William*, B. Passus XV, lines 337–8.

51 ibid.: B. Passus IX, lines 67–9. John of Salisbury, *Policraticus*, book VIII, pp. 307–8: 'It is quite proper to give to everyone that asketh us . . . at times, however, it is more beneficial to chide the sluggard and to disconcert the harlot or actor than to lavish upon them what they are demanding.' Also see wills in which testators provide dowries only to maidens who are 'honest' or 'pure'. For example, T.C.B. Timmins (ed.), *The Register of John Chandler, Dean of Salisbury, 1404–17*, Devizes: Wiltshire Record Society, 39:404, 1984. J. Raines (ed.), *Testamenta Eboracensia*, vol. XXX, Durham: Surtees Society 1885, p. 208.

52 *Piers Plowman*, Passus VIII, lines 139–40.

53 ibid.: Passus IX, lines 168–72. For references to children who were deliberately maimed and forced to beg, see John Capgrave, *The Chronicle of England*,

edited by F.C. Hingeston, London: Rolls Series 1858, vol. I, p. 316; T.H. Jamieson (ed.), *The Ship of Fools by Sebastian Brant*, vol. I. London: Henry Southern 1874, p. 304. Also see J. Boswell, *The Kindness of Strangers: The Abandonment of Children in Western Europe from Late Antiquity to the Renaissance*, New York: Vintage Books 1990, pp. 60, 113 n. 77.

54 Barnum (ed.), *Dives and Pauper*, vol. 1, pt 1, p. 311; Pecock, *The Reule of Crysten Religioun*, p. 319.

55 Francis (ed.), *The Book of Virtues and Vices*, p. 325; Barnum (ed.), *Dives and Pauper*, vol. 1, pt 1, p. 314.

56 Francis (ed.), *The Book of Virtues and Vices*, p. 325.

57 Brundage, *Law*, pp. 479–80.

58 Schimmelpfennig, 'Ex Fornicatione Nati', p. 31.

59 R.H. Helmholz, *Marriage Litigation in Medieval England*, Cambridge: Cambridge University Press 1974, pp. 108–9.

60 ibid.

61 For support cases reported in the records of coroners and manor courts, see Hanawalt, *Ties That Bound*, p. 209; G.C. Homans, *English Villagers of the Thirteenth Century*, Cambridge, Mass.: Harvard University Press 1941, reissued New York: W.W. Norton 1975, p. 174.

62 R.A. Wilson (ed.), *The Register of Walter Reynolds: Bishop of Worcester, 1308–1313*, vol. IX, London: Dugdale Society 1928, pp. 47–9. Also, Helmholz, 'Support orders', pp. 437–8.

63 F. Pollock and F.W. Maitland, *The History of English Law*, 2nd edn, vol. II, Cambridge: Cambridge University Press 1968, pp. 396–8.

64 For discussion of manorial evidence, see Hanawalt, *Ties That Bound*, p. 72; R.M. Smith, 'Marriage processes in the English past: Some continuities', in L. Bonfield, R.M. Smith and K. Wrightson (eds), *The World We Have Gained*, Oxford: Basil Blackwell 1986, pp. 57–8; R.M. Smith, 'Some thoughts on "hereditary" and "proprietary" rights in land under customary law', *Law and History Review*, 1, 1983, pp. 112–4. For a case where the court and the lord granted the land of a deceased father to his illegitimate son, rather than his lawfully born daughter, see Norfolk Record Office: court of Heacham for 25 March 1309.

65 Powicke and Cheney (eds), *Councils and Synods*, vol. II, p. 1014.

66 ibid.

67 The problems are discussed in the essays included in P. Laslett, K. Oosterveen and R.M. Smith (eds), *Bastardy and its Comparative History*, Cambridge, Mass.: Harvard University Press 1980.

68 Wilson (ed.), *The Register of Walter Reynolds*, p. 29.

69 A.T. Bannister (ed.), 'Visitation returns of the Diocese of Hereford in 1397', *English Historical Review*, xliv, 1929, pp. 279–89; ibid., xlv, 1930, pp. 92–101, 444–63.

70 For comparative data, see A. Grandsen (ed.), 'Some late thirteenth century records of an ecclesiastical court in the Archdeaconry of Sudbury', *Bulletin of the Institute of Historical Research*, 32, 1959, pp. 62–9; A. Jessop (ed.), *Visitations of the Diocese of Norwich, 1492–1532*, Camden Society, 2nd series, vol. 43, 1888; S.L. Parker and L.R. Poos (eds), 'A consistory court from the Diocese of Rochester, 1363–4', *English Historical Review*, CVI, 1991, pp. 652–65; F.S. Pearson (ed.), 'Records of a ruridecanal court of 1300', in S.G. Hamilton (ed.), *Collectanea*, Worcestershire Historical Society, 1912, pp. 70–80; C.E. Woodruff (ed.), 'Some early visitation rolls preserved at Canterbury', *Archaelogia Cantiana*, 32, 1917, pp. 143–80.

71 Amercements for *legerwite* and *childwite* are discussed by E. Britton, *The Community of the Vill: A Study in the History of the Family and Village Life in*

Fourteenth-Century England, Toronto: Macmillan 1977, pp. 35–7, 52; A.E. Levett, *Studies in Manorial History*, New York: Barnes & Noble 1963, pp. 235ff.; R.M. Smith 'Marriage processes', pp. 53–6; T. North, 'Legerwite in the thirteenth and fourteenth centuries', *Past and Present*, III, 1986, pp. 3–16.

72 H.S. Bennett, *Life on the English Manor*, Cambridge: Cambridge University Press 1937, reprinted 1971, p. 246.

73 During the thirteenth century, the fathers of pregnant girls were sometimes amerced, but by the fourteenth century the girl alone was fined. For the lord's involvement, see Cambridge University Library: court for Abbots Langley, held in 1267: 'Hugo Clericus in misericordia xij d. eo quod filia sua inpregnata erat ad hutagium domini sui.'

74 This case is cited and edited in Homans, *English Villagers*, p. 438, n. 14.

75 Norfolk Record Office (hereafter NRO) Horsham court, 23 November 1282.

76 NRO Horsham court, 25 April 1284.

77 NRO Horsham courts, 30 June 1287 and 5 February 1288.

78 NRO Horsham court, 18 October 1285.

79 NRO Horsham court, 7 July 1291. For a similar case, see NRO Salle courts, 2 February 1344 and 1 August 1351.

80 M. Ingram, 'The reform of popular culture? Sex and marriage in early modern England', in B. Reay (ed), *Popular Culture in Seventeenth-Century England*, London: Croom Helm 1985, pp. 150–3; M. Ingram, *Church Courts, Sex and Marriage in England, 1570–1640*, Cambridge: Cambridge University Press 1987, pp. 19, 162–6, 264–7; Amussen, *An Ordered Society*, pp. 111–17, 132; P. Laslett, *Family Life and Illicit Love in Earlier Generations*, Cambridge: Cambridge University Press 1977, p. 107, 147–51.

81 See Appendix, p. 159 for archival references.

82 Cambridge University Library (hereafter CUL), Abbots Langley court, 6 May 1329. CUL Lakenheath court, 11 June 1310.

83 For fuller discussion of widows and wards, see Clark, 'Custody of Orphans', pp. 342–3.

84 NRO Hindolvestone court, 7 July 1401.

85 Deathbed settlements of customary land routinely included clauses directing widows to consult with manorial officials. NRO Gymingham court, 22 February 1384. Suffolk Record Office (hereafter SRO) South Elmham court, 1 May 1419. SRO Westwood court, 12 March 1428.

86 SRO Flixton court, 10 August 1421.

87 NRO Newton court, 5 April 1276. NRO Horsham court, 28 October 1431. SRO South Elmham court, 14 February 1417.

88 Public Record Office (hereafter PRO) Brightwalton court, 11 June 1325.

89 PRO Dunmow court, 13 April 1337. Essex Record Office (hereafter ERO) Ingatestone court, 30 May 1393. ERO Abbess Roothing court, 14 April 1382. Dorset Record Office, Gillingham court, 13 March 1423.

90 For a carefully argued but differing point of view, see P. Franklin, 'Peasant widows' "liberation" and remarriage before the Black Death', *Economic History Review*, 39, 1986, pp. 186–204.

91 The courts, which cover the period 1313–77, are Wells, Horsham St Faith, Salle, Barnet, Codicote, Cashio, Abbots Langley, Park Winslow.

92 At Horsham, Salle and Wells, 58 per cent of the thirty-six widows, who acted as guardians of children under 14 years of age, purchased licenses to remarry.

APPENDIX MANOR COURTS

The manorial documents used in this chapter are for the most part on deposit in English record offices and have not been published in edited form. For a detailed introduction to manor court rolls, see J.A. Raftis, *Tenure and Mobility: Studies in the Social History of the Mediaeval English Village*, Toronto: Pontifical Institute of Mediaeval Studies 1972. For specific references to court cases involving unwed mothers and widows with dependent children, see:

British Library, Barnet Add MS 40167. Cashio Add MS 40626. Codicote MS Stowe 849. Park Add MS 40625.

Cambridge University Library, Langley MS A 1.1. Lakenheath E DC 7/15/II. Winslow MS Dd 7 22.

Dorset Record Office, Gillingham D4/55/1.

Essex Record Office, Ingatestone D/DP M5−8. Abbess Roothing D/DH/ 1382− 1484.

Holkham Hall, Wells Bundle 2 nos 2−13. The Holkham material is on microfilm at the University of Michigan, Harlan Hatcher Graduate Library.

Norfolk Record Office, Hindolvestone DCN 4814, 4869. Horsham St Faith 19495−19507, 1245. Salle 2605/1−5. Gymingham, 5741−91. Newton 5065, 5074. Heacham DC 1.

Public Record Office, Brightwalton SC2 153−69. Dunmow SC2 171/63.

Suffolk Record Office, South Elmham HA 12/C2/23−25. Westwood HA 30/369/390. Flixton HA 12/C3/2.

7 Women, children and poverty in Florence at the time of the Black Death*

John Henderson

1 INTRODUCTION

> In addition to the sons, the grandsons and all others born of our blood
> should be regarded as useful [members of the *famiglia*]. At the begin-
> ning, a house is whole in itself. . . . But, by giving and receiving spouses
> in legitimate marriage, they gather in, through *parenti* and through the
> love that unites them, a large part of the city. Thus, conjoined by kin-
> ship, men help one another in charity . . . and they give council, favours
> and assistance to one another.[1]

This passage from the *Della vita civile* by the humanist Matteo Palmieri
suggests that the family in mid-fifteenth-century Florence was seen in terms
of a series of concentric circles, which radiated out from the household to
close blood relatives, to the *consorteria* or lineage. Such a broad inclusive
definition has, moreover, important implications for the survival of the
weaker and poorer members of the family, especially those suffering from
the life cycle poverty associated with youth and old age. This is particularly
true for girls and elderly women, whom Palmieri significantly fails to
mention, underlining still further the vulnerability of their position.

Recent books on the family in late medieval and Renaissance Florence
have confirmed contemporary belief in the vital role of the extended family
in providing political and social support to its members.[2] However, because
these studies have been concerned predominantly with patrician lineages,
what remains less clear is how far this sense of kin solidarity went down the
social scale, especially among that substantial sector of society who found it
difficult enough to support their immediate family members, let alone their
relatives. This historiographical bias reflects the nature of surviving
evidence; documentation about the kin networks of patricians is much more
readily available than that concerning the poor.

One important source of information about the family structure of the
lower echelons of society is the Catasto of 1427, detailed tax registers which
enable one to examine the demographic and family systems of the whole of
early fifteenth-century Tuscany. While further evidence is provided to
support Palmieri's concept of family, that many patrician families were

extended, these records suggest that the size and structure of the households of the poor were more restricted. In Florence the average size of the household was 3.8, falling to below three for those in the lower income brackets.[3]

It is sometimes assumed that an important corollary of the fact that the poor had small households is that their kin networks were inadequate to support those in most need. Much more work still needs to be done on how the poor in this period managed to survive. Clearly they were forced to turn to charity to make up the shortfall between their various sources of income and expenditure. What remains unclear is the full extent of the informal charity of neighbourhood and kinship. The relatively high rate of parish endogomy, as measured by the marriage patterns of the Florentine poor,[4] suggests that the family structure as reflected in tax records hides their potential networks of support.

Informal charity, an area which is very difficult to document for the later medieval period, has only recently come under historical scrutiny.[5] More accessible to analysis are the records of the religious fraternities and hospitals which provided the main institutional source of support for the poor. This, of course, raises the wider debate concerning the nature and value of charity in this period. Traditionally it has been suggested that medieval almsgiving was merely symbolic. It aimed, so the argument runs, to help simply the traditional biblical categories of the 'Poor of Christ' rather than the really poor. This begs the question, for while pilgrims, for example, may have been voluntarily poor, widows and orphans – the focus of this chapter – were very much victims of life cycle poverty and remain important objects of modern welfare systems to this day.[6]

This traditional picture has been modified by recent research, but there remains an underlying prejudice among modernists that medieval poor relief was inefficient because it was based on rigid categories. This chapter will examine how far medieval charity really did adapt itself to changing demographic and family systems. In particular, we shall look at female poverty in relation to two phases of the life cycle, children as orphans and elderly widows.

Evidence will be drawn from fourteenth-century Florence, which came to foster an enviable reputation among contemporaries as a model for poor relief, not only in other parts of Italy but as far afield as England.[7] This chapter will concentrate on the decades surrounding the Black Death in order to discover whether late medieval charity might have been characterized by some of the features usually regarded as more typical of the early modern period: the close relationship between private charity and the state and the adaptability of institutional poor relief. The main source of information about poor relief will be the records of what became the single most affluent charitable institution in mid-fourteenth-century Florence, a religious fraternity of laymen called the company of the Madonna of Orsanmichele.

While the underlying theme of this chapter is by definition institutional, our main emphasis will be on the poor themselves, for only in this way can we begin to approach the thorny problem of separating poverty from charity, in other words discovering how far the clients of charitable institutions really did represent the poor rather than, as has been argued, just the prejudices and predelictions of benefactors and canon lawyers.

Two separate periods have been chosen for analysis: 1324–5 and 1350–6. The first will enable us to establish a typology of poverty in a period before the Black Death, when the cost of living was quite high but prices remained relatively stable. The second period provides data to explore the effects on the poor of the Black Death, one of the worst mortality crises Europe has ever suffered. We shall preface these main sections by comparing both the population levels and standards of living in the city before and after the Great Plague and thus by implication summarizing the effects of this epidemic on Florentine society.

2   POPULATION AND STANDARDS OF LIVING BEFORE AND AFTER THE BLACK DEATH

The demographic profile of Florence in the first half of the fourteenth century remains shadowy because of the lack of any surviving comprehensive fiscal survey.[8] However, the picture which emerges from the surviving records suggests that Florence followed a similar development to other parts of Europe. The population saw a gradual increase from the late twelfth century which speeded up in the second half of the thirteenth century, the city achieving its maximum density around 1300, with about 110,000 inhabitants. Over the subsequent forty years population growth slowed and, after taking into account the impact of famines and epidemics between 1340 and 1347, on the eve of the Black Death Florence contained somewhere in the region of 90–95,000 inhabitants.[9]

In common with much of Europe, Florence then lost between a half and two-thirds of its population. According to the first reasonably reliable source following the plague, a hearth tax of 1352, the city now numbered about 42,000. The following fifty years saw an initial rapid growth through the arrival of large numbers of immigrants, but the recurrence of epidemics almost every decade led the population to stabilize at around 50–60,000.[10]

With this general demographic picture in mind, we will turn to standards of living. Figure 7.1 presents nominal wages for workers in the Florentine construction industry between 1310 and 1399 and the price of wheat in the same period.[11] The lowest two cycles represent nominal wages for skilled and unskilled workers in the construction industry, although unfortunately the earlier decades are presented in a very schematic form due to the method of data collection. The third cycle calculates the price of wheat, which is the only available price series to cover the whole period. Although wheat was, of course, not the only foodstuff consumed by a fourteenth-century Florentine, it was the main staple and therefore can be taken as some measure of the cost-of-living index.

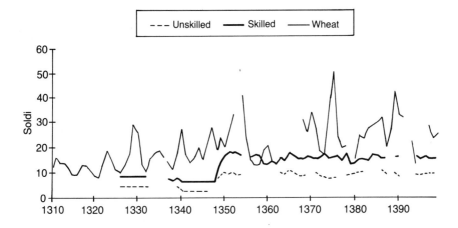

Figure 7.1 Daily wages of construction workers and price of a bushel of wheat in Florence, 1310–99 (*Soldi di piccioli*)

Sources: C. de La Roncière, *Prix et salaires à Florence au XIVe siècle, 1280–1380*, Rome: Ecole Française de Rome 1982, pp. 280, 326, 821; R.A. Goldthwaite, *The Building of Renaissance Florence. An Economic and Social History*, Baltimore, Md.: Johns Hopkins University Press 1980, pp. 436–7.

In the period leading up to the Black Death there was a gradual rise in the price of wheat, with a number of peaks corresponding to a series of grain shortages. The highest represented here was in 1329, although by far the worst was in spring 1347, when the city experienced near famine conditions, and the price of grain rose to more than 60s. a bushel, over three times the normal level.[12] In the same period there was a fall in wages, especially during the decades preceding the Black Death; the average wage of an unskilled labourer dropped from 4s. 6d. in the years 1326–31 to 2s. 7d. in 1340–6 (see Table 7.1).[13]

In an attempt to produce a more accurate account of changes in standards of living, Charles de La Roncière created a model budget for both a family of four and a bachelor to include food, clothing, rent and even working tools. This model he then placed against the fluctuating level of wages. Before the Black Death even the skilled mason who had a family to support could hardly meet this budget and during the 1340s fell well below subsistence to the level of the unskilled labourer who was never able to meet more than half his expenses (see Table 7.1).

Despite the tragic consequences of the Black Death and subsequent epidemics for individuals and families, the high mortality – especially that

Table 7.1 Monthly budget and wages of skilled and unskilled workers in Florentine construction industry, 1289–1360

	1289–93	*1326–32*	*1340–7*	*1350–60*
1 Monthly budget (*soldi*)				
a Bachelor				
Food	35.0	64.0	71.0	90.0
Lodging, clothing, etc.	8.0	14.0	13.0	17.0
Total	43.0	78.0	84.0	107.0
(Wheat as per cent of total)	30.0	39.0	38.0	31.8
b Family of four				
Food	83.0	147.0	168.0	202.0
Lodging, clothing, etc.	16.0	30.0	29.0	39.0
Total	99.0	177.0	197.0	241.0
(Wheat as per cent of total)	32.0	42.0	41.0	35.4
2 Wages (*soldi* and *denari*)				
a Daily				
Labourer	2.4	4.6	2.7	9.2
Skilled	4.8	8.6	6.4	17.3
b Monthly (21 days a month)				
Labourer	50.0	97.0	57.0	193.2
Skilled	100.0	181.0	134.0	363.3

Source: C. de La Roncière, *Prix et salaires à Florence au XIVe siècle, 1280–1380*, Rome: École Française de Rome 1982, pp. 280, 326, 394–5.

of 1348 – had immediately beneficial results on the standards of living for survivors. The drastic drop in the population led to an increased demand for labour, resulting in the doubling of wages, as can be seen from Figure 7.1. By 1351 daily wages for skilled labourers rose to over 18s., compared with those before the Black Death which climbed no higher than 9s. and in the 1340s fell as low as 6.5s. The same picture is true of unskilled labourers, who had earned an average of 4.4s. a day in the 1340s and now earned 10s. At the same time the cost of many staple products rose, due partly to shortages and partly to the increase of indirect taxes. This was reflected by the price of wheat, which for the seven years following the Black Death averaged at the relatively high level of 26s. Even in these circumstances the typical Florentine was much better off because rises in the cost of wheat were much lower than the rises in wage levels. Therefore the mason was now able to earn a 66 per cent surplus to the basic requirements of his family and the unskilled labourer could manage to cover 80 per cent.

With this general demographic and economic picture in mind, it is now possible to assess more clearly Orsanmichele's contribution to poor relief and the extent to which the confraternity came to adapt its policy according to the changing circumstances of the poor.

3 ATTRIBUTES OF THE POOR IN NON-CRISIS YEARS: THE 1320s

The bulk of Orsanmichele's charitable budget was directed to a carefully controlled category, who were subsidized under a system called the *limosina per la città*, 'charity throughout the city'.[14] These people were chosen by the company's almoners who toured the city every four months in search of people in particular need. The maximum any individual might receive each month was 5s., which in the 1320s was equivalent to about one day's work for an unskilled labourer. The only larger sums were the 10s. paid to women in childbed (*una donna in parto*) or to men to be released from the debtors' prison of the Stinche, but these were always one-off payments. The policy of the company was evidently to meet an individual's short-term rather than long-term needs, and although the sums were relatively small, the poor evidently found them worth collecting as one among many strategies of survival.

This system involved the disbursal of quite considerable sums of money: already by the mid-1320s the company spent about £3,500 per annum, which was almost double the charitable budget of the commune itself.[15] The provision of large sums led to the necessity for careful accounting and the statutes insisted on officials making a precise description of recipients of alms to include name, street or parish of residence and the reason they required assistance, as in the case of 'Monna Dada, wife of Martino, lodger of Neri del Giudice; in childbed, extremely poor, in the Parish of S. Michele Visdomini'.[16]

The attributes of those people in receipt of relief in the four-month period from October 1324 to January 1325 are summarized in Table 7.2. To avoid confusion it should be pointed out that each category was not exclusive, which explains why the columns do not add up to 100 per cent. An individual pauper might be given money for a number of reasons and therefore be counted simultaneously under more than one heading, as, for example, being described as poor, sick and widowed.

Two general observations about Orsanmichele's clientele can be made before descending to the particular. The first is that over this four-month period 1,640 nominative alms were distributed, which suggests that if this period was representative, about 5,000 alms would have been handed out over the year.[17] Second, in common with most other relief agencies in pre-industrial Europe, females received a higher percentage of Orsanmichele's charity than males: 72 per cent. In other words, an average of about 3,600 women and girls would have been given alms over the course of the year and 1,400 men and boys.

Table 7.2 shows that males and females were given alms for similar

Table 7.2   Characteristics of Orsanmichele's clientele, October 1324 to January 1325*

Reason for support	Female Month		Male Months Oct. – Jan. (%)
	Oct. (%)	*Jan. (%)*	
With children	42	44	46
Poor	27	19	25
Sick	52	20	42
Orphan	1	1	2
Old	—	—	2
Widowed	13	16	—
Shame-faced	6	—	5
In childbed	12	16	—

Note: *Columns do not add up to 100 per cent because some clients appear in more than one category.

Source: OSM 248.

reasons, although men were never identified as widowers. A substantial number of their clients were described as sick or poor and the majority (see Table 7.3) represented a household with a higher than average number of children. Orsanmichele's concern for poor families was underlined by the provision of double the normal subsidy to women in childbed. This would obviously have interrupted temporarily the household economy, as these women would not have worked.

After physical disability – of which 'sickness' was the most common – the main reason for men and women receiving aid was that they represented a household containing children: 42 to 44 per cent of females and 46 per cent of males. To look at this phenomenon in more detail Table 7.3 sets out the distribution of children per household.

Although there is no reliable guide to household size in pre-Black Death Florence, the average household size in nearby Prato in 1339 was 3.9.[18] If we assume that the conjugal unit was the most common residential unit in Florence in 1325, the average household would have contained two adults and two children. But the captains of Orsanmichele concentrated on families with a larger than average number of children (3.8), thus probably containing five to six people. This would have been considerably higher than the proportion of households of that size in the population of Florence at large, and even more so among the poorer levels of society, who tended to live in smaller residential units.[19]

If an important feature of Orsanmichele's policy in 1324–5 was to provide subsidies to those with larger than average conjugal units, they also showed concern to help single women and men, and especially widows. Table 7.4 analyses the marital status of the poor helped by the company in January 1325. After married women, widows at 16 per cent were the largest

Table 7.3 Orsanmichele's clientele: number of children per household, January 1325

No. of children per household	No. of households	%
1	6	2.7
2	14	6.3
3	57	25.5
4	60	26.8
5	30	13.4
6	29	13.0
7	18	8.0
8	6	2.7
9	3	1.3
10	1	0.5
Total	224	100

Source: OSM 248.

Table 7.4 Marital status of Orsanmichele's clientele, January 1325

	Females		Males	
	N	%	N	%
1 Adults				
a Unknown	—	—	189	93.6
b Ever-married				
Monna or Donna[1]	240	69.2	—	—
Widow[2]	57	16.4	—	—
Subtotal	297	85.6	189	93.6
c Presumed single				
Religious	3	0.9	—	—
Christian name[3]	32	9.2	—	—
Subtotal	35	10.1	—	—
2 Children				
Daughter/son	5	1.4	3	1.5
Father dead/orphan	4	1.2	4	2.0
Girl/boy	5	1.4	6	3.0
Young person	1	0.3	—	—
Subtotal	15	4.3	13	6.4
Total	347	100.0	202	100.0

Notes: [1] Of whom in childbed: 48.
[2] Of whom in childbed: 3.
[3] Of whom in childbed: 3.

Source: OSM 248.

single category of females helped by Orsanmichele. This figure was probably roughly the same as or slightly less than the proportion of widowed
heads of household in Florence as a whole in this period. In, for example,
the contemporary Pratese tax known as the 'Lira', 19.1 per cent of heads of
household were women, although not all were widows. Orsanmichele's
records give little specific information concerning the age of the widows,
although up to half may have been relatively young, since twenty-five of the
fifty-seven were described as having young children in their care and three
more were in childbed. The incidence of widowhood was much more common for women during early adulthood than it was for men, given the
normal age gap between spouses of ten to twelve years and the greater likelihood of remarriage for men than women.[20]

Whether young or old, widows from the lower levels of society were
particularly vulnerable, especially when elderly and infirm. For the more
affluent, a woman who had been widowed was likely to have been provided
with some protection through her dowry. On the death of her husband the
dowry was in theory returned to her family, who then felt some obligation
to support her for the rest of her life.[21] There was not such a simple solution
for the widow who came from a poor background; she might have faced the
real threat of indigence on the death of her husband. Even if her partner
had not already spent her dowry, there was no guarantee that she herself
would obtain it immediately. There are numerous instances of the
husband's family only returning the dowry after lengthy and expensive legal
proceedings or other cases when the individual's own relatives opted to
retain the capital to reinvest in the marriage of a younger sister.[22]

Even if the recent historiography on the position of women in late
medieval Italy has tended to concentrate on those records which provide
evidence for their misery rather than how they might have managed to
survive through work or the informal support of family and neighbours, the
economic hardship experienced by many of these women is evident. The
earning capacity of women was much lower than that of men and their legal
rights were very restricted. Furthermore, contemporaries made it clear that
women living alone were regarded with suspicion as attracting potential dis-
honour to their family.[23] If this was the case for the widow, how much more
true it must have been for the unmarried woman or girl. Indeed, the next
most sizeable category identified by Orsanmichele's captains as in need of
support were women who are presumed to have been single because they
were identified simply by their Christian name. Once again an important
qualification for receiving aid was that they had children in their care. The
twelve girls in this case may have been sisters or maiden aunts, who had
been left with the responsibility of looking after young relatives on the
decease of parents, as in the pathetic case of the Tertiary La Prima, who
was described as being in manifest need as she was blind and had two
children in her care.[24] Some of these women may also have been unmarried
mothers. Three were in childbed, as in the case of 'Brunetta, who is in

great necessity, from Sant'Orsola, in childbed, [from the] parish of San Lorenzo'.[25]

The smallest category of Orsanmichele's clients were children by themselves: female 4.3 per cent and male 6.4 per cent. Their dire position was obvious, as in the case of an entry which by its very baldness indicates the plight of this anonymous girl: 'A poor girl, sick, without a father, had one shilling'.[26] Slightly older girls considering marriage were also placed in an invidious position if their fathers died leaving them without a dowry. Orsanmichele stepped in to provide at least a contribution, as in the case of 'Giovanna, daughter of the apothecary Masi, deceased, who died in the prison of the Stinche in debt; help towards [buying] a gown and to marry her . . . 25 shillings'.[27]

These examples suggest that there was much poverty among both larger families and widows in early Trecento Florence, even before standards of living dropped dramatically during the epidemics and dearths of the following two decades. Many of these individuals receiving relief, either on their own behalf or for their family, were suffering from the life cycle poverty familiar from studies of the indigent from the middle ages to the present day. What seems to distinguish the clientele of Orsanmichele is the vulnerability of not just the disadvantaged solitaries, especially widows, but also the large number of households with two or more children.

In short, Orsanmichele's records reveal that the alms provided by the captains, though limited, did respond to real cases of indigence. The argument which is sometimes advanced that medieval charity failed to help in relieving poverty because it concentrated on women and children misses the point. Evidently religious and economic categories coincided. However, we should not allow the highly feminized nature of Orsanmichele's clientele in the 1320s to lead us to assume that the captains therefore entirely ignored the working poor. As we have seen, the vast majority of women given alms by Orsanmichele were married and had children. This suggests that it was regarded as the women's job to collect alms, as can be seen in the case of the money given to 'Monna Vanna and Meo, wife and husband, sick, from Lucca, lodger of Bianciardo in Borgo S. Lorenzo, 5s.'[28]

We shall now turn to the early 1350s to discover whether the company modified its policies to deal with the very different demographic and social regime which prevailed in Florence in the years immediately following the Black Death. If charity had been merely symbolic, there would have been little change in the way the confraternity distributed the bulk of its alms.

4 THE POOR AFTER THE BLACK DEATH

In the introduction to this chapter we outlined the immediate effects of the Black Death on Florence: the dramatic reduction of the population by between a third and a half, the doubling of wages through the shortage of labour and the consequent rise in the standard of living for most of those who survived the plague. Even with this striking improvement in the finances of many Florentines, the Black Death had a considerable impact on the structure of the family, leaving some – and particularly women – in precarious economic circumstances.

It is a topos of contemporary chronicles that families were disrupted during the plague: 'Son abandoned father, husband wife and wife husband, one brother the other, one sister the other.'[29] Even if this picture of a dissolving social fabric is exaggerated, the Black Death did cause untold disruption of family life by the sudden death of heads of households, who left their wives and offspring without adequate means of support. Furthermore, many survivors became involved in court cases to claim their inheritances which proved difficult to obtain as a result of challenges from other interested parties or the intestacy of relatives.[30]

There were two particular groups of society whom contemporaries saw as having fallen victim to confusion over inheritance: orphaned minors and widows. Their position was eloquently described in a law of 29 August 1348:[31]

> the aforesaid minors and women are found and remain deprived of care, of their necessities and sustenance. . . . And who will not pity such youth? who will console the weakness of their sex? and who will nourish a tranquil and peaceful marriage?

While this emotive statement could be interpreted as simply a continuation of traditional evangelical approaches to poverty, evidence from other Italian cities (Orvieto and Siena) suggests that governments were concerned by the wider implications of the plague's decimation of the family, and in particular the necessity for communal action to protect the rights of orphans and widows, the majority of whom had no legal personality. This meant that they could not in law own property and required male relatives or representatives to witness official documents; it was precisely these 'false friends' who are reputed to have deprived them of their 'sustenance'.[32] The concern of the Florentine commune went further than rhetoric and the company of Orsanmichele was seen as vital to government policy. The captains of Orsanmichele were instructed to give minors and widows a substantial proportion of all the money received by the confraternity from the liquidation of its considerable inheritance during the Black Death.[33]

The necessity to administer these very substantial sums led to the emergence of a two-tier system for the distribution of charitable funds. In the long term the *limosina per la città* remained an important feature, but in the short term larger sums were provided as 'sealed alms' (*limosine suggellate*), payments authorized directly by the captains rather than deputed through almoners.

There were two main features of this new system which distinguished it from those in operation before the Black Death. The first was that the confraternity distributed much larger individual sums, reflecting the greatly increased affluence of Orsanmichele. In November 1350, for example, the average donation was £15, equivalent to twenty days' wages for an unskilled labourer, rising to £23 in 1351, compared with 5s. to 10s. three years earlier.[34]

Second, partly following their own tradition and partly in response to government pressure, females received an even higher proportion of alms, on average 90 per cent. This increased feminization of charity may be seen, on the one hand, as a response to the greater vulnerability of females after the disruption of the plague. On the other hand, it can be seen as an unprecedented official intervention in the life of the Florentine family for most of the money went to fund dowries, which between 1350–2 accounted for 62–72 per cent of the company's charitable budget. The amounts given to individual girls were much more substantial than they had been before the Black Death – £14 to £24 compared with only 10s. Orsanmichele now provided a significant rather than a merely symbolic contribution to a dowry. However, very few payments were made to dower girls to enter a convent. Whether or not this was a deliberate company policy or reflected a drop in the number of people wanting to join religious orders after the plague remains unclear at the present state of research.

This emphasis on the marriage market would certainly have been encouraged by a government which wished to repopulate the city after the high mortality caused by the epidemics and severe dearths of the previous decade. There would have been some urgency if, in common with other epidemics of 'plague' in Trecento Florence, a large number of deaths during the Black Death occurred among children, the parents of future generations.[35] Furthermore, it was precisely this section of society which was most vulnerable after the Black Death, having been deprived of support by the disruption of their rightful inheritance.

While the increase in nuptiality can be seen as part of a government policy, we must not underplay the desire of young couples to get married, as is attested by contemporary chroniclers such as Matteo Villani.[36] Marriage may have been facilitated for some by early inheritance through the death of their parents, making them economically independent at an earlier age than usual, but this was far from a universal pattern.

The higher number of people seeking partners led to a greater demand for dowries, a demand which the captains of Orsanmichele, following the directives of government, were able to meet for a significant number of girls following the Black Death. Although it is impossible to say exactly how many girls did receive dowries from the company, if we extrapolate from the surviving records, Orsanmichele could have provided contributions for *circa* 1,300 dowries between 1350 and 1352. Even taking into account that some of these girls may have been from the countryside, Orsanmichele may have partly funded up to 20 per cent of all marriages in the city during these years, if the surviving records are representative.[37]

One group of the population which may have been affected adversely by the tendency of men to marry younger were women who had been widowed during the plague. Not only did young men look for spouses earlier, but older widowers apparently sought younger, more fertile partners. We know little in this period about attitudes towards remarriage, but the records of Orsanmichele suggest that charities underlined the general tendency of Florentine society to discourage remarriage by providing dowries to girls who had not previously been married rather than to widows.

Although the elderly in general and widows in particular may not have benefited from the way Orsanmichele distributed these larger sums, they did from the traditional city-wide *limosina per la città*. Table 7.5 shows that nearly 30 per cent of female recipients were described as either widowed or elderly. Given that most elderly women had lost their husbands, these figures suggest that the rate of widowhood among Orsanmichele's clientele was double that of thirty years earlier. The support to elderly women is part of a wider phenomenon, the even greater emphasis on female clients by spring 1356. In March and April, they received 78 per cent of the 1,465 nominative alms and in the whole period (October 1356 to May 1357) the proportion rose as high as 85 per cent, up to 20 per cent more than the mid-1320s. Once again just less than half of women had children, some of whom may have represented the households whose formation had been facilitated by Orsanmichele through the provision of dowries and marriage subsidies.

Table 7.5 Characteristics of Orsanmichele's clientele, March and April 1356*

Reason for support	Females		Males	
	N	%	N	%
With children	442	43.0	77	26.0
Poor	3	0.3	7	2.3
Sick	165	16.0	110	36.9
Orphan	94	9.1	57	19.1
Old	239	23.1	52	17.4
Widowed	58	5.6	—	—
Shame-faced	—	—	1	0.3
In childbed	21	1.4	—	—

Note: * Columns do not add up to 100 per cent because some people appear in more than one category.

Source: OSM 254.

Table 7.6 develops this point further by relating the frequency of help to both sexes to the number of children per household. The average number of children per household was 3.8, exactly the same as thirty years earlier. At first sight this result seems curious considering the devastation suffered by families during the Black Death. But looking more closely at the distribution of households with children shows that families were on average much smaller in 1356 than in 1325: the number of women with one to five children had risen from 75 to 86 per cent, and consequently those with six to ten children had shrunk from 25 to 14 per cent (see Table 7.6). More specifically, those families with only two children were now 21 per cent of the total, about 15 per cent more than thirty years earlier, and almost 50 per cent of these clients had three or fewer children, compared with 35 per cent in 1325.

Table 7.6 Orsanmichele's clientele: number of children per household, March and April 1356

No. of children per household	No. of households	
	N	%
1	2	0.4
2	110	21.2
3	144	27.7
4	115	22.1
5	78	15.0
6	51	9.8
7	15	2.9
8	4	0.7
9	—	—
10	1	0.2
Total	520	100

Source: OSM 254.

This preponderance of smaller family units suggests that the captains of Orsanmichele were responding to the new demographic regime following the Black Death. Many of these children may have belonged to couples who had married during the years immediately following the great plague, helped by inheritance or the contributions from charitable institutions. If this was the case, these children would have been young, and although there is little quantitative data available for the effect on the Florentine population of the presumed rise in nuptiality following the Black Death, it is possible to assess the effect of the same phenomenon on the city of Prato eight years after the epidemic of 1363: by 1371–2, 38 per cent of the population were children less than 8 years old compared with 23 per cent in Florence in 1427. While this represents a response of older cohorts to replace the exceptionally large number of children who had died in what has been called the 'children's plague' of 1363, there would have been a similar rise in fertility in Florence following the Black Death.[38]

Orsanmichele's support of the nuclear family also becomes clear when examining the marital status of the company's clients in 1356 (see Table 7.7). As in January 1325, the highest proportion of charity went to ever-married women, although there was a marked bias towards those whose spouses were alive rather than dead. This reduction in the proportion of widows receiving support from 16 per cent in 1325 to 6 per cent may be more imagined than real because, as seen in Table 7.5 (p. 172), the company did seek to help the elderly: in 1356, 23 per cent of their female clients were described as 'old' and another 6 per cent widowed, compared with no elderly thirty years earlier. There was also a much higher number of elderly men receiving help than in 1324–5 (17 against 2 per cent).

Table 7.7 Marital status of Orsanmichele's clientele, March and April 1356

	Females		*Males*	
	N	%	N	%
1 Adults				
a Unknown	0	—	152	51.0
b Ever-married	—	—	77	25.8[1]
Monna or Donna[2]	661	63.8	—	—
Widow	58	5.6	—	—
Subtotal	719	69.4	229	76.8
c Presumed single				
Religious	10	1.0	1	0.3
Christian name	212	20.5	0	—
Subtotal	222	21.5	1	0.3
2 Children				
Daughter/son	0	—	0	—
Father dead/orphan	95	9.2	60	20.1
Girl/boy	0	—	8	2.7
Young person	0	—	0	—
Subtotal	95	9.2	68	22.8
Total	1,036	100.0	298	100.0

Notes: [1] With children.
       [2] Of whom in childbed: 18.

Source: OSM 254.

In addition to the company's interest in the elderly, the captains were concerned about the young, and orphans in particular. Whereas few children had been given alms in 1324–5 (4 to 6 per cent), now 9 per cent of females were helped because they had been orphaned and about 20 per cent of males. This was a good seven years after the Black Death, reflecting the longer-term consequences of the massive mortality in 1348 on the Florentine social structure. An attempt to mitigate the effects of this disruption was also evident in the company's concern for unmarried women, whose share of alms had doubled since 1324–5 from 10 to 22 per cent. Only one in three of these women was described as 'old', suggesting that in this case the company was concentrating on younger or middle-aged spinsters. They may have been left even more unprotected by the Black Death if their close male relatives had died during the plague, especially given Florentine suspicion of unmarried women living on their own. Some of these women may have been adolescents who had been left bereft by the death of their parents, and a quarter had the additional burden of younger brothers and sisters in their care.

These examples of the charity provided by Orsanmichele during the 1350s underline the confraternity's continued commitment to contributing to the budget of the poor during the decade following the Black Death, and in particular to female casualties of the life cycle. The financial standing of single women, whether orphaned or widowed, was clearly a special cause for concern. The difficulty comes when attempting to calculate what proportion of the city's population might have been helped by the captains in these years. Orsanmichele's fragmentary records mean that our answer is bound to be speculative. When discussing the company's policy in the early 1350s, we suggested that Orsanmichele may have contributed to the dowries of up to 20 per cent of girls getting married in Florence between 1350 and 1352, assuming (and this is a big assumption) that dowries were provided at the same rate during the periods when the records are missing.

Orsanmichele's female clientele also benefited most from the company's city-wide charity. They received 81 per cent of the 4,250 alms provided by the company to named individuals in the first six months of 1357, representing 1,721 subsidies if each one had been helped twice. Given a population of about 42,000 and a sex ratio of 118, there would have been about 19,270 women in Florence in the early 1350s. Excluding children, who had always represented a small percentage of female clientele under this system (see Tables 7.4 and 7.7, pp. 167 and 174), the 1,567 adult females helped by Orsanmichele represented about 14 per cent of Florentine women aged 15 and over and even more if a greater number received only one subsidy.[39]

5 CONCLUSION

The poor relief provided by the company of Orsanmichele during the twelve years following the Black Death changed in a number of significant ways in response to the new social and economic conditions. The first new characteristic was greater specialization in almsgiving, the beginning of a trend shared by many poor relief agencies throughout Italy in the second half of the fourteenth century. Specialization was a direct response to high mortality: the scale of poverty had been reduced drastically so that poor relief administrators could now concentrate on select categories of the poor rather than seeking to spread their charity over a wide range of paupers. The second major new feature of Orsanmichele's almsgiving was its increased feminization, which reflected the concerns of contemporaries. The moralist Paolo da Certaldo, for example, advised that charity should be given 'rather to women, widows, or to young girls who do not have a dowry rather than to men'.[40] The concentration on females reflects the greater legal and financial vulnerability of young and old women alike during the years following the Black Death. They were unable to defend themselves personally in court and the employment of male representatives meant that at worst they were cheated by 'false friends', and at best unable to control the minutiae of their bequests. Orphans and widows were those whom contemporaries saw as suffering most among the survivors of the Black Death, and it was the former in particular who benefited from the confraternity's large contributions towards dowries.

If Orsanmichele's provision of dowries on such a lavish scale may have been a short-term consequence of the confraternity's enrichment in 1348, in the 1350s other changes were made to the traditional system of city-wide charity to take into account the social and demographic impact of high mortality. Three main characteristics of Orsanmichele's clientele in the mid-1350s reflect the longer-term consequences of the Black Death. The first was the concentration on the elderly and particularly widows, impoverished through the death of the male head of household and members of their kin networks who might normally have provided them with informal relief. The second feature, the increase in the number of orphans, would also have been caused by the same financial circumstances as the rise in the number of elderly clients. Third, there was a change in the size of the average family helped by Orsanmichele. While the single most important reason for a family to receive aid was still their possession of a larger than average number of children, Orsanmichele's clientele now had significantly smaller families: 50 per cent had three children or less in 1355–6 compared with only 35 per cent in 1325.

Behind some of the major changes in the confraternity's poor relief lay government responses to the social and economic climate after the Black Death, underlining the close connection between public and private charity. The regimes which ran the Florentine commune in this period had a self-conscious policy to repopulate the city. The best-known measure was the encouragement of *contadini* to settle in Florence, thus enabling the city to maintain fairly stable population levels, despite repeated outbreaks of epidemic disease.[41] The second measure, the effect of which is more difficult to calculate, was financial encouragement to young couples to create new household units through marriage. The provision of dowries through the medium of Orsanmichele was obviously an important part of this policy, taking advantage of the confraternity's inheritance during the great plague.

Thus the records of an institution such as Orsanmichele suggest that the larger late medieval charities did change their policy in accordance with shifts in the typology of poverty, which in themselves reflected changes in the social, demographic and economic circumstances. Furthermore, despite traditional interpretations of medieval charity as merely symbolic, we have shown that the really indigent lay behind the evangelical categories of the poor. Even before the Black Death these were young and elderly victims of life cycle poverty – orphans and widows – and only to a lesser extent the households of the working poor for whom women appeared as the main recipients of alms.

NOTES

* This chapter summarizes the findings of two sections of my forthcoming book *Piety and Charity in Late Medieval Florence*, Oxford: Clarendon Press 1994, chs 7–8. I am grateful to Oxford University Press for giving me permission to publish these findings here. All manuscripts, unless otherwise stated, are in the Archivio di Stato di Firenze.

1 M. Palmieri, *Della vita civile*, Milan: G. Silvestri 1825, p. 222, as cited in D. Herlihy and C. Klapisch-Zuber, *Tuscans and Their Families. A Study of the Florentine Catasto of 1427*, New Haven, Conn. and London: Yale University Press 1985, p. 353.

2 Recent studies include: R.A. Goldthwaite, *Private Wealth in Renaissance Florence. A Study of Four Families*, Princeton, NJ: Princeton University Press 1968; F.W. Kent, *Household and Lineage in Renaissance Florence. The Family Life of the Capponi, Ginori and Rucellai*, Princeton, NJ: Princeton University Press 1977; D.V. Kent, *The Rise of the Medici. Faction in Florence, 1426–1434*, Oxford: Oxford University Press 1978; C. Lansing, *The Florentine Magnates. Lineage and Faction in a Medieval Commune*, Princeton, NJ: Princeton University Press 1991.

3 Herlihy and Klapisch-Zuber, *Tuscans and Their Families*, ch. 10 and esp. pp. 319–25.

4 See Philip Gavitt's contribution to this volume, Chapter 3; S.K. Cohn Jr, *The Laboring Classes of Renaissance Florence*, New York and London: Academic Press 1980, p. 38.

5 See C. Klapisch-Zuber, *Women, Family and Ritual in Renaissance Florence*, Chicago, Ill.: Chicago University Press 1985, ch. 4; F.W. and D.V. Kent, *Neighbours and Neighbourhood in Renaissance Florence. The District of the Red Lion in the Fifteenth Century*, Locust Valley, NY: J.J. Augustin 1982; and J. Henderson, 'The parish and the poor in Florence at the time of the Black Death: The case of S. Frediano', in J. Henderson (ed.), *Charity and the Poor in Medieval and Renaissance Europe*, in *Continuity and Change*, 3, 1988, pp. 247–72.

6 For a discussion of this point see: B. Tierney, *Medieval Poor Law. A Sketch of Canonical Theory and its Application in England*, Berkeley and Los Angeles, Calif.: University of California Press 1959, ch. 3. More recently on the nature of medieval charity: C. Lis and H. Soly, *Poverty and Capitalism in Pre-Industrial Europe*, Brighton: Harvester Press 1983 edn, chs 1–2; B. Geremek, *La pietà e la forca. Storia della miseria e della carità in Europa*, Rome and Bari: La Terza 1986, ch. 1.

7 On poor relief in Florence see: C. de La Roncière, 'Pauvres et pauvreté à Florence au XIVe siècle', in M. Mollat (ed.), *Etudes sur l'histoire de la pauvreté*, vol. 2, Paris: La Sorbonne 1974, pp. 661–745; and on the reputation of Florence: J. Henderson, 'The hospitals of late-medieval Florence: A preliminary survey', in L. Granshaw and R. Porter (eds), *The Hospital in History*, London: Routledge 1989, pp. 63–92.

8 For the population of Florence in this period see: C. de La Roncière, *Prix et salaires à Florence au XIVe siècle, 1280–1380*, Rome: École Française de Rome

1982, pp. 625–41; and Herlihy and Klapisch-Zuber, *Tuscans and Their Families*, pp. 67–9.

9 Herlihy and Klapisch-Zuber, *Tuscans and Their Families*, pp. 67–70; La Roncière, *Prix et salaires*, pp. 625–41.

10 Herlihy and Klapisch-Zuber, *Tuscans and Their Families*, p. 69; La Roncière, *Prix et salaires*, pp. 638–40, 674.

11 Data for these series have been derived from La Roncière, *Prix et salaires*, and R.A. Goldthwaite, *The Building of Renaissance Florence. An Economic and Social History*, Baltimore, Md.: Johns Hopkins University Press 1980, pp. 436–9, and *idem*, 'I prezzi del grano a Firenze dal XIV al XVI secolo', *Quaderni storici*, 28, 1975, pp. 32–3.

12 La Roncière, 'Pauvres', pp. 671–85.

13 ibid. The Florentine monetary system was a complex intermeshing of the silver and gold currencies as well as money of account. For the sake of simplicity I have chosen to present all figures in pounds (*lire*), shillings (*soldi*) and pence (*denari*).

14 On these systems see the company's 1333 statutes in Biblioteca Medicea Laurenziana di Firenze, Antinori 29, ch. vi: ff. 6v–7r; and ASF, Capitani di Or S. Michele (henceforth OSM) 248 for names.

15 Calculated from OSM 248; for communal subsidies see R. Davidsohn, *Storia di Firenze*, transl. E. Dupré-Theseider, Florence: Sansoni 1977, vol. v, p. 326.

16 OSM 248, f. 5r (1.x.1324).

17 Calculated from OSM 248.

18 E. Fiumi, *Demografia, movimento urbanistico e classi sociali in Prato dall'età comunale ai tempi moderni*, Biblioteca storica toscana, 14, Florence 1968, p. 72, on Prato.

19 Herlihy and Klapisch-Zuber, *Tuscans and Their Families*, pp. 216–17, 282–3, 286–7, 291–2.

20 Fiumi, *Demografia*, p. 70; cf. Herlihy and Klapisch-Zuber, *Tuscans and Their Families*, p. 301: Table 10.4 for 1427.

21 E.G. Rosenthal, 'The position of women in Renaissance Florence: Neither autonomy nor subjection', in P. Denley and C. Elam (eds), *Florence and Italy. Renaissance Studies in Honour of Nicolai Rubinstein*, London: Westfield Publications in Medieval Studies 1988, pp. 369–82.

22 See Klapisch-Zuber, *Women, Family and Ritual*, ch. 6; and C. Chabot, 'Poverty and the widow in later medieval Florence', in Henderson (ed.), *Charity and the Poor*, pp. 291–311.

23 Klapisch-Zuber, *Women, Family and Ritual*, ch. 6.

24 OSM 248, f. 49v.

25 ibid.: f. 70r.

26 ibid.: f. 59v.

27 ibid.: f. 44v.

28 ibid.: f. 5v.

29 Marco di Coppo Stefani, 'Cronica fiorentina', edited by N. Rodolico, *Rerum Italicarum Scriptores*, new edn, 30.1, Città di Castello: S. Lapi 1903, p. 634.

30 See A.B. Falsini, 'Firenze dopo il 1348. Le consequenze della peste nera', *Archivio Storico Italiano*, 129, 1971, pp. 423–503; and Henderson, *Piety and Charity*, chs 5 and 8.

31 Provvisioni Registri 36, f. 3r: 29.viii.1348, printed in S. La Sorsa, *La compagnia d'Or San Michele ovvero una pagina della beneficenza in Toscana nel secolo XIV*, Trani: V. Vecchi 1902, pp. 229–30.

32 E. Carpentier, *Une ville devant la peste. Orvieto et la peste noire de 1348*, Paris: Ecole Pratique des Hautes Etudes 1962, pp. 146, 190; W.M. Bowsky, 'The impact of the Black Death upon Sienese government and society', *Speculum*, 39, 1964, p. 27.

33 Provv. Reg. 36, f. 3r: 28.viii.1348: La Sorsa, *La compagnia*, pp. 229–30; and Falsini, 'Firenze dopo il 1348', pp. 460–1.
34 See Henderson, *Piety and Charity*, ch. 8 and table 8.3.
35 Herlihy and Klapisch-Zuber, *Tuscans and Their Families*, pp. 205–7, 188.
36 *Cronica di Matteo Villani a miglior lezione ridotta*, Florence: Magheri 1825, I.iv.
37 Calculated from OSM 146 and 252, and for a more detailed discussion of these sources see Henderson, *Piety and Charity*, ch. 8. See E.A. Wrigley and R.S. Schofield, *The Population History of England, 1541–1871. A Reconstruction*, Cambridge: Cambridge University Press 1989 edn, p. 312 for marriage rates and pp. 359–63 for the effect of mortality on nuptiality.
38 Cf. Herlihy and Klapisch-Zuber, *Tuscans and Their Families*, pp. 273–4; P. Slack, *The Impact of Plague in Tudor and Stuart England*, London: Routledge 1985, pp. 181–3. The figure for Florence in 1427 has been calculated from D. Herlihy and C. Klapisch-Zuber, *Les toscans et leur familles. Une étude du catasto Florentin de 1427*, Paris: Editions de l'École des Hautes Etudes en Sciences Sociales 1978, app. 5, table 2, pp. 660–3.
39 Herlihy and Klapisch-Zuber, *Tuscans and Their Families*, p. 157, table 5.4 for the sex ratio in Florence in 1427; and ibid.: p. 187, table 6.6, for overall age distributions in Prato (1371) and Florence (1427). The proportion of females over 14 has been calculated from Herlihy and Klapisch-Zuber, *Les toscans*, app. 5, table 2, pp. 660–3.
40 Paolo da Certaldo, *Il libro di buoni costumi*, edited by A. Schiaffini, Florence: Le Monnier 1945, pp. 149, 162 and 238.
41 La Roncière, *Prix et salaires*, p. 674.

8 The status of widows in sixteenth-century rural Castile

David E. Vassberg

The purpose of this chapter is to take a brief exploratory look at the status of widows living in villages in sixteenth-century Castile. The chapter is based principally upon censuses (*padrones de vecindad*) from the Expedientes de Hacienda section of the Archivo General de Simancas. These censuses were drawn up for fiscal purposes, and the data that they contain is usually limited in scope. But the compilers of *some* censuses included detailed information about the composition and property of each household. Unfortunately, these highly detailed censuses are rare. But those that do exist offer an unparalleled opportunity to examine the demographic and economic characteristics of selected communities throughout the Kingdom of Castile.

WIVES AND WIDOWS BEFORE THE LAW

The *fueros* (basic law codes) of late medieval and early modern Spain placed married women under the legal tutelage of their husbands. Generally speaking, a wife was totally subject to her husband's will and could take no major actions without his consent. The *fueros* envisioned wives as weak beings keeping to their homes and protected by their husbands, hence needing no special legal protection. In a legal sense, widows were much better off than married women: for example, widows were the only women who officially could be family heads (for administrative and fiscal purposes). Widows were permitted to live alone with their children, administering their property and making their own decisions – even to remarry – without the consent of some male relative.[1]

Nevertheless, widows in the Spanish *fueros* were distinctly inferior to men. For example, the *Fuero Real* (introduced by Alfonso X in 1255) obliged widows to wait a full year before remarrying, whereas widowers were not forced into an obligatory period of mourning. And if a widow remarried, she risked losing the guardianship over her children, as well as any property from her first husband's estate. Nevertheless, medieval Spanish law treated the widow as more of a real person than the wife.[2]

In practice, however, economic realities permitted medieval and early modern Spanish women to enjoy far more autonomy than the *fueros* had intended. Municipal ordinances throughout Spain allowed women considerable freedom of action outside the home. Women actively participated in the economic life of the municipalities, even monopolizing numerous trades. This permitted many Spanish women of this period to act quite independently when it came to handling their property. But women with a profession – in the sixteenth century as today – were expected to continue to fulfil their role in the household. Thus their work load may have actually *increased*, and this factor must be weighed against their enhanced economic freedom.[3]

The medieval rural woman had an important role in the formation of family property holdings, through her dowry and *arras*, a gift from the husband to his bride. The *arras* were considered to be a type of widow's insurance, and were used even by families with meagre resources. In theory, the *arras* were supposed to represent at least one-tenth of the bridegroom's net worth, and sometimes went as high as one-half. But the actual value of the *arras* varied greatly, according to regional customs and the economic and social status of the family. The medieval Spanish *fueros* stipulated that the *arras* were to be maintained intact during the lifetime of the husband. But a widow was legally entitled to use them, so long as she did not remarry. In that case, the *arras* were passed down to the children from the former marriage or returned to the former husband's family, if the marriage had been childless.[4]

The wife's dowry (Spanish *dote*) was deposited under the care of her husband or her father-in-law, whoever was the official head of the household.[5] The value of the dowry depended upon local tradition and family standing. According to the noted early seventeenth-century writer, Barbón y Castañeda, the typical dowry in Castilian villages in the late 1500s was 'a donkey and 4 or 5 head of cattle'.[6] But the dowry could include any type of property. So long as the wife's husband remained alive, her dowry remained under male control, although the wife might be assigned an allowance (*alimentos*) from the dowry. But Spanish law provided that the property brought by each spouse to the marriage should be kept legally separate. This applied to the dowry as well as to the *arras* and to other parental gifts. The reason for this legal separation was to permit the property to be returned to the family of a spouse who died, if the marriage had produced no children to inherit it. The underlying principle was that the property of a family line should be protected, to prevent it from leaving the family where it belonged.[7]

In sum, the married woman had legal ownership of her *arras* and her dowry, as well as one-half of any community property (*gananciales*) acquired during the marriage. But she could not freely dispose of this property, or administer it, until she became a widow. At the moment of widowhood, a woman gained full economic and legal rights over her property, until the day that she remarried, at which point she forfeited her *arras* and her deceased husband's half-interest of their community property.[8] Furthermore, a widow was the trustee (*curadora*) of her dead husband's property during their children's minority, which often gave her considerable economic power.[9]

So long as a widow maintained her own separate household, she could avoid falling under the domination of some male – be it her father, a son or some other relative. By living in her own house, the widow could maintain her independence and self-esteem in a male-dominated and highly misogynistic society. A widow in Spanish society was accorded considerable respect, but was often suspected of neglecting her deceased husband's children. Given these factors, and the frequent lawsuits endured by widows who remarried, it is hardly surprising that most widows were content to remain widows, and that there was a high incidence of widowhood in early modern Spain.[10]

The society of medieval and early modern Spain reserved full political rights for men alone. A person with citizenship in a Spanish town or village was called a *vecino*. It was essential to secure citizenship, because in principle only citizens – that is, *vecinos* – had the right to the communal rights that formed the economic foundation of the lives of most rural inhabitants.[11] Normally, only an adult male property-owner could become a *vecino*. Some places specified that only a married man or a widower with his own separate household could be a *vecino*. And sometimes *vecino* status was limited to those who cultivated land, however small the amount. Women – whether married or widows – were not considered to have *vecino* status, and they could not participate in *concejos abiertos*, or town meetings.[12]

In practice, however, women *were* allowed partial rights of citizenship. Censuses from medieval and early modern Spain show that a substantial minority of rural households were headed by women. Most of these were widows, who had been left at the head of the family productive unit when their spouses died. Since these widows often were left in legal control of the family's property and agro-pastoral operations, they were permitted to continue to enjoy the communitarian rights formerly held by their husbands. The town of Montamarta (Zamora province), for example, specifically allowed widows to participate in the annual allotment of common lands.[13]

Thus, widows occupied an ambiguous position in the socio/administrative life of the Spanish municipalities of the day: although they had no political rights, they were recognized as the heads of households; they controlled property, operated productive enterprises, participated in communal activities and paid taxes. Early modern Spain was too *machista* to accord full equality to widows, but many censuses gave official recognition of their special status by counting each widow as one-half *vecino* in formal rosters of household heads and for purposes of taxation.[14]

THE PROPORTION OF WIDOWS

Spain had a high proportion of widows during the early modern period. A census taken in 1531 in the village of La Serradilla (Cáceres) showed 330 households, of which sixty-eight (or 21 per cent) were headed by widows.[15] There were similar proportions in Alcalá de Guadaira (Seville) in 1484, 1493 and 1519.[16] But it appears that the norm for the sixteenth century was around 15 per cent. This was true of villages in Valladolid and Burgos provinces, as well as Olvera (Cadiz) in 1534[17] and of seven Castilian villages in the 1550s.[18]

Our data from the 1560s suggests a higher proportion of widows, but this is probably merely variation within the norm. A 1561 census of 2,328 households in Piedrahita (Avila) and its surrounding territory (*Tierra*) shows 24 per cent headed by widows,[19] and the proportion of households headed by widows in fourteen Castilian villages in the 1560s averaged 22 per cent. But the range within this last group was from 5 to 41 per cent. The proportion of widow-headed households in eight villages in the 1570s was 16 per cent,[21] while eleven villages in the 1580s averaged 15 per cent widows[22] and nine villages in the 1590s averaged 14 per cent widows.[23]

Why were there so many widows heading households in Spanish rural areas, particularly in comparison[24] with other parts of Europe? Unfortunately, we have no satisfactory answer, although we can venture some guesses. We do know that there was a large disproportion of widows to widowers in rural Spain. A previous study[25] found that widows in Castilian villages were from four to twelve times more numerous than widowers – a much higher disproportion than that in rural England at the same time.[26] One would expect widows to be more numerous than widowers, because wives tended to be younger than their husbands. Furthermore, male mortality may have been higher than that of females, despite the dangers of childbirth, because of male deaths in dangerous work activities and in Spain's imperial adventures during this period.[27] Also, we must remember that widowers could remarry with greater ease than widows. But widowers preferred not to marry widows with children, because the children's inheritance and upbringing might be troublesome. And finally, because of the previously mentioned advantages of widowhood, many widows probably preferred to maintain their independence, rather than to fall again under the domination of a husband.

Nevertheless, there were good reasons for wanting to remarry: emotional fulfilment, need for help with fields and flocks and managing the household, and assistance in rearing small children. Moreover, there is some evidence of social prejudice against single persons living alone, particularly young women or widows.[28] Spanish Golden Age folkloric tales depict the widow as happy to be free from the yoke of matrimony, yet, almost immediately laying plans to remarry, out of economic necessity. The widow's motto, in Golden Age folklore,[29] was 'to weep little, and look for another' (*'llorar poco y buscar otro'*). The stereotype is illuminating, even if it does not represent the norm. Census evidence, in fact, suggests that widows were less likely than widowers to remarry.

Unfortunately, we have no data for the frequency of remarriage in sixteenth-century Spain. But there is ample documentary proof that many widows remarried; some censuses take pains to identify previously married persons, particularly if they had children from earlier marriages. For example, seven out of eighty households in a 1578 census of Poveda de Obispalía (Cuenca) included children from previous marriages.[30] And a 1558 census of Monleón (Salamanca) found that 17 per cent of households with co-resident children had children from at least one previous marriage of one of the spouses;[31] while a 1589 census of Puebla del Príncipe (Ciudad Real) had 20 per cent of households with children from a previous marriage.[32]

WIDOWHOOD IN THE FAMILY CYCLE

The family continuously had to adapt itself to changing conditions. Although the overwhelming majority of sixteenth-century Castilian families were of the nuclear type at any given moment,[33] most families probably became extended at some time in their history, as they felt obliged to take in a relative faced with adverse conditions. This especially concerned orphans,[34] widowed daughters, or elderly parents – particularly widows.[35] In fact, parents expected their offspring to help them in their old age, and might even threaten to disinherit them in favour of a more solicitous niece or cousin if they did not.[36] Thus it is not surprising to find widows living with their children.[37]

Women who were widowed often were obliged to place their children under the care of someone else. Usually this was true because of remarriage, but could also be brought about by economic necessity.[38] The children of widows who remarried were typically sent to live with their paternal grand-parents. But they might be sent to live with some other relative. The willing-ness of peasant families to take in poor relatives may be taken as an indication of family solidarity. But children living with relatives were expected to work, usually without pay. It appears that they were not treated exactly as servants, nor as the household's own children, but somewhere in between.[39]

Widows – and other poor parents – often pushed their children into service in wealthier households. This not only relieved the parents of an economic burden, but also furnished the most impoverished children in society with a type of apprenticeship. This movement of children from poorer to more prosperous households helped preserve a sort of societal equilibrium. It supplied additional workers for the larger farms, and it gave the transferred children the advantage of growing up in households with better living conditions.[40] This caused the wealthier households to swell in size, while the poorer ones shrank, thus accentuating an already-existing positive correlation between household size and wealth.[41]

WIDOWS AND POVERTY

Most widows in medieval and early modern Spain were poor. In fact, the phrase 'poor widow' was employed so frequently in documents of that time that it almost seems to be a single word. Widows in *fueros*, and other legal texts, are viewed as poor, weak and needy because they have lost their husband's protection. However, the idea of feminine poverty may be more related to gender than to economic circumstances, because these same texts do not consider widowers to be automatically 'poor'.[42] Nevertheless, we know that many widows owned little or no property, and that they survived on charity, or by working as domestic servants, or as spinners or weavers. Fiscal censuses usually considered widows to be 'poor', and municipal authorities often assumed that they should not be assessed for a tax contribution. However, many of the 'poor' on fiscal censuses were not totally destitute. Some owned animals, tools or other property, and were included in the 'poor' category on the fiscal census because they *declared* themselves to be poor, and were able to convince the census-takers that they should not pay taxes.[43]

'Poverty' in medieval and early modern Spain referred to a precarious material situation. The state of poverty existed in various degrees, but its typical defining characteristic was a situation in which the individual could not live from rents or accumulated savings, and had to resort to personal labour or some other means of subsistence. Literary, religious and legal texts dealing with individual poverty described it as a situation of dependence and helplessness, especially with reference to the sick, orphans, the elderly, captives, poor maidens (*doncellas pobres*) and widows. It is noteworthy that individuals in the last two categories were considered to be 'poor' not because a temporary physical condition made it impossible for them to work for a living, but rather because of their gender.[44]

Table 8.1 provides a simplistic view of poverty in rural society, as depicted in a census of Piedrahita (Avila) in 1563. Here the heads of households are dichotomized into the 'poor' (giving no indication of how 'poverty' was defined) and the non-poor (unspecified), the former constituting 66 per cent of the village. The married men in Table 8.1 were nearly twice as likely to be non-poor (39 per cent) as were widows (22 per cent). Thus, widows are shown to be significantly worse off than their male neighbours.

Table 8.2 divides the household heads of La Nava de Arévalo (Avila) into socio-economic categories, as employed in a census of 1561. The top category is *Labrador*, used for independent peasant farmers – a class representing social status and wealth in rural society.[45] Forty-seven per cent of the household heads in the village were ranked in this group. But whereas 48 per cent of the males were *labradores*, only 19 per cent of widows were in

Table 8.1 Poor and non-poor heads of household in Piedrahita in 1563

Economic category	Married men		Widows		Total	
	N	%	N	%	N	%
Unspecified	77	39	16	22	93	34
Poor	122	61	57	78	179	66
Totals	199		73		272	

Notes: In addition to the household heads listed above, there were thirty-three *hidalgos* and nineteen *viudas hidalgas* in Piedrahita, but the document did not categorize these according to economic status, hence they could not be included here. The term *hidalgo* is defined below in the note to Table 8.4.

Source: Archivo General de Simancas, Expedientes de Hacienda (henceforth AGS, EH), 142–4–i.

Table 8.2 Socio-economic characteristics of household heads in La Nava de Arévalo in 1561

Category	Men		Never-married women		Widows		Total	
	N	%	N	%	N	%	N	%
Labrador	33	48	0	—	3	19	36	42
Poor *labrador*	2	3	0	—	0	—	2	2
Unspecified	9	13	0	—	2	13	11	13
Poor	20	29	0	—	5	31	25	29
Very poor	5	7	0	—	6	38	11	13
Totals	69		0		16		85	

Source: AGS, EH, 1^0, 43.

that category. The widows of the village were overwhelmingly clustered in the two lowest socio-economic categories: 69 per cent were either 'poor' or 'very poor'. By contrast, only 36 per cent of male household heads were in these categories. Table 8.2 indicates that widows were, on the average, far worse off than their male neighbours in La Nava de Arévalo. They were much less likely to occupy the highest socio-economic rank, and they were nearly twice as likely to be 'poor'.

But 'poor' is a subjective, or comparative, term which is difficult to assess without reference to specific details. We should not give too much importance to the fact that 66 per cent of the family heads in Table 8.1 were identified as 'poor', whereas in Table 8.2 it was only 44 per cent, because these censuses did not reveal what criteria were used to determine 'poverty'.

Nevertheless, we can use the designation as an indicator of relative economic well-being. One useful criterion of wealth, or poverty, is the ownership of property. Table 8.3, based upon a 1566 census of Quintana de Loranza (apparently the current Quintanaloranco, Burgos province), divides household heads into six categories based upon property ownership. Widows in this small village fared relatively well *vis-à-vis* their male counterparts. Whereas 48 per cent of the village men were placed in the top two categories, 44 per cent of the widows were placed there. However, the percentage of widows who were 'very poor' is more than twice that for men. The census does not indicate to what extent this represents the social displacement of women when they were widowed, and to what extent it represents the distribution of widows by previous economic status. But here, and in other villages, there seems to be a tendency for women household heads to be either very poor or wealthy.

Table 8.3 Property-owning and poor household heads in Quintana de Loranza in 1566

Category	Men		Never-married women		Widows		Total	
	N	*%*	*N*	*%*	*N*	*%*	*N*	*%*
Well-off	1	4	0	—	0	—	1	3
Moderately well-off	10	44	0	—	7	44	17	44
Owns little property	4	17	0	—	2	13	6	15
Owns no property	1	4	0	—	0	—	1	3
Poor	5	22	0	—	4	25	9	23
Very poor	2	9	0	—	3	19	5	13
Totals	23		0		16		39	

Note: The categories, given by town officials, in the original Spanish were: *vive buenamente, de razonable* [(or) *de mediana*] *hacienda, de poca hacienda, sin hacienda, pobre* and *muy pobre*.
Source: AGS, EH, 130–18–i.

Livestock ownership was a good measurement of wealth in rural Spain. A wealthy person almost invariably owned many animals of differing types, whereas the poor owned few animals or none at all. Table 8.4 shows the distribution of large livestock ownership among the men, never-married women and widows who headed households in Ruanes (Cáceres) in 1561. In this case, widows are present in all livestock-owning categories, and the proportion of widows is actually greater than that of men in several of the higher categories. But widows were more likely than men to own only one animal or no animals. In general, widows seem to have fared relatively well in Ruanes in comparison with men, and they certainly fared far better than non-widowed women (presumably spinsters).

Table 8.4 The ownership of large livestock by household heads in Ruanes in 1561

Number of large livestock	Men		Never-married women		Widows		Total	
	N	%	N	%	N	%	N	%
14–43	2	5	0	—	1	8	3	6
7–9	5	13	0	—	2	17	7	13
5–6	7	18	0	—	1	8	8	15
4	6	15	0	—	2	17	8	15
3	9	23	0	—	2	17	11	20
2	6	15	2	67	1	8	9	17
1	4	10	0	—	2	17	6	11
0	0	—	1	33	1	8	2	4
Totals	39		3		12		54	

Notes: Large livestock (*ganado mayor*) included oxen, cows, horses, mules and asses – of all ages. Ruanes was virtually an all-*hidalgo* village: all *vecinos* were listed as *hidalgos*, except for one *labrador*, the village priest, and a *casero* of a priest from the nearby city of Trujillo. *Hidalgo* was a hereditary title for a member of the lesser (non-titled) nobility or of the gentry. Because *hidalgos* were supposed to enjoy certain tax exemptions, they were invariably identified in fiscal censuses.

Source: AGS, EH, 189–56.

The situation was similar in Plasenzuela (Cáceres) according to a census taken in 1575. Table 8.5 ranks the household heads of Plasenzuela according to the number of large livestock owned. In the top category were three men and three widows, each owning from six to nineteen animals. Men predominated among the middling groups (owning one to five animals), but on a proportional basis, widows were more likely than men (17 to 13 per cent) to own two animals. However, only 13 per cent of men owned no large animals compared with 38 per cent of widows. In Plasenzuela, as in Ruanes, widows as a group fared better than the lone never-married woman.

Other villages showed a similar distribution. In Monleón (Salamanca), for example, a census of 1558 showed ninety-one household heads. One of these was a widow who was by far the largest owner of large livestock in the village. She owned 115 animals, whereas the wealthiest man had only thirty-eight. But the rich widow was an exception: only 16 per cent of the widows of the village were listed as owners of large animals, compared to 53 per cent of the men.[46] The imbalance of large animal-ownership was even more striking in Ibahernando (Cáceres), a village with 177 households in 1561. Here 75 per cent of the male householders owned more than one large animal, whereas only 30 per cent of widows were in that class.[47]

Another useful gauge of an individual's economic well-being was the amount of grain that he or she planted. Large fields, or numerous fields, were associated with wealth, and small or non-existent fields with poverty.

Table 8.5 The ownership of large livestock by household heads in Plasenzuela in 1575

Number of large livestock	Men		Never-married women		Widows		Total	
	N	%	N	%	N	%	N	%
6–19	3	4	0	—	3	13	6	6
4–5	18	24	0	—	1	4	19	19
3	19	25	0	—	3	13	22	22
2	10	13	0	—	4	17	14	14
1	16	21	0	—	4	17	20	20
0	10	13	1	100	9	38	20	20
Totals	76		1		24		101	

Note: Large livestock (*ganado mayor*) included oxen, cows, horses, mules and asses – of all ages.

Source: AGS, EH, 906.

Table 8.6 Amount of grain planted by household heads in Plasenzuela in 1575

Fanegas *of* grain planted	Men		Never-married women		Widows		Total	
	N	%	N	%	N	%	N	%
15–30	8	10	0	—	3	13	11	11
11–14	14	18	0	—	2	8	16	16
9–10	9	12	0	—	1	4	10	10
7–8	11	14	0	—	2	8	13	13
1–6	10	13	0	—	1	4	11	11
0	24	32	1	100	15	63	40	40
Totals	76		1		24		101	

Source: AGS, EH, 906.

Table 8.6 shows the amount of grain planted by the household heads of Plasenzuela in 1575. Widows are present in each of the categories of Table 8.6, and they are proportionately more numerous than men (13 to 10 per cent) in the top category. But widows are nearly twice as likely as men to be in the very bottom category (63 versus 32 per cent). Again, widows as a group were better off than the lone never-married woman in the census. One would expect the distribution of individuals in Table 8.6 to be quite similar to that in Table 8.5, because oxen, mules and other large animals provided power for field-work and transport. The widows in Table 8.5, however, appear to have owned a disproportionately large number of animals, given the amount of grain that they planted. There may be several explanations. Perhaps the widows under-utilized their animals, or perhaps they rented or lent them to their male neighbours or relatives rather than using them in their own fields. Or perhaps widows were more likely to inherit animals than land.

When their husbands died, some widows were unwilling or unable to continue the household farming operations. But it appears that most widows continued to operate the family farm, with the help of their children and/or servants.[48] And we have evidence that widows often performed even the most demanding tasks, including reaping, rather than hiring a man to do it.[49] The national ordinances approved by the Cortes of Castile-Leon between 1258 and 1505 depict women working at practically all agricultural tasks.[50] Some jobs, however, were considered to be 'women's work'. One of these was the harvesting and preparation of linen. For example, in Garrafe (León) a widow named Francisca Vélez supported herself and four children by planting flax, from which she made thread to sell in regional markets. This particular widow did not plant grain, but she kept livestock and she worked at various other jobs.[51]

Local ordinances in some places attempted to alleviate the economic hardship of widows by giving them special privileges. For example, widows might be permitted to take an extra turn with their grain at the flour mill. Since widows usually did not grow much grain, this concession was probably not burdensome to the miller. And Castilian law reserved the post-harvest gleaning of grain – and other crops – for the old and infirm, women (including widows, of course), minors and others who were unable to work for wages.[52]

As we have seen, widows were often among the neediest members of society. This is further confirmed in a census for the village of Argijuela (apparently the current La Herguijuela, Avila province), which had sixty-eight households in 1563. This census listed the net worth of all heads of households, based upon the value of all real estate and animals, minus any indebtedness. Table 8.7 shows the position of widows in the net-worth assessments. As in the previous tables widows are under-represented in the wealthier categories, and over-represented in the poorer categories. We need not belabour the point.

We should remember, however, that the position of widows varied enormously from household to household and from village to village. In some places, widows appear to have been relatively well-off, compared with males in the community. A good example is provided in Table 8.8, which gives the distribution of *alcabala* tax assessments in Trigueros del Valle (Valladolid) in 1587. Here widows were only marginally inferior to men in terms of their taxable sales.

Table 8.7 Net worth assessments of household heads in Argijuela in 1563

Net worth in Maravedís	Men		Never-married women		Widows		Total	
	N	%	N	%	N	%	N	%
50,000–150,000	3	6	0	—	0	—	3	4
30,000–49,999	5	10	0	—	1	5	6	8
20,000–29,999	7	14	0	—	1	5	8	12
10,000–19,999	18	37	0	—	3	16	21	31
2,000–9,999	11	22	0	—	7	37	18	27
0	5	10	0	—	7	37	12	18
Totals	49		0		19		68	

Source: AGS, EH, 142–4–i.

Table 8.8 *Alcabala* tax assessments of household heads in Trigueros del Valle in 1587

Alcabala *tax* in Maravedís	Men		Never-married women		Widows		Total	
	N	%	N	%	N	%	N	%
4,000	1	1	0	—	0	—	1	1
200–399	6	6	0	—	2	13	8	6
100–199	15	14	0	—	2	13	17	14
50–99	17	16	0	—	0	—	17	14
10–49	13	12	0	—	4	25	17	14
0	56	52	0	—	8	50	64	52
Totals	108		0		16		124	

Notes: Although the *alcabala* was theoretically a 10 per cent sales tax, it was actually paid at predetermined fixed amounts negotiated with the Royal Treasury. Each village collected what it deemed an appropriate amount from its citizens, using various criteria: typically, the amount of property owned by each individual. But the officials of Trigueros made their assessments based upon estimates of sales subject to the *alcabala*. Five of the men in the "0" category were priests.

Source: AGS, EH, 189–21.

CONCLUSION

Census data from the aforementioned sixteenth-century Castilian villages indicates that widows as a group occupied a significantly lower socio-economic position than their male neighbours. Widows were far more likely to be considered 'poor', they owned less property and they had lower incomes. Ideally, we should confirm this by analysing data from a much larger number of villages. And other detailed censuses must certainly exist; it is simply a question of finding them among the thousands of bundles of documents at Simancas.

We should be aware, however, that the census data may be misleading. Many of the 'poor' widows listed in the censuses as independent household heads, actually may have been linked economically with the more prosperous households of their married children or other family members. We have no way of knowing how prevalent this was, but it would have caused widows to appear poorer than they actually were. This question may be clarified by research utilizing documents from municipal, parish, notarial and other archives. But whatever its shortcomings, the data that we have from the Expedientes de Hacienda Section at Simancas confirms the stereotype of the 'poor widow' in Golden Age Spain.[53]

NOTES

1 C. Segura Graíño, 'Situación jurídica y realidad social de casadas y viudas en el medievo hispano (Andalucía)', in *La condición de la mujer en la Edad Media; Actas del coloquio celebrado en la Casa de Velázquez, del 5 al 7 de noviembre de 1984*, Madrid: Casa de Velázquez/Universidad Complutense 1986, pp. 128–33; and A. Molina Molina, *La Vida cotidiana en la Murcia bajomedieval*, Murcia: Academia Alfonso X El Sabio (Comúnidad Autónoma de la Región de Murcia) 1987, pp. 189–90. Cf. E. Clark, Chapter 6 in this volume.

2 E. Montanos Ferrín, *La familia en la Alta Edad Media española*, Pamplona: Ediciones Universidad de Navarra 1980, pp. 45–7, 55–6; Segura Graíño, 'Situación jurídica', pp. 128–33.

3 Segura Graíño, 'Situación jurídica', pp. 130–2; J.C. Martín Cea, *El campesinado castellano de la Cuenca del Duero: Aproximaciones a su estudio durante los siglos XIII al XV*, 2nd edn, Valladolid: Junta de Castilla y León 1986, p. 88; P. Rojo Alboreca, 'El trabajo femenino en Extremadura durante la Baja Edad Media a través de la documentación testamentaria', in A. Munoz Fernández and C. Segura Graíño (eds), *El trabajo de las mujeres en la Edad Media hispana*, Madrid: Asociación Cultural Al-Mudayna 1988, pp. 171–2; T. Ruíz. 'Notas para el estudio de la mujer en el área del Burgos medieval', in *El pasado histórico de Castilla y León*, vol.1: *Edad Media,* Burgos: Junta de Castilla y León 1983, pp. 419–24.

4 R. Lanza García, *Población y familia campesina en el Antiguo Régimen: Liébana, siglos XVI–XIX*, Santander: Universidad de Cantabria, Ediciones de Librería Estudio 1988, p. 147; Segura Graíño, 'Situación jurídica', pp. 125–6; Molina Molina, *La Vida cotidiana*, pp. 193–4.

5 For tax and voting purposes, the head of a household was designated a *vecino* (citizen). Each *vecino* normally represented a married couple plus any children, other relatives or servants living in the house. See H. Nader, *Liberty in Absolutist Spain: The Habsburg Sale of Towns, 1516–1700*, Baltimore, Md.: Johns Hopkins University Press 1990, pp. 27–45.

6 G. Barbón y Castañeda, *Provechosos arbitrios al consumo del vellón, conservación de plata, población de España y relación de avisos importantes a las cosas que en ellas necesitan de remedio, compuesto por el capitán . . .*, Madrid 1628, folio 9.

7 Lanza García, *Población*, pp. 147–63; Segura Graíño, 'Situación jurídica',

pp. 124−9; P. Pereiro, *Vida cotidiana y élite local: Málaga a mediados del Siglo de Oro*, Málaga: Diputación Provincial 1987, pp. 36−7.

8 Segura Graíño, 'Situación jurídica', pp. 125−6.

9 Lanza García, *Población*, pp. 150−1.

10 ibid.: pp. 150−1.

11 D.E. Vassberg, *Land and Society in Golden Age Castile*, Cambridge: Cambridge University Press 1984, pp. 27−8, 33−5, 48−9; Nader, *Liberty*, pp. 27−45; A. Alvar Ezquerra, 'Control social, cuestionarios, riqueza y pobreza en el último cuarto del siglo XVI; algunas noticias referidas al mundo rural madrileño', *Hispania*, XLVIII: 170, September−December 1988, pp. 875−907.

12 J.F. O'Callaghan, *A History of Medieval Spain*, Ithaca, NY: Cornell University Press 1975, p. 270; A. Rodríguez Fernández, *Alcaldes y regidores: Administración territorial y gobierno municipal en Cantabria durante la Edad Moderna*, Santander: Institución Cultural de Cantabria, Ediciones de Librería Estudio 1986, p. 31; Lanza García, *Población*, p. 127.

13 Vassberg, *Land and Society*, p. 46; Alvar Ezquerra, 'Control social'.

14 A. Franco Silva, *El concejo de Alcalá de Guadaira a finales de la Edad Media (1426−1533)*, Seville: Diputación Provincial 1974, pp. 58−9; Lanza García, *Población*, pp. 133−4; Alvar Ezquerra, 'Control social'.

15 Archivo de la Chancillería de Valladolid, Pleitos Civiles, Fernando Alonso (Fenecidos), p. 64.

16 Franco Silva, *El concejo*, pp. 58−9.

17 B. Bennassar, *Valladolid au siècle d'or; Une ville de Castille et sa campagne au XVIe siècle*, Paris: Mouton 1967, p. 191; F. Brumont, *Campo y Campesinos de Castilla la Vieja en tiempos de Felipe II*, Madrid: Siglo Veintiuno 1984, p. 79; M. Rojas Gabriel, *Olvera en la Baja Edad Media (Siglos XIV−XV)*, Cádiz: Diputación Provincial 1988, p. 117.

18 The villages are Castañar de Ibor, Fuente el Saz, Horcajo de las Torres, La Zarza, Monleón, Morales de Toro and Puebla del Príncipe. Sources: Archivo General de Simancas, Expedientes de Hacienda (henceforth AGS, EH), 177, 292, 911, 323, 131, 906; and AGS, Consejo y Juntas de Hacienda, 14 moderno.

19 AGS, EH, 142−4−1.

20 The villages were Abellaneda, Castellanos de la Sierra, El Alameda, El Argijuela, Langa, Palacios de Goda, Pero Rodríguez, Quintana de Loranza, Ruanes, San Martín de la Vega, Villanueva del Horcajo, Vinaderos, Ibahernando and Zarza de Montánchez. Source: AGS, EH, 178, 176, 209, 142, 43, 130, 189.

21 The villages were Abellaneda, Calabazanos, Montaragón, Monteagudo, Navalvillar, Plasenzuela, Poveda de Obispalía, and Santa Cruz (de Talavera) and the range was 8 to 41 per cent. Source: AGS, EH, 209, 240, 323, 394, 906, 360, 382.

22 The villages were Abadengo de Palacio, Abelgas, Castilblanco, Castañar de Ibor, Montiel, Pilas, Puebla del Príncipe, Terrinches, Valderrillas and Trigueros del Valle, and the range was 10 to 34 per cent. Source: AGS, EH, 187, 209, 74, 130, 142, 146, 366, 178, 187, 189.

23 The villages were Torrenteras, Montenegro (S^to. Domingo de Silos), Castañar (de Talamanca), Palacios de Goda, Pineda-Trasmonte, Pino, Poveda de la Sierra, Pozantiguo and Trigueros del Valle. If we added the large agro-town of Arévalo (with 25 per cent widows), the overall total for the 1590s group would be 19 per cent widows − a considerably larger figure, and perhaps more reflective of the demographic crisis sweeping the peninsula in the last decade of the sixteenth century. Source: AGS, EH, 189, 130, 177, 43, 142, 187.

24 P. Laslett, 'Introduction: The history of the family' and C. Klapisch, 'Household and family in Tuscany in 1427', both in P. Laslett and R. Wall (eds), *Household and Family in Past Time*, Cambridge: Cambridge University Press 1972, pp. 54−5, 275.

25 D.E. Vassberg, 'The structure of the rural household in sixteenth-century Castile', a paper presented at the 18th annual meeting of the Society for Spanish and Portuguese Historical Studies, University of Texas at Austin, 1987.
26 According to Laslett, 'Introduction', p. 78, the ratio of widows to widowers in rural England was around five to one.
27 The relative mortality levels of men and women were also influenced by their different roles in society, which exposed them to different disease environments. See S.R. Johansson, 'Welfare, mortality and gender. Continuity and change in explanations for male/female mortality differences over three centuries', *Continuity and Change*, 6: pt 2, August 1991, pp. 135–77.
28 For the prejudice against single people living alone, see M.R. Weisser, *The Peasants of the Montes: The Roots of Rural Rebellion in Spain*, Chicago, Ill.: University of Chicago Press 1976, pp. 78–9. Cf. Klapisch, 'Household and family', pp. 275–9.
29 M. Chevalier, *Tipos cómicos y folklore (siglos XVI–XVII)*, Madrid: EDI-6, S.A. 1982, pp. 86–7, 91.
30 AGS, EH, 360.
31 ibid.: 323.
32 ibid.: 366.
33 Vassberg, 'The structure of the rural household'.
34 Some aspects of the treatment of orphans are covered in L. Valverde, Chapter 2 in this volume.
35 The 1575 census of Monteagudo (Cuenca) included numerous examples of this. AGS, EH, 323.
36 Lanza García, *Población*, pp. 141, 151–2.
37 For example, the widow Catalina Thomé was living with her son in Morales de Toro in 1569. AGS, EH, 360.
38 There is considerable information about widows' children, and their guardians, for Monteagudo (Cuenca, in 1575) in AGS, EH, 323; for Abelgas (León, in 1582) in ibid.: 323; and for Morales de Toro (Zamora, in 1569) in ibid.: 360.
39 Lanza García, *Población*, p. 136.
40 D.E. Vassberg, 'Juveniles in the rural work force of sixteenth-century Castile', *Journal of Peasant Studies*, 11:1, 1983, pp. 62–75; Lanza García, *Población*, pp. 136–7.
41 D.E. Vassberg, 'Household size and socioeconomic status in rural Castile in the 16th century', a paper presented at the 20th annual meeting of the Society for Spanish and Portuguese Historical Studies, St Louis, Missouri, 1989; F. Chacón Jiménez, *Los murcianos del siglo XVII: Evolución, familia y trabajo*, Murcia: Editora Regional 1986, pp. 115–17.
42 C. López Alonso, *La pobreza en la Espana medieval: Estudio histórico-social*, Madrid: Centro de Publicaciones, Ministerio de Trabajo y Seguridad Social 1986, pp. 45–6.
43 Franco Silva, *El concejo*, pp. 68, 82.
44 C. López Alonso, 'Mujer medieval y pobreza', in *La condición de la mujer en la Edad Media; Actas del Coloquio celebrado en la Casa de Velázquez, del 5 al 7 de noviembre de 1984*, Madrid: 1986, pp. 261–2.
45 Vassberg, *Land and Society*, p. 142.
46 AGS, EH, 323.
47 ibid.: 189–56.
48 There are numerous examples of both types of widows in a 1558 census of Monleón: ibid.: 323.
49 M.E. Contreras Jiménez, 'La mujer trabajadora en los fueros castellano-leoneses', in Muñoz Fernández and Segura Graíño (eds), *El trabajo*, p. 109.
50 M. del P. Rábade Obradó, 'La mujer trabajadora en los Ordenamientos de

Cortes, 1258–1505', in Muñoz Fernández and Segura Graíño (eds), *El trabajo*, pp. 136–9.

51 AGS, EH, 187.

52 Rábade Obradó, 'La mujer trabajadora', pp. 124–5; Contreras Jiménez, 'La mujer trabajadora', p. 104; Vassberg, *Land and Society*, p. 55.

53 This conclusion was also reached by Brumont, *Campo y Campesinos*, p. 223, for the village of La Bureba, in the province of Burgos. In fact, Brumont concludes his section entitled 'Feminine pauperism' with the observation that: 'En un mundo pobre, las mujeres, y singularmente las viudas, aparecen, pues, como las más menesterosas' ('In a poor world, women – and particularly widows – stand out as the most needy of all').

9 Never-married women in town and country in eighteenth-century Denmark

Hans Chr. Johansen

Eighteenth-century Denmark had, like most European contemporary societies, a very unequal income distribution. There was a small upper class including estate-owners, top civil servants and merchants, a somewhat larger middle class of which typical elements were tenant farmers and master artisans, and a lower class of cottagers and day labourers.

It is difficult to determine a meaningful poverty line in such a society, but it is quite obvious that the cottagers and day labourers were more at risk than the rest of the population, having no access to assistance from members of their families or from a guild, and living under conditions which made saving in kind or money impossible even in good years. Demographic data, on the other hand, do not demonstrate very large differences between classes in the expectation of life, nor do death rates rise and fall according to the success or otherwise of the harvest.[1] This may indicate that poverty did not persist over the whole of the life cycle of the eighteenth-century Danish labourer. Being already at that time a net exporter of foodstuffs, Denmark probably better than many other European countries could ensure that the population did not starve, in spite of the absence of an economic and political situation which would have permitted the creation of a worthwhile public assistance system.

As will be made clear below, it was in old age that members of the lower classes were most at risk of poverty, and those most liable to be dependent on begging and charity were the women who had never married. Yet the period of risk covered only a small part of the life cycle and, as demonstrated below, involved only a small section of the population, although a larger one in urban than rural areas.

In order to illuminate the living conditions of this section of the population a variety of Danish communities in the eighteenth century have been selected for a detailed analysis at the micro-level, taking census lists as a starting-point. Census-taking started in Denmark in 1769, and from 1787 the enumerators' books have survived from the whole of the kingdom.[2] In Table 9.1 an extract from a contemporary statistical analysis of the nominal lists of the 1801 census sets out the marital status of women over the age of 40. As expected most women in their 40s and 50s were married, while in their later years the majority were widowed. There were, however, in all age groups a considerable number of never-married women – relatively more in urban than in rural areas – and it is the purpose of this chapter to describe the living conditions of this segment of the Danish population in the eighteenth century.

Table 9.1 Marital status of women aged over 40 in Denmark, 1801

Age	Copenhagen			Provincial towns			Rural areas		
	Unm.	*Marr.*	*Wid.*	*Unm.*	*Marr.*	*Wid.*	*Unm.*	*Marr.*	*Wid.*
	Percentage of women in the area and age group								
40–9	14	67	19	15	72	13	8	86	6
50–9	14	50	36	14	58	28	6	78	16
60–9	13	32	55	13	39	48	5	59	36
70+	10	15	75	13	20	67	5	35	60

Source: National Archives, Tabeller over folkemængden i Danmark den 1. februar 1801.

The total number of single women in Denmark aged over 40 in 1801 was nearly 11,000 or about 1 per cent of the total population, but amounting to between 5 and 15 per cent of older age groups depending on the area concerned. The contemporary publications from which the figures in Table 9.1 have been compiled also show that when the single women were still in their 40s, most were listed as servants, whereas the largest group of older single women were simply described as 'poor people'. For those aged over 70 years the poor constituted over half of all the never-married women. It is not clear, however, how the contemporary statisticians were able to identify the poor since the enumerators recorded in the column, where they should have stated the source of each individual's livelihood, a much smaller number of persons in receipt of alms or poor in other ways than they later designated as poor in the statistical tables. The most likely solution is that many without any occupation were counted as poor when the tabulations were compiled at the beginning of the nineteenth century.

Such tabulations do not contain any further details about the life cycles of the old single women but, fortunately, material in two databases created at the University of Odense has supplementary information on some of them. The earliest database is a family reconstitution study of a nationwide sample of twenty-six rural parishes.[3] The second contains demographic, social and economic data on all individuals living in the largest provincial town, Odense, in the late eighteenth century.[4]

URBAN LIVING CONDITIONS

The enumerators' books of the 1801 census have information on 126 never-married women over the age of 40 resident in Odense. The town had by then a total population of 5,782, which means that about 2 per cent of the inhabitants belonged to this group. The age and household status of these women are set out in Table 9.2 (p. 199).

Those who maintained their own household were normally women who were in receipt of some sort of pension or who had inherited a sizeable fortune from their family. They would often own a house in Odense and their means were sufficient to pay for a female servant who looked after them in their old age. Most of these women had lived in Odense for the whole of their lives, at first living with their parents and then, following the death of their parents, buying a smaller house, which is where they can be found in 1801.

Those women who lived in the household of a relative in 1801 were on average younger than those who had their own household. The vast majority were either daughters of the head of the household or sisters of the head or his wife. Most had grown up in Odense. Daughters would often stay with their father because the mother had died, a pattern found in both upper-class and middle-class households, whereas the never-married 'aunts' were usually only to be found in upper-class homes. Women from these two groups probably furnished many of those who later in their lives ended up with their own households.

Two examples can give an impression of the lives of these women. First there is Margrethe Christine Sibbern. She was baptized on 12 February 1729 in the cathedral, where her father was organist. She had three brothers and two sisters. The family seems to have enjoyed a comfortable standard of living and after 1740, when her father bought a large house, Overgade 3, in the finest street in the town, they were well-housed. During the 1770s her two sisters married and moved to Jutland, while two of the brothers became teachers at the local grammar school and moved out of the parental home. However, Margrethe and the third brother, who became an organist and at the same time a watchmaker, remained with the parents, their father dying in 1775 and their mother in 1782. In the 1787 census the third brother was listed as head of the household in Overgade 3 with Margrethe as house-keeper, assisted by two female servants, aged 33 and 30. At this time Margrethe was undoubtedly comfortably off.

In 1790 the brother died and the probate inventory indicates that no division of the parents' estate had yet taken place. This was, however, carried out a few years later, but much care was taken to ensure that Margrethe would have a reasonable standard of living. Although the house was sold, a smaller one in the same neighbourhood, Nørregade 6, was bought in her name and out of the total net assets of approximately 3,000 rixdollars, she was allotted 900. A useful reference point is provided by the

annual income of an unskilled worker at this time, approximately 50 rixdollars, which sufficed for the maintenance of a family. Nevertheless, she
could not afford an affluent lifestyle from the interest alone,[5] and this
income was supplemented by a yearly pension of 20 rixdollars.

Table 9.2 Never-married women in Odense, 1801, according to position in
household and age group

Age group	Independent household	With relatives	Servants	Lodgers
40–9	5	14	18	15
50–9	7	6	7	12
60–9	3	5	5	16
70+	—	—	2	11
Total	15	25	32	54

Source: Funen Provincial Archives, Folketællingen 1801.

Margrethe can be found in the house at Nørregade 6 in the 1801 census,
living with one of the female servants who had been with the family in 1787.
There was also a bachelor tradesman living as a lodger in the house.
Margrethe continued her life in this way until she died in 1819 at the age of
90. In her will it was decreed that the same servant who had stayed with her
all these years should live rent free in some of the rooms of the house for the
rest of her life. It is not known how Margrethe managed during the years of
hyper-inflation between 1807 and 1814, but until then she was probably able
to maintain a middle-class living standard. During the years following the
death of her brother, Margrethe still had relatives in the town, but it is not
known to what extent these relatives took care of the old woman.

The second woman is Christiane Rudolphine Bjørnsen, baptized on 9
August 1754 as a daughter of a goldsmith who later became a member of
the city council. Until 1758 the family lived in a rented house, but then
bought a large house in one of the main streets, Vestergade 2. Two of her
brothers died as infants, and Christiane grew up with a brother and a sister.

According to the tax lists, their father was a relatively wealthy man in the
1770s and 1780s. Their mother died in 1779 at the age of 50 and the two
sisters, who were then about 20 years old, appear to have taken over the
housekeeping for their father. In the 1787 census the household consisted of
the father, the three children who were now aged 36, 32 and 26 years, the
son listed as a surveyor, and a female servant.

During the 1790s, however, first Christiane's brother and sister died, and
then in 1797 also her father. She inherited 613 rixdollars and this made it
possible for her to stay in the house, but the 1801 census discloses that it had
become necessary for her to take in a lodger and to let half of the house to a
merchant. She had, however, sufficient means to have a resident female
servant, but the census also recorded that she 'lives from sewing'. The

probate inventory after her death in 1827 confirms that she had been living in modest, but not poor, conditions in her final years, since she still owned the house and the inventory lists clothes and furniture comparable to those of typical middle-class families. The size of her income in the last years of her life, however, is unknown.

The life cycles of such women as Margrethe and Christiane contrast markedly with those who lived as servants or lodgers. The latter were typically women who often moved from one house in the town to another. Only a few of the servants were as lucky as the one who stayed with Margrethe Sibbern for more than thirty years. A majority had migrated to the town from the rural hinterland earlier in their lives and they had few, if any, relations in the town. As long as possible they earned their livelihood from service or from spinning and sewing.

The possibilities for the latter type of work were especially good in Odense in the late eighteenth century.[6] The reason for this was that enterprising merchants had established a putting-out system for the manufacture of gloves. The markets for the gloves were found all over Europe, at first in northern Germany and along the Baltic coasts, but later Odense gloves were also sold in more distant places, such as Milan, Vienna and Amsterdam. The demand was so strong that it was impossible to train a sufficient number of journeymen within the guild system and from the 1770s so-called 'out-sewers', women without any connection to the guild, were sewing in their private homes. They received raw materials from a guild master who was financed by a merchant, and the master would later pick up the finished gloves. Production figures from the late eighteenth century indicate that a labour force of some 800 was required to complete the tanning, cutting and sewing, or about one-fourth of the total labour force of the town. This may explain why Odense had more single women and widows living as lodgers than other Danish towns at this date, and also the considerable in-migration of this type of labour.

The income the women could earn from this type of work was modest and when they lost their ability to work in order to survive they were thrown upon the very inefficient public social security system or they had to beg. Throughout most of the eighteenth century, public assistance was based on an act of 1708 which laid down that each town should have a Board of Guardians, and that poor people should apply to the Board for assistance. Only the deserving people should be given help by being inscribed on a special list of poor people. The Act failed to stipulate any scale of allowances and it was not until the 1730s that subsequent Acts authorized the levying of taxes on the citizens in order that the Boards could discharge their duties to the poor.

In the second half of the eighteenth century there were normally between 100 and 200 people on the Odense poor lists. The poor were divided into six or seven classes. Those in the first class received half a rixdollar every fortnight and those in the lowest class about one-eighth of a rixdollar. This translates into a rate of assistance between 3 and 13 rixdollars per year,[7] and even the highest of these amounts would hardly cover the costs of a person living at the lowest possible subsistence level. Begging was consequently a necessity for the members of the lower classes, and contemporary accounts of the daily life in the town confirm that dozens of beggars would gather around travellers and pedestrians.

In view of their frequent changes of addresses and very common names, the poor never-married women are difficult to identify, and since most of them also had spent part of their life outside Odense, the database can give little information about them. To describe the conditions of these women an approach which differs from that used for more affluent persons has therefore been chosen. In 1792 the city council made an inventory of all the people in receipt of public charity. This list has been taken as a starting-point, but where possible individuals have been traced in the more comprehensive database mentioned above. The list of 1792 contains 199 names. Of these thirty-two were single women over the age of 40, the rest being widows and old men plus a few orphans and younger disabled persons without any family to support them. If the number of single women and their ages are compared with the women listed in Table 9.2 and a corresponding list from the 1787 census, it is clear that nearly all lodgers in their mid-50s or older received some form of public assistance, and that the detailed living conditions described in the 1792 list consequently cover this segment of the population.

The first characteristic is that only one of the persons received some help, and very modest help at that, from their family. The rest had no family in the town. A second observation is that their health was poor. Typical descriptions are 'very frail', 'very decrepit', 'bedridden' or 'a cripple' and there are also more direct indications of handicap, such as blindness, insanity and rupture. The poor health of these women and the resulting higher mortality risk may be an explanation why they constitute a declining proportion of all women at higher ages (see Table 9.1, p. 197). The council's list of 1792 also mentions that their ability to work was in most cases very limited, although it was added that many did a little spinning or sewing (of gloves) despite the fact that their capacity for self-support was limited. A few had small grandchildren living with them, the illegitimate children of their own illegitimate daughters. The addresses of the women indicate that they lived in very small and overcrowded houses in side-streets or just outside the town gates.

As an example it is appropriate to choose Kirstine Hansdatter Juel. Her first appearance in the database is in 1775 when she resided as a lodger in a small house outside the eastern gate. She was then 69 years old, and her landlord was a journeyman in the glove trade who had become a widower in 1772. She may have been in the town earlier as a servant, but since the data used for earlier years fail to name female servants, the necessary information is lacking. She must, however, have arrived in Odense after 1758, since the illegitimate daughter mentioned below was not baptized in any of

Odense churches. In 1779 a list of the poor reports Kirstine Hansdatter as living in great distress and needing more than the 5 rixdollars a year which she received in alms. In 1787 she was living in a neighbouring house and enumerated as a beggar of 72 years, but co-residing with her daughter who had married a few months earlier. The daughter's husband was a servant and resident on a nearby farm, but when the first child to this marriage was born in 1789 the husband was a day labourer and the young couple had established a separate home.

In the 1792 list of the poor she is described as 80 years old, 'very frail, can do nothing, begs' and her alms were now 13 rixdollars a year. This means that she had been admitted to the first class in the poor list and given the very slight inflation that occurred between 1779 and 1792, the implication is that her economic condition had improved. As mentioned earlier the assistance may have been able to provide her with very modest maintenance at the lowest possible subsistence level. After 1792 she disappears from the records and since there is no record of her burial it may be inferred that, despite her age, she left the town soon after 1792.

Other descriptions of this type relating to old never-married women in the sources used for the database include pieces of information which confirm that the poor had no relatives who could support them, and when, after their death, the Overseers of the Poor came to seize their belongings all that was left in most cases were a few pieces of clothing, the bed and perhaps a table and a chair. The town had little else but the poor relief to offer the destitute old never-married women. There were a few institutions, established by rich people in their wills, which gave shelter to old people, but they seem in most cases to have preferred widows to never-married women, and sometimes the by-laws for the institutions expressly prohibited the acceptance of persons other than widows as inmates.

The main reason why so many never-married women had no family who could support them when they grew old was the extraordinarily high mobility in urban populations of the time. Among those who were born in Odense, a mid-eighteenth-century cohort study[8] has revealed that only 13 per cent were still living in the town when they were in their 30s. About 40 per cent had died and the rest had left the town. At the same time only about one-fourth of the registered out-migrants had been born in the town, which means that there must have been a very large turnover of people who tried their luck in Odense but after a stay of a few years returned to their birthplace or moved on, in the hope of having better luck in another place.

Thus, the citizens of Odense would more often than not see their relatives leave the town and after a short time they would lose contact with the migrants. An heir in the probate ledgers would often be described as, 'Has left Odense about ten years ago and no one in the family knows where he or she now lives', or 'Is said to be in Germany, but the exact place is unknown'. For a girl who had migrated to Odense from a Funen rural parish in her youth and become a servant in a middle- or upper-class home the chances of having relatives in the town would be still smaller. Consequently, it would seem that the only chance these women would have to prosper would be either to marry a person such as a guild master, and hope that it would be possible to stay on in the house after widowhood, or to find a job as a servant in a house where the landlord would take care of them after a long and faithful period of service. For the rest begging and insufficient public assistance would provide their only available resources when they lost the ability to work.

RURAL LIVING CONDITIONS

The sample of twenty-six rural parishes contains just eighty-four never-married women aged over 40 in 1801. Out of a total population of 7,360 persons in the twenty-six parishes, the percentage never-married and aged over 40 is only about half that found in Odense. The reason for this is not that there were relatively fewer women in these age groups in rural areas, but that a larger proportion were married or widowed (see Table 9.1, p. 197). It is difficult to say from existing research whether this was due to a higher propensity in rural areas to marry or to better chances for a middle-aged never-married woman to support herself in a town. The latter in turn might indicate either a push effect from the rural society involving those who failed to marry or, alternatively, the migration of female servants from the countryside into a town and the smaller chances these girls had to find a partner in the new environment.

Table 9.3 Never-married women in twenty-six rural parishes, 1801, according to position in household and age group

Age group	Independent household	With relatives	Servants	Lodgers
40–9	5	15	6	3
50–9	13	6	8	2
60–9	4	9	—	3
70+	5	2	—	3
Total	27	32	14	11

Source: Demographic database at the Institute of History, University of Odense.

The position of the eighty-four never-married women in rural districts and their ages are set out in Table 9.3. Compared with the distribution in Table 9.2 (p. 199) the rural areas had more single women living in the households of relatives and in independent households, and a much smaller proportion of servants and lodgers. As a consequence it is most likely that these women on average had better living conditions than the never-married women resident in Odense.

A closer study of the information in the database reveals a distinct geographical pattern. Most of the never-married women were resident in the poor parishes in western and northern Jutland, whereas there were very few in the more prosperous regions, such as Sealand. The parish of Rindom in western Jutland with 4 per cent of the population in the sample thus contained thirteen never-married women out of the eighty-four in the sample, and Tved parish in northern Jutland with about the same population had eleven of the sample women. On the other hand, there are Sealand parishes without any old never-married women. The Jutland parishes were situated in regions which experienced heavy out-migration to eastern Denmark and this migration included more men than women and normally took place when the young people were in their early 20s. Consequently, in these parishes it may have been more difficult for a girl to find a husband once she passed the normal age of marriage in her late 20s.

Information in the database furthermore shows that the rural never-married women in most cases were the daughters of farmers and not of cottagers, and that farmers' daughters were the least mobile element in these societies. They were educated to become wives of farmers, usually receiving this education in their own home or as servants on neighbouring farms, often where the occupier or his wife was a relative. The daughters of cottagers, on the other hand, would be much more mobile, and any surplus girls from this group would have emigrated to urban areas at an early age.

Life stories indicative of the experience of the farmer class are those of Karen Mortensdatter in Rindom and her sister Maren. Karen was born in 1744, her father being a farmer. She was the oldest child and five younger brothers and sisters were born in the years from 1747 to 1757, two of them dying very young. Maren was born in 1753. A sister was married to a local carpenter, but by 1781 he was a widower. Their mother died in 1786. In both the censuses of 1787 and 1801 the father appeared as head of the farm household living together with his three unmarried children, the two daughters and a son. Both daughters died in Rindom when they were in their 70s and would appear to have stayed on the farm for the whole of their lives.

The small group of aged lodgers and some of those living in independent households were, according to the censuses, given alms from the parish, but the public assistance in rural areas was at that time even less adequate than that provided in the towns,[9] and a parish would often try to drive away poor old people born in other parishes in order to save money. Most of the few old lodgers in the sample were children of cottagers and in the censuses they were described as poor and as beggars, without any information on their general health.

CONCLUSION

The overall impression left by this survey is that in rural areas farmers were able to support their unmarried daughters on the farm, whereas unmarried women from the lower social classes would often migrate to Copenhagen or other towns. In most rural areas there were only a few old never-married women, and poor relief was therefore very largely reserved for old widows and widowers from the cottager and day-labourer class and for orphans from the same section of society. Even so the farmers often complained that the burden of the poor relief was very heavy. Since the long-distance flow of migrants between rural areas involved larger numbers of men than of women, the number of old never-married women was largest in the western parts of the country where there was a net out-migration.

The towns had a large in-migration of young people of both sexes, but there was a surplus of men who later left the towns for Copenhagen or abroad. Since older men experienced a higher mortality than older women among the population aged over 60 living in the towns, there were many more women in relation to men than in rural areas. In 1787 the number of women per 1000 inhabitants in this age group was 529 in rural areas, 588 in Copenhagen and 615 in the provincial towns. The need to provide public assistance to old women was therefore much greater in the towns and the never-married women who could not stay with their family or had not inherited a fortune experienced extreme poverty.

The living conditions described above are probably not only typical for Denmark in the eighteenth century, but also for the first half of the nineteenth. The agrarian reforms which took place late in the eighteenth century increased the number of cottagers and landless labourers, but the number of old never-married women in the countryside remained relatively low during the first half of the nineteenth century. Industrialization, on the other hand, came late to Denmark, and it was not until after 1870 that it left a distinct mark on the largest towns, creating a working class with new social problems. Before 1870, many of the characteristics which were documented for Odense in about 1800 could still be found in most provincial towns.

NOTES

1 See Hans Chr. Johansen, 'Regional mortality fluctuations in Denmark 1735–1849', paper presented at the ninth International Economic History Congress, Berne, 1986. See, however, also for an analysis of Aarhus diocese, Patrick R. Galloway, 'Short-run population dynamics among the rich and poor in European countries, rural Jutland, and urban Rouen', paper presented at the IUSSP seminar at Majorca, 1991.
2 They are kept at the Rigsarkiv (Danish National Archives) in Copenhagen.
3 The database links information on individuals in both censuses and parish registers. See Hans Chr. Johansen, *Befolkningsudvikling og familiestruktur i det 18 århundrede*, Odense: Odense University Press 1975.
4 This database uses information from a wider range of sources including censuses, parish registers, probate inventories, guilds, tax lists, registrations of poor people, land registers, criminal records and municipal trade licences. See Hans Chr. Johansen, *Næring og bystyre*, Odense: Odense University Press 1983.
5 The issuing of non-convertible notes by the Kurantbank meant that interest rates were kept low in Denmark throughout this period. It would be difficult to get more than 4 per cent per annum on loans.

6 On glove-making in Odense see Johansen, *Næring og bystyre*, pp. 91–101.
7 For comparison a barrel of rye, the staple food of the population, cost in normal harvest years in the 1770s and 1780s 2–3 rixdollars, and the average yearly consumption of rye in Odense was three to four barrels per capita.
8 Johansen, *Næring og bystyre*, pp. 28ff. Cf. also Hans Chr. Johansen, 'Migration into and out of the Danish city of Odense', in Ad van der Woude, Jan de Vries and Akira Hayami (eds), *Urbanization in History*, Oxford: Clarendon Press 1990, pp. 152–64.
9 Information from several parishes in 1787 indicates that even when assistance in kind was included, the normal yearly allowance was only 2–3 rixdollars per poor person. Although the cost of living was cheaper in rural areas than in the towns, such a small sum was far from adequate to meet the costs of maintenance, perhaps covering one-third of what was needed to survive, and begging was therefore also common in rural areas.

10 The household position of elderly widows in poverty
Evidence from two English communities in the late eighteenth and early nineteenth centuries

Thomas Sokoll

OLD AGE, POVERTY AND THE FAMILY SYSTEM

In the history of ageing, as well as that of the Poor Law, the close association of poverty with old age, especially for women, has become a commonplace. It is somewhat surprising, therefore, that one of the chief demographic variables which determine the situation of elderly people in poverty has been neglected in previous research: their household position. Admittedly, it is a characteristic which does not apply universally, since a certain proportion of the aged poor did not live in households but were placed in institutions. And, of course, the knowledge of whether, say, an old widow on poor relief lived in a household of her own, or with someone else as a relative or lodger, does not in itself tell us anything about her actual standard of living.

Nevertheless, knowledge of that kind is important to the discussion of the demographic context and the wider social implications of old-age poverty. It is crucial, for example, to the understanding of the model of the poverty life cycle, because it enables that model to be considered from the comparative perspective within different family systems. Thus, in complex family systems we would not expect to find elderly people (not even those who are well off) living on their own. But in a nuclear family system this should be a frequent occurrence, even among those who are poor. In this sense, old people in poverty, and old women in particular, can be regarded as a test case. In a strict nuclear family system, an elderly widow, for example, would *have* to live alone even if she lacked sufficient means to support herself. If she had married children, these might be expected to assist her in various ways, but certainly *not* by taking her into one of their households – since this would break the rule of the system that households be nuclear in structure and not incorporate additional relatives, becoming extended family households, to use the terminology of Peter Laslett. Under such conditions the responsibility for the support of the elderly would only to a limited extent be fulfilled through the family system, and as a result systems of public welfare provision would play the decisive part. For England, with both the nuclear family and the Poor Law having been firmly established at comparatively early times, this seems indeed a plausible proposition.[1]

Other issues are closely related. For example, if elderly paupers were generally maintained in their own households by means of public support, the question arises as to what extent their residential independence would be accompanied by social isolation. Again, it is a widely-held belief that in early modern England this was often the case. Paul Slack, for example, in his masterly account of poverty and poor relief in early modern England, has written precisely to this effect: 'A lonely old age was . . . the lot of most of the labouring poor.'[2]

THE NUMERICAL STUDY OF THE PAUPER HOUSEHOLD

The discussion of such issues is complicated by the fact that detailed information on the household position of elderly paupers is not readily available. However, for the last two decades or so research in historical demography and, more specifically, in the social history of ageing has produced an ever-growing amount of data on the household arrangements of the elderly, and many of these data, especially those from case-studies like that by Anderson on Preston in 1851 or, more recently, by Quadagno on Chilvers Coton in 1851 and 1881, refer to the poorest sections of the labouring classes.[3] But even data of the latter kind cannot be taken as evidence of the household position of the aged poor in any strict sense as it is not clear to what extent the people covered were in actual need. On the other hand, this lack of specific data on the household position of elderly paupers is perhaps not all that surprising, given that, whatever claims have been made in previous research, we still do not even possess reliable data on pauper households in general.

Previous attempts at the numerical study of the households of the poor, which have drawn on listings of inhabitants or on 'pauper censuses', would have us believe that pauper households were particularly small in size and simple in structure, with high proportions of solitaries especially among the elderly.[4] But this view is highly misleading. It results from misplaced reliance on such records at face value.

As a matter of fact, neither listings of inhabitants nor 'pauper censuses' are in themselves suitable sources for the statistical study of the pauper household. As has been shown elsewhere,[5] listings of inhabitants do not normally indicate more than a small fraction of all households in the community which were actually in need because the label 'pauper' was apparently only used as a residual category in those few cases where the normal labels to characterize the social position of a household (social status and/or occupation for male and marital status for female heads) would not apply. At best, listings yield extremely small and completely unrepresentative sub-samples of pauper households. What is worse, the so-called 'pauper censuses' do not normally record households at all, because they were concerned with individuals or families as 'relief-receiving units', but not with co-resident domestic groups. Reliable statistical data on the size, composition and structure of pauper households can only be obtained on the basis of a nominal record linkage of both types of document, whereby the pauper households in a community are identified in a proper census or listing of inhabitants of that community by means of a 'pauper census' or, more precisely, a list of the poor relief recipients for the same community at the same point in time.

The findings reported in what follows are based on the latter method. They come from a larger study of two Essex communities in which that method has been applied for the first time: the agricultural village of Ardleigh as recorded in 1796 and the market town of Braintree as recorded in 1821.[6] The results show that in both places the households of the poor were by no means smaller and less complex than those of the remaining population. Needless to say, this is not the place to dwell on this at length. But since this newly-established evidence on pauper households makes such a contrast to the hitherto accepted view, it will be necessary to make at least some overall reference to it, thus enabling the special data concerning the household position of elderly paupers, and here particularly of women, to be put in context. For each place, therefore, we shall take a brief look at the distribution of pauper households by structure (and compare it with the rest of the population), before we deal in more detail with those household forms which are of particular interest to the question of the household position of the elderly poor, especially of widows whose case, as we shall see, is the most revealing.

First, a further point needs to be made concerning the level – and implicit social meaning – of poverty to which our data refer. On the basis of the method of obtaining statistics of the pauper household as outlined above, this is a pretty straightforward matter, if only in an operational sense, since through the linking of a pauper list with a listing of inhabitants the proportion of identifiable pauper households in all households in the community is automatically yielded as well. In Ardleigh, 41 per cent of all households were pauper households in this sense, comprising 43 per cent of the population. In Braintree, where a set of different pauper lists enables us to distinguish between a primary and a secondary group of paupers, the proportion of pauper households amounted to 13 and 25 per cent respectively, representing 12 and 24 per cent of the total population. For reasons which will become plain as we turn to the two communities in question, these differences in the level of acknowledged poverty are mainly due to the different economic and demographic conditions at the moment when their populations were enumerated.

ARDLEIGH IN 1796: POOR ELDERLY WIDOWS IN COMPLEX HOUSEHOLDS

In the case of Ardleigh in 1796, the community was still suffering from the severe subsistence crisis of the previous winter. Poverty was widespread among the rural proletariat that formed the bulk of the population. But that condition was also acknowledged by the small group of grain-producing tenant farmers who managed the economy as well as the local government of the village. Thus, in a typical 'Speenhamland' situation it was especially young agricultural labouring families who were given relief in the form of fairly generous child allowances.

It is no wonder, therefore, that most pauper households consisted of nuclear family households, more precisely of young couples with children (class 3b): nearly 75 per cent of all pauper households belonged to this category, as compared with just over half of all non-pauper households (Table 10.1).

This extreme disparity also explains some of the quirks in the distribution of pauper households by structure. For instance, couples without children (class 3a) made up just 1 per cent of the pauper households, but nearly 20 per cent of others. Given that a fifth of these households consisted of elderly couples (in five of the twenty-four couples both partners were aged 60 or above), it should perhaps be expected that a higher proportion of them were poor. What is even more surprising is that there was almost no difference between the poor and the remaining population in the proportion of widows with children (class 3d), and the proportion of households headed by a widow (which includes solitary widows as well as widows heading complex households) was actually smaller among the poor. However, to some extent such findings have to be attributed to the small numbers involved. With only twenty-one pauper households left to be distributed among all household types other than couples with children, there is bound to arise a number of unexpected observations which are simply due to random variation.

On the other hand, there are two points at which the evidence stands out so clearly as to suggest real differences between the two groups. One is the extreme paucity of solitaries among the poor, the other one the fact that pauper households showed a higher degree of household complexity.

Just one of the eighty-two pauper households at Ardleigh in 1796 was a solitary household, and not even this was a household in which a pauper lived all alone. It was headed by an elderly widow by the name of Abigail Johnson (aged 64), who received a regular pension of 2s. a week from the parish. But with her were Martha Loft (26) and her daughter Charlotte (1), who were also on poor relief.[7]

Among complex households, that is extended family households and multiple family households, those with an upward extension are of particular interest because in this class the proportion of pauper households

Table 10.1 Distribution of households by structure, Ardleigh, 1796

	Pauper households		Non-pauper households	
	%	(N)	%	(N)
1 Solitaries				
a Widowed	1.2	(1)	1.7	(2)
b Single or of unknown marital status	—		4.2	(5)
Subtotal 1	1.2	(1)	5.9	(7)
2 No family				
a Co-resident siblings	—		0.8	(1)
b Co-resident relatives of other kinds	—		0.8	(1)
c Persons not evidently related	—		—	
Subtotal 2	—		1.7	(2)
3 Nuclear family households				
a Married couples alone	1.2	(1)	19.3	(23)
b Married couples with child(ren)	74.4	(61)	51.3	(61)
c Widowers with child(ren)	2.4	(2)	5.0	(6)
d Widows with child(ren)	6.1	(5)	5.0	(6)
Subtotal 3	84.1	(69)	80.7	(96)
4 Extended family households				
a Extended upwards	9.8	(8)	5.0	(6)
b Extended downwards	3.7	(3)	5.0	(6)
c Extended laterally	1.2	(1)	0.8	(1)
d Combinations of 4a–4c	—		—	
Subtotal 4	14.6	(12)	10.9	(13)
5 Multiple family households				
a Secondary units up	—		0.8	(1)
b Secondary units down	—		—	
c Secondary units lateral	—		—	
d *Frérèches*	—		—	
e Other multiple family households	—		—	
Subtotal 5	—		0.8	(1)
6 Households of indeterminate structure	—		—	
Total	100.0	(82)	100.0	(119)

Source: Essex Record Office, Chelmsford, D/P 263/1/5, Ardleigh baptisms and burials, 1790–1812 (1796 listing of inhabitants in the middle of the volume); D/P 263/12/1, Ardleigh overseers' accounts, 1794–8 (various pauper lists).

was almost twice as high as that of non-pauper households: 9.8 against 5.0 per cent (category 4a). They are worthy of more detailed consideration, even if the absolute numbers involved are very small indeed. Of the eight upwardly extended family households among the poor, five consisted of a young couple, two of them without, the other three with children, who all had the wife's mother residing with them. The men in these households were all agricultural labourers. In a further two households we find a young family with the man's own mother. One of the two men was again an agricultural labourer, the other one a small farmer who had also two servants. Finally, we have the household of a young shoemaker with his wife, four children and two journeymen, and the wife's father and her grandfather (aged 86) – the only four-generational household in the entire community.

In all these eight poor extended family households it was the young man (the mean age was a little under 27, with the oldest one being 36) who held the headship. This would suggest, especially in those cases where the wife's mother was present, that the widowed parent had been taken into the young couple's household, presumably after the death of his or her spouse.[8]

By contrast, in four of the six non-pauper households with an upward extension to the nuclear family unit it was the father of one of the spouses who held the headship, even though the couples in these households were somewhat older than their counterparts among the poor (the mean age of the men was just over 30, the oldest one was 41). A possible explanation is suggested by the occupations of these elderly household heads. Two of them were blacksmiths, one a brickmaker and one an innkeeper. Thus, in the wealthier households of the community it might have been common for the newly-wed couple to join one of the parental households, presumably that where the father was still running a business.

The evidence presented so far suggests that in Ardleigh in 1796 the lack of residential isolation among the poor was closely related to the comparatively high proportion of complex pauper households. Elderly widows on poor relief, we may contend, did not live as solitaries because they resided with their married children.

It is worth carrying this hypothesis a little further and considering the association of both household complexity and solitary householding with the position of the elderly in a more systematic fashion. In pre-industrial English communities, solitary households were primarily those of widowed persons, especially women, and widowhood was very much a function of old age.[9] But the possibility of the formation of complex households was also very much, though again not exclusively, a function of the availability of elderly people. The more elderly people there were in the community, the more households might be expected to be either solitary or complex, or both. This is because in most English historical communities, the overwhelming majority of complex households consisted of lineally extended family households or multiple family households with lineal disposition.[10] These types of household (classes 4a, 4b, 5a and 5b in Peter Laslett's classification scheme) involve either a span, if not necessarily the actual presence, of three generations among its members (extensions downwards), or a (set of) parent(s) with a child old enough to be married (extensions upwards and secondary units up or down) (see Figure 10.1). In any community at a particular moment, therefore, the number of households spanning three

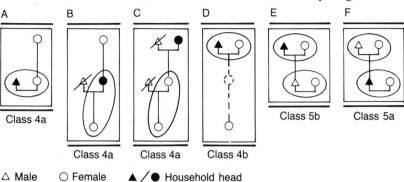

△ Male   ○ Female   ▲/● Household head

Figure 10.1 Examples of lineally extended family households and multiple family households with lineal disposition

Notes: Examples A, E and F are the only possible forms of complex households other than those with lateral extensions or secondary unit sideways to involve no more than two generations. (D spans three generations, although only two are actually present.) But they too require a parental generation old enough to have married children. Types B and C are distinguished by the fact that the middle generation female in B is illegitimate.

generations (examples B, C and D) cannot be higher than the total number of grandparents present. Assuming a mean age at marriage for women around 25, it would follow that if a community happened not to possess anybody who was over 50, we should not expect it to possess households of these types either. The same would be true of households which require the presence of only two generations (examples A, E and F). For here the members of the younger generation would have to be married, which again would require their parents to be, on average, at least 50 years old.[11]

Admittedly, this simple check of household complexity against the age structure of household members cannot be regarded as a precise control measure.[12] But it provides at least some sort of external standard against which to judge a given degree of household complexity.

Applied to the comparison of household structure between the poor and the rest of the population at Ardleigh in 1796, this simple test lends further support to the suggestion that the taking-in of elderly people, especially widows, into households of their married children seems to have been a distinctive behavioural pattern among the poor. As we have seen above, complex households comprised 15 per cent of all pauper households, compared with 12 per cent of all non-pauper households. This difference is very slight indeed, but then it is striking that the proportion of complex households was higher among the poor although the proportion of elderly paupers was so surprisingly low. Given that the proportion of people aged 50 and over was much higher in the non-pauper population, it is the non-pauper households which should be expected to show greater complexity.

Looking at the evidence more closely, it appears that among paupers, thirteen out of thirty-seven household members of age 50 and upwards (excluding servants and lodgers)[13] lived in lineally extended family households, whereas this was true for only twenty out of seventy-seven non-paupers. In other words, the proportion of the elderly population 'at risk' that actually lived in vertically complex households was 35 per cent among paupers, as compared to only 26 per cent among non-paupers. For women this contrast was even more pronounced. Half of all poor women aged 50 and over (nine out of seventeen) lived in lineally extended family households, but only a quarter of the women who were not poor (nine out of thirty-three).[14]

To conclude that the proportion of complex pauper households would have been far higher than among non-paupers if the proportion of elderly people, particularly elderly women, among the poor had been considerably higher than in the rest of the population would of course be mere speculation. On the other hand, the evidence might indeed indicate different practices of household formation between the two groups, in that the poor at Ardleigh in 1796 would be more inclined, provided they were not prevented from doing so by demographic constraints, to live in complex households.

BRAINTREE IN 1821: POOR ELDERLY WIDOWS WITH CHILDREN AND AS 'JOINT SOLITARIES'

Braintree in 1821 provides a contrasting case. After a century of decline during which the town had lost its former role as a centre of proto-industrial cloth production, the community was entering a period of economic and demographic recovery. Under the more prosperous conditions of a mixed urban economy, poverty was less pronounced than in the case of Ardleigh. But it was also acknowledged to a lesser extent, as the newly established Select Vestry, in their attempts at enhancing the social control of the poor, made efforts to restrict the qualifications for relief. Hence the higher proportions of such 'classical' types of recipients as widows with children or elderly couples among that group of primary paupers to which our figures refer.

The proportion of complex households was almost twice as high among the poorest people in the community as among those who were not poor (Table 10.2). As in Ardleigh, the contrast was most pronounced in upwardly extended family households (class 4a), while again the only multiple family household in the entire community was a non-pauper household. On this occasion, however, the secondary family unit was located in a younger generation than that of the household head (class 5b). With almost twice as high a proportion of complex households among the poor, the contrast with the remaining population would seem to have been even stronger than in Ardleigh. On the other hand, the proportions of complex households to be compared here were all of a much lower order than those found in Ardleigh.[15] The same is true of the overall proportion of complex households in the community, where Braintree had only 5 per cent, against 13 per cent in Ardleigh.

Table 10.2 Distribution of households by structure, Braintree, 1821

	Primary pauper households		Non-pauper households	
	%	(N)	%	(N)
1 Solitaries				
a Widowed	1.2	(1)	3.1	(15)
b Single or of unknown marital status	3.7	(3)	5.2	(25)
Subtotal 1	4.9	(4)	8.3	(40)
2 No family				
a Co-resident siblings	1.2	(1)	1.5	(7)
b Co-resident relatives of other kinds	—		1.5	(7)
c Persons not evidently related	6.2	(5)	1.0	(5)
Subtotal 2	7.4	(6)	4.0	(19)
3 Nuclear family households				
a Married couples alone	13.6	(11)	17.9	(86)
b Married couples with child(ren)	42.0	(34)	56.3	(271)
c Widowers with child(ren)	1.2	(1)	2.9	(14)
d Widows with child(ren)	21.0	(17)	6.2	(30)
Subtotal 3	77.8	(63)	83.4	(401)
4 Extended family households				
a Extended upwards	4.9	(4)	1.9	(9)
b Extended downwards	2.5	(2)	1.9	(9)
c Extended laterally	—		0.2	(1)
d Combinations of 4a–4c	1.2	(1)	0.2	(1)
Subtotal 4	8.6	(7)	4.2	(20)
5 Multiple family households				
a Secondary units up	—		—	
b Secondary units down	—		0.2	(1)
c Secondary units lateral	—		—	
d *Frérèches*	—		—	
e Other multiple family households	—		—	
Subtotal 5	—		0.2	(1)
6 Households of indeterminate structure	1.2	(1)	—	
Total	99.9	(81)	100.1	(481)

Source: Essex Record Office, Chelmsford, D/DU 65/83, Braintree census return 1821; D/DO 09, Braintree 'Poor Book', 1821.

With only about one in twelve of the poorest households being complex, Braintree in 1821 decidedly does not provide a case for a strong tendency among the poor to live with relatives. Moreover, an analysis of more refined age-specific data shows that this relatively low level of household complexity here cannot in any way be attributed to age-structural peculiarities as suggested in the case of Ardleigh in 1796.[16] But as in Ardleigh, it is the case of widows which is of particular interest to the question of the household position of elderly paupers.

In Ardleigh, poor widows tended to live with their married children, and only a very small proportion of all pauper households consisted of widows with children. In Braintree, however, the situation was quite different. Here more than one in five of the poorest households consisted of widows with children (class 3d), as opposed to less than one in fifteen of the households which were not poor (Table 10.2, class 3d).

Most of the widows with children in primary poverty were elderly women. Out of seventeen in all, eleven were aged 50 and over, and of these seven were over 60. Nine of them had children with them who were 20 years or older (eleven such children in all), but only three of these children were male. Two of these three male children headed the household. This suggests the possibility that poor elderly widows would be more inclined to live with their daughters and to retain the headship of their household even if their daughters had come of age, and that, by contrast, if an adult son stayed with his widowed mother, which was rather exceptional, he would be likely to take over the headship of the household when he became adult.

However, these residential patterns were not specific to widows in poverty. As they became older, widows who were not poor also tended to live almost exclusively with their daughters. Among the children aged under 20 found in non-pauper households of class 3d, one in two was male, but less than one in three were male among the children over 20. The most extreme case was that of Rebecca Thompson, a widow aged 95. She was the oldest person recorded in Braintree in 1821 and lived with her daughter Mary, who was 70.[17]

If the households of widows with children did not, then, differ a great deal between the poorest people and those who were not on relief, an important conclusion may be drawn. A widow with unmarried children would seem to have been able at all events to maintain an independent household – even if she fell into poverty, in which case she would receive public assistance. This would confirm the point made by Peter Laslett, that in pre-industrial English society elderly people, especially if widowed, tended to stay in the same households as before rather than to join the households of others.[18] But only to some extent. An important qualification has to be made with respect to solitary widows, that is widows who never had children or whose children had already left home.

Here the evidence from Braintree in 1821 strongly suggests that, just as in Ardleigh, a solitary widow in poverty should not normally be expected to have kept an independent household. Among the 330 people in primary poverty there was no more than one widow who lived all alone, a certain widow Slaughter aged 61 (see Table 10.2, class 1a).[19]

If residential independence was not, then, an option normally chosen by a poor widow without dependent children, joining the household of a married child does not seem to have been common either. In Braintree, there were only four poor widows in that position, who all lived in the household of a married son, rather than with a married daughter as in Ardleigh.[20]

Most solitary widows in primary poverty lived together with other widows or single women who were also poor. There were eleven such women, aged between 50 and 81, who lived in the five households shown in Figure 10.2. In Table 10.2, these households are to be found under 'persons not evidently related to each other' (class 2c), and it is striking that all pauper households of that class were occupied only by elderly women. By contrast, the five non-pauper households of the same kind were occupied by six men and seven women, though these were also mainly elderly.

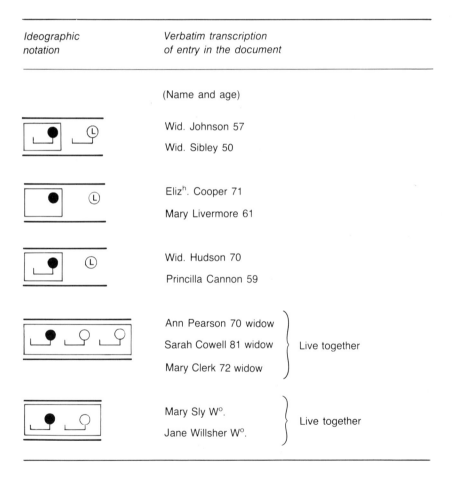

Ideographic notation	Verbatim transcription of entry in the document
	(Name and age)
	Wid. Johnson 57 Wid. Sibley 50
	Eliz^h. Cooper 71 Mary Livermore 61
	Wid. Hudson 70 Princilla Cannon 59
	Ann Pearson 70 widow Sarah Cowell 81 widow } Live together Mary Clerk 72 widow
	Mary Sly W^o. } Live together Jane Willsher W^o.

Figure 10.2 Braintree, 1821: primary pauper households of persons not evidently related to each other (household class 2c)

Source: Essex Record Office, Chelmsford, D/DU 65/83, Braintree census return 1821.

The point that the women in the five pauper households were all elderly, without a family and on regular poor relief raises the question of whether it may have been the case that these similar circumstances made them share their living spaces. It would be plausible, for example, to argue that for an elderly woman it was cheaper to live in a 'joint' household with another woman in the same situation.[21] Perhaps it was even the parish officers who applied that logic and urged poor elderly people to form such common households.

That such considerations are not groundless may be illustrated by an instance which neatly shows how closely the living arrangements of paupers could be related to the administration of poor relief. Upon his death in 1685, a Braintree gentleman by the name of Joseph Clarke left a sum of £20 for the relief of the poor. From this endowment the trustees bought a tenement with land in Coggeshall Lane, 'to the intent and purpose that some of the poor of Braintree should from time to time and at all times hereafter inhabit and dwell in the premises'. Unfortunately, as early as 1715 that house was burnt down and apparently never rebuilt,[22] and it is unclear how the charity was administered after that date.[23] But there is reason to believe that as late as the early nineteenth century the parish provided such common lodgings for the poor.

Lack of evidence makes it impossible to carry this point any further as far as the case of Braintree is concerned. But of course we know, indeed we have known for a long time, that under the Old Poor Law communal housing in parochial tenements was a common form of provision for the poor, especially for the elderly, and again most especially for elderly women.[24]

CONCLUSION

The most obvious conclusion to be drawn from the evidence presented here seems to be that the widely held notion of the pauper household as being small and simple ought to be revised. In particular, there seems to be little justification for the view that a large proportion of paupers, especially among the elderly, and most particularly elderly women, lived in residential isolation. The poor old widows and 'maidens' who feature so prominently in 'pauper censuses' must not be presumed to have been solitary house-holders. Instead, they were found either to have lived in other people's households, whether as relatives or lodgers, or to have shared their own premises with other people, whether related or unrelated. In both the villages we have been discussing, 'a lonely old age' was decidedly not the lot of the poor, at least not in the sense that they lived alone. This finding is all the more striking as the communities of Ardleigh in 1796 and Braintree in 1821 were completely different in social structure, economic condition and demographic profile as well as in their policy towards the poor.

Two questions arise. The first one is whether the findings for Ardleigh or

Braintree are in any way exceptional. This question is impossible to answer at the present state of our knowledge. The data on the household position of elderly paupers presented in this chapter are the first ones of their kind to have been generated. We can only hope that comparable data for other places and points in time will be supplied in future research. And we should add that in order to yield reliable results such studies ought to apply the same method of obtaining the required figures as that employed here. In other words, future research into the size, composition and structure of pauper households should no longer draw on either 'pauper censuses' or listings of inhabitants alone, but be firmly based on a combined quantitative analysis of both types of record.

The second question is why it was that in neither of the two places we have been looking at elderly people who received poor relief lived on their own, and more particularly, to what extent this was related to the system of poor relief. For example, did the overseers of Ardleigh force those elderly widows to live with their married daughters, while the overseers of Braintree made them form 'joint' households of two or three women? As already stated, as far as the evidence from the Poor Law records of these two places goes, such questions have to be left open as well.

But if placed in a comparative perspective, even the limited data from these two English communities should help us to see the issue more clearly. As Josef Ehmer has recently argued, there is every reason to believe that in early modern society the household position of old people mainly depended on whether they had ever married, due to the close link between marriage and household formation. Such persons would stand a good chance of spending their old age in the household they had entered upon marriage, even after their marriage had been broken up by the death of their spouse. A widow, for example, providing she did not remarry, would normally maintain her own household, more typically as a nuclear household with co-residing children, but also as a solitary householder in those cases where she had no children or after they had left home to marry and set up their own households.[25]

But what happened if she became poor? Here the question is whether the principle that you stayed in the household you had entered on marriage was strong enough as a social norm to guarantee that she was given the means to do so if she was unable to support herself. Another critical factor would be the extent to which that norm would overrule other considerations, most notably financial considerations, for in the case of solitary households the rule of maintaining residential independence must usually have incurred higher costs than arranging for such elderly poor to be placed in the households of others.

As to the latter option, perhaps the most extreme example comes from nineteenth-century Iceland. Not only were, according to the Icelandic poor law, individual paupers to be 'taken in' by prosperous members of the community, but pauper families, elderly couples for example, were actually split up by the local authorities to 'make' them into individual paupers.[26] In England, on the other hand, it would seem that parish officers always had a free choice between several alternatives. From the very beginning of the Elizabethan Poor Law, there is evidence of a variety of practices of relief to the aged poor: 'boarding-out' as well as rent allowances or the provision of housing were all possible strategies that might be followed. Housing provided by the community would also include smaller workhouses, which were in fact often old people's homes.[27]

Most importantly, in England the variety of provision for the aged poor is not only found between places, but also within the same community at the same time. In Braintree in 1821, as we have seen, the parish officers provided for elderly widows with co-residing children as well as for those who lived in the households of their children or with other widows.[28] A few years later, the Select Vestry had to decide on the application from a certain widow Parmenter who had her settlement in Braintree but lived in Bromsgrove (near Birmingham) and wanted to move to Wordsley where 'sume Friend will take her to make her Comfortable and Mr Jones the Over[se]er [paper torn] of that Parish could Allow her the Weekly Allowance'. They agreed to that proposal, and informed the parish officers of Bromsgrove that they would remit the relief expenses to widow Parmenter by quarterly payments, 'as is our useal way'.[29]

Judged from this instance and similar ones witnessed in overseers' correspondence from other Essex communities, it would seem that in England under the Old Poor Law, that is up to 1834, the parish authorities did not, in their administration of outdoor relief, favour living arrangements of the aged poor of a particular kind, but rather tended to support them in the households in which they found them, providing that, other things being equal, this would not incur extraordinary costs. But this is a tentative suggestion, made in the hope that further research will show to what extent it is tenable.

NOTES

1 For the English case, see P. Laslett, 'The family and the collectivity', *Sociology and Social Research*, 63, 1979, pp. 432–42; P. Laslett, 'Family, kinship and collectivity as systems of support in pre-industrial Europe: A consideration of the "nuclear-hardship" hypothesis', *Continuity and Change*, 3, 1988, pp. 153–75; R.M. Smith, 'Incomes, risk and security: The roles of the family and the collectivity in recent theories of fertility change', in D. Coleman and R. Schofield (eds), *The State of Population Theory: Forward from Malthus*, Oxford: Blackwell 1986, pp. 188–211. A succinct comparison of the western (nuclear) and 'eastern' (complex) family systems in their impact on the household position of the elderly is provided by M. Mitterauer, 'Problemfelder einer Sozialgeschichte des Alters', in H. Konrad (ed.), *Der alte Mensch in der Geschichte*, Vienna: Verlag für Gesellschaftskritik 1982, pp. 37–40.

2 P. Slack, *Poverty and Policy in Tudor and Stuart England*, London: Longman 1989, p. 85.

3 M. Anderson, *Family Structure in Nineteenth-Century Lancashire*, Cambridge: Cambridge University Press 1971, pp. 55–6, 95–6, 139–47; J. Quadagno, *Aging in Early Industrial Society. Work, Family and Social Policy in Nineteenth-Century England*, New York: Academic Press 1982, pp. 77–90. Other case studies include H.P. Chudacoff and T.K. Hareven, 'Family transitions into old age', in T.K. Hareven (ed.), *Transitions. The Family and the Life Course in Historical Perspective*, New York: Academic Press, 1978, pp. 216–43; T.K. Hareven, *Family Time and Industrial Time. The Relationship Between the Family and Work in a New England Industrial Community*, Cambridge: Cambridge University Press 1982, pp. 173–85; J. Robin, 'Family care of the elderly in a nineteenth-century Devonshire parish', *Ageing and Society*, 4, 1984, pp. 505–16; S.O. Rose, 'The varying household arrangements of the elderly in three English villages: Nottinghamshire, 1851–1881', *Continuity and Change*, 3, 1988, pp. 101–22, and Chapter 13 this volume; N. Folbre, 'Women on their own: Residential independence in Massachusetts in 1880', *Continuity and Change*, 6, 1991, pp. 87–105.

General surveys are provided by P. Laslett, 'The history of ageing and the aged', in his *Family Life and Illicit Love in Earlier Generations*, Cambridge: Cambridge University Press 1977, pp. 196–208; P. Laslett, 'Societal development and aging', in E. Shanas and R. Binstock (eds), *Handbook of Aging and the Social Sciences*, vol. 1, New York: Van Nostrand Reinhold Co. 1978, pp. 87–116; D.S. Smith, 'Historical change in the household structure of the elderly in economically developed societies', in P.N. Stearns (ed.), *Old Age in Preindustrial Society*, New York: Croom Helm 1982, pp. 248–73; J. Ehmer, 'Zur Stellung alter Menschen in Haushalt und Familie. Thesen auf der Grundlage von quantitativen Quellen aus europäischen Städten seit dem 17. Jahrhundert', in Konrad (ed.), *Der alte Mensch*, pp. 62–103; R. Wall, 'Residential isolation of the elderly: A comparison over time', *Ageing and Society*, 4, 1984, pp. 483–503; P. Laslett, *A Fresh Map of Life. The Emergence of the Third Age*, London: Weidenfeld & Nicolson 1989, pp. 111–15; J. Ehmer, *Sozialgeschichte des Alters*, Frankfurt am Main: Suhrkamp 1990, pp. 177–87.

4 Slack, *Poverty and Policy*, pp. 73–85, provides an excellent summary of the research undertaken on the basis of 'pauper censuses' (with comprehensive references).

5 T. Sokoll, 'The pauper household small and simple? The evidence from listings of inhabitants and pauper lists of early modern England reassessed', *Ethnologia Europaea*, 17, 1987, pp. 26–33; T. Sokoll, *Household and Family Among the Poor: The Case of Two Essex Communities in the Late Eighteenth and Early Nineteenth Centuries*, Bochum: Brockmeyer 1993, ch. 2.

6 Sokoll, *Household and Family*, chs 3–10. A different attempt was undertaken in the path-breaking study by T. Wales, 'Poverty, poor relief and the life cycle: Some evidence from seventeenth-century Norfolk', in R.M. Smith (ed.), *Land, Kinship and Life Cycle*, Cambridge: Cambridge University Press 1984, pp. 351–404, linking lists of poor families with other Poor Law records. But then, these 'pauper censuses' suffer from the same inaccuracies in recording the households of the poor as other documents of that type.

7 According to Peter Laslett's classification scheme a solitary household is not necessarily a household with no more than one person. This is why there is no contradiction between the appearance of a solitary pauper household in Table 10.1 (p. 211) and the fact that there was no pauper household of size 1.

8 Unfortunately, we know nothing about the relationship of those mothers-in-law in pauper households to their daughters. Later studies on working-class households have stressed the importance of the bond between married women and their mothers. See M. Young and P. Willmott, *Family and Kinship in East*

London, Harmondsworth: Penguin 1962, chs 3 and 4; P. Willmott and M. Young, *Family and Class in a London Suburb*, London: Routledge & Kegan Paul 1960, ch. 6. But note also the critique of such studies in P. Laslett, 'Introduction', in P. Laslett and R. Wall (eds), *Household and Family in Past Time*, Cambridge: Cambridge University Press 1972, pp. 22–3.

9 Laslett, 'The history of ageing', pp. 196–208; J.E. Smith, 'Widowhood and ageing in traditional English society', *Ageing and Society*, 4, 1984, pp. 430–7.

10 In Laslett's sample of the thirty most reliable English community listings, laterally extended family households and multiple family households with lateral disposition made up 3 per cent of all households, as compared to 12 per cent for complex households involving a lineal relationship. P. Laslett, 'The stem family hypothesis and its privileged position', in K.W. Wachter, E.A. Hammel and P. Laslett (eds), *Statistical Studies of Historical Social Structure*, New York: Academic Press 1978, p. 75, exhibit 5.3.

11 For the sake of simplicity, the model developed here has been confined to (grand)parental involvement in the formation of complex households. To consider lateral extensions or multiplicity (households to be classified as 4d or 5e), such as a co-residing maternal aunt of the wife (instead of her mother) in case A of Figure 10.1 (p. 213), would complicate the argument in so far as such relationships, although involving the same generational spans as those discussed here, might well imply different age ranges. For instance, if ego's mother has many younger sisters, then he might well be little younger than his youngest aunt. For a statistical formulation of ego's possible kin relationships according to age, number of siblings, number and order of parents' siblings, etc., see H. Le Bras, 'Living forebears in stable populations', in Wachter, Hammel and Laslett (eds), *Statistical Studies*, pp. 163–88.

12 Apart from the already mentioned fact that it does not make allowance for the minority of complex households which involve lateral relationships to the household head, there is the further complication that the exact number of those parents over 50 who would be able to form, or be available in the formation of, complex households cannot, of course, be gathered from the information provided in a listing of inhabitants. The analysis of a listing may yield the total numbers of males and females over 50, but a complete family reconstitution would be necessary to establish the number of those who had married children (or widowed ones with their own children) and were thus potential partners for complex households. In other words, the number of men and women in a listing who are over 50 would in most cases probably considerably overstate the actual group at risk in the formation of lineally extended family households or multiple family households with a lineal disposition.

For a more exact analysis of the propensity of the elderly to live in complex households, see H.C. Johansen, 'The position of the old in the rural household in a traditional society', in S. Akerman, H.C. Johansen and D. Gaunt (eds), *Chance and Change. Social and Economic Studies in Historical Demography in the Baltic Area*, Odense: Odense University Press 1978, pp. 122–30. He found that, under the demographic conditions obtaining in late eighteenth-century Denmark,

> if all old people of 60 years or more who had married children stayed with them, then between 51 and 61 per cent of all old women and between 37 and 49 per cent of all old men would [have] live[d] with them
>
> (ibid.: p. 127)

and that about half of the elderly population at risk thus defined did actually live in complex households in Denmark in 1787 and 1891 (ibid.: pp. 127–9).

13 Servants and lodgers were excluded from these calculations since according to Peter Laslett's classification scheme they do not influence the structure of the household.

14 Neither of these differences between paupers and non-paupers is statistically significant, but it should be noted that in the case of women, despite the smaller absolute numbers involved, the degree of random variation was much lower than in the pooled data for both sexes. According to a chi-square test, where $chi^2 = 3.209$; $df = 1$; $0.10 > p > 0.05$ for women, as compared to $chi^2 = 1.020$; $df = 1$; $0.50 > p > 0.30$ for both sexes.

15 Even so, because of the higher absolute numbers involved in the case of Braintree, the difference observed there shows less random variation than that for Ardleigh. According to a chi-square test, where the 2×2 contingency table compares complex households against all other households for paupers against the rest of the population, we find: $chi^2 = 2.678$; $df = 1$; $0.20 > p > 0.10$ for Braintree; and $chi^2 = 0.355$; $df = 1$; $p < 0.50$ for Ardleigh.

16 See Sokoll, *Household and Family*, pp. 267–9.

17 That girls and young women were more inclined than boys and young men to live with their widowed mother was by no means specific to Braintree in 1821. Rather, it seems to have been a common feature of pre-industrial English society. See R. Wall, 'Leaving home and the process of household formation in pre-industrial England', *Continuity and Change*, 2, 1987, pp. 92–4.

18 Laslett, 'The history of ageing', p. 199.

19 Solitary households of poor women who were single or of unknown marital status were also extremely rare, and the same holds for male paupers. In this household class (1b) we find only two people who lived on their own, a woman (aged 89) and a man (73), while the third pauper household in this class consisted of a man (69) with a male lodger, presumably a widower (55), and his son (11).

20 Three of them lived in an upwardly extended family household (class 4a), and the youngest of them (aged 59) actually headed the household. The fourth one was found in a combined extended family household (class 4d), also involving the presence of an unmarried daughter.

21 To avoid confusion it should be noted that the term 'joint household' is not normally used in this sense. Rather, it usually refers to complex households consisting of several brothers and their families, as, for instance, the *frérèches* of southern France.

22 H.J. Cunnington, *An Account of the Charities and Charitable Benefactions of Braintree*, London 1904, p. 29.

23 There is no reference to it in the *Abstract of Returns of Charitable Donations for the Benefit of Poor Persons* of 1788, *Parliamentary Papers* (henceforth *PP*) 1816, XVI, A, pp. 368–71, under Braintree. But in the mammoth report of the Charity Commission of the 1830s it is mentioned as 'Clarke's charity' with an annual income of £1. *Thirty-Second Report, Part I, of the Commissioners Appointed to Continue the Inquiries Concerning Charities in England and Wales, Until 1 March 1837, PP*, 1837–8, XXV, p. 780.

24 Both the *Abstract of Returns of Charitable Donations* and the *Report* of the Charity Commission quoted in the previous note are replete with references to charities providing housing to poor people. To quote a few instances from Essex: at Steeple Bumpstead, a tenement 'for the poor to live in, rent-free'; at Boxted, the three tenements 'for the residence of poor widows'; at Dedham, five tenements 'for the poor to dwell in' (*PP*, 1816, XVI, A, pp. 370, 374). More specifically, we hear of a row of houses with six dwellings provided for old people, single ones or couples, but without children (Winnock's almshouses, bequeathed at Colchester in 1679; *PP*, 1837–8, XXV, p. 537). See also the *Analytical Digest of the Reports Made by the Commissioners of Inquiry into Charities, PP*, 1843, XVI

and XVII, where the additional comments make it clear that houses and tenements were often occupied by paupers even though the original purpose of the charity was such as to provide for the poor in cash or kind by means of the profits to be made from such property.

25 Ehmer, *Sozialgeschichte des Alters*, ch. 9. For similar considerations, see Laslett, *A Fresh Map of Life*, chs 8 and 9.
26 Gísli Á. Gunnlaugsson, *Family and Household in Iceland 1801–1930. Studies in the Relationship Between Demographic and Socio-Economic Development, Social Legislation, Family and Household Structures*, Uppsala: Uppsala University 1988, pp. 94–5. See also Chapter 12 with Loftur Guttormsson in this volume.
27 E.M. Leonard, *The Early History of English Poor Relief*, Cambridge: Cambridge University Press 1900, pp. 213–15; G.W. Oxley, *Poor Relief in England and Wales 1601–1834*, Newton Abbot: David and Charles 1974, p. 92.
28 Four women aged 50 and above were also recorded in the workhouse (with sixteen inmates in all). Unfortunately, neither their names nor their marital status have been recorded. Essex Record Office (ERO), Chelmsford, D/DU 65/83, Braintree census return 1821.
29 ERO, D/P 264/9/18, Braintree overseers' correspondence, letter of 18 September 1827 (a copy of an answer by the Braintree vestry clerk to the parish officers of Bromsgrove).

11 Poverty, the life cycle of the household and female life course in eighteenth-century Corsica

Antoine Marchini

INTRODUCTION

This study focuses on the links between the descent into poverty and the composition of the household, an issue which is particularly relevant in the case of Vescovato and the villages of Loreto and Porri all in Casinca, a region of Corsica about 20 kilometres to the south of Bastia in the hills overlooking the Mediterranean. Particularly striking in this population is the important part played by women as heads of households in a rural and seemingly male-orientated world and that many of these women were identified by the census enumerators as '*poveri*'. One of the main purposes of this chapter will be to investigate the family and household patterns of this group.

FEMALE POVERTY: A SEXUAL DIMENSION TO THE SOCIAL HIERARCHY?

Twenty-five households (14.3 per cent of all the households in Vescovato in 1786) were classified as *poveri*. The *poveri* would hire themselves out by the day as wage-earners,[1] and constitute the second largest group after the *travagliatori* or *colons*. The members of this latter group were also poor, renting land, but usually in insufficient quantities to provide them with a livelihood and in addition had to find rent, the *terratico*, the level of which varied between a quarter and a half of the total value of the harvest. Their contracts might be written but were more commonly oral and often of an uncertain duration.

The proportion of household heads in poverty in Vescovato is less than in Gangi, the Sicilian village studied by Maurice Aymard (22 per cent).[2] It is also below Fernand Braudel's estimate of 20 per cent in the sixteenth century for the Mediterranean as a whole, although the incidence of poverty in Vescovato is close to that in Migliacciaro, a more southerly region of Corsica.[3] Of the twenty-five heads of household described as *poveri*, only one was male, and he was an adolescent; of the thirty households headed by women, only six were not identified as *poveri*. These figures demonstrate that women ran a far greater risk of destitution. They also suggest that

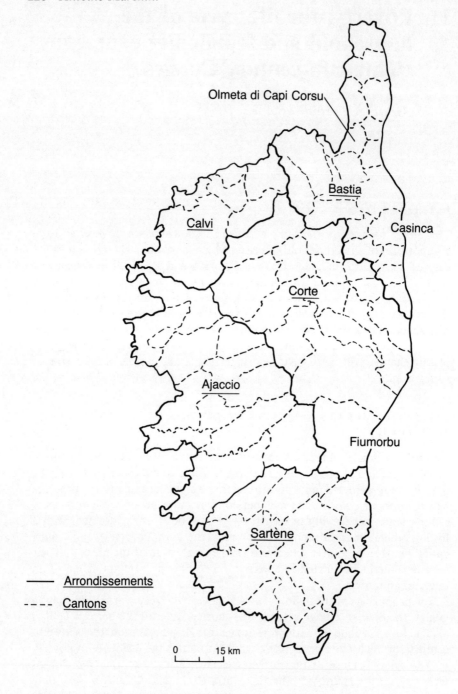

Figure 11.1   Corsica showing administrative boundaries of 1812

when they became heads of households there was a price to be paid in terms of their own and their co-residents downward social mobility. This is not only a Corsican model, but a phenomenon characteristic of the rest of the western Mediterranean, where women often formed a significant proportion of the poor. In many instances they constituted the majority, as did the 700 Andalusian women who headed 70 per cent of the households of the poor of Malaga in 1559.[4] By contrast, at Gangi they represented less than half (42.3 per cent) of the heads of destitute households.[5] Even here, however, it appears that they made up more than half of the number of all women who headed households.

In order to understand how women became destitute, we shall continue to focus on the village of Vescovato in 1786. The majority of the women who were heads of households were not recorded by name, a fact which implies their marginal role in society and possibly to their own family. Contemporaries may also have perceived the poverty of these women as an absence of identity, indicative of someone bereft of power. No less significant than their material deprivation is the inability of these people to exercise any control over their own future and their exclusion from the domain of family politics.[6]

Table 11.1 Vescovato: percentage of household heads in each age group classed as *poveri* in 1786

Age group	Household heads	Poveri *heading households*	
		N	%
0–20	2	0	0.0
20–4	14	1	7.1
25–9	14	1	7.1
30–9	53	9	16.9
40–9	43	7	16.2
50–9	22	5	22.7
60+	25	2	8.0
Total	173	25	14.4

The age distribution of heads of households classed as poor in the 1786 census as compared with that of all heads of households is set out in Table 11.1. This serves to identify the ages when a decline into poverty was particularly likely. The descent into poverty was clearly an ever-present threat. Nevertheless, women became more vulnerable in this respect after the age of 30 and their vulnerability peaked when they were in their 50s. The reason why fewer elderly household heads were listed as *poveri* reflected in all probability the fact that the more prosperous and stable households were more likely to survive until the household heads became elderly. The decrease in the number of households whose heads were over the age of 50 is very evident. The 50s marked a critical threshold in the history of many households in which some disappeared and others became destitute. The latter faced great odds in the struggle to survive – hence the fact that there were relatively fewer *poveri* heading households over the age of 60 (see Table 11.1).

THE POOR AND THE WEAKNESS OF THEIR HOUSEHOLDS

The mean size of the household and its variation according to the social position and age of its head casts some light on the weakness of the households of the *poveri*. The mean size of the twenty-five *poveri* headed households was 2.24. The fifty-six members of these households represented 9 per cent of the population. By contrast, the households whose heads were over the age of 60 sheltered many more persons than was possible for the *poveri*, containing an average of 4.04 members.

The small size of the household is, therefore, one of the factors which signal the risk of poverty. The women of Vescovato, unlike those from the neighbouring villages of Loreto and Porri, had the opportunity to head a household. But in this state of freedom they not only experienced poverty in its social, economic and political dimensions but also could only forge a limited range of interpersonal relationships within these households, and then in many cases only with other women or with children. The autonomous woman was 'liberated', but not in the present-day sense of the word. In official documents she was often not recorded by the name which would have proclaimed her identity. Headship of a household, and any independence that went with it, was obtained at a very considerable price.

The small size of the households of the *poveri* thus indicates that as a rule the poor failed to establish large households, and that their personality was formed and developed in an environment where there were few opportunities for interpersonal relationships to operate within the household. This will be particularly clear if we compare the average household size of high status members of the village, *nobili* and 'gentlemen', with those of the *travagliatori* and *poveri*. Table 11.2 shows that the higher the status of the household head, the larger on average was the household. Yet, the gap between *travagliatori* and *nobili* was no greater than 0.5 persons per household, not very large especially given that the former are represented by twenty-four groups and the latter by eleven. Moreover, since the majority of households of *poveri* were headed by widows, like is not being compared with like, since widow-headed households were one person short. In addition, the female-headed households, lacking a marital unit, were obviously less likely to expand than were couple-headed households.

In Table 11.3 we expand our study to include two villages near Vescovato (Loreto and Porri). This shows the variation in the average size of the household according to the age and sex of the head of the household in 1786. The size of households headed by women is clearly less than that of

Table 11.2 Vescovato: mean household size by social status of household head in 1786

High status		Low status	
Gentry	4.6	*Travagliatori*	3.8
Nobili	4.3	*Poveri*	2.2
Mean	4.4		3.0

Table 11.3 Vescovato, Loreto and Porri: mean household size by age and sex of household head in 1786

Age group	Male-headed households	Female-headed households
0–25	3.3	2.0
25–34	3.5	2.8
35–44	4.5	3.4
45–54	4.7	3.7
55–64	4.4	1.3
65 +	4.2	1.0
Mean	4.1	2.3
N	298	61

households where there was a male head. The average was 3.7 persons per household when the woman heading the household was aged between 45 and 54. Older women had much smaller households. While between the ages of 20 and 54 the average difference in the size of the male- and female-headed households was about one person per household, the difference widened to three persons for older household heads. In other words, from their late 50s these women were likely to be living alone just at the time when they were approaching old age. Households headed by a male who survived into old age managed to survive longer. Adaptations in the composition of these households took place to ensure the continuing stability of the group – a solution which was not open to women, whose households consequently fragmented.

THE *POVERI*: MARRIAGE DISSOLUTION AND THE FORMATION OF WOMEN'S HOUSEHOLDS

The fragmentation process is primarily linked to the high mortality rate, the most obvious effects of which are seen in the fact that the development of certain households was suddenly arrested. As a rule these households did not succeed in re-establishing themselves and, predominantly, it was the female members of the family who remained. Let us, therefore, consider the proportion of women who were married at different ages. The censuses of

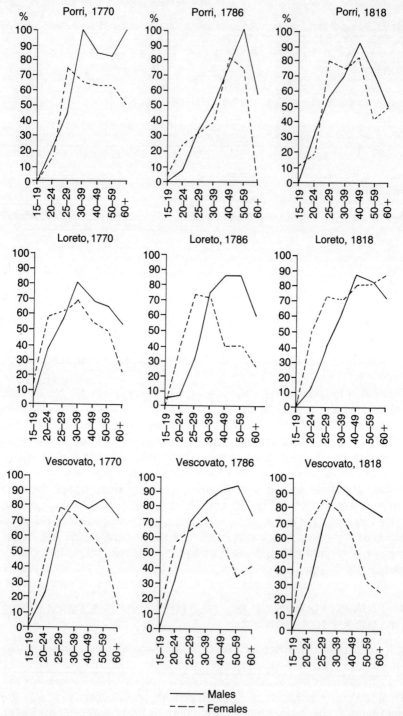

Figure 11.2 Vescovato, Loreto and Porri: percentage married by age and sex, 1770–1818

1770, 1786 and 1818 suggest that, once widowed, women would find it difficult to remarry (see Figure 11.2). Marriage was an easily available option when women were in their 20s and 30s. Thereafter, the proportion of women who were married declined steadily, a situation that still applied even at the beginning of the nineteenth century, when people were inclined to marry a little younger. In all three years men found it easier than did women to remarry.

There is therefore an association between the age from which women experienced an increased risk of poverty and the age which marks the beginning of a decline in the proportion of women who were married. The 30s represented a watershed in the life of women, a period during which their households were increasingly likely to be disrupted by the death of their husbands and consequent poverty. The fate of these women was sealed in many cases by the failure on the part of the remaining family members to support all the new dependants. The response of the families was to minimize the numbers of their dependants, a process which might even lead to the abandonment of those women who were no longer involved in the process of reproduction. According to Giovanni Levi, such solutions were also employed in seventeenth-century Piedmont.[7] Thus it was that some of the *poveri* came to live entirely on their own.

Admittedly, the nuclear family household was the predominant form since it describes fourteen out of twenty-five households listed as *poveri* in 1786 in Vescovato. However, none of these households was complete. Each one had at its head a widow: the household was, for a time at least, barred from further development.[8] Nine of the fourteen were organized along the mother−daughter axis, in a regular pattern which is the basis of groups which were very largely female. However, there were other groupings which did not include a conjugal family unit, the 'no family' households of the Laslett−Hammel classification scheme.[9] First were two *frérèches*, one involving three brothers and a sister and the other three sisters. In the first of these, three children were specified as dependants of Guiseppe Simeoni, the only 'man' (although still an adolescent) who was both the head of a household and identified as poor. The reference to *poveri pupilli* is indicative of their living conditions and of the origin of this *frérèche*. Orphans were unable to preserve effectively the identity of either their household or their parents' family. In Corsican communities of the time, orphans would have as their guardians members of their family or neighbours.[10] A development of a similar kind would also seem to explain the origin of the second grouping, comprising the sisters Elisabeth, Anna and Maria Caterina, an exclusively female world sustained by the close blood relationship, with each sister identified as *povera*.

The second category comprises apparently unrelated women who were living together. There were six such groupings in Vescovato in 1786 and their origin is unknown. Conceivably in the absence of a daughter or a sister such women may have sought out others who were in a similar situation hoping that a combined household would reduce their living costs. Women who lived entirely on their own were unusual: in 1786 among the poor of Vescovato there were just five of them.

POVERTY IN ITS ECONOMIC DIMENSION: THE ROLE OF WOMEN AS AN INDICATOR

It is impossible to be satisfied with the description of the *poveri* that is provided in the census. Whether the description which has been left us is an oversimplification can be considered by placing alongside it the information we have concerning the economic background.[11] According to the census of 1786, the *poveri* clearly may be considered genuinely poor as far as the possession of animals is concerned as they owned none, yet they were not alone in this respect. Almost three-quarters of the *travagliatori* were in the same position. However, none of the latter were described as *poveri*, at least so long as husband and wife remained together.[12] This information allows us to refine the social classifications adopted above (cf. Table 11.2, p. 229). It reveals a more subtle form of hierarchy and broadens our conception of what poverty entailed in this locality, even as it reveals a highly stratified society. It is also evident that a close correlation existed between the position of household heads in the social scale and the degree of control they exercised over the means of production.

Table 11.4 Vescovato: number and percentage of households by status of household head, owning at least one animal for transport or labour in 1786

Social category	Availability of animals for transport/labour			Percentage with 1+ animal
	None	1+	Total	
Poveri	25	0	25	0.0
Travagliatori	88	34	122	27.9
Nobili	9	18	27	66.6
Total	122	52	174	29.9

Two other conclusions also follow. First, this information justifies the use of the term *poveri* as applied to certain household heads. Second, these details illustrate the danger of placing too much reliance on contemporary labelling of persons as poor or not poor, as only one-quarter of the *travagliatori* had the means to live independently. Three-quarters suffered the same kind of deprivation as the *poveri* and were forced to resort to the renting of animals in order to work the land which was also owned by others. Finally, the proportion of the gentry (*nobili*) who were owners (66.6 per cent) confirms their position as the leaders of society.

There is also another source to which we can turn for information on the economic standing of these families: the inventories of the possessions of the deceased. In all, 212 estates were described between 1815 and 1830.[13] By studying these further light is thrown on the different situations of men and women in Vescovato, and also in Porri and Loreto.

Table 11.5 Vescovato, Loreto and Porri, 1815–30: distribution of estates by sex of the deceased and value of estate

Value (francs)	Men	Women	Total
10,000 +	1	2	3
5,000–9,999	2	0	2
1,000–4,999	32	8	40
500–999	39	30	69
100–499	38	47	85
0–99	7	6	13
Total	119	93	212
Average value[1]	1,292	1,068	1,180
Average value[2]	922	397	—

Notes: [1] All estates.
[2] Calculation excluding inheritances of more than 10,000 frs.

Table 11.5 shows both the average value and range of estates left by men and women. It is evident that the wealth bequeathed by men exceeded that left by women. The average value of all estates (measure 1) includes three inheritances of exceptional value and two of these were left by women. These two women, therefore, played an important part in the circulation of wealth from one generation to the next within the family. Most women, however, were not in this position and the value of their estates, excluding these three cases, should be considered more typical (measure 2). The difference in value between the average estate left by females and that left by males should therefore be considered relatively substantial, with men leaving about 500 frs more than women. The distribution of the deceased by marital status and sex indicates some of the factors which contributed to this difference. Two points are worthy of note. First, the average value of the estate left by those who were still married exceeded the amounts bequeathed by widows and widowers and those we have presumed to be single. The end of a marriage appears to have entailed a serious loss of 'wealth'. It should be noted that there were no known instances of a family's wealth being passed on to the next generation during the lifetime of the testator. Second, those who never married may never have acquired much wealth of their own. Both observations apply to men as well as to women.

However, these initial findings require qualification because of the inequality in the situations of men and women. Married women left less than

Table 11.6 Vescovato, Loreto and Porri, 1815–30: mean value of estates by sex and marital status of the deceased

	Men			Women		
	Married	Widowers	Unmarried[1]	Married	Widows	Unmarried[1]
Vescovato	29,845[2]	30,156	20,799	2,172	21,974	17,159[2]
Loreto	3,160	23,987	4,552	17,334[2]	13,060	637
Porri	4,118	7,102	5,260	300	2,468	217
Total	37,123	61,245	30,611	19,806	37,502	18,013
Number of cases	18	67	34	12	62	19
Average[3]	2,062	914	900	1,650	605	948
Average[4]	1,573	914	900	437	605	328

Notes: [1] In the absence of direct information the assumption has been made that when the marital status of the deceased was not specified the person concerned was unmarried.
[2] Including one estate of exceptional value (10,000+ frs).
[3] All estates.
[4] Calculation excluding inheritances of more than 10,000 frs.

married men; when a widow died she left less than a widower (a difference of 300 frs). The difference is even more significant in the case of those presumed to be single, at least if we eliminate the largest inheritance (12,117 frs, at Vescovato). Thus an estate declined in value when a woman was widowed. Poverty is also suggested by their failure to remarry, their fate dependent on the number and age of the children whom they had to support. The death of the husband seems to be the decisive factor. These points illustrate the legal context in which Corsican women lived. Custom distanced women from the inheritance of the means of production. In the absence of a will, property was transmitted through the male line.[14] Daughters were excluded, yet they needed to find a dowry if they were to marry and their economic plight worsened in the nineteenth century, because, with the inception of the Civil Code, the dowry system disappeared but daughters continued to be denied any share of the inheritance.[15] Table 11.6, therefore, takes on an even greater significance in that male wealth reflects, in effect, inheritances they have received, while female wealth often consisted of the dowry of the daughter. Men were able, therefore, to accumulate wealth, while women strove to mitigate the almost inevitable erosion of their dowry.

To conclude, poverty in these communities was the result of a process which involved an interplay between the life cycle of the couple, and the mode in which inheritance was managed and transmitted. Due to the status of women within society, 'downward mobility' rendered women particularly vulnerable to the instability which followed the dissolution of marriage. Yet there is not one single means by which individuals were channelled to their allotted positions within the social structure. The inhabitants of Vescovato were distributed among at least four major groups: fifty-five individuals were characterized as poor, sixty-four were salaried officials, forty-eight of these originating from groups of *nobili*, sixty-four were craftsmen and, finally, there were the 332 undergoing the uncertainties of life as *travagliatori*. Each of these groups followed its own social rules despite regular contact and avenues of mobility which drew them together. The composition of these groups was determined by their degree of success in reproduction. Only the *nobili* succeeded in establishing enduring lineages which they used to cement interfamily alliances and consanguineous marriages. Other social groups were very largely excluded from this process. Admittedly, the better-off *travagliatori* occasionally behaved in a similar fashion, but most were dependent on the marriage market rather than being in a position to control it. Social reproduction did not constitute a goal or a realistic possibility for many of the *travagliatori* and even less so for the *poveri*. An inability to form such alliances constitutes another criterion of social differentiation, and exclusion from this process was yet another sign of poverty. In the next section we will consider the influence exerted by such factors on the potential for stability or instability of the household.

EPHEMERAL MARRIAGE BONDS IN CENTRIFUGAL SYSTEMS

A comparison of the censuses of 1770 and of 1786 reveals a marked loss of households who had been resident in the earlier year. At Vescovato thirty-eight households survived from 1770 to 1786, that is 27 per cent of the total in 1770 and 22 per cent of the households of 1786.[16] The identity of the 'village' varied a great deal. If we look closely at the names of the families, it is clear that few family networks had survived.[17] The continuous process of renewal emphasizes the fact that the environment was not necessarily hostile; nevertheless only the well-established families persisted.

Fewer households survived in Vescovato where society was more hierarchical and the division of labour more highly developed than in the neighbouring villages. At the same time, the fact that a great number of these households did not survive very long was also a direct result of the way in which the political and social structure acted as a support for the well-established households who monopolized the opportunities for social reproduction by their firm grasp on the levers of power and the system of inheritance.

The aim of the following analysis is to determine whether a given level of wealth, forms of collaboration between households or the employment of servants had any bearing on the survival chances of a household. Our consideration of the issues will focus upon the situation in 1770,[18] when the 'traditional' strategies of the established families[19] still operated, though there was little security for individuals and households at the lower levels of society.

THE FATE OF FAMILY UNITS AND THE POSSESSION OF PROPERTY: A BROADER CONCEPT OF POVERTY

A first approach involves using the information we have concerning the number of animals which belonged to each household head, such possession being itself a vehicle of social differentiation. Table 11.7 indicates a correlation between the ownership of animals and the chances that a household would survive. In the three villages considered together, nearly two-thirds of the households which disappeared owned no animals. There was, however, some variation between one village and another in the strength of this association. For example, a higher proportion of the households in Loreto which persisted over the period possessed animals. Special factors also affected households at Vescovato, where the absence of animals almost appeared to guarantee the disappearance of the household. In the two other villages the situation was apparently more complex because ownership did not of itself guarantee the continuity of the household.

This pattern reveals the social differences between the villages, distinguishing Vescovato from the other two. In Vescovato the division of labour operated to tighten the relationship between the individual and the

Table 11.7 Household persistence in relation to ownership of animals in Vescovato, Loreto and Porri

Village	Households persisting		Households not persisting	
	No animals	*Total*	*No animals*	*Total*
Porri	5	31	11	24
Vescovato	5	38	89	105
Loreto	5	46	22	56
Total	15	115	122	185
Per cent not owning animals	13.0		65.9	

household. The possession of some land, however small, defined a family and offered the possibility of continuity. Social relations, therefore, determined the chances of survival, and of the continuity of the household. Excluded from the system were most of those who did not succeed in amassing economic and social capital. It was a society in which it was difficult to put down roots, as any enterprise not based on a social foundation ran the risk of imminent extinction.

Even in Loreto and Porri, however, the proportion owning animals was clearly higher among the households which persisted than among the unstable households. In addition, there were differences between one village and another, both in the type of animal owned and in the size of properties. Table 11.8 sets out the number and types of animal owned according to the persistence or non-persistence of the households.

This table highlights some aspects of the support which the ownership of land was able to provide and which contributed to the longevity of households. At the same time it also becomes clear how complex the quest for a determining variable can be. An overall comparison of the animal capital owned by each of the two categories of domestic group, the long-lived and the ephemeral, shows that in large measure the former controlled the means of production. Nevertheless, there were also significant spatial differences. Certain kinds of animal also seemed to have had greater significance for the local economy than others. There was a clear difference between Vescovato and Loreto. In the former, a system of cereal production, characterized by the use of draught oxen, existed alongside the breeding of ewes for sale, systems which were increasingly in competition[20] as demographic pressure increased. However, in Vescovato the breeding of ewes for sale seems to have been restricted to households which enjoyed continuity (of 2,650 ewes, the stable households owned 2,276), and in Loreto and Porri the proportion owned by the stable households was even greater. Pastoralism in the midst of crop farming permitted these few families to ensure their continuity. The Giamarchi and the Buttafoco families had the major part of these flocks, with the preponderance being held by the former due to specialization.

Gio Battista Giamarchi and Gio Stefano Giamarchi each possessed over 1,000 ewes.

Table 11.8 Numbers and types of animal owned by persisting and non-persisting households in Vescovato, Loreto and Porri

Village	Households	Number and type of animals owned										
		⅓A	½A	½B	½C	A	B	C	D	E	F	G
Vescovato	Persisting	—	—	—	—	8	4	19	37	45	83	2,276
	Non-persisting	—	—	—	—	3	1	7	21	29	0	374
Porri	Persisting	—	—	—	—	8	8	15	6	14	41	95
	Non-persisting	—	—	—	—	3	4	3	4	6	22	7
Loreto	Persisting	2	5	2	3	6	14	16	12	16	68	95
	Non-persisting	1	4	2	2	5	10	7	21	29	67	1
Total	Persisting	2	5	2	3	22	26	50	55	75	192	2,466
	Non-persisting	1	4	2	2	11	15	17	46	64	89	382

Notes: ⅓A Households having one-third share in a mule.
     ½A Households having one-half share in a mule.
     ½B Households having one-half share in an ass.
     ½C Households having one-half share in a horse.
     A mule
     B ass
     C horse
     D ox
     E cow
     F goat
     G lamb

In Vescovato animals were not kept mainly for home consumption, as was the case at Loreto and Porri where several households owned one or two goats for the milk and wool. The ownership of goats was not, there-fore, a significant indication of social or economic status. Moreover, in Loreto there is evidence of forms of collective ownership involving the sharing of a beast of burden between two or three families. Shared owner-ship of an animal did not automatically guarantee that the families partici-pating in this scheme would survive. Both the ownership of animals, such as asses, mules or goats, for the purpose of domestic consumption and reliance on others through a form of collective ownership signified a quest for security in the present rather than for the future. Such practices reveal a very fragile environment leaving little scope for breeding animals to supply the market.

This leads us to the issues raised by Peter Laslett in his 'nuclear-hardship' hypothesis: in particular how families solved the problem of the excessive nuclearization of the family unit.[21] At Vescovato the means adopted was exclusion – the continual thrusting of a part of the population into a spiral of poverty, with no access to the resources of the collectivity, since the community represented the interests of a few well-established families. At Loreto, and probably also at Porri, the community took the form of the common ownership and shared use of certain means of production. Schemes whereby families co-operated with each other became more effective in a world in which the job market was so limited that individuals faced an uncertain future, even when in regular employment. Yet as we have seen, the discovery of one set of interrelationships can reveal the existence of a whole host of others. Family patterns were not determined solely by the degree of wealth. For a deeper understanding it is necessary to take into account the interplay of other factors and in particular the structure of the household for each of these two groups.

THE EMPLOYMENT OF SERVANTS: AN EQUILIBRIUM BETWEEN CONTINUITY AND STABILITY

Of the 110 stable households, 40 per cent were complex in structure: this means they could make adjustments in the event of a structural disequilibrium. This was far more difficult for the unstable households. Scarcely 20 per cent of these were complex in form. A household's chances of survival therefore depended in part on the fact that they formed part of a larger family network capable of giving them the support they needed in a time of crisis. The threat of poverty was more acute in those groups which could not rely on the support of co-resident relatives. Complex households may even have come into being in advance of a crisis which could emerge to threaten destitution in any of the successive phases of the household's development. This can be seen in the context of the 1770s when it was still possible for larger family groups to co-reside, whereas by the 1780s this was no longer possible. With the increase in the number of nuclear family households, other strategies had to be implemented. In particular, the nuclear households which had emerged from the older traditional households co-operated with non-resident relatives to form self-help networks. The position of the other households, the majority, was of course unchanged.

Table 11.9 demonstrates just how insecure was the situation of the household containing just one married couple. Three-quarters of the unstable households were of the nuclear family type, 22 per cent were headed by widows, of whom the majority were identified as *poveri* in 1786. The death of the household head in a nuclear family household rendered it unstable, pushing it rapidly towards the point of dissolution. This relationship was clearly much stronger in the villages of Loreto and Vescovato than in Porri, where only 29 per cent of the stable families were complex against 49 per cent in 1770 at Loreto and 38 per cent at Vescovato. Let us recall that, of the three villages, Porri was the furthest advanced in terms of the increasing dominance of the nuclear family. This explains why the married couple was the linchpin of the family, even in the case of stable families. Nevertheless, the proportion of complex households among the stable families clearly exceeded the proportion among the unstable forms.

Table 11.9 Structure of persisting and non-persisting households in Vescovato, Loreto and Porri

Village	Household type[1]	1	2	3 a	3 b	3 c	3 d	4	5	F	S	Total
Vescovato	Persisting	0	0	2	14	2	3	4	7	2	7	34
	Non-persisting	1	2	16	41	2	19	5	7	9	8	102
Loreto	Persisting	0	0	1	18	2	2	9	4	9	0	45
	Non-persisting	0	3	5	20	1	16	6	2	3	0	56
Porri	Persisting	0	0	2	18	2	0	5	2	2	0	31
	Non-persisting	2	1	3	10	0	6	3	0	2	0	27
Total	Persisting	0	0	5	50	6	5	18	13	13	7	110
	Non-persisting	3	6	24	71	3	41	14	9	14	8	185
	Persisting (%)	0	0	5	45	5	5	16	12	12	—	100
	Non-persisting (%)	2	3	13	38	2	22	8	5	8	—	100

Notes:
[1]Household types largely follow the categorization scheme set out in Peter Laslett and Richard Wall (eds), *Household and Family in Past Time*, Cambridge: Cambridge University Press 1972, pp. 28–31. *Frérèches* (co-resident siblings) have, however, been categorized separately (type F), while households with servants (type S) have been noted but in this case have been already included in the totals. The remaining types of household indicate solitaries (1), no family households of related or non-related persons (2), nuclear family households (3), subdivided into married couples living alone (3a), married couples with children (3b), widowers with unmarried children (3c) and widows with unmarried children (3d). Extended households, households consisting of a nuclear family plus additional relative(s) not forming a family in their own right, comprise type 4, and multiple family households type 5.

Households in Vescovato, and in particular the Buttafoco, made use of the assistance of external labour by employing servants. Such households were typically nuclear in character, suffering structural instability due to their age or sex composition. The servant or servants were employed to meet immediate economic needs. Yet a large number of the households employing servants did not survive, particularly among *frérèches*, as if the employment of a servant represented a last chance to escape from a situation of chronic instability.[22] *Frérèches* were not durable structures in Vescovato where the majority of them dissolved swiftly, lending support to the hypothesis that a community of brothers was not an effective solution in a harsh, individualistic society in which family forms reinforced social divisions. On the other hand, at Loreto, where such communities did provide a successful solution, *frérèches* constituted a successful model for family continuity, since only three out of twelve failed to survive until 1786.

Thus these data make clear that the most destitute households were those least likely to survive. They bear witness to the limitations in this society of the practices of mutual help and co-operation and to the inability of society to promote efficient self-regulation. In a social context in which the law gave women no right to independence, the erosion of the larger family networks, or their absence, left women without guidance, liberated in practice through the lack of male partners. Yet this was not the breaking-point in the life cycle of the family. That is the focus of the inquiry which follows.

THE MEASUREMENT OF LIFE CYCLE POVERTY

Although the instability of the nuclear family households is now clear,[23] we still need to establish whether poverty varied over the life cycle. Three aspects are considered: the proportion of heads of families in each generation who did not own animals for the purposes of transport or labour, the comparative fate of households headed by males and females of different ages and, finally, the age at which the children from nuclear family households left home and the impact of the social status of the household head on the age of their departure.

Table 11.10 Vescovato, Loreto and Porri: percentage of household heads in each age group who owned no animals in 1786

Age group	Male heads (%)	Female heads (%)	All heads (%)
20–9	55.5	16.6	72.1
30–9	46.7	11.9	58.6
40–9	37.2	16.2	53.4
50–9	34.5	20.0	54.5
60+	38.7	8.1	46.8
Not owning animals	155	51	206
Total	298	61	359

Table 11.10 and Figure 11.3 show the percentage of household heads in 1786 owning no animals for transport or labour. The upper line in Figure 11.3 shows the variation with age in the proportion of all heads of households who did not own any animals. The second line does the same for households with a male head, the difference between the two representing the proportion of such households headed by women, that is to say for those households whose development had been interrupted.

Overall, the proportion of households who did not own any animals declined with advancing age. In other words, the acquisition of the means of production was one way to secure the survival of a household. Clearly, however, it was not the only one, since a significant proportion of household heads over 60 were non-owners (47 per cent). Nevertheless, after the

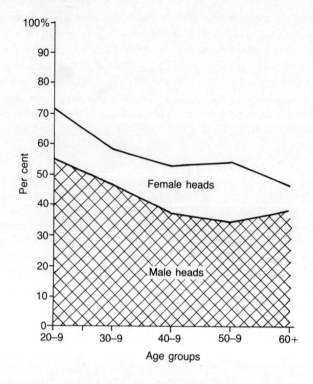

Figure 11.3 Vescovato, Loreto and Porri: percentage of household heads by age and sex who did not own animals for transport or labour, 1786

age of 40, fewer than four in ten male household heads owned no animals. Thus, a proportion close to two-thirds of older males owned animals at a time in life when fewer males were heading households and members of failed households dispersed. The youngest household heads clearly found it difficult to obtain ownership of the means of production and thus to provide a firm basis for the family which they had formed. The period in which they experienced these difficulties lasted for approximately twenty years. Between the ages of 30 and 39, 59 per cent of household heads, 47 per cent of them male, still possessed no animals. This occurred at a time when the formation of a family was somewhat easier. The increasing proportions of nuclear family households therefore involved the creation of less stable families in which the balance between income and expenditure was particularly precarious.

Overall, 84 per cent of women who headed households owned no animals, a far higher proportion than among the male-headed households (52 per cent). Not surprisingly, given the increasing risk of widowhood and household headship by older women, there was also a steady rise with age, between 30 and 59, in the proportion of women among the household heads who did not own any animals.

An alternative approach involves a comparison of the number of women in successive age groups owning and not owning animals. It then becomes apparent that the youngest women aged 20–49 were also the most deprived, the percentage owning animals being greater after the age of 50. It is therefore necessary to understand why women in their 50s were better able to share in the control of some elements of the means of production, and to ascertain whether this situation persisted over time. For this perspective we shall make use of a preliminary indicator: the comparative study of the male and female life course once they had reached the age of 15. Table 11.11 sets out the distribution of men and women classified according to their relationship to the household head and, in the case of household heads, according to the structure of the household. It is immediately apparent that males had a wider range of choice than females, and that the position of unmarried

Table 11.11 The male and female life course in 1786 in Vescovato, Loreto and Porri

Age group	Unmarried son	Male household heads[1]				Other non-married	Married	Total
		3d	2	Alone	3c			
15–19	39	3	2	0	0	3	1	48
20–9	48	9	3	1	0	3	33	97
30–9	10	3	6	5	0	3	85	112
40–9	0	2	1	1	1	2	67	74
50–9	0	0	0	0	2	3	37	42
60–9	0	0	0	3	7	1	31	42
70–9	0	0	0	0	1	0	3	4
80+	0	0	0	0	0	2	0	2
Total	97	17	12	10	11	17	257	421
Per cent	23	4	3	2	3	4	61	—

Age group	Unmarried daughter	Female household heads[1]				Other non-married	Married	Total
		2	Alone		3d			
15–19	43	6	0		0	0	5	54
20–9	35	8	3		2	1	58	107
30–9	9	7	2		10	4	93	125
40–9	0	2	1		15	3	58	79
50–9	0	1	1		20	10	31	63
60–9	0	2	2		12	4	10	30
70–9	0	0	0		0	1	2	3
80+	0	0	0		0	3	0	3
Total	87	26	9		59	26	257	464
Per cent	19	6	2		13	6	56	—

Note: [1] For definitions of household types see note to Table 11.9.

individuals deserves particular attention. The 257 married couples represented the norm which presumably most wished to achieve.

Unmarried women outnumbered unmarried men. Forty-four per cent of women were unmarried but only 39 per cent of men. A quarter of the women were no longer part of the nuclear family (neither daughters nor married), but only 16 per cent of men were in this situation. There is, therefore, a typical life pattern which is distinct for women; the latter were often marginalized relative to the dominant position of the married couple.

In order to determine the major transition points in the life cycle of individuals, four distinct roles within the household will be examined. First, there is the transition from that of unmarried son or daughter to that of married family head. The majority of persons aged 20–9 were still single. Only nineteen individuals over 30 lived with their parents. Women, as is customary, were in general a little younger on marriage than their partners. More significant differences in the household positions of the two sexes applied when they did not marry or were widowed. Between the ages of 15 and 40 a man who did not marry would typically succeed his widowed mother as head of the denuded simple family household (type 3d); a few might unite with their brothers and sisters to form a *frérèche* (type 2 in the Laslett classification scheme). Those who lived alone, as did a few men once they had entered their 20s, represented no more than 0.3 per cent of the total. All such residence patterns, however, were unusual. After the age of 40, some widowers lived alone with their unmarried children (household type 3c). A few more joined the household of a relative. This was more typical of the very youngest or the old but was again rare at all ages.

For women, on the other hand, residence outside a complete nuclear family was both more prevalent and almost certainly longer lasting. Some women still in their 20s were in this position and were joined by many others up to the age of 70. Although some women, and more than was the case with men, were able to join other households (4 per cent of men, 6 per cent of women), there were few relatives able to provide such support. Family solidarity was limited.

After the age of 50 a significant difference opens up between the life course of men and women. The majority of women were no longer married. Of women aged 50–9, thirty-two were not married, thirty-one married; of those aged 60–9, twenty had no husband compared with ten who were still married. Residence in the household of a relative was not the usual solution for these women. They lived as widows surrounded by children or alone, while groups of related females (type 2) were most common among unmarried women under the age of 40. There was therefore no social mechanism to support the older individual, even less for women than for men, although women seem to be the more devalued through the ageing process, at least if we take as a criterion the chances of remarriage. The difference between the experiences of men and women aged 60 and over is considerable. Seventy-one per cent of the former were married, and only one-third of the latter.

These figures may be compared with those reported by Richard Wall with regard to Great Britain, which indicate smaller proportions of both men and women aged over 60 who were married.[24]

This interruption of the female life course after the age of 50 caused by the severance of the marriage bond provides another perspective on the material support available to households headed by women (see Table 11.10, p. 241). The decline in the standard of living of these women does not, therefore, occur in the period immediately following the termination of their married life. More critical was that they inherited very little. The hypothesis we would now advance is that in these populations poverty took on another dimension, which condemned women to participate in a system whose purpose was biological reproduction while excluding them from profitable economic activity and depriving them of family support. To this legal aspect should be added the instability of the widow-centred households (type 3d).

Let us, therefore, return to Vescovato to look in more detail at the internal dynamics of the family units headed by women who constituted most of the *poveri*, in relation to the dynamics of other residential groups. True, the sample is a small one, but it provides a certain number of insights into the precarious state of such households. Households described as *poveri* had to resort to a number of temporary strategies in the pursuit of stability, in the first instance because of the early departure of male children.

Table 11.12 shows the age distribution of children within nuclear family households, without distinguishing the various subcategories, according to the social status of the family head. The four major social groups are identified: *nobili* and gentry, craftsmen, *travagliatori* and *poveri*. Only young children were present in the households of craftsmen, even though out of a total of fourteen households ten were headed by individuals over the age of 40. One married couple was all that was required to run the craft workshop and thus the co-residence of parents and adult children was unlikely. The case of the *poveri* is just as revealing in this context, by making clear what residence choices were made by the offspring of a poor family. Sons did not remain in the home under the tutelage of their mother beyond the age of 19 and these households became heavily feminized in character. Confronted by poverty, daughters remained with their mother for longer, yet most also departed as they approached 20. With a widowed head, the fortunes of the household declined, and hence the reduction in the average size of households headed by women of 60 and over (see Table 11.3, p. 229).

By contrast, for property-owners and *travagliatori* sons were more useful than daughters. The differences between owners (*nobili* and gentry) and *colons* (*travagliatori*) imply the presence of intergenerational ties. Apart from a few instances of children remaining within the parental home beyond the age of 25, a practice more often followed by sons than daughters, the break with the parental home usually came after the children

Table 11.12 Vescovato: age distribution of children in nuclear family households according to the social status of the head of the family

	0–4	5–9	10–14	15–19	20–4	25–9	30–4	35–9	Percentage of families with	
									Sons of 15+	Daughters of 20+
Craftsmen										
boys	4	6	5	0	2	0	0	0	7.6	7.6
girls	2	6	3	1	0	0	0	0		
Poveri										
boys	0	1	1	2	0	0	0	0	14.2	14.2
girls	1	3	3	7	1	1	0	0		
Nobili and gentry										
boys	4	3	4	2	0	2	2	2	25.0	12.5
girls	6	6	4	3	1	0	2	0		
Travagliatori										
boys	10	15	6	10	11	2	2	0	27.9	11.7
girls	8	13	18	9	5	1	1	0		
Total										
boys	18	25	16	14	13	4	4	2	18.6	23.0
girls	17	28	28	20	7	2	3	0		

had reached the age of 20. In the case of the *travagliatori* the transition was delayed, and a higher proportion of the children remained with their parents through into their early 20s.

The delayed departure from the parental home of the offspring of the *travagliatori* increased the chances that they would be able to achieve economic independence. In some instances openings may have been foreseen and their anticipation initiated a series of readjustments in the structure of the group in terms of both its age and sex composition, notably because it was the departure of the sons which was postponed. The contribution made by this extra manpower ensured a greater level of productivity within the parental household. None the less, such expectations could be overturned by an untimely death in the parental generation.

The instability of the female-headed household is also evident from a perusal of wills. These reveal that it was essential if the interests of the widow were to be protected that the relationships with her children, and in particular with her sons, should be enshrined in a legal code. Without this, and in the absence of a will, the widow was left unprotected. Many of the wills show that the co-residence of mother and children was unlikely following the death of the father. Indeed, the family was, in a legal sense, the creation of a father. In the absence of specific clauses protecting a woman either as a wife or mother she had no guarantee of assistance from her sons, or a share of the family wealth. Such instances are even more common in the north of Corsica (Cap Corse) than in the south (Fiumorbu).[25] As it was not common practice to leave a will, it is clear that the position of the widow was insecure and the future of her family at risk.

THE FAILURE OF FAMILY AND COMMUNITY AS WELFARE INSTITUTIONS

This study has demonstrated that in these particular Mediterranean communities the family coped poorly with critical life situations. Nor was there any effective state support of the needy. As a result, widowhood and a failure to marry reduced people to poverty. The households of the poor were both deprived of family solidarity and cut off from communal support. It is obvious that poverty prevented families from following the desired course of development. Unforeseen events, a death in early adulthood, for example, could thrust individuals, more especially the women, into a spiral of downward mobility. This situation was exacerbated by the legal framework. To a certain extent the plight of women arose from the inability of family groups to care for those, always numerous, who were cast aside when offspring left to form their own households. Women were also likely to be poorer than men because once no longer married they lost many of their social and legal rights. They became heads of households without the benefit of the legal support accorded a male head of household. Such women lived in a state of unenviable independence, reduced to using up the family inheritance.

What may appear surprising in this Mediterranean and rural context is that there were numbers of women living independently even in the eighteenth century, more indeed than at the end of the nineteenth century and the beginning of the twentieth century, when women were reintegrated into the family.[26] The increased proportion of nuclear family households, the numbers of female household heads and the growth of a wage-earning class were all interlinked. In the eighteenth century women could live independently because of the existence of a labour market offering very ill-paid work.

This case-study, based on the experience of three small communities in an island population, also indicates that the nuclear family household, although the most commonly adopted mode of family organization, offered no guarantee of stability. It is one thing to measure the prevalence of a certain form of the family, but quite another to establish its viability. This depends on the wider demographic and economic context. In Corsica the maintenance of a family over a large part of the individual life cycle and from generation to generation was not easily achieved: it was the privilege of the few. In fact, the fundamental cleavage in the three villages studied was that between a minority able to live through the support provided by the extended family, and the great majority who found it impossible to form family networks.

Nevertheless, the two groups were interdependent as the poor were required to work the land of their richer neighbours, thereby retaining, or even increasing, the value of their power base. Yet it comes as no surprise to discover that when the strategy for family reproduction mentioned above was in some jeopardy, as in Vescovato at the beginning of the nineteenth century, attempts were made to control the movement of labour and, indeed, to expel those without a secure base in the community. While the *nobili* and gentry were happy enough to enjoy the benefits of generous returns on a minimal outlay, they were less enthusiastic when it came to bearing the social costs.[27]

NOTES

1 Antoine Casanova, 'Evolution historique des sociétés et voies de la Corse. Essai d'approche', *Etudes Corses*, 18–19, 1982, pp. 105–46.
2 Maurice Aymard, 'Un bourg de Sicile entre XVI et XVIIième siècle: Gangi', in F. Braudel (president of editors) (ed.), *Conjoncture économique, structures sociales, hommage à Ernest Labrousse*, Paris 1974, pp. 353–73 and esp. 367–8.
3 Fernand Braudel, *La Méditerranée*, Paris 1976, vol. 1, pp. 413–16; vol. 2, pp. 75–94; Migliacciario, see Casanova, 'Evolution historique', 17 per cent of the population were destitute.
4 Fernand Braudel, *La Méditerranée*; on the western Mediterranean women see José Gentil Da Silva, 'As mulheres dos homens: o outro para a vida', *Actes 1er Simposio Interdisciplinar de Estudas Portugueses sur dimensoes da alteridade nas culturas de lingua portuguesa – o outro*, vol. 2, Departamento de Estudos Portugueses, Universidade Nova, Lisbon, pp. 565–613.

5 Aymard, 'Un bourg de Sicile'.

6 Georges Duby, 'Ouverture: pouvoir privé, pouvoir public', in G. Duby and P. Ariès, *Histoire de la vie privée*, vol. 2, Paris 1985, pp. 37–9.

7 Giovanni Levi, *Le pouvoir au village-histoire d'un exorciste dans le Piemont du XVIIième siècle*, Paris 1989, pp. 202–3.

8 This type of household constitutes type 3d in the Laslett–Hammel typology of household forms; see Peter Laslett and Richard Wall (eds), *Household and Family in Past Time*, Cambridge 1972, pp. 28–31.

9 ibid.

10 This hypothesis originates with Jacques Dupâquier and Louis Jadin, 'Structure of household and family in Corsica, 1769–71', in Laslett and Wall (eds), *Household and Family*, pp. 283–97.

11 Archives de l'enregistrement, série Q, Archives Corse du Sud, Ajaccio.

12 The facts which appear below nevertheless indicate the precarious situation of the *travagliatori*. The criterion chosen here is the possession of at least one animal used as a means of transport or for labour. This is in accordance with the generally accepted classification.

13 Archives de l'enregistrement. All inventories relating to Vescovato, Loreto and Porri drawn up between 1813 and 1830 were examined.

14 R.J. Pommereul, *Histoire de l'Isle de Corse*, Paris 1990, pp. 180–1 (1st edn, 1779).

15 Leca Antoine, *L'Esprit du droit Corse*, Ajaccio 1989, pp. 98–101.

16 The termination of a household is defined here by its disappearance either as a result of the death of the last surviving member or because of the lack of any male descendant. A comparison of family names in the censuses of 1770 and 1786 shows that thirty-seven out of seventy persisted – that is 53 per cent. The rate of population turnover (movement into and out of the commune) was quite similar to that in north-west Europe, although closer to the situation in Hallines in the north of France than to that in Clayworth in England as reported by Peter Laslett, *Family Life and Illicit Love in Earlier Generations*, Cambridge 1977, ch. 2. However, mortality was higher in Vescovato than in Hallines. That certain names are repeated does not mean that people who shared the same surname are necessarily related. Between 1770 and 1786 there were 122 more deaths than births and only the immigration of 205 persons enabled the population to grow. This population was therefore characterized by a high mobility which militated against the establishment and stability of households.

17 These networks were those of lineages which had lasted at least since the end of the middle ages.

18 In the case of Casinca, public space was extremely circumscribed: on the concepts of public and private space see Duby and Ariès, *L'histoire de la vie privée*.

19 These strategies embodied a 'genealogical consciousness' which families incapable of self-perpetuation found impossible to formulate. The term genealogical consciousness is taken from Pierre Guichard, *Structures sociales 'orientales' et 'occidentales' dans l'Espagne musulmane*, Paris 1977.

20 Evidenced by the proceedings of the Municipal Council of Vescovato, Série archives communales, EJ/16, Archives Haute-Corse, Bastia.

21 Peter Laslett, 'Family, kinship and collectivity as systems of support in pre-industrial Europe: A consideration of the "nuclear-hardship" hypothesis', *Continuity and Change*, 3:2, 1988.

22 Yet *Frérèche* type households were wealthier than average.

23 These examples would seem to confirm the conclusion of Frederic Le Play concerning the instability of the nuclear family; cf. the summary in R. Wall, J. Robin and P. Laslett (eds), *Family Forms in Historic Europe*, Cambridge 1983, pp. 18–34.

24 Richard Wall, 'Les relations entre générations en Europe autrefois', *Annales de démographie historique*, Paris 1991, pp. 136–7, although it should be noted that Wall uses a different age distribution.

25 For examples of these wills see Paul Felix Vecchioli, *La communauté d'Olmeta di Capicorsu*, 2, pp. 215–7; for the Fiumorbu see Sauveur Nicolini, *Actes, notariés du Fiumorbu – Le notaire Fabbio Agostini à Ventiseri 1691–1703*, *Cahiers Corsica*, 117–118–119, Bastia 1987. Over an eleven-year period wills constituted less than 3 per cent of all deeds executed by this notary.

26 Antoine Marchini, 'Sur le développement d'un système domestique à relations complexes à la fin du XIXième siècle', *Bulletin de la société des sciences historiques et naturelles de la Corse*, Bastia 1990.

27 The situation of the *travagliatori* who were obliged to pay a proportion of the harvest to the owner (at least a quarter including the seed) was strongly criticized in the nineteenth century by agronomists who considered that it was one of the factors retarding agricultural development; see Eugène Burnouf, *Essai sur les assolements en Corse*, Bastia 1885, p. 143. Comparable arrangements governing access to land were concluded in other parts of the Mediterranean, see Aymard, 'Un bourg de Sicile'. The system weakened the social structure by condemning a part of the population to permanent insecurity. In a meeting held on 1 November 1815, the Municipal Council of Vescovato strongly criticized the behaviour of families who had 'come to live there less than three years ago' and who had not integrated into village life, perceiving them as a danger to the social fabric of the community.

12 Transitions into old age

Poverty and retirement possibilities in late eighteenth- and nineteenth-century Iceland

Gísli Ágúst Gunnlaugsson and Loftur Guttormsson

INTRODUCTION

If it is problematic to delimit the phase of 'old age' within the life course of our contemporaries, it turns out to be much more so in the context of traditional society. One notes, for example, that in Icelandic rural society age tended to be perceived not so much as a function of a chronological order, but rather as a function of the social/civil position of the individual. This is a well-established fact as regards the highly indistinct phase of youth in traditional rural society; here, unmarried persons counted as youths until the age of approximately 40 years.[1] When such persons, most often servants, who according to modern standards used to be prematurely marked by hard work, approached the age of 50 years, they were already considered likely to show signs of 'old age'.[2] For the individuals in question 'adulthood' hardly existed as a distinct and recognized phase of life.

When studying age transitions across time it is therefore very important to keep in mind the varying, culture-bound meanings of the terms in use for designating the different stages of the life course. However, if any kind of comparison across time and place is to be effective, precise chronological limits have to be assigned to the different phases of life. In accordance with conventional definitions, the age of 60 will be used here as the transitional point between adult life ('prime working age') and old age.[3]

In earlier times retirement possibilities in rural societies were largely dependent upon the nature of landownership, inheritance customs, family structure and the economic situation of the population in question. 'In all periods the variety of family patterns and care of the elderly have to be assessed in their appropriate economic context', writes Peter Borscheid.[4] He also points out that inheritance often played a key role in determining the lives of the younger generation; by using inheritance as a kind of blackmail, the head of household could determine the marriage prospects of his children, the timing of their marriages and, to a certain degree, his own economic prospects in retirement.[5]

Research has shown that in several European countries the establishment of a household by one couple was closely tied to the retirement of another.

As a rule a married son took over a farm previously occupied and run by his parents. Often a formal contract was negotiated, stating the terms under which the young couple took over from the older one. These contracts frequently included clauses making it obligatory for the young couple to build a small house on the farm for the parents, and guaranteeing them a certain percentage of the yearly profit. This was a common procedure in both central and northern Europe.[6] The retiring couple was thus provided for and could, if economic conditions allowed, enjoy a reasonably secure old age in the immediate neighbourhood of their family.

It is clear that this system could only function in societies where owner-occupancy was widespread or where tenants were awarded long-term, often hereditary, leases for the farms they worked. But what were retirement possibilities like in societies where owner-occupancy was the exception rather than the rule, and tenants did not enjoy secure long-term leases for the farms they occupied? Eighteenth- and nineteenth-century Iceland constitutes an example of such a society. Around 1800, 90 per cent of farmers were tenants of limited economic means, most of whom only leased their farms for a year at a time.[7] Owner-occupancy became slightly more common during the course of the nineteenth century, and at the turn of the twentieth century around 70 per cent of farmers were tenants. Even if legislation passed during the 1880s slightly improved terms of leases, most tenants were still in a precarious position at the end of the century. This had important implications for their own life cycles, as well as for those of their children. First, migration of tenants was common.[8] Second, it was unlikely that young people would take over a farm previously run by their parents when they founded a family and household of their own. Third, the majority of farmers, and their spouses, could not expect to be able to negotiate a retirement contract when handing over their farm to a married offspring. The 'typical' life cycle of an individual in eighteenth- and nineteenth-century Iceland is likely to have been affected by these factors.[9]

Here, we shall limit our discussion to the following questions: what were the options left open for people who had reached the age of 60 in Icelandic society during the late eighteenth and nineteenth centuries? Could they retire within the household of an offspring or were they forced to enter service or depend on poor relief should illness or other circumstances prevent them from functioning as heads of households and carrying on farming (or another occupation) on their own? Were there changes in the retirement arrangements for farmers as owner-occupancy and more favourable terms of leases became more common during the course of the nineteenth century?

We shall address these questions on two separate levels. First, we will present an account of typical ways of entry into old age in a coastal parish, Hvalsnes, in the fishing district of Gullbringusýsla in south-west Iceland during the latter part of the eighteenth century. The evidence is based on parish and catechetical registers. When analysing the results of this study we found it necessary to examine closely the household position of the elderly in pre-industrial Icelandic society. Second, we will therefore present and discuss evidence relating to the household position of people over the age of 60 in two of the country's counties (Gullbringusýsla and Árnessýsla) in 1801, 1845 and 1901. The counties are chosen to represent different socio-economic structures. Farming was the main source of income in Árnessýsla, while fishing constituted the principal livelihood in Gull-bringusýsla. The evidence is drawn from Icelandic censuses.

Before turning to the questions presented above, brief accounts of the socio-economic situation of the country and the system of poor relief during the eighteenth and nineteenth centuries are appropriate.

THE SOCIO-ECONOMIC SITUATION OF ICELAND DURING THE EIGHTEENTH AND NINETEENTH CENTURIES

During the eighteenth century and the first eight decades of the nineteenth century Iceland was almost entirely a rural society. The majority of the population derived its livelihood from animal husbandry, while farmers along the coast augmented their income by operating small open boats during the fishing seasons. Only a small proportion of the population, chiefly cottars in the south-western and western parts of the country, depended on fishing as their only source of livelihood.[10] During the eighteenth century the population was periodically reduced by several thousand, mainly due to famines, epidemics or natural catastrophes. The worst years in this respect were between 1707−8, 1754−9 and 1783−6. In the first and last of these phases, more than 20 per cent of the population died.[11] As a result of these demographic catastrophes the population declined from 50,000 to 48,000 during the eighteenth century. However, the nineteenth century saw a gradual rise in population, although external con-ditions did not change dramatically until the 1880s.[12] By 1870 the population had risen to 70,000. The period up to 1860 saw an expansion of habitation into areas previously unoccupied. However, the new farms that were founded were often unprofitable and many were deserted between 1860 and 1880, partly due to unfavourable climatic conditions and partly because of emigration.

During the period 1850−80 symptoms of overpopulation in relation to utilized economic resources are detectable in Iceland: it became ever more difficult to found new households in the country because local authorities implemented legislation which prevented people of limited economic means from settling in towns and villages on the coast, while there was no more land available inland for new farms in rural areas.[13] This had important consequences. First, households on average became larger, since their number remained practically constant at a time of population growth. Second, the proportional number of unmarried servants in the population rose. Third, the marriage rate declined, while the average age at marriage rose. Fourth, illegitimacy rose because it proved more difficult for the local authorities to control the sexuality of the poor than their marriage prospects.[14] Fifth, the number of paupers rose. In 1870 over 10 per cent of the population was dependent on poor relief.[15]

It has been argued that by 1870 the country could not have catered for a larger population (70,000 people) without drastic changes in the modes of production and the pattern of habitation. The period 1870–1900 witnessed the introduction of such changes.[16] During this period at least 12,000 people emigrated to Canada and the USA.[17] Internal migration accelerated, with people settling in coastal towns and villages without first seeking the consent of the relevant local authority. This migration became far too extensive for the local authorities to be able to enforce the strict social control they had previously been able to exercise. At the same time it is possible to detect important changes in socio-economic structures. Fishing became ever-more important for the national economy. The number of large fishing boats and decked sailing vessels rose during the last few decades of the nineteenth century, and during the first decade of the twentieth century motor boats and trawlers were introduced. The growing fish industry required a considerable and stable workforce ashore in the fishing villages to process the catches. As a result of this, urbanization did not lead to an increasing proportion of paupers in the population, as conservative elements within Icelandic society had predicted. On the contrary, the percentage of paupers fell during the last three decades of the nineteenth century.[18] Moreover, the growth of towns and villages created a demand for various services. In 1860 only 3 per cent of the population lived in urban areas, but by 1890 12 per cent were resident in towns and in 1920 44 per cent.[19]

After 1880 age at marriage fell, as did mean household size, the illegitimacy ratio and the percentage of servants in the population, while the marriage rate and the number of households increased.

POVERTY AND POOR RELIEF

The system of poor relief in Iceland during the eighteenth and nineteenth centuries had its origins in medieval legislation. According to the law, communes were obliged to provide for paupers if no members of their immediate families were able to support them. Paupers were provided for by their communes of birth if they had not acquired the rights to relief elsewhere by continuous residence within another commune for a specified length of time.[20]

There were two main ways of administering poor relief during the eighteenth and nineteenth centuries. First, individual paupers were, on the orders of the local authorities, 'taken in' by farmers in the commune and provided with board and care for an agreed period of time. Second, farming families were given aid so they could continue to work their farms. The former alternative was that most commonly used in Iceland prior to the late nineteenth century. Families were usually not supported by the local authorities unless it seemed likely that their difficulties were temporary. Otherwise the family was dissolved (although the marriage of the farming couple was not annulled) and the members supported as individual paupers if they could not provide for themselves.[21] By splitting up families the local authorities achieved several objectives: the reproductive functions of the poverty-stricken family were curtailed, a farm was made vacant for another family, support and care was provided for those members of the family who were not fit to work and the limited working capacities of these members were utilized.

Pauperism posed a very real threat for a large proportion of the population. In 1703 more than 15 per cent of the population received poor relief, 4.6 per cent in 1801, more than 10 per cent benefited from poor relief in 1870 and 7.3 per cent in 1902.[22] The majority of paupers apportioned among taxpaying farmers were either children or elderly persons.[23] The poor laws constituted the only instrument available to solve different types of social problems, including those facing elderly persons unable to support themselves. Since people lost most of their civil rights by accepting poor relief, it is likely that they tried for as long as possible to postpone requesting the aid of local authorities. According to a survey carried out in 1901–2 the majority of paupers received relief owing to old age and/or failing health.[24] During the 1890s the parliament discussed the necessity of dealing with the problems of the aged in a different, and more humane, manner. A uniform system of old-age benefits, administered outside the scope of the poor laws, was, however, not introduced until after the turn of the century.[25]

The traditional poor law system had important implications for the situation of the elderly within Icelandic society during the eighteenth and nineteenth centuries. If people could not, for various reasons, remain in an independent household position as heads of household (or spouses), and did not have the possibility of retiring within a household of an offspring, they were forced to either enter service or request poor relief.

As we move on, this general background will hopefully help to clarify some of the structural features which tended to affect the condition of old people in Icelandic society.

TRANSITIONS INTO OLD AGE: THE CASE OF HVALSNES IN THE LATE EIGHTEENTH CENTURY

The following account of the typical ways of entry into old age in eighteenth-century Iceland is based on a micro-demographic study of a single parish, Hvalsnes. Like many Icelandic parishes, this one has standard parish registers preserved from the middle of the eighteenth century as well as catechetical registers ('soul registers'). The latter type of record is particularly valuable for the study of individual life cycles because for every individual household it lists the name, age and social position of all its members. For the period in question, information is lacking on movements in and out of the parish, but the parish register makes it possible to determine whether the disappearance of a particular person was due to death or migration. This, however, does not prevent our 'sample' of individuals from including a disproportionate number of stable residents at the cost of the more mobile elements of the population.

Hvalsnes is a coastal parish situated at the extremity of the peninsula of Reykjanes in south-west Iceland. During this period its 400–500 inhabitants were normally divided between seventy-five to eighty households (mean household size 5.5–6.0). Fishing was by far the most important source of livelihood, since the limited agricultural resources meant that human habitation was limited to a narrow strip of land along the coast. Here, as elsewhere in the country, the settlement was dispersed, but in each locality it took the special form of a cluster of households (*hverfi*) centring around a main farm to which several outlying farms (*hjáleiga*) and cottages (*tómthús*) were attached. Most of the farms were Crown possessions, the rest being private properties. The *hjáleiga* tenants and the cottars were obliged to work as fishermen on the landowners' boats. Some of the privately owned farms were occupied by their owners, while the majority of the Crown's holdings were let to tenants.[26]

It is likely that the inherently unstable nature of traditional fisheries, as well as the heavy work duties to which the Crown tenants were subject, are among the factors explaining the unusually high rate of population turnover in the parish. During the decade of 1774–84 it amounted to no less than 65 per cent, as compared with 46 and 42 per cent respectively in two farming parishes during the third quarter of the century.[27] It can be established that these differences in population turnover did not result from differences in nuptiality rates between the three parishes in question. Thus the population of Hvalsnes did not contain a higher proportion of servants (who, here as elsewhere, were noticeably more mobile than householders) than the two farming parishes where animal husbandry constituted the principal livelihood.

Table 12.1 shows that Hvalsnes has a higher proportion of elderly inhabitants than the country as a whole; this is substantiated by the national census of 1785.[28] It is also evident that in Hvalsnes the sex ratio is less skewed in favour of women. Further research will be needed to clarify the reasons for these age-structural peculiarities.

Consideration now needs to be given to the factors most markedly affecting the kind of social/household position which the inhabitants of Hvalsnes were likely to occupy when entering old age. In order to examine this issue we have reconstructed the life course of a number of individuals in the period 1766–75, who had reached adult status (i.e. passed the age of 40) and who continued to live in the parish at least till the age of 60. The choice

Table 12.1 Proportion of elderly persons by age and sex in the parish of Hvalsnes in 1784 as compared with Iceland as a whole in 1785

	Population	Aged 60 and above				Aged 70 and above			
		M (%)	F (%)	Both (%)	Sex ratio	M (%)	F (%)	Both (%)	Sex ratio
Hvalsnes 1784	478	8.5	12.7	10.7	65	1.7	2.9	2.3	57
Iceland 1785	40,623	6.5	8.7	7.8	58	1.6	2.5	2.1	48

Sources: Hvalsnes: unpublished catechetical registers, National Archives of Iceland (NAI), Reykjavik. Iceland: Hans Oluf Hansen (ed.), *Manntal 1729 í þremur sýslum* (Population census 1729 in three counties), *Statistics of Iceland*, vol. II, 59, Reykjavik 1975, p. 38.

of persons to be followed up in this way was determined by the necessity of including in the 'sample' representatives of the major social categories of rural society. It proved to be possible to reconstruct in this manner the transitions in household position during old age of approximately thirty persons. The following account aims to identify the factors which seemingly had the greatest impact on the characteristics of the social position people occupied in their old age.

Not surprisingly, the most important social determinant was connected with the headship of a household which in turn was intimately tied up with the marital status of the individual. As a rule, household headship and married life went hand in hand.[29] As shown in Table 12.2, the majority of men over the age of 60 were married. Table 12.4 (p. 261) shows that the majority of married persons of both sexes over the age of 60 remained at the head of a household. It has to be emphasized that in Iceland, a country of very scarce resources, it was particularly difficult to obtain the position of a household head. Thus our sample includes one man, an unmarried one, who did not become household head until he was more than 60 years of age, a reminder of the high degree of irregularity characterizing life course patterns in traditional society.[30] An additional manifestation of this irregularity – (to be commented on in Tables 12.4–12.6, pp. 261, 262, 263) – was the tendency of household heads to retain their position until the last few days of their lives.

An important aspect of the impact of marital status in adult life on the social position of the individual in old age relates to widowhood. Here sex differences become obvious. Not unexpectedly, Hvalsnes in 1784 had three times as many widows as widowers.[31] Our sample shows that on the death of her partner an elderly woman was much more likely than a man of the same age to lose her position at the head of a household. Even if remarriage was a rare occurrence for widowers at this advanced age it was, practically speaking, relatively easy for them to compensate for the loss of the housewife by hiring a housekeeper or a responsible servant-girl. Thus when Runólfur Sigurðsson, one of the few owner-occupiers in the parish, lost his wife in

Table 12.2 Marital status of elderly and aged persons by sex and age in the parish of Hvalsnes in 1784

	Aged 60 and above		Aged 70 and above	
	Male	Female	Male	Female
Married	13	11	3	2
Widowed	4	12	1	2
Single	3	8		3
Total	20	31	4	7

Sources: Hvalsnes: unpublished catechetical registers, National Archives of Iceland (NAI), Reykjavik.

1779 at the age of 64, he did not retire in favour of his only son who was then 31 years old. Instead, with the help of a servant who, exceptionally, was married, he continued to occupy his farm until his death in 1792. It was not until his father's death that the son, who anyway had founded an independent household in the neighbourhood some fifteen years earlier, took over the 'family farm'.

Whether or not widows succeeded in retaining their position at the head of a household in old age depended largely on their chances of finding a new partner.[32] With a good deal of luck they might even remarry in their old age. The case of Signý Jónsdóttir is a telling one in this respect, even if it is somewhat exceptional. In 1787, at the age of 52, she became a widow for the third time in her life. Signý remained at the head of a household until 1799 when (at the age of 64) she was hired as housekeeper by Jón Sigurðsson, 38 years of age, whom she married the same year. Signý continued to live as the spouse of a household head until she lost her fourth husband in 1803 at the age of 68. She died two years later in widowhood.

In addition to her many marriages, Signý's case is an exception to the rule according to which women widowed in their 60s were doomed to remain in that position to the end of their lives. If they were not taken in by their kin they usually ended their days as either servants or paupers, depending on their health. As such they would join the ranks of elderly women who had never married nor attained the status of household heads. Our sample contains three representatives of this latter group, noticeably less than their numerical importance in Hvalsnes and in the country as a whole would suggest; undoubtedly their scarcity is due to the high degree of geographical mobility characteristic of people in service.[33] None of the three was lucky enough to be taken in by a relative.

Among the never-marrying part of the population, which as regards women in traditional Iceland was larger than in any other north-west European country,[34] transitions into old age were marked by important sex differences. Thus, unmarried men were more likely than women to retain in old age the kind of semi-independence most of them (with the exception of disabled persons) had attained in adulthood, whether as lodgers or labourers exempt from service (*lausamenn*). Compared with their female counterparts, they were less at risk of being reduced to pauperism in their old age.[35] The same kind of difference between the sexes is revealed by a life course analysis of the eleven single individuals included in Table 12.2 (p. 258), but not detailed here because of space constraints.

Behind the old age transitions discussed above we have been able to detect the combined effects of marital status and gender. Concurrently, the problem of attaining household headship in adult life stands out as a factor of critical importance for the social placement of the individual in old age. Even if a household status achieved in the prime of life had in many cases (particularly in the case of widowhood) to be abandoned in old age, it acted as an insurance against the cruder forms of dependency (such as communal poor relief). Thus our sample contains only a few examples of household heads and spouses of heads who were reduced to pauperism in widowhood.

The evidence discussed above illuminates the situation of the elderly in one coastal parish in late eighteenth-century Iceland. In order to check the validity of the findings we have undertaken a study of the household position of the elderly in two of the country's counties according to the censuses of 1801, 1845 and 1901.

THE HOUSEHOLD POSITION OF THE ELDERLY IN 1801, 1845 AND 1901

Research has shown that the kin composition of households varied considerably between coastal fishing parishes and inland farming ones in nineteenth-century Iceland. This is shown in Table 12.3.

The parish of Garðar is a coastal parish in the county of Gullbringusýsla in south-west Iceland, the parishes of Ingjaldshóll and Fróðá are fishing parishes in the county of Snaefellsnessýsla in western Iceland, while the parish of Hruni is situated in the southern farming region of Árnessýsla. It is clear from Table 12.3 that the possibilities for parents to 'retire' within the household of an offspring were far better in the farming parishes than in the coastal ones. It should not, however, be concluded that residence within a household of an offspring meant that the parent in question enjoyed retirement in the modern sense of the term. It seems more likely that the parent contributed to the household's workforce as far as his or her health and capabilities allowed. There is extremely limited evidence of retirement contracts in pre-industrial Iceland.

Households in the farming districts of nineteenth-century Iceland were on average considerably larger than in the coastal areas. Labour requirements were greater in farming districts, and they were to a large extent met by hiring servants on a yearly basis. The nuclear family dominated, although a

Table 12.3 Composition of the kin group within the household: number of relatives per 100 households in seven Icelandic parishes, 1880

Relationship to the head of household	Garðar 1880	Hruni 1880*	Ingjaldshóll/ Fróðá 1880
Parents[1]	6	19	5
Siblings[1]	7	4	7
Son/daughter-in-law	1	3	1
Nephew/niece	1	1	2
Grandchild	8	4	3
Other relatives	0	0	1
Total per 100 households	23	31	19

Notes: * Also includes four neighbouring parishes.
        [1] Includes in-laws.

Sources: National Archives of Iceland. *Manntal á Íslandi 1880*.

considerable percentage of households (20–30 per cent) in farming parishes included three generations living together under one roof. Stem families were extremely rare.[36]

A more detailed investigation into the household position of those over the age of 60 in Árnessýsla and Gullbringusýsla, based on the censuses of 1801, 1845 and 1901, reveals that retirement possibilities, in the sense of residing within the household of an offspring, differed not only between farming and fishing districts, but also according to sex and marital status, as our findings for Hvalsnes suggested (see Tables 12.4–6). In both counties married persons gave up their positions as heads of households relatively late in life, although somewhat earlier in the farming district of Árnessýsla than in the fishing district of Gullbringusýsla. In Gullbringusýsla it was common for around 80 per cent of married men and women to head a household at the age of 60 or above, while the corresponding proportion was usually between 60 and 70 per cent in Árnessýsla.

This suggests that retirement possibilities for married couples were limited in both counties, but more so in Gullbringusýsla than in Árnessýsla. Widows were more likely to retire within the household of an offspring. Between 40 and 50 per cent of widows resided in the households of their children. It was not as usual for widowers to reside within a household of their children, partly because more widowers headed households of their own. This agrees with the findings presented in the preceding section. A relatively high proportion of widowers and widows are categorized as 'other' in the later censuses of 1845 and 1901 (see Tables 12.5–12.6, pp. 262, 263). This is due to the fact that many widowers and widows were recorded as 'disabled' in 1845, whereas in 1901 many were boarders and lodgers.

Table 12.4 The household position of people aged 60 and above in Árnessýsla and Gullbringusýsla, 1801 (percentage of each marital status group)

	Head/ spouse	Household of an offspring	Household of a relative	Servants	Paupers	Other	N
A Árnessýsla							
Married							
women	66.7	20.5	1.7	2.6	4.3	4.3	117
Widows	18.4	38.6	7.0	14.6	13.9	7.5	158
Unmarried							
women	1.1	1.1	14.9	39.1	37.9	5.7	87
All women	29.8	23.8	7.2	16.6	16.6	6.1	362
Married							
men	81.0	12.4	1.3	2.6	0.7	2.0	157
Widowers	37.8	33.3	11.1	2.2	13.3	2.2	45
Unmarried							
men	11.1	0.0	27.8	27.8	22.2	11.1	18
All men	66.2	15.7	5.6	4.6	5.1	2.8	220
B Gullbringusýsla							
Married							
women	73.2	9.8	1.2	6.1	2.4	7.3	82
Widows	5.4	39.8	4.3	25.8	7.5	17.2	93
Unmarried							
women	0.0	5.0	20.0	50.0	15.0	10.0	20
All women	33.3	23.6	4.6	20.0	6.2	12.3	195
Married							
men	82.0	7.9	0.0	4.5	0.0	5.6	89
Widowers	28.6	17.9	3.6	17.9	14.3	17.9	28
Unmarried							
men	0.0	0.0	22.2	44.4	11.1	22.2	9
All men	64.3	9.5	2.4	10.3	4.0	9.5	126

Source: Manntal á Íslandi 1801. Suðuramt, Reykjavik 1978.

It is difficult to explain why elderly widows seem to have been more readily accepted than widowers into the households of their offspring. As Booth suggested for England in the 1890s, it is possible that they made the adjustment to living with their offspring more easily than did widowers.[37] A second hypothesis is that households broke up more frequently on the death of an elderly man than a woman. It is also conceivable that elderly widowers were more reluctant to give up the prestige inherent in headship than were widows. Much research is still required to answer these questions with any accuracy.

It is necessary to point out that many persons over the age of 60 may have been able to remain heads of households by hiring servant labour or by

Table 12.5 The household position of people aged 60 and above in Árnessýsla and Gullbringusýsla, 1845 (percentage of each marital status group)

	Head/ spouse	Household of an offspring	Household of a relative	Servants	Paupers	Other	N
A Árnessýsla							
Married							
women	56.3	16.9	0.0	5.6	5.6	15.5	71
Widows	8.3	51.7	2.1	9.0	19.3	9.6	145
Unmarried							
women	0.0	1.7	0.0	32.2	55.9	10.2	59
All women	18.9	32.0	1.1	13.1	23.3	11.3	275
Married							
men	65.9	18.2	0.0	2.3	4.5	9.0	88
Widowers	19.0	41.4	1.7	5.2	15.5	17.2	58
Unmarried							
men	0.0	0.0	0.0	63.6	27.3	9.1	11
All men	43.9	25.5	0.6	7.6	10.2	12.1	157
B Gullbringusýsla							
Married							
women	88.5	1.9	0.0	3.8	3.8	3.8	52
Widows	15.9	42.1	1.9	6.5	11.2	22.4	107
Unmarried							
women	0.0	12.5	6.3	12.5	37.5	31.3	16
All women	36.0	27.4	1.7	5.7	11.4	17.7	175
Married							
men	82.9	4.3	0.0	1.4	5.7	5.7	70
Widowers	26.0	26.0	0.0	10.0	24.0	14.0	50
Unmarried							
men	25.0	0.0	8.3	16.7	8.3	41.7	12
All men	56.1	12.1	0.8	6.1	12.9	12.1	132

Source: *Manntal á Íslandi 1845. Suðuramt*, Reykjavik 1982.

retaining grown-up children within the parental household. An inquiry based on the census of 1845 indicates that this was often the case.[38] The elderly rarely lived alone: only 5.1 per cent of heads of households over the age of 60 in Árnessýsla lived entirely alone or only with their spouse, while the corresponding proportion was 11 per cent in Gullbringusýsla. Furthermore, 75.5 per cent of heads over the age of 60 in Árnessýsla had children residing at home, while only 49 per cent were in a similar position in Gullbringusýsla.[39] As previously mentioned, the evidence presented above points to an important difference between the coastal and the inland region.

Although the retirement possibilities of married or widowed persons were far better than those of people who had never married, many widowers and

Table 12.6 The household position of people aged 60 and above in Árnessýsla and Gullbringusýsla, 1901 (percentage of each marital status group)

	Head/ spouse	Household of an offspring	Household of a relative	Servants	Paupers	Other	N
A Árnessýsla							
Married							
women	62.9	11.2	3.4	8.6	2.6	11.2	116
Widows	7.8	41.9	9.3	12.4	7.8	20.9	129
Unmarried							
women	5.8	9.1	4.5	46.1	21.4	13.0	154
All women	23.1	20.3	5.8	24.3	11.5	15.0	399
Married							
men	62.6	12.9	3.4	8.8	4.8	7.5	147
Widowers	16.1	25.8	11.3	8.1	12.9	25.8	62
Unmarried							
men	19.7	4.9	6.6	23.0	21.3	24.6	61
All men	42.2	14.1	5.9	11.9	10.4	15.6	270
B Gullbringusýsla							
Married							
women	81.1	10.8	0.0	2.7	4.1	1.4	74
Widows	15.2	45.5	6.3	8.0	5.4	19.7	112
Unmarried							
women	11.6	20.3	4.3	27.5	13.0	23.2	69
All women	33.3	28.6	3.9	11.8	7.1	15.3	255
Married							
men	82.1	8.3	0.0	2.4	1.2	6.0	84
Widowers	18.2	25.5	1.8	7.3	14.5	32.7	55
Unmarried							
men	24.1	3.7	0.0	29.6	27.8	14.8	54
All men	47.7	11.9	0.5	11.4	12.4	16.1	193

Source: National Archives of Iceland. *Manntal á Íslandi 1901.*

widows in both counties were forced to enter service or accept poor relief in order to support themselves in old age. Poverty and pauperism clearly posed a more real threat to the elderly in nineteenth-century Iceland than was suggested by the evidence from Hvalsnes. According to the census, a high proportion of unmarried persons were dependent on poor relief in old age. It was not uncommon for more than 40 per cent of unmarried people above the age of 60 to spend their old age as servants, while between 10 and 20 per cent were paupers (and in some years this proportion was much higher). Service or pauperism was also the fate of a considerable percentage of both married and widowed persons.

The evidence presented in Tables 12.4–6 (pp. 261–3) clearly indicates some improvements in the household position of elderly unmarried persons towards the end of the nineteenth century. In 1901 the percentage of unmarried women heading households of their own or residing within the households of illegitimate children had risen markedly, as had the percentage of unmarried men living with illegitimate children.

The evidence presented in Tables 12.4–6 also clearly reveals one of the characteristics of pre-industrial Icelandic society: the unequal sex ratio.[40] There were far more women in the age groups over 60 than there were men (people in the age groups over 60 constituted between 8 and 12 per cent of the population of the two counties). Tables 12.4–12.6 demonstrate too the limited marriage prospects for women in nineteenth-century Iceland. In particular, marriage prospects were extremely poor for both sexes between 1860 and 1880.[41] This is clear from the evidence drawn from the census of 1901 (see Table 12.6, p. 263). The illegitimacy ratio was very high during the period 1860–80 (around 18 per cent of all births were illegitimate). Because of this, a considerable percentage of unmarried persons over 60 years of age are reported as residing within a household of an offspring in the census of 1901.

CONCLUDING DISCUSSION

The relatively restricted arrangements for retirement of persons aged 60 or more in nineteenth-century Iceland can in part be explained in terms of the limited possibility for achieving owner-occupancy and in part with reference to the high proportion of elderly persons (especially women) who had never married. 'Household headship rates of older [married] people remained high throughout the nineteenth century', as was the case in England and the United States, but contrary to the experience of many countries in western and central Europe.[42] The great majority of farmers were tenants who frequently migrated. It was, therefore, relatively uncommon for a married child to take over a farm previously worked by the parents. Parents could only use inheritance as a guarantee for care and support in old age to a limited extent, in contrast to the practices of many other European regions.[43] Although the rate of owner-occupany rose during the nineteenth century (around 10 per cent in 1801, 17 per cent in 1845 and 37.5 per cent in 1910)[44] and terms of leases became more favourable for tenants, retirement possibilities do not seem to have improved correspondingly.

Although inheritance and the nature of landownership were important in determining retirement arrangements in rural societies, these variables should not be used in isolation to attempt to explain the relatively limited choices available to married couples to retire within a household of a child in nineteenth-century Iceland. Irrespective of inheritance and nature of landownership, many children would undoubtedly have wanted to provide care and support for their elderly parents. If this was the case, why did not more people over the age of 60 reside within the households of their children?

There can be three explanations for this. First, as Michael Anderson has pointed out, the high age of marriage in European societies meant that 'the children's own families are costing most just at the time of [greatest parental] need'.[45] As a result children were incapable of offering support when their elderly parents needed it. Since age at marriage, even by European standards, was extremely high in nineteenth-century Iceland (over 30 years of age for men and 28 for women in the latter part of the century),[46] this is likely to have affected retirement possibilities. Second, the availability of kin played a critical role in determining the option for retirement in pre-industrial societies.[47] In Iceland, retiring within the household of a relative was largely restricted to the children of the persons in question. Only a small percentage of those over the age of 60 resided in the households of other relatives (see Tables 12.4–12.6, pp. 261–3). Infant mortality was extremely high in Iceland during much of the nineteenth century (thirty-five per cent around 1850 and over twenty per cent until 1880),[48] as was the death rate during youth (of every 1,000 born there were only 564 survivors at the age of 15 and 347 at the age of 50 between 1850 and 1860).[49] Therefore, it seems likely that in some cases the elderly had no children alive by the time they needed support. The low life expectancy in eighteenth- and nineteenth-century Iceland also resulted in a high rate of remarriage, which often led to a considerable age difference between the spouses.[50] This age difference often allowed one of the spouses to remain at the head of a household longer than otherwise would have been the case.[51]

Third, there remains the question of whether or not it was in part culturally determined that people should remain as the head of household for as long as possible. As we have stressed, it was relatively difficult to attain the position of household head. Bearing in mind the importance of patriarchal authority in eighteenth- and nineteenth-century Iceland,[52] it seems likely that those holding this desired position were tempted to retain it as long as possible. Being forced to 'retire' into the household of an offspring, not to speak of being forced into service or to seek communal relief, in all probability signalled publicly a fall in social status. However, as yet, this last point remains speculative and certainly one on which future research will focus.

Our findings indicate that retirement arrangements were relatively limited in late eighteenth- and nineteenth-century Iceland. There was a clear difference in this respect between farming and fishing districts. Sex and marital status were, however, even more influential determinants. A high percentage of married and widowed persons remained heads of households long past the age of 60.

Arthur E. Imhof has pointed out that in at least one German region people would not have 'considered running the farm at such an advanced age'. The rule was that a farm was turned over to the next generation at 'sixty or sixty-five'.[53] This certainly was not the case in Iceland. Farmers headed households long after the age of 60, and, as in many other regions in

Scandinavia, the 'possessionless elderly' were frequently 'circulated by agreement within the community from household to household'.[54] Poverty was an ever-present threat for the elderly in pre-industrial Iceland. Peter Laslett has stated that the Scandinavian evidence points to kin support having been conspicuous by its absence.[55] He suggested that the system of circulating the elderly poor from household to household can be seen as an example of 'nuclear-hardship'.[56] The evidence relating to the household position of the elderly in Icelandic society during the eighteenth and nineteenth centuries, especially that concerning single men and women, may suggest that until 1900 Iceland constituted an extreme case of such 'nuclear-hardship'. During the first decades of this century increased rates of owner-occupancy and the emergence of a modern welfare system drastically changed retirement possibilities in Iceland for the better.[57]

NOTES

1 Loftur Guttormsson, *Bernska, ungdómur og uppeldi á einveldisöld. Tilraun til félagslegrar og lýðfræðilegrar greiningar*, Reykjavik: Sagnfraeðistofnun Háskóla Islands 1983, pp. 85–8.
2 ibid.: pp. 155, 161.
3 Peter Laslett, *Family Life and Illicit Love in Earlier Generations*, Cambridge: Cambridge University Press 1977, p. 184; Richard Wall, 'Introduction', in R. Wall, J. Robin and P. Laslett (eds), *Family Forms in Historic Europe*, Cambridge: Cambridge University Press 1983, p. 41.
4 Peter Borscheid, *Geschichte des Alters. Vom Spätmittelalter zum 18. Jahrhundert*, Munster: F. Coppenrath Verlag 1989, p. 52: 'Familie und Alterversorgung haben sich in ihrer Form und ihren Möglichkeiten zu allen Zeiten nach den jeweiligen wirtschaftlichen Verhältnissen ausrichten müssen.'
5 ibid.: p. 53.
6 See, for instance, L.K. Berkner, 'The stem family and the developmental cycle of the peasant household: An eighteenth century Austrian example', *American Historical Review*, LXXV, 1972; D. Gaunt, 'The property and kin relationships of retired farmers in northern and central Europe', in Wall, Robin and Laslett (eds), *Family Forms*; D.G. Troyansky, 'Old age in the rural family of Enlightened Provence', in Peter N. Stearns (ed.), *Old Age in Preindustrial Society*, London: Croom Helm 1982, p. 220.
7 Björn Lárusson, *The Old Icelandic Land Registers*, Lund: Gerup 1967.
8 Gísli Ágúst Gunnlaugsson, *Family and Household in Iceland 1801–1930: Studies in the Relationship Between Demographic and Socio-Economic Development, Social Legislation and Family and Household Structures*, Uppsala: Uppsala University 1988, pp. 74–83; Loftur Guttormsson, 'Staðfesti í flökkusamfélagi? Ábúðarhættir í Reykholtsprestakalli á 18. öld', *Skírnir*, 163, 1989, pp. 9–40.
9 See a discussion in Gunnlaugsson, *Family and Household*, pp. 60–2.
10 The socio-economic situation of the country during the eighteenth and nineteenth centuries is discussed in the following books: Gísli Gunnarsson, *Monopoly Trade and Economic Stagnation: Studies in the Foreign Trade of Iceland 1602–1787*, Lund: Lund University 1983; Gunnlaugsson, *Family and Household*; Magnús S. Magnússon, *Iceland in Transition: Labour and Socio-*

Economic Change Before 1940, Lund: Economic History Society 1985; Guttormsson, *Bernska, ungdómur og uppeldi á einveldisöld*.

11 Gunnlaugsson, *Family and Household*, p. 17.

12 Aðalgeir Kristjánsson and Gísli Ágúst Gunnlaugsson, 'Félags-og hagþróun á Íslandi á fyrri hluta 19. aldar', *Saga*, 1990, pp. 7–62.

13 Gísli Ágúst Gunnlaugsson, 'The poor laws and the family in 19th century Iceland', in John Rogers and Hans Norman (eds), *The Nordic Family: Perspectives on Family Research*, Uppsala: Uppsala University 1985, pp. 16–42; Gunnlaugsson, *Family and Household*, pp. 32–41.

14 See Gunnlaugsson, *Family and Household*, pp. 90–118. Gísli Gunnarsson, *Fertility and Nuptiality in Iceland's Demographic History* (Meddelande från ekonomisk–historiska institutionen, Lunds Universitet, nr. 12, Lund 1980.

15 Gísli Ágúst Gunnlaugsson, *Ómagar og utangarðsfólk. Fátækramál Reykjavíkur 1786–1907*, Reykjavik: Sögufélag 1982, pp. 101–6.

16 See Magnússon, *Iceland in Transition*; and Gunnlaugsson, *Family and Household*, for a discussion of the socio-economic development of Iceland in the period 1870–1940.

17 Helgi Skúli Kjartansson, 'Emigrant fares and emigration from Iceland to North America 1874–1893', *Scandinavian Economic History Review*, 28, 1980.

18 Gunnlaugsson, *Ómagar og utangarðsfólk*, pp. 130–9.

19 *Statistics of Iceland II, 63. Statistical Abstract of Iceland*, Reykjavik: 1976, pp. 24–5.

20 This time could vary between ten and twenty years until 1834 when it was limited to five years, only to be extended again to ten years in 1848: see Gunnlaugsson, *Family and Household*, pp. 93–5.

21 ibid.: pp. 94–5.

22 Gunnlaugsson, *Ómagar og utangarðsfólk*, pp. 29, 32, 101–6 and 166.

23 ibid.: p. 167.

24 ibid.: p 167.

25 Jón Blöndal, *Félagsmál á Íslandi*, Reykjavik 1942.

26 A detailed contempory survey of the county to which Hvalsnes belongs is given by Skúli Magnússon, 'Lýsing Gullbringuog Kjósarsýslu', *Landnám Ingólfs. Safn til sögu þess*, 1, Reykjavik 1936.

27 Guttormsson, 'Staðfesti í flökkusamfélagi?', pp. 12–13. A comparison is also made here with seventeenth-century English parishes and with eighteenth-century Danish parishes.

28 Table 12.1 (p. 257) has been explicitly designed to facilitate comparison with data tabulated by Peter Laslett, 'The history of aging and the aged', in Laslett, *Family Life*, pp. 186–7, table 5.2, 190–1, table 5.5. The data relating to the Icelandic census of 1785 is included in the first of Laslett's tables.

29 Guttormsson, *Bernska, ungdómur og uppeldi á einveldisöld*, pp. 105–6.

30 John Modell and Tamara K. Hareven, 'Transitions: Patterns of timing', in T.K. Hareven (ed.), *Transitions. The Family and the Life Course in Historical Perspective*, New York: Academic Press 1978, pp. 264–8.

31 For the country as a whole the proportion of widows/widowers among the population aged 20 years and above was 15.0 and 7.8 respectively; see Guttormsson, *Bernska, ungdómur og uppeldi á einveldisöld*, p. 109.

32 As regards England and France, the problem is discussed by Olwen Hufton, 'Women without men: Widows and spinsters in Britain and France in the eighteenth century', *Journal of Family History*, 9, 1984, pp. 364ff.

33 Gunnlaugsson, *Family and Household*, pp. 60–2.

34 Guttormsson, *Bernska, ungdómur og uppeldi á einveldisöld*, p. 114, table 16.

35 This sex difference is manifested clearly in the census of 1703: see, *Population Census 1703. Statistics of Iceland II, 23*, Reykjavik 1960, pp. 48–50.

36 See Gunnlaugsson, *Family and Household*, pp. 72 and 133.
37 Charles Booth, *The Aged Poor in England and Wales*, London: Macmillan 1894 and New York: Garland Publishing Inc. 1980.
38 Calculations based on *Manntal á Íslandi 1845. Suðuramt*, Reykjavik 1982.
39 In Arnessýsla seventy-one out of seventy-four households with children included one or more offspring over the age of 15, whereas forty-seven out of fifty-four did in Gullbringusýsla. *Manntal á Íslandi 1845. Suðuramt.*
40 See Gísli Gunnarsson, *The Sex Ratio, the Infant Mortality and Adjoining Social Response in Pre-Transitional Iceland* (Meddelande från ekonomisk-historiska institutionen Lunds universitet, nr. 32), Lund 1983.
41 Gunnlaugsson, *Family and Household*, pp. 119–37.
42 See Sonya O. Rose, Chapter 13 this volume.
43 Borscheid, *Geschichte des Alters*, p. 53.
44 Björn Teitsson, *Eignarhald og ábúð á jörðum í Suður-þingeyjarsýslu*, Reykjavik: Bókaútgáfa Menningarsjóðs 1973, pp. 149–50.
45 Cited from Richard M. Smith, 'The structured dependence of the elderly as a recent development: Some sceptical historical thoughts', *Ageing and Society*, 4, 1984, p. 425.
46 *Statistics of Iceland II, 82. Statistical Abstract of Iceland 1984*, Reykjavik: 1984, p. 40.
47 Smith, 'The structured dependence', pp. 417–25; H.C. Johansen, 'The position of the old in the rural household in a traditional society', in Sune Åkerman, H.C. Johansen and D. Gaunt (eds), *Chance and Change*, Odense: Odense University Press 1978, pp. 122–30.
48 *Statistical Abstract of Iceland 1984*, p. 13.
49 ibid.: p. 56. For a discussion of the implications of the high mortality, see H.O. Hansen, 'The importance of remarriage in traditional and modern societies: Iceland during the eighteenth and nineteenth centuries and the cohort of Danish women born between 1926 and 1935', in J. Dupâquier, E. Hélin, P. Laslett, M. Livi-Bacci and S. Sogner (eds), *Marriage and Remarriage in Populations of the Past*, London: Academic Press 1981, pp. 307–24.
50 See Hansen, 'The importance of remarriage'; Gunnlaugsson, *Family and Household*, pp. 112–14.
51 During the middle of the nineteenth century 18.2 per cent of women marrying were widows and 14.6 per cent of the men, widowers. In 1870 there was an age difference of more than fifteen years between spouses in 37 per cent of all marriages. See Gunnlaugsson, *Family and Household*, pp. 114–15.
52 See Guttormsson, *Bernska, ungdómur og uppeldi á einveldisöld*.
53 Arthur E. Imhof, 'Planning full-size life careers: Consequences of the increase in the length and certainty of our life spans over the last three hundred years', *Ethnologia Europeae*, 17, 1987, pp. 12–13.
54 Peter Laslett, 'Family, kinship and collectivity as systems of support in pre-industrial Europe: A consideration of the 'nuclear-hardship' hypothesis', *Continuity and Change*, 3, 1988, p. 166. See also Gaunt, 'The property and kin relationships'.
55 Laslett, 'Family, kinship and collectivity', p. 168.
56 ibid.
57 Gunnlaugsson, *Family and Household*, pp. 160–3.

13 Widowhood and poverty in nineteenth-century Nottinghamshire

Sonya O. Rose

In nineteenth-century England the large majority of working-class families faced an insecure economic existence. Although wages for men in a number of industries rose during the third quarter of the nineteenth century, economic slumps frequently meant that they were laid off from work, or they were put on short-time. Except for the most secure working-class men, and those who belonged to unions and friendly societies, they were able to save little for their old age. If economic security for ageing men was problematic, it was even more so for women. Generally women had fewer opportunities for employment than did men, and, when they were employed, they worked at low waged jobs.

Most working-class families frequently needed more than one wage-earner to make ends meet, and men often relied on their wives and/or children to contribute to household subsistence. However, most men could survive economically on their own if forced to do so. For women, marriage was something of an economic necessity; when their husbands were employed, their earnings provided them and their children with a cushion against destitution. Widowhood, therefore, threatened poor women with profound economic insecurity.[1] B. Seebohm Rowntree, for example, found that in York at the end of the nineteenth century, about 15 per cent of households were below the poverty line due to the death of the 'chief wage earner'.[2]

Yet, Rowntree's model of the poverty cycle of families was based on the experiences of male heads of households. Central to Rowntree's model of poverty and the family life cycle was the presence or absence of children in the household coupled with the relative age of the father. The presence of children served as a drain on family resources when the children were too young to earn wages, but they helped the family to rise above the poverty line when they were old enough to contribute to household coffers. When household heads were old, it was the absence of children that made for a precarious economic existence.[3] According to Rowntree, women were poor during much of the period when they were bearing children. Additionally, Rowntree developed his ideas about poverty and the family life cycle on the assumption that as people aged they remained in their own households, and did not become resident in the households of their relatives. As far as their living situations were concerned, then, Rowntree presumed that men lived independently, as household heads, into their old age. Because Rowntree had the male life course in mind as a model for thinking about families and poverty, he omitted direct consideration of women as they aged, especially when there was no male head of household to earn a large share of the family's subsistence. In other words, Rowntree did not consider death of a spouse, an experience more common for women than for men, as a stage in the poverty cycle of households. This chapter explores the Rowntree model for women, viewing widowhood as well as old age as significant amplifiers of poverty, and investigates women's residence patterns and earnings strategies.

Discussions about who has been responsible for the various tasks involved in maintaining life on a day-to-day basis and intergenerationally and, most importantly, the care of dependants have stressed the centrality of families, and especially the women in them.[4] A presumption has been that domestic units or households were the key settings in which care of dependants took place.

Old age for working-class women and men was a particularly precarious time, and the question of how poor people managed when they were elderly has increasingly been the subject of historical investigations. A central pre-occupation of scholars has been the extent to which family involvement with elderly kin or the community through Poor Law relief were sources of support for older residents. What seems to have puzzled scholars is why more elderly were not found living in the households of their adult children. In England this form of co-residence was a special strategy which families adopted under unusual circumstances. Michael Anderson, for example, found that in Preston in 1851, households were flexible to cope with housing shortages and rural–urban migration and so they expanded to include elderly parents, especially mothers. Generally, the large majority of the elderly did not live in extended family households.[5] Unlike today, however, widows even in old age, rarely lived alone. Generally, a child remained in the household, or another relative moved in with them.[6]

A key question about family involvement with elderly kin is whether or not the relative absence of households in which elderly parents lived with their married children can be interpreted to mean that there was no assistance passing between relatives residing separately.[7] There is a differ-ence of scholarly opinion on the question of kin support for the elderly in nineteenth-century England. Some scholars have argued that kin supported one another with small amounts of money or aid in kind to stretch the sums available from employment or public assistance. Pat Thane, for example, has argued that when work was unavailable, and people were impoverished, the extended family gave support, most often in the form of food.[8]

Other scholars have maintained that family members could not or would not have been responsible for their ageing relatives. According to this view, large numbers of elderly widows would not have surviving children who could have helped them because of mortality and out-migration rates.[9] In working-class communities, elderly parents would have been the most in need when their adult children faced the point in their life cycle when they had more dependants than could be supported by their wages.[10] Richard Wall, using data from the contemporary studies of Le Play and Charles Booth, has reported that while the majority of elderly in the nineteenth century and earlier may have been assisted by their close kin with aid in kind, families played only a minor role in securing the financial well-being of the elderly.[11] Some scholars, arguing that families were insignificant sources of assistance for the working-class aged, suggest that such inter-generational ties were not an aspect of proletarian culture.[12] Giving help to an aged parent was not, according to this view, an obligation of kinship.

David Thomson has proposed that in England public assistance, through Poor Law relief given as pensions to the very old, was the primary source of support for the working-class elderly until the last quarter of the nineteenth century.[13] He has argued that levels of public assistance for the elderly have declined since the mid-Victorian period.[14] His work has been important in highlighting a tradition of community support for the elderly which was only transformed by Poor Law reformers in the 1870s. He suggests that until then public assistance would have allowed the working-class elderly person to subsist at about 80 to 100 per cent of the levels of most non-elderly adult working-class people.[15]

Thomson's work has been challenged by E.H. Hunt who has argued that the sums distributed by Poor Law authorities, even during the times that Thomson proposes that the elderly poor were given a 'pension', were too small to maintain them.[16] Hunt maintains that they were far from the levels of 80 to 100 per cent of earnings of non-elderly working-class people suggested by Thomson. Instead, Hunt argues that the elderly were primarily dependent on their own wage-earning, and survived mostly by piecing together sums of money from different sources, especially their own earnings.

In what follows I examine the living arrangements and sources of economic support for widows in two industrial villages in Nottinghamshire, a county in the East Midlands, over a thirty-year period. Using evidence gleaned from the censuses of 1851 and 1881, I explore how age differentiated the survival strategies of widows, and I contrast the living arrangements and sources of economic support of widows and wives. I examine, in particular, employment as a source of income for widowed women, and investigate whether or not they were entirely self-supporting or whether their wages were supplemented by or were supplements to the wages of others. Finally, I analyse patterns of Poor Law relief in the region. Because much of the evidence for this analysis is based on census data for two relatively small communities, and the numbers of widows and elderly people are small, the study is necessarily an exploratory rather than a definitive one.

The two villages were selected because of the differences between them in their staple industries. One of the villages, Brinsley, was a small hamlet of approximately 250 households clustered near a coal-mine. Coal-mining was the staple industry of the village throughout the period. Most of the male inhabitants worked in the coal-mine. The next largest category of occupation was agricultural worker, and approximately 10 per cent of residents worked as shopkeepers or public servants. No large landowners or mine-owners lived in Brinsley in either census year. In 1881 it is likely that the residents of Brinsley had fallen on hard times. Beginning in the mid-1870s coal prices went into a sharp decline due to a general trade depression, and miners' wages also declined as they were set on a sliding scale dependent on the price of coal.[17] The Derbyshire and Nottinghamshire Miners' Association, founded in 1863, collapsed with the price of coal at the end of the 1870s.[18]

Arnold was an industrial village almost twice the size of Brinsley. It was a community whose staple industry was domestic framework knitting. By 1881 framework knitting was declining as a source of employment for men, but there were increased opportunities for women to do home-based employment by seaming factory-made hosiery as well as stockings that were hand-loomed.[19] Only around 10 per cent of the male heads of households were in occupations such as shopkeeping or public service. While a small number of the men worked as middlemen and framesmiths in the domestic hosiery trade, the vast majority in the hosiery industry worked as framework knitters. One resident in the sample was classified as a large property-owner in Arnold. Thus, both communities were largely made up of proletarians.

By examining data from the census enumerators' records, I trace changes in the living arrangements of widows and their employment status over the time period. Half of the households in Arnold (N = 488) in 1851 were sampled and one-third of the households in 1881 (N = 405) were sampled. All of the households in Brinsley were examined for 1851 (N = 244) and 1881 (N = 255). Information about all of the individuals in the sampled households in addition to the characteristics of the households in which the individuals lived was recorded. These individual data are the basis for the analysis that follows.

Although generally I present data for three age groups of women, those aged 20–54, 55–64 and 65 and older, I also group the women aged 55 and older together. I do this primarily because of the very small numbers of people in the age group 65 and older. Using age 55 to demarcate the population of older people to be studied is somewhat arbitrary but, as Janet Roebuck has argued, there was considerable variation in who was considered old in the nineteenth century, and no uniform understanding existed of when old age began.[20] Also, discussing those aged 55 and older as elderly can be justified on the grounds that in the nineteenth century, workers would have passed the period of their peak earnings.[21] While Poor Law officials considered 60 to be the age at which people could be considered 'aged and infirm',[22] they also expected people to be able to earn some wages, even if they were not entirely self-supporting, until their late 60s.[23] However, the Friendly Society Acts of 1875 and 1887 defined old age as over 50.[24]

In addition to the census materials, I examined records from the Basford Union, the Poor Law authority for both villages during the period. These records reveal the numbers of people assisted by the Union, suggest patterns of kin support and provide hints about how relief, kin assistance and employment may have worked in combination to support elderly women. Although there were not complete records for these villages for the whole period, there were a variety of different records for Arnold and Brinsley, and for villages which are very similar to them. These include relieving officers' books, Poor Law Guardians' minutes and a very useful set of biannual parish reports on the numbers and categories of persons given relief both in and out of the workhouse from the mid-1860s to 1883.[25]

RATES OF WIDOWHOOD AND LIVING ARRANGEMENTS

Loss of a spouse was far from an infrequent experience for women and men in these nineteenth-century villages, especially in the older age groups. As Table 13.1 shows, generally women were more likely to be widowed than men, especially in the older age groups, and, as expected, the percentage of women and men who were widowed increased with age. What is somewhat surprising is that rates of widowhood for women over age 65 decreased in both villages over the time period, while they remained the same for men of this age group. None the less, the percentage of women aged 65 and older who were widowed ranged from a low of 40 per cent to a high of 70.4 per cent.

Although widows were less likely than their married counterparts to live in their own households, the majority of widows remained heads or nominal heads of their own households even when they were elderly. As Table 13.2 shows, both married women and widows tended to remain in their own households as they aged. In addition, headship rates of women appeared to have *increased* in Arnold over the thirty-year period, especially the rates for widows. The changes occurring in Brinsley are difficult to interpret because of small numbers in the older age groups. However, when the older age groups of women are combined, the data show that whereas there is no change in headship rates for married women 55 and older over the period concerned, the rates of headship for elderly widows *decreased* in Brinsley from 76.5 per cent in 1851 to 66.7 per cent in 1881.

Even though headship rates for widows remained high, only a small percentage of widows lived alone. As Table 13.3 shows, at most one-fifth of widows lived by themselves, and, generally, it was the oldest widows who resided alone. Examining the living arrangements of widows aged 55 and older as a group, the data show that the percentages of widows living on their own varied from a high of 15.6 per cent to a low of 8.3 per cent.

Table 13.1 Number and percentage of widows and widowers in Arnold and Brinsley by age, sex and year

	Arnold								Brinsley							
	1851				1881				1851				1881			
	Men		Women		Men		Women		Men		Women		Men		Women	
Age group	%	N	%	N	%	N	%	N	%	N	%	N	%	N	%	N
25–54	2.8	14	4.6	22	5.0	19	2.8	10	3.2	7	4.9	11	2.7	7	5.4	11
55–64	15.4	12	23.5	16	28.6	16	32.6	14	19.4	7	17.2	5	11.6	5	21.6	8
65+	35.3	18	60.4	29	22.4	11	47.5	19	45.8	11	70.4	19	44.0	11	40.0	10

Table 13.2 Number and percentage of women heading households in Arnold and Brinsley by age, marital status and year

	Arnold								Brinsley							
	1851				1881				1851				1881			
	Married		Widowed		Married		Widowed		Married		Widowed		Married		Widowed	
Age group	%	N	%	N	%	N	%	N	%	N	%	N	%	N	%	N
20–54	92.4	316	77.3	17	94.7	265	50.0	5	89.8	141	81.8	9	90.5	161	90.9	10
55–64	97.9	48	64.3	9	100.0	28	75.0	9	100.0	20	100.0	5	92.6	25	62.5	5
65+	82.3	14	66.7	18	94.7	18	83.3	15	66.7	5	76.5	13	100.0	12	66.7	6

Table 13.3 Percentage of widows living alone in Arnold and Brinsley by age and year

Age group	Arnold				Brinsley			
	1851		1881		1851		1881	
	%	N*	%	N*	%	N*	%	N*
20–54	0.0	24	0.0	10	8.3	12	0.0	12
55 +	15.6	45	9.1	33	8.3	24	11.1	18

Note: *N = Total number of widows in each age group.

The small minority of widows who did not head their own households generally resided with their parents when they were young and with their adult children when they were older. Of the widows in these communities in both census years who co-resided with relatives, only two lived with a relation other than their parents or adult children (in both cases with siblings). Only small numbers of widows in these communities lived as lodgers in the households of non-relatives. The percentages of widows who were lodgers ranged from zero in Brinsley in 1881 to 12.5 per cent in Arnold in 1881. Of the small number of widows who were lodgers, the majority were in the age group 55–64.

The frequency with which married and widowed women lived in households in which they had children at home with them is considered in Table 13.4. Unfortunately the findings are difficult to interpret because of the small number of cases in the oldest age group. As one might expect, the vast majority of younger married and widowed women had children living with them in their households. The data appear to indicate (with the exception of women aged 55–64 in Arnold in 1851) that in both communities there was a *decrease* from 1851 to 1881 in the percentage of older married women who had children living with them. Among widows in Arnold there also was a *decrease* over the thirty-year period in the percentage who had children residing in their households.

Patterns of difference become clearer when women aged 55 and older are grouped together, and women co-residing with children either as heads or in the households of their adult children are considered. Table 13.5 reveals that there was an overall decrease in the percentage of elderly married women living with their children as described above. Among the widowed elderly in Arnold there was a decrease in the percentage living with their children between 1851 and 1881, but in Brinsley the percentage of elderly widows living with children *increased* over the thirty-year period. In addition, elderly widows in Arnold were about as likely as their married counterparts to live with children. In Brinsley, however, there were major differences in the frequency with which elderly married and widowed women co-resided with children.

Table 13.4 Number and percentage of female household heads with children in Arnold and Brinsley by marital status, age and year

	Arnold								Brinsley							
	1851				1881				1851				1881			
	Married		Widowed		Married		Widowed		Married		Widowed		Married		Widowed	
Age group	%	N	%	N	%	N	%	N	%	N	%	N	%	N	%	N
20–54	84.2	266	94.1	16	80.8	214	80.0	5	87.9	174	77.8	7	88.8	143	90.0	9
55–64	68.8	33	77.8	7	71.4	20	66.7	6	85.0	17	60.0	3	52.0	13	100.0	5
65+	50.0	7	61.1	11	22.2	4	53.3	8	80.0	4	46.1	6	50.0	6	50.0	3

Table 13.5 Number and percentage of elderly* women living with children** in Arnold and Brinsley by marital status and year

| | Arnold | | | | Brinsley | | | |
| | 1851 | | 1881 | | 1851 | | 1881 | |
	%	N*	%	N*	%	N*	%	N*
Married	65.1	41	52.2	24	84.6	22	53.9	21
Widowed	64.4	29	60.0	15	45.4	12	72.2	13

Notes: * Aged 55 and older, living with children.
      ** Women who live with their children or who have children living with them.

These patterns of residence illuminate a number of differences and similarities between married and widowed women as they aged. First, it is clear that headship rates remained high throughout the period, although elderly widows were generally less likely to remain in their own households than were their married counterparts, especially in Brinsley in 1881. Second, there is confirmation of the findings of other studies, notably by Richard Wall, that very few widows of any age group lived alone.[26] It was established that except in Arnold in 1881, a majority of elderly women lived with their children, and that elderly widows in Arnold in both 1851 and 1881 were as likely, and in Brinsley in 1881 more likely, than their married counterparts to co-reside with their children. These data suggest, first, that the Rowntree hypothesis regarding the importance of children to household poverty may be applicable to both married and widowed women. Second, the data suggest that for elderly widows, living with children may have been at least a partial solution to the economic difficulties they may have been facing. The data also raise questions about why elderly widows in Brinsley in 1881 tended to be both less likely to head their own households and much more likely to be living with children than both married women in Brinsley and widows in Arnold. To explore possible answers to these questions, we turn next to an analysis of the economic strategies of the widowed women in these villages.

HOUSEHOLD ECONOMIC ARRANGEMENTS

As Table 13.6 makes clear, women who were widowed were likely to find a job. Higher percentages of widows in each age group were working in both census years and in both communities than were married women from the same age group. Although again we are dealing with small numbers of widows and older married women, the consistency of the direction of differences of these numbers and percentages is convincing. In addition to the differences between married and widowed women, there were consistent differences in the percentages of women who were employed by age, village and year.

Table 13.6 Number and percentage of women employed in Arnold and Brinsley by marital status, age and year

	Arnold								Brinsley							
	1851				1881				1851				1881			
	Married		Widowed		Married		Widowed		Married		Widowed		Married		Widowed	
Age group	%	N	%	N	%	N	%	N	%	N	%	N	%	N	%	N
20–54	43.9	150	91.7	22	55.7	156	100.0	10	21.0	33	91.7	11	3.5	6	50.0	6
55–64	32.6	16	75.0	12	57.1	16	85.7	12	11.1	2	60.0	3	0.0	0	37.5	3
65+	29.4	5	44.8	13	52.6	10	64.7	11	0.0	0	47.4	9	9.0	1	20.0	2

Generally, women were less likely to be employed as they aged. The youngest group of women were the most likely and the oldest group were the least likely to be employed in both villages and census years. With the exception of young widows in 1851 when more than 90 per cent were listed with an occupation in both Arnold and Brinsley, generally higher percentages of women were employed in Arnold than were employed in Brinsley. Finally, the percentage of women who were employed increased in Arnold from 1851 to 1881, but decreased in Brinsley in the same time period.

These differences in women's employment patterns may be accounted for by two factors: need and opportunity for employment. That widows were employed at much higher rates than were comparably aged married women suggests that with work opportunities held constant, widowhood dramatically changed women's economic security. Marriage, as suggested earlier, often provided women and their children with something of a buffer against economic adversity. Thus, need for employment is important in explaining some of the variation in the data presented in Table 13.6.

What we know about the differences in the staple industries of the two communities helps to explain why women in Brinsley were less likely to work than were women in Arnold. There were simply fewer job opportunities for women in Brinsley than there were in Arnold. Brinsley was a coal-mining village in both census years. There is evidence that a colliery owned by Barber Walker and Company was in existence as early as 1739.[27] The hosiery industry, the dominant industry in Nottinghamshire until the mid-Victorian period, never became a significant source of employment in Brinsley, although a minority of the male residents of the town in 1851 were framework knitters. By 1881, only very small numbers of Brinsley residents were employed in hosiery. If anything, mining became even more dominant in the economy of the village over the thirty-year period.[28]

Brinsley was probably very much like mining communities elsewhere in that there were very few opportunities for women's employment.[29] Mining itself offered few if any jobs for women, and except for Lancashire, where textile mills were located reasonably close to coal-mines, mining communities were generally isolated. It was particularly married women who were unlikely to be employed in mining areas.[30] Their low rate of employment has been attributed to their extraordinary household duties in addition to lack of opportunity. Household responsibilities of wives in Brinsley were probably not much different than in the following description: 'Three or four black men coming in makes plenty of hard work for the women-folk! The nature of the work makes heavy washing days, and the dust of collier villages invades the homes and must be continually fought against.'[31]

By contrast with mining, the hosiery industry employed large numbers of women. Throughout the period under investigation, Arnold's staple industry was framework knitting organized as a domestic industry. In 1851 Arnold's knitters specialized in making wrought stockings on narrow-gauge machines. Narrow frames were physically less demanding than wide frames, and therefore women and old people generally might have contributed to the production process by working frames. Although women were frame-work knitters in Arnold, they were principally employed seaming the stockings made by other members of their households. Arnold remained a village specializing in wrought-hose made on hand-powered knitting frames in 1881. By the end of the 1870s and early 1880s wrought-hose-makers would have experienced a decline in demand for their products as factory production in Nottingham and its suburbs became increasingly competitive.[32] Although men were less likely to work in the hosiery industry in 1881 than they were in 1851, the reverse was true for women. Opportunities for seaming hosiery expanded along with the factory industry.

Thus the two communities differed from one another in the opportunities women had to earn wages and this difference might well account for the differential rate of women's employment. With the data that are available for this study, however, it is impossible to disentangle need and opportunity. What we can do is to explore further the ways that women were helped to sustain themselves when their husbands were dead.

Although once again interpretation of findings is difficult because of the small number of widows in the two populations at the time of the enumeration, Table 13.7 presents data showing that for the most part only a very small number of widows had no discernible means of support as indicated by the census. Furthermore, with the exception of Brinsley in 1881, the majority of both young and old widows either earned wages in order to subsist on their own, or had their wages supplemented by a relative who lived with them. The proportion of widows who did not earn wages, but were helped to subsist by a working relative who lived with them increased with the age of the widow. Older widows, in other words, were more likely than younger widows to be economically dependent on a co-residing relative. In addition, while the percentage of young and old widows who either supported themselves with wages or added their wages to those of a co-residing relative in the two villages was virtually identical in 1851 (in both villages approximately 90 per cent of young widows and slightly more than 50 per cent of old widows), if anything the percentage increased in Arnold over the thirty-year period (100 per cent of young and 79 per cent of older widows). In Brinsley, however, the percentage of widows who were so supported decreased rather markedly over the thirty-year period (45.5 per cent of young and 29.4 per cent of older widows). There was a corresponding rise of widows in Brinsley who, according to census estimates at least, appeared to be economically dependent on relatives (from 23.8 per cent of older widows in 1851 to 58.8 per cent of their counterparts in 1881). What we do not know, however, is whether or not these widows may have been in receipt of a pension which helped to support the households in which they were residing.

Taken as a whole, these data suggest that opportunities for women's

Table 13.7 Sources of support for widows as inferred from the censuses of Arnold and Brinsley, 1851 and 1881

Age group	Self only*		Self + relative**		Relative only		No discernible support		Total
	%	N	%	N	%	N	%	N	N
A Arnold 1851									
20–54	25	5	65	13	5.0	1	5.0	1	20
55+	15.8	6	36.8	14	39.5	15	7.9	3	38
B Arnold 1881									
20–54	22.2	2	77.8	7	—	—	—	—	9
55+	26.9	7	42.3	11	19.2	5	11.5	3	26
C Brinsley 1851									
20–54	27.3	3	63.6	7	—	—	9.1	1	11
55+	33.3	7	23.8	5	23.8	5	19.0	4	21
D Brinsley 1881									
20–54	27.3	3	18.2	2	27.3	3	27.3	3	11
55+	5.9	1	23.5	4	58.8	10	11.8	2	17

Notes: * Self = employed.
** Relative = lives with working relative.

employment in Arnold in 1881 made it possible for widows there to be somewhat more economically independent than widows in Brinsley. Without opportunities for work, widows in Brinsley appear to have increasingly relied on their working relatives, especially their children, to support them. It is also possible that adult children in Brinsley were more able to help their widowed mothers than were their counterparts in Arnold in 1881. Although miners were far from affluent, especially considering the decline in miners' wages that occurred after 1878, they were probably paid more than were framework knitters. What evidence there is suggests that with the demise of the domestic hosiery trade accompanying the growth of the factory hosiery industry, men in Arnold were increasingly hard-pressed.

Thus, a combination of factors helps to explain the differences between the living and working situations of widows in Brinsley and Arnold. Employment opportunities for women in Arnold helped elderly widows survive there, whereas, in Brinsley, marginally more prosperous sons helped elderly widows to survive. In any case, the census suggests that in both villages only a minority of widows had no discernible means of support, and would have been totally dependent on private pensions if they were lucky enough to have them, or, more often, on the Poor Law or other charity aid.

POOR LAW RELIEF

While the employment rates of widows increased in Arnold but decreased in Brinsley between 1851 and 1881, both villages experienced a severe cutback, beginning in the early 1870s, in the numbers of people who were given public assistance outside of the workhouse. These reductions were general in Poor Law Unions throughout the country, and Basford Union to which Brinsley and Arnold belonged was no exception. The cuts were especially designed to eliminate the award of public assistance to able-bodied people, especially assistance in support of wages. The cuts affected support for the elderly generally, including women.

The New Poor Law of 1834 was intended to stop public assistance outside of the workhouse to 'able-bodied' men, especially relief in support of wages. In the Act of 1834, women as a class were not mentioned.[33] The definitions of both 'able-bodied' and 'whether or not a person was wholly unable to work' were left up to the local Guardians. In 1844 the Central Poor Law Authority made Basford and numerous other Unions subject to the Outdoor Relief Prohibitory Order and the Outdoor Labour Test Order. In combination, these regulations sanctioned outdoor relief to able-bodied men and their families subject to test work by the man, which meant a man on outdoor relief had to do hard and demeaning work such as stone-breaking. However, the new rules prohibited outdoor relief to able-bodied single women.[34] In addition, widows were exempted from the rules governing single women for only the first six months of widowhood, but the aged and infirm continued to be considered not able-bodied, and the local

Guardians were the ones who decided what it meant to be 'able-bodied'. They still had a great deal of latitude when it came to allowing older people to remain outside the workhouse by giving them aid in support of wages.[35]

Poor Law Guardians in Basford continued to sanction outdoor relief to elderly persons between 1844 and 1871 as long as Relieving Officers defined them as not able-bodied.[36] They supported them even when they earned wages and when they were given support by their families. For example, in 1850 in Brinsley a 62-year-old disabled collier and his 54-year-old disabled wife who worked as a seamer were given relief half in kind and half in money.[37] Elizabeth Ward, a 70-year-old widow with no dependants, living in the mining community of Kimberly, and who had no occupation listed, was given relief in kind and with money even though she was residing with her daughter.[38] In contrast John Gregory, a 34-year-old collier whose wife did 'housework', was refused the relief he had requested because he could not support his five children (the eldest two, aged 12 and 10, were working in the pits). In Hucknall, a framework knitting village similar in many respects to Arnold in 1850, a 63-year-old widow who earned money charring was given outdoor relief. Martha Spray, a 66-year-old widow living with her son George who was a framework knitter was given Poor Law assistance when she sprained her ankle. Evidence about non-elderly widows suggests that in 1850 Poor Law Guardians were relatively strict about applying the Prohibitory Order to which reference was made above.[39] For example, a 47-year-old widow with five children was described as 'ordinarily able-bodied', and because she and three of her children were earning 8 shillings a week between them, seaming and winding in the domestic framework knitting trade, she was denied relief.

Beginning in 1871 the centralized Poor Law Governing Board began a concerted (and successful) campaign to persuade local Guardians to reduce the numbers of people who were relieved out of the workhouse, forcing them either to enter the workhouse, find work that would support them, or in the case of the aged and infirm, demand help from relatives. In spite of the relatively strict enforcement of the 1844 Prohibitory Order by the Basford Guardians and the relatively meagre aid they gave the elderly generally before 1871, after that date the numbers of people given outdoor relief were reduced.[40] This decline is indicated in Table 13.8. As Table 13.8 shows, in both communities the overall decline in the numbers of people given outdoor relief was dramatic between the earlier and later periods. However, the reduction in the numbers of non-able-bodied women (many of whom would have been elderly) and widows was less extreme than the reduction in the total numbers given outdoor relief.[41] None the less, these data suggest that there was an increase in 1881 in the numbers of elderly women in these communities who were poor and who had to find a way to live without assistance from the Poor Law in 1881 as compared with 1851. As Table 13.9 suggests, there was no concomitant increase in the numbers of old women from those communities in the Basford workhouse over the same time periods.

Table 13.8 Average numbers on outdoor relief* in Arnold and Eastwood by type of recipient

| | Arnold | | | Eastwood | | |
| | Framework knitting | | | Mining | | |
	Pre 1872 N	Post 1875 N	Decrease %	Pre 1872 N	Post 1875 N	Decrease %
Total	542	161	70.3	125.7	46	63.4
Non-able-bodied women	87.3	49.4	43.4	26.3	18.4	30.0
Widows	12.6	9.2	26.9	5.0	2.6	48.0
Non-able-bodied men	66.0	26.2	60.3	15.7	9.2	41.4

Note: * Calculated by averaging the numbers reported in half-yearly reports ending in the month of September, for the early period the years 1867, 1869, 1871; for the latter period, 1875, 1877, 1879, 1881, 1883.

Table 13.9 Numbers in the Basford workhouse by community and year

| | Arnold | | Eastwood | |
	Pre 1872	Post 1875	Pre 1872	Post 1875
Total	35.0	34.5	15.7	15.6
Non-able-bodied women*	3.0	4.2	3.3	4.8**

Notes: * Married adult women, both able-bodied and not able-bodied were listed separately from 'other' non-able-bodied women. It is the latter category that was used in this calculation. ** There was a sharp rise in the numbers of such women from Eastwood in the workhouse in the reports of 1881 and 1883 when compared with all other years between 1871 and 1881. From 1867 to 1879 the modal number was three. In 1881 and 1883 there were nine and eight such women in the workhouse respectively. In Arnold the numbers of such women in the workhouse varied between three and four from 1867 to 1881. In 1883 the number jumped to seven. I have no way of explaining these shifts.

Application and report books of 1882 for Ruddington, a framework knitting community similar to Arnold, and for Eastwood in 1888 suggest that very elderly people continued to be supported out of the workhouse after the tightened Poor Law policy. However, those who were given outdoor relief in this later period were, on average, older than those given outdoor relief in 1850.[42] In 1850, the average age of those receiving outdoor relief was 49.9 and 53.5, and in the 1880s, it was 64.8 and 72.2.

In addition, the relatively full information about those who applied for relief, and the disposition of their cases in the later record books indicate that elderly people often were given outdoor relief that supplemented both employment and family support. Report books for the earlier period only mentioned the person's family situation when a relation was helping the applicant. In the later period, mention was made in each case of whether or not there were relatives who could and did assist the person. A 64-year-old widow living with her son in Ruddington was earning 1 shilling a week and was given 2 shillings by the parish. Mary Pike, a 72-year-old widowed seamer earned 1 shilling weekly, her son gave her an allowance of 2 shillings and she was given 2 shillings in outdoor relief. In Eastwood in 1888 relief was given to elderly widows, in only a very few cases as a supplement to wages and more frequently to help out, even when the widow was living with relatives.

Whether the relatives of the elderly were compelled by Poor Law officials to help, or whether such kin assistance was given freely are questions which unfortunately cannot be answered with these data.[43] However, the issue of whether or not the aged were being cared for by kin was certainly a part of the rhetoric about Poor Law relief for the elderly in the last quarter of the century. For example, the report of a House of Lords Commission investigating Poor Law relief argued against the practice of giving outdoor relief to the elderly in the following way:

> In the case of the aged and infirm . . . if the doles were withdrawn, it would be found that there are relatives who are in a position to afford the necessary support and who would do so when aid was not forthcoming from the rates.[44]

Evidence collected on the condition of the aged in the Midland districts (which included Nottinghamshire) by Charles Booth in the 1890s suggests, however, that in only rare instances were relatives perceived to be unwilling to help and had to be forced to contribute to their ageing kin.[45] The reports to Booth indicate none the less that the sums of money passed from adult children to their ageing parents may have been small and irregular, especially from adult children who themselves were poor. For example:

> Children cannot give aged parents much help; their own families are costing the most just at the time of need. Not much assistance is given as a rule, often the other way. Married children have to depend on parents for help; they marry so young and without prospects.[46]

Poverty, exacerbated by the stage of the life cycle of adult children of the elderly, might have made it very difficult indeed for the elderly to be cared for in their children's households. As I suggested above, it is possible that in 1881 Brinsley miners would have been marginally better able to afford to include an ageing widowed mother or mother-in-law than would Arnold's framework knitters. In any case there may have been no other option, given that there were so few job opportunities for women in the village.

The evidence reported in this chapter suggests the likelihood that in mid-

Victorian Nottinghamshire elderly widows were supported by help from relatives when possible in combination with earnings and parish relief. When the Poor Law Guardians began to be more restrictive about outdoor relief beginning in 1871, the very old were less affected than the young old. In the framework knitting village where there was an expansion in the opportunities for women to earn very small sums of money by seaming hosiery, elderly women were able to remain heads of households. They did not do so solely on their own earnings, however, but rather they were helped by co-residing children. In the mining community where employment opportunities for women were very limited, the cut-backs in public assistance probably induced some of the elderly widowed women to leave their own households in order to live with their relatives rather than go into the workhouse. In any case, relatives in Brinsley took on more responsibility for elderly widows in the later time period.

These findings are very preliminary. Our understanding of the lives of the elderly in past times awaits the difficult task of linking census and Poor Law records over time in a variety of different communities. If my findings hold up in such subsequent research, they suggest that throughout much of the nineteenth century the elderly pieced together a very meagre subsistence, probably barely enough to remain out of the workhouse and in their own households. They did this with help from relatives, supplemented by parish relief and earnings. When there were no earnings, and public assistance was reduced or non-existent, any available kin who were able to help served as a last resort before the elderly person entered a public institution. The fear of the workhouse was palpable.[47] Public assistance to the widowed elderly in the form of outdoor relief in nineteenth-century England, even in small amounts, supported both family interdependence and the independence of the elderly.

NOTES

1 For an overview of research on the history of widowhood see I. Blom, 'The history of widowhood: A bibliographic overview', *Journal of Family History*, 16, 1991, pp. 191–210. For research on widows in the west of the United States in the nineteenth century and early twentieth century, see A. Scadron (ed.), *On Their Own: Widows and Widowhood in the American Southwest, 1848–1939*, Urbana and Chicago, Ill.: University of Illinois Press 1988.

2 B. Seebohm Rowntree, *Poverty: A Study of Town Life*, London: Macmillan 1901, p. 120. Included in the 15.63 per cent of households below the poverty line because of the loss of the 'chief wage-earner's' wages were fourteen cases of women deserted by or separated from their husbands.

3 ibid.: pp. 136–7.

4 J. Brenner and B. Laslett, 'Social reproduction and the family', in U. Himmelstrand (ed.), *Sociology from Crisis to Science?*, vol. 2: *The Social Reproduction of Organization and Culture*, London: Sage 1988; M. Anderson, *Family Structure in Nineteenth Century Lancashire*, Cambridge: Cambridge University Press 1971; M. Anderson, 'The impact on the family relationships of the elderly since Victorian times in governmental income-maintenance provision', in

E. Shanas and M. Sussman (eds), *Family, Bureaucracy and the Elderly*, Durham, NC: Duke University Press 1977; P. Thane, *Foundations of the Welfare State*, London: Longmans 1982.

5 Anderson, *Family Structure*.

6 R. Wall has shown that only about 5 per cent of women over the age of 65 were living alone in 1891. See his 'Elderly persons and the members of their households in England and Wales from pre-industrial times to the present day', in D. Kertzer and P. Laslett (eds), *Aging in the Past. Demography, Society and Old Age*, Berkeley, Calif.: University of California Press 1994.

7 R. Wall, 'Residential isolation of the elderly: A comparison over time', *Ageing and Society*, 4, 1984; R. Wall, 'Relationships between the generations in British families past and present', in C. Marsh and S. Arber (eds), *Household and Family: Division and Change*, Basingstoke: Macmillan 1992.

8 Thane, *Foundations*; Anderson, 'The impact on the family relationships'.

9 D. Thomson, 'The decline of social welfare: Falling state support for the elderly since early Victorian times', *Ageing and Society*, 4, 1984, pp. 451–82.

10 R.M. Smith, 'The structured dependence of the elderly as a recent development: Some sceptical historical thoughts', *Ageing and Society*, 4, 1984, pp. 409–28; Thomson, 'Decline of social welfare'.

11 Wall, 'Relationships'.

12 D. Thomson, ' "I am not my father's keeper": Families and the elderly in nineteenth century England', *Law and History Review*, 2, 1984, pp. 265–86.

13 Smith, 'Structured dependence'; D. Thomson, 'Workhouse to nursing home: Residential care of elderly people in England since 1840', *Ageing and Society*, 3, 1983, pp. 43–70; Thomson, 'The decline of social welfare'; Thomson, ' "I am not my father's keeper" '.

14 Thomson, 'The decline of social welfare'.

15 ibid.: p. 477.

16 E.H. Hunt, 'Paupers and pensioners: Past and present', *Ageing and Society*, 9, 1990, pp. 407–30.

17 H. Pelling, *A History of British Trade Unionism*, London: Macmillan 1966, p. 72.

18 ibid.; B.J. McCormick, *Industrial Relations in the Coal Industry*, London: Macmillan 1979, p. 11; S. Webb and B. Webb, *The History of Trade Unionism*, London: Longmans, Green 1896, p. 372.

19 S.O. Rose, 'The varying household arrangements of the elderly in three English villages: Nottinghamshire, 1851–1881', *Continuity and Change*, 3, 1988, pp. 101–22.

20 J. Roebuck, 'When does old age begin? The evolution of the English definition', *Journal of Social History*, 12, 1979, pp. 416–29.

21 See P. Stearns, *Old Age in European Society: The Case of France*, London: Croom Helm 1977, p. 26. Stearns also considers those aged 55 and older as elderly.

22 Anderson, 'The impact on the family relationships'; Thomson, 'Workhouse to nursing home'.

23 ibid.

24 Anderson, 'The impact on the family relationships', p. 40.

25 For example, application and report books for outdoor relief in 1850 survive for Greasley, the parish in which Brinsley was located, but not Arnold. However, surviving from 1850 were some records from Hucknall, a framework knitting village. See PUB 4/2/3 at the Nottinghamshire County Records Office. Application and report books survive for Ruddington (a framework knitting community) as well as the parish of Basford in 1882: PUB 4/5/1 at the Nottinghamshire County Records Office. Such records from 1888 survive for Eastwood,

a coal-mining community (where D.H. Lawrence was born and grew up) which was near Brinsley. In addition twice yearly parish statistical statements of the "Classes of Paupers Relieved" from 1868 to 1883 survive for Arnold and Eastwood (but not Brinsley). Eastwood was very similar to Brinsley except that it was a somewhat larger community. The two coal-mining communities were similar enough so that the records for Eastwood can be used to suggest what might have been happening to parish relief in Brinsley. For the Statistical Statements of Classes of Paupers Relieved, see PUB 1/26/1. Other evidence about the operation of the Poor Law concerns Basford Union as a whole which included Arnold and Brinsley.

26 Wall, 'Elderly persons'.
27 A.P. Griffen, *The Nottinghamshire Coalfield, 1881–1981*, Nottingham: University of Nottingham Press 1981, p. 10.
28 See my discussion of the changes in the industry and its consequences for older men in Rose, 'The varying household arrangements', p. 107.
29 However, as Angela John has shown, in Lancashire the textile mills provided employment, especially for single women, in areas where husbands worked in the mines. Generally, however, there tended to be few opportunities for women to be employed in mining towns. See A. John, *By the Sweat of Their Brow: Women Workers at Victorian Coal Mines*, London: Routledge 1984, pp. 117–18.
30 ibid.: p. 117; also see, M. Haines, 'Fertility, nuptiality, and occupation: A study of coal mining populations and regions in England and Wales in the mid-nineteenth century', in T. Rabb and R. Rotberg (eds), *Industrialization and Urbanization: Studies in Interdisciplinary History*, Princeton: Princeton University Press 1981, p. 120.
31 *Woman Worker*, 3 July 1908, p. 149.
32 S.O. Rose, 'Proto-industry, women's work and the household economy in the transition to industrial capitalism', *Journal of Family History*, 13, 1988.
33 S. Webb and B. Webb, *English Poor Law Policy*, London: Longmans, Green 1910, p. 18.
34 The Central Authority encouraged Guardians to put women with illegitimate children into the workhouse and not to support them on outdoor relief.
35 M.E. Rose, 'The allowance system under the New Poor Law', *Economic History Review*, 19, 1966, pp. 607–20.
36 No evidence survives that identifies the criteria they followed when deciding whether a person was 'able-bodied'.
37 Application and Report Books for Outdoor Relief, Basford Union, PUB/4/2/3, p. 18.
38 PUB/4/2/3, p. 14.
39 M. Caplan has argued that between 1836 and 1846, the Guardians at Basford interpreted the New Poor Law in their own way, granting outdoor relief both to the unemployed and to the partially employed because of the continuing problem of underemployment and depression in the framework knitting industry. The Central Authority and the Local Guardians disagreed on assistance. The former wished for the Basford Guardians to enlarge the workhouse, the latter were under pressure from residents of the parishes in the Union to keep costs and rates low (outdoor relief was generally cheaper than indoor relief). As a consequence, Caplan estimates that between 80 to 90 per cent of all poor relief continued as out-relief in the County of Nottinghamshire: M. Caplan, 'In the shadow of the workhouse: The implementation of the New Poor Law throughout Nottinghamshire, 1836–46', *Centre for Local History, Occasional Papers* no. 3, University of Nottingham, 1984, pp. 14–42. Also see M. Caplan, 'The Poor Law in Nottinghamshire, 1836–71', *Transactions of the Thoroton Society*, 74, 1970, p. 93.

40 An inspector who visited Basford Union in January 1872 wrote, 'The present practice of the Guardians is almost entirely in conformity with the recommendations of the Board' (Letter Books of Local Governing Boards, 1872. MH 12/9254 dated 29 January 1872 at the Public Records Office, Kew Gardens).

41 It is most likely the case that it was the younger women with children who were most affected by the reduction in outrelief. The proportion of the total numbers given outdoor relief who were non-able-bodied women or widows remained virtually the same over the time period. From one-third to one-half of all those who were given relief outside the workhouse were children. In Arnold in both 1867 and 1881, 36.8 per cent of adults on outdoor relief were either widows or non-able-bodied women. In Eastwood 36 per cent of adults on outdoor relief were in this category in 1867, and 43 per cent of adults were in this category in 1881.

42 For Ruddington, see PUB 4/5/1, pp. 66–75. For Eastwood, see PUB 4/3/1, pp. 25–31. I averaged the ages of those for whom there was complete information.

43 D. Thomson shows that in Cambridge after 1871, Poor Law Guardians prosecuted relatives who did not support their ageing kin. I found no indication of such prosecutions in the Basford Poor Law records themselves. There is no question, however, that the Poor Law Guardians were very concerned about payments by relatives and were probably more systematic in their questions about such assistance and in collecting contributions from kin: Thomson, ' "I am not my Father's Keeper" '. For an insightful discussion of the complex attitudes of adult children to supporting their ageing parents, as well as parental desire to be independent of their children, see Anderson, 'The impact on the family relationships', pp. 50–7. Anderson argues that the cut-backs in aid to the elderly and concomitant pressure by Poor Law authorities to force adult children to support ageing parents led to an increase in institutionalization of the elderly. The data presented here are consistent with this thesis, but do not show an increase in the numbers of elderly women who were institutionalized. During the nineteenth century in England, the workhouse was primarily filled with old men and young women with illegitimate children. It was not until the twentieth century that the proportion of elderly women in the workhouses began to rise significantly. On the complex issue of extended family households and social class, see S. Ruggles, *Prolonged Connections: The Rise of the Extended Family in Nineteenth-Century England and America*, Madison, Wisc.: University of Wisconsin Press 1987.

44 'Report of the Select Committee of the House of Lords on Poor Law Relief', Parliamentary Papers, xv, 1888, p. iv.

45 Charles Booth, *The Aged Poor in England and Wales*, New York: Garland Press 1980 (originally published in 1894), pp. 225–6.

46 ibid.: p. 226.

47 In his autobiography, Robert Roberts poignantly describes how a man in his community in the early years of the twentieth century carried his sick and disabled father to the door of the workhouse because his father had asked him to do it, but in the end he turned back and carried him home again. This remarkable work contains many references to the ways in which poor people depended on one another, their fear of pauperization and the particular problems of the aged: R. Roberts, *The Classic Slum*, Harmondsworth: Penguin 1974, p. 74. Recently, however, historians are questioning the extent to which the distaste for charity and poor relief kept working-class people from using it. See P. Mandler, 'Poverty and charity in the nineteenth-century metropolis: An introduction', in P. Mandler (ed.), *The Uses of Charity: The Poor on Relief in the Nineteenth-Century Metropolis*, Philadelphia, Pa.: University of Pennsylvania Press 1990,

p. 19. For an insightful overview of how poor people combined aid from kin, Poor Law Relief and wages, see L. Hollen Lees, 'Survival of the unfit: Welfare policies and family maintenance in nineteenth-century London', in Mandler (ed.), *The Uses of Charity*, pp. 68–91.

14 Avoiding poverty

Strategies for women in rural Ireland, 1880–1914

Joanna Bourke

> Little Girl (aged 8): 'If I am married shall I have to marry a man like papa?'
> Mother: 'Yes, I suppose so, my child.'
> Little Girl: 'And if I don't marry, shall I be an old maid like Aunt Julia?'
> Mother: 'Yes.'
> Little Girl: 'Well, it's very hard on women.'[1]

In Ireland between 1890 and 1914, the position of women within the paid labour markets deteriorated. Married women were increasingly dependent on the husband's wage. Economic opportunities for unmarried women collapsed. Rural women entered the fields only during times of peak agricultural demand, if at all. Unwaged domestic production – housework – became increasingly important. In the same period, the Irish economy was undergoing rapid growth. Part of this growth resulted from the massive public and private investment in agricultural and social reform. Living standards for a wide spectrum of the population improved dramatically. The effects of improvements in living standards differed for men and women. The pattern of growth and development did improve female well-being: women were better fed, housed and educated in 1911 than in 1891. Economic progress brought new aspirations. The desire for domestic labour intensified. Economic growth released capital (as well as labour) for investment in the unwaged household sector. Inevitably, the dynamic relationship between housework and rising living standards was complex. Improving living standards stimulated housework which, in turn, raised living standards. Similarly, the collapse of certain employment sectors conventionally reserved for women stimulated a shift of female labour into the home which, in turn, encouraged the further substitution of men for women in the employment market. The coincidence of sectoral shifts in the employment market, investment in the rural economy and the growth of a labour-intensive household sector was crucial.

STRATEGIES FOR AVOIDING POVERTY

Irish women attempted to minimize their risk of poverty by adopting one of four strategies: paid employment; emigration, followed by employment or marriage abroad; marriage and the performance of domestic labour for one's spouse and household; or celibacy and the performance of housework for another household, generally a member of the family. Each of these options was restricted by life cycle considerations. Marriage was unlikely before a woman reached her mid-20s. Elderly women did not emigrate: age severely restricted the options of a woman abroad. To remain unmarried and performing domestic labour, a woman needed a widowed father, a brother, a nephew or a cousin who required her unwaged labour. Furthermore, the decision about which strategy to adopt was not made by the woman alone. The co-operation of the family – and especially parents – was needed. Life options depended to a large extent on the placing of a daughter in the line of siblings. All the options depended on the household's economic position at the time the decision had to be made. A young woman could lose her chance to escape an oppressive household because of the demands of younger siblings or elderly parents, or because the inheriting son brought an 'empty' (or dowerless) bride into the household. Nevertheless, within the context of the household, Irish women sought the 'best deal'. Increasingly, women remaining in Ireland chose to perform housework rather than engaging in paid employment or labouring on the familial farm. What choices were women making? Why did their choices change over time? What were the costs and benefits of these long-term trends?

Option: employment

Tracing changes in female labour is no easy task. The movement of Irish women out of the paid employment markets from the end of the nineteenth century was, however, attested to by commentators from all sections of the community. Although the inaccuracy of census statistics on female labour prevents placing too great a weight on the precise nature of the decline, according to this source, from the last few decades of the nineteenth century to 1911 paid employment for men remained stable, in contrast to female employment which was rapidly declining.[2] Between 1891 and 1911 the percentage of all rural men with designated occupations remained steady at 64 per cent while the proportion of rural women with designated occupations dropped from 23 to 15 per cent. In 1891, 641,000 women were employed, compared with only 430,000 twenty years later. The decline in female participation was steepest between the age categories 20–4 and 25–44, and affected single, married and widowed women to similar degrees.

The census proves useless when it comes to the labour of women on the family farm: it eliminates entirely the labour of female members of the household on their farm, while assuming maximum levels of labour power from all adult male members of the household. Every census to 1911 asserted that farmers' sons, grandsons, brothers and nephews over 15 years of age would be designated 'employed in fields and pastures' if they had not been given another occupation. Corresponding female relatives would be referred to the 'unoccupied' category. Fortunately, there is a great deal of discussion of farm labour in this period – Royal Commissions, annual regional reports from the Department of Agriculture, Congested Districts Board and the Irish Agricultural Organisation Society (the co-operative society), agricultural pamphlets of an 'improving' as well as descriptive nature, massive oral history collections, newspaper reports and so on. This literature universally affirms that the daughters and wives of male farmers were increasingly ceasing to work on the family farm.

What caused the rapid acceleration of female unemployment? Labour historians generally answer this type of question in terms of changes in demand for female labour or changes in the supply of female labour. For instance, the 'tastes' school argues that women no longer wanted to work at particular jobs (such as heavy agricultural labour or domestic service) and/or that certain jobs were no longer considered appropriate for women. A more plausible version of this argument introduces the notion of 'income effect'. In this view, tastes were always opposed to female employment in particular occupations and when average household income reached a certain level this taste was able to be acted upon, or that there was a threshold effect, so that people reaching a certain income level always disliked particular forms of female labour and as more and more households reached this level, more and more women withdrew from these jobs. This type of supply-based argument is useful in explaining the withdrawal of Irish women from domestic service. In 1911, 72,000 fewer women worked as indoor domestic servants than in 1891. As I show elsewhere, the demand among wealthier households for domestic servants remained buoyant: increasingly, however, women from poorer households were refusing to enter into service, preferring to devote a larger proportion of their domestic labour to their own families.[3]

Demand-based arguments include the shift from tillage to pastoral agriculture and changes in farm technology. This argument requires an explanation of why female labourers were more liable to be made redundant than male labourers. A useful demand-based argument in the late nineteenth-century Irish context is the effect of legislation in restricting female employment in certain jobs and the establishment of new institutions concerned with labour which excluded women. An example might be the development of creameries. The replacement of home dairying with creameries (either co-operatively run or privately owned) dramatically reduced the need for female labour in what had been a (female) labour-intensive operation. The cream of 100 farms was churned in two churns instead of 100. Institutional discrimination also had some impact, particularly when it concerned education in new forms of employment.[4]

There is no space here to discuss the reasons for the declining participation of women in each of the main employment sectors but for the purposes of this chapter, it is important to note that their participation in paid employment and work on the family farm was rapidly declining.

Option: emigration

Emigration was considered a very favourable option. Whereas in many other European countries surplus siblings could be dispersed to urban centres, in Ireland surplus family members migrated to England, America, Canada or Australia. While a young unmarried woman might choose to perform unwaged housework for her family as long as there was a chance of marrying, once marriage was no longer a probable outcome her best option was to emigrate. Every year 20,000 women, mostly between the ages of 18 and 26, emigrated. In contrast to migration on the European mainland, Irish migration was composed of nearly as many women as men. Most of the female emigrants left the country alone, and most were unmarried. For instance, of the 2,147 women emigrating from county Mayo in 1892, 90 per cent were unmarried.[5] If a woman emigrated, her labour as a houseworker would pay off in America or Australia. The wealth of her parental household and her position in the line of siblings determined whether a daughter even attempted to find a position for herself in the Irish marriage market. The benefits of emigration were substantial both for the prospective female emigrant and for her family. Families might prefer to send daughters rather than sons abroad: at the very least, while daughters required a dowry, sons brought in a dowry. Furthermore, daughters were reputedly more generous with remittances.[6] Daughters might choose to emigrate rather than contract an Irish marriage outside their region: New York might seem nearer to friends and relatives than a home in a village only 30 miles away.[7] Although emigration continued to be an important option, it declined over the period. Thus, the percentage probability that a woman initially aged 15 years would emigrate before reaching 55 years was 55 for women in the 1831 cohort, declining to 43 for women in the 1871 cohort.[8]

Option: housework

The performance of unwaged domestic labour was an option which grew in importance, especially for those women choosing to remain in Ireland. The economic significance of female labour in the household was accelerating rapidly. Investment of capital and labour in the household sector was booming. Economic 'development' changed the material and labour requirements of the home. It is misleading to focus solely upon increasing consumption. Households did not consume unprocessed products from the farm or shop. Potatoes were washed, cabbages were cut. Consumption did not start when the cow was slaughtered. Increased consumption required increased production.[9] The role of women performing labour necessary for consumption was crucial. Women were already performing housework: intensification of this on the English and urban model required increased specialization. The expansion of a market for commodities – preferably Irish commodities – required the energies of women. It was this view which galvanized nationalist opinion behind the movement to improve house-wifery (for instance, the 'Buy Irish' campaigns). The role of 'consumption' has been most clearly expressed by John Kenneth Galbraith in his *Economics and Public Purpose*. But while Galbraith correctly argues that increased consumption requires greater inputs of time, he sees the force driving women to perform housework as social virtue rather than economic reward. However, it also made better welfare sense for women to do house-work rather than other forms of labour. This was true for rural parts of Ireland because of the rapid changes in domestic production. Expansion occurred particularly in four areas: housing, diet, domestic goods and child care.[10]

The house was the workplace. Improvements in rural housing radically affected labour requirements inside houses. In each decade between 1841 and 1911 the census enumerators collected data on the 'class' of inhabited housing in rural and urban areas. The condition of housing was judged by the number of rooms, the number of windows and the materials from which the house was built. While in 1891 nearly half of all rural houses were third- or fourth-class houses (that is, tiny mud huts or houses with a small number of rooms and very few windows), within twenty years nearly three-quarters were first- or second-class houses (that is, good farm houses, having five to nine rooms and windows – or better). Most of these changes in housing were the result of the investment of surplus household funds into the home, but state sponsorship of housing was also crucial. Although important Acts of Parliament aimed at improving rural housing in Ireland were passed in 1856, 1860, 1870, 1872, 1881, 1883 and 1892, the most radical housing reforms resulted from the Labourers' Act of 1906. At a time when the average agricultural wage in Ireland was less than 11 shillings a week, this Act empowered local councils to provide all manual workers earning under 15 shillings with cottages. Other groups were investing heavily in housing. For instance, the Congested Districts Board alone built or substantially improved over 36,000 houses in the two decades prior to the war. Improved houses would (and were expected to) increase domestic workloads. The public – men and women – discussed the planning and construction of these houses extensively. Everything from the style of the hearth, to the distance from water supplies, to the type of floors was discussed in relation to the impact on housework.

Diet had been changing since the famine.[11] There was an increasing diversity of diet, especially in the form of 'luxury' goods. Assuming that the increased import of food products meant increased consumption of these goods rather than the substitution of imports for home production (a reasonable assumption in the Irish case), we can get some measure of the extent of dietary expansion. Data on imports exist from 1904. Comparing import levels in 1904 with 1911 levels, sugar (and sugar manufactures) increased between 6 and 10 per cent, imports of fruit and vegetables increased by almost 20 per cent, imports of spices and condensed milk increased between 40 and 50 per cent and imports of luxury items such as chocolate increased by 132 per cent.[12] Contemporaries noted rising levels of protein intake by rural households. More butter was being consumed.[13] Farming households ate more of their own eggs.[14] Agricultural statistics show expanding vegetable and fruit cultivation.[15] As incomes increased, meat consumption increased. Meat required more time to cook and a more extensive array of cooking equipment. As diet diversified, so did the degree of specialized knowledge required by houseworkers. No longer was cooking a job that was perceived as being able to be performed by everyone in the household. A degree of elementary training was required. One of the things which gave status to certain types of food was preparation time. Food variety had higher time costs, in terms of preparation and administration.

The material of the home also vitally affected housework. The improving economy saw increased accumulation of household goods.[16] In Ireland, investment in these goods substantially increased the amount of work women performed in the home, both by altering expectations of the goods and services which houseworkers should supply and by increasing the time spent maintaining the new products. One indicator of increased investment in the home can be found by looking at the importation of household goods.[17] This increased by 50 per cent in the nine years between 1904 and 1913, and increased by a further 23 per cent in the years 1913–14. Of course, we have trouble knowing precisely what this means – a real increase in demand for household goods or simply part of the substitution of Irish-made goods with imported goods. However, the fact that *exports* of these household goods increased even more rapidly, suggests that local production was buoyant.

Turning to the labour involved in human reproduction, the labour of child care was undergoing change. The most convincing fertility estimates have been supplied by David Fitzpatrick. Using his estimates based on census survivors, Fitzpatrick's index of marital fertility decreases steadily from 796 in the decade 1871–81 to 743 in the decade 1901–11.[18] Although fertility in Ireland was declining, there was a marked intensification of child care. Children were dependent for longer, partly as a result of declining employment opportunities for the young and partly due to increased pressure for regular school attendance. Imports of toys and other fancy goods increased from just under 12,000 hundredweight in 1904 to over 18,000 by 1911. Increased domestic production of toys is suggested by the increase in exports of toys from only 99 hundredweight in 1904 to over 700 by 1911.[19]

The demands of housework substantially increased the need for girls to remain at school for longer periods. Although David Fitzpatrick argues that girls remained at school longer because education provided them with more options after emigration, they also stayed longer because housework could be significantly improved by education.[20] Educated women made better housewives and good housekeeping increased status. It is only by taking housework seriously, *from the inside* (that is, not simply as a labour market that responds only to economic stimuli from the employment market), that we can understand the boom in domestic education classes. Questions to be addressed include why hundreds of thousands of rural Irish women started attending courses in cookery, laundry-work, domestic hygiene and general housewifery from the 1890s and why rural parents insisted that their daughters were taught compulsory domestic education in local schools. The number of organizations teaching young girls and women how to cook, clean and make clothes was enormous. While similar groups were faltering in England, they were booming in Ireland, with high attendance rates in every county. The importance of these classes was not lost on people at the time. Although the usual arguments based on notions of health, national pride and ideologies regarding 'womanhood' were all put forward, in the final analysis what all the protagonists have in common is their vision of a prosperous countryside which could only be realized by women putting more time into home-making. It is only by tracing the relatively rapid increases in labour requirements of the rural household that we can understand the sudden popularity of the ideology of domesticity.[21]

FEMALE WELL-BEING

The effect on Irish women's lives of the increasing movement into full-time, and exclusive, housework now needs consideration. Historians like to say that the late nineteenth century was a 'dismal period' for Irishwomen, a period when women became increasingly vulnerable.[22] This is only true if we accept the idea that housework was a 'bad' option. Many women thought differently. The costs of the movement into full-time unwaged domestic work were substantial. However, it would be wrong to deny that many women found housework fulfilling. The intensification of the two 'spheres of labour' was part of an attempt by women in this period to minimize their risk of poverty. The costs and benefits of the movement to full-time, unwaged housework will be examined in turn.

The costs of unwaged domestic labour

To identify the beneficiaries of economic growth is not easy. There are very few indicators of the distribution of benefits. Economists working in 'Third World' countries stress that discrimination against women *increases* as households become wealthier: unequal distribution of goods within households can only take place once there are surpluses. The most common types of inequality are those relating to food and housing. Diet improved in

Ireland at the end of the nineteenth century, but children, the aged and women received less food than men of 'working' ages. When there was meat it was generally for the 'breadwinner' of the family.[23] Even in the workhouses and hospitals, men were given more meat and bread.[24] Female labourers were excluded from the attempts by the reforming organizations to improve the housing of rural Irish workers. Houses for agricultural labourers were generally given to male heads of families. Local councils even debated whether women could really be classed as 'labourers'.[25] Houses were disproportionately given to families containing young male labourers, on the grounds that if men were persuaded to remain in Ireland, young women would 'naturally' remain behind also, attracted by increasing marriage opportunities. Current owners of the relatively scarce factor of production − land − benefited from the changes to a much greater extent than other groups.

One of the main ways in which the position of women deteriorated was through the narrowing of their employment opportunities and the correlative reduction in female access to cash resources. The direct impact of agricultural growth on women depended on their access to opportunities for income-earning. This is not to ignore the indirect impact of agricultural growth, which may improve the *household's* economic position. In the dairying industry, capital was transferred to male heads of families. Women expressed concern with the way control over the household's income affected household consumption. Many women ceased receiving the money from the sale of butter or eggs: 'her lord taking this regularly to the nearest bank to deposit'.[26] The increased seasonality of work for female members of small farming families and for female labourers limited their independent access to an income to particular times of the year. By focusing on the needs of male 'heads', the institutional reforms resulted in women losing their right to independent control of the products of their own labour. By not earning cash themselves, women became even more dependent on the generosity, or 'love', of the male earner:

> Before that I went out to day [*sic*], my wife she said says she,
> Be very careful of your pay, and bring it home to me,
> You know you're wanting a Sunday hat and the children wanting shoes,
> So bring me home yez overtime and not go on the booze.
> Says I, my darling that I will, I'll bring yez ivery cent,
> For your the girl knows the way that money should be spent
> But I'm absent minded and the warning soon forgot,
> I got a drop, and now of course I mean to spend the lot.[27]

However, the increased female dependency occasioned by the movement of women out of the waged market should not be exaggerated. Wages *may* have increased female independence, widened their number of choices and provided access to status outside the family. The extent to which this could actually occur is very doubtful, however, as female employment options in rural areas were customarily based on the social standing of the male 'head', and opportunities to move beyond this depended more on geographical mobility than on the labour market.

The most startling change was the movement of women into full-time housework. Although statements such as 'For the labourer, who is abroad from early morning to nightfall, a wife is a necessity' were common, male dependence on female domestic labour did not necessarily require any transfer of power.[28] Indeed, male dependency itself drew some of its acceptability from the increased status it gave to men.[29] Furthermore, the stress on housework carried certain threats with it. Domestic violence centred increasingly on accusations of poor housework. Assaults were admitted by men ('he said it [aggravated assault on his mother] was too little for her'), but excused because the woman was not performing her duties adequately ('as she had no supper ready for him').[30] 'Grania' of the *Irish Homestead* was not at all surprised that men 'drink and beat their wives', and she wished men would 'beat them a great deal more, until they served proper meals, and kept the children in order'.[31] Lawyers testified that only if a woman were a good cook and housekeeper could she be confident that her husband would not abandon her.[32] The basis of domestic bliss was good housekeeping, and bad housekeeping was criminal.[33]

> The truth is, and few women blink it now, women have made a mess of their business, the home. . . . After thousands of years' apprenticeship to their trade they are as ignorant of it as the poor woman who when remonstrated with on her improper feeding of her infant said, 'You needn't teach me how to bring up children, I buried nine of them.' Women have murdered their homes, their health, their children and their husbands for long enough, and have been as thoroughly satisfied with themselves as our friend who had only nine victims. But they are awakening to a conviction of their criminality . . .[34]

Improved housework brought a new sense of guilt and responsibility.

Power can be measured by the amount of control a particular group has over crucial societal resources. One of these resources was children. Housework within marriage involved child-bearing and the childless wife could be stigmatized by the community. In Ireland, women's reproductive capacities were accorded greater and increasing status, but fewer women were allowed access to the only legitimate means to attain this goal – marriage. In 1891, 17 per cent of women aged between 45 and 55 who remained in Ireland were single, compared with 25 per cent by 1911.

Women's role in the new order was not easy. Not only were women supposed to be ideal houseworkers, but they were also responsible for 'making an ideal husband' – and the recipe was complex, ranging from instructions on how to 'feed him well' to exhortations that he must always 'feel that your interest centres chiefly in him'.[35] Mothers had equally onerous obligations: 'Don't forget to live so that your memory will be the tenderest and holiest upon earth to your children.'[36] On the one side, the wife had to act as intermediary between the father and the children. On the other side, her power to achieve her goals against the resistance of her children lay with him. Mrs Hogan had to explain to her husband that their son had decided not to return to school:

> How to so arrange matters with her husband that Jack's surrender may be prevented is now the poor woman's critical perplexity. Even with his own family Tom Hogan is very distant. His word is law; his command never disobeyed or questioned. Tomorrow evening he is expected home, and being naturally supposed after his retreat to be in the state of grace, and consequently in good humour, he will, Mrs. Hogan hopes, be comparatively easily managed.[37]

Women's role as mediator was strictly limited to the domestic sphere. Women were excluded increasingly from nationalist aspirations. For instance, *Sinn Fein* published a column aimed at women, entitled 'Letters to Nora'. The letter on the 19 May 1906 began:

> The work is calling, I said. It awaits us in our own homes. We must be clear about that point. No Irishwoman can afford to claim a part in the public duties of patriotism until she has fully satisfied the claims her 'home' makes on her.[38]

After this the writer declares that 'Nora' may feel that the burden of housework is too great for her, but she is not afraid of hard work, and, after all, 'it is a step in nation building all the same'.

Unmarried women in the poorest households suffered most in the new order. In households which did not benefit from growth in the rural economy, the prevailing poverty meant that the unmarried woman had to find paid employment to supplement her dowry. Since the size of the dowry determined the size and fertility of the farm on which she would eventually reside, a good dowry was the most sensible way to avoid poverty in married life. These women might reduce their risk of poverty by accumulating a higher dowry by working either in Ireland or − more realistically − in England or the United States. In Ireland, she had to find paid employment in an unfavourable market. In some cases, young unmarried women might do best not to seek employment, but rather concentrate on increasing the family's income by substituting as a domestic servant in the familial household; but there was no guarantee that the household would, later on, fulfil its obligations by providing a dowry.

Since a woman who was born into a very poor household was not likely to be able to either marry or emigrate, she was at greatest risk of poverty in old age. If she came from a large family, and if the parents refused to make a settlement of the land until their deaths, she was *less* liable to face destitution in the future. However, the unmarried elderly woman without a kinship network − especially without a network of unmarried brothers or uncles – was vulnerable. In 1901, 68 per cent of women in the Roscrea work-house were over the age of 60. Nearly 80 per cent of women in the Glenties workhouses were elderly. The vulnerability of elderly women was greater if they had remained unmarried. In two Donegal workhouses in 1911, 71 and 77 per cent of the women had never been married. Most of these women claimed to have been domestic servants.[39] The economic vulnerability of single unmarried women must not, however, be exaggerated. These women were vulnerable whether or not they were restricted to household labour because the paid labour market was substantially closed to them. The greater value of elderly women in the house, compared with elderly men, should also be acknowledged. Men over the age of 65 were more liable to end up in Irish workhouses than women over the age of 65. According to David Fitzpatrick, 6.4 per cent of all unmarried men over the age of 65 in 1911 were in work-houses, compared with 5.2 per cent of all unmarried women over the age of 65.[40] Women remained productive by performing domestic tasks from which men were increasingly excluded. The greater productive activity of women, however, did not necessarily confer higher status on them than on the leisured men. Was status more likely to be attained by an old patriarch smoking by the fire and creating work for other members of the household, or by an elderly woman busily minding children and repairing stockings?

The tendency for women to enjoy less leisure than men was accentuated when the primary labour was housework.[41] The theme was stressed in the papers of the period:

> In a home there is no limit to the possibilities for occupation, and when leisure time does come it brings with it the opportunity for assisting those less fortunate.[42]

> A man often works much harder than a woman whilst at work, but through all his labour runs the consciousness that it has a finish. The busy wife and mother has no such consciousness to sustain her in her manifold duties and worries . . . and when utterly too tired and worn out to do another hands turn, [she] turns to the family mending basket as a source of recreation.[43]

> The two facts noticeable in connection with womenkind in rural districts are: Their recreation is nonexistent and their work is never done. . . . That mythological gentleman who was perpetually employed in rolling a stone into a place where it would not stay is the prototype of the modern country girl; at least he has no counterpart nearly so accurate in our time – the only thing differentiating the daily routine of brushing, sweeping, cooking and cleaning from the eternal stone-rolling process being the zest for usefulness.[44]

The houseworker did not know any real sabbatical rest – after mass, her duties resumed.[45] Housework was a continual process: no sooner was the house cleaned than it was dirty.[46]

The benefits of unwaged domestic labour

The changes in female labour were not always experienced negatively by women. For the women making the decision to quit paid employment, or never to engage in it, housework offered them a chance to increase their status and improve the quality of their lives. Anything which alleviated poverty was in the interests of women. There was no necessary trade-off between household living standards (met by increased division of labour) and women's status (allegedly declining as women moved out of the two other labour markets). At the very least, during periods when the paid and farming labour markets were unfavourable to women, attempts by women to work in the market as well as in the domestic sphere might have increased poverty for the individual woman as well as for the household. By concentrating on domestic production a woman could increase her own consumption as well as the consumption of the household, strengthen moral ties of dependency and independence and increase her own power to an extent that would exceed her potential power in the paid workforce and in the familial farming market where she was subject to the dictates of the 'head' of the farming family. The increasing movement of women into full-time housework was a sensible strategy for reducing their risk of poverty and maximizing possible control over their own lives and the lives of their family. This was true for rural parts of Ireland because of the rapid changes in the domestic sphere.

It is useful to distinguish between production within the household (that is, cooking, cleaning, making clothes and so on) and reproduction (that is, child-bearing and child-rearing). While productive housework was an immediate way to maintain a certain standard of living, children were the long-term strategy that a woman might have chosen. As a long-term strategy, children were more important for female members of the household than for male members. Since women tended to marry when younger, they tended to outlive their husbands. With the general improvement in diet, health care and living standards, women were less liable to die giving birth.[47] They were more liable to be dependent on the future resources of their children, whether those children were male or female. Particularly in the period before old-age pensions, reproductive housework was crucial. The effect of the increased dependency of children reduced the immediate value of children while, simultaneously, increasing their long-term value. Children also cemented the economic contract between the couple. The rights of a woman to the property of her husband's farm were not clearly established until, through the birth of children, the succession to the farm through her husband's line had been assured. Thus, there was an acute loss of economic power and security if a woman remained childless. Once she had children, the wife's position was stronger since, if widowed, she was allowed to hold the land in trust for her husband's heirs. If she were childless and made a widow, the collateral kin of the dead might oust her from the farm, returning the cash equivalent of the dowry. *Male* children, in particular, were an immensely important long-term investment for married women. A woman might try to avoid poverty in old age by marrying her son to a woman with a good dowry. As the probability of women living to old age improved, and age of marriage rose for both men and women, it became increasingly likely that it was the widow (rather than the married couple or widower) who would benefit from the dowry brought by the son's wife.

The importance of the dowry in marriage negotiations in Ireland has been seen by many historians as an indication of the *low* status of Irish women. There has been considerable confusion in Irish historiography about the role of the dowry. Unlike the dowry in many European countries, in Ireland the father of the bride gave the dowry to the father of the groom, who generally used it to facilitate the emigration of the other offspring or to dower a daughter. The dowry in Ireland has been viewed as moving along generations, rather than flowing between generations. Richard Breen has seen the dowry as the way women 'bought' social position – unmarried women were part of a 'floating' population which would only be settled once married.[48] David Fitzpatrick has called it a 'fine for the transfer of one redundant female from one family to another'.[49] Cormac O'Grada has also viewed dowry payments as some indication of the relative worth of the labour of the incoming bride.[50] A more plausible interpretation of the dowry takes into account the crucial fact that, in Ireland, the dowry is a payment across generations. Dowry payments were similar to payments of 'tenant right'. In both cases, the incoming person paid the present incumbents (in the case of the dowry, other siblings) compensation for their labour on the farm. This explanation is consistent with the increasing prevalence of the dowry in Ireland in the late nineteenth century: as the productive aspects of housework became more important, it became increasingly relevant that the daughters of a household should be given some compensation for their labour. The payment of the dowry has less to do with the status of the incoming bride and more to do with the productive potential of the farm and household as prepared by family members forced to disperse.

Elderly widowed women benefited from the emphasis on domestic work. Their labour was liable to be much more valuable to the household than the labour of elderly widowed men. Widowed men over the age of 65 were more liable to end up in a workhouse than widowed women over 65. In 1911, 4.5 per cent of widowed men over the age of 65 were in workhouses, compared with 2 per cent of widowed women over the age of 65.[51] The land inheritance system favoured widows with children. It assured widowed women of a place in the household. If the widow handed the land over to a son, certain customary rights provided important economic resources.[52] The provision of pensions to old people created incentives to 'retire', while simultaneously reducing pressure on the parents to compensate for their 'dependency' by performing domestic labour. In Ireland, the old age pension was seen as a significant sum of money. It enabled elderly women (whether married or not) to have some freedom from the constraints of family:

> When the affairs of house or land
> Go clean against her will,
> She boasts: 'I have my Pension
> And I'm independent still.'[53]

Not all women married. Over one-quarter of all women in Ireland never married; yet, even women who remained unmarried were affected by the economic demands of increased housework. In part, this was due to the particularly late transfer of land in many Irish communities (especially in the west) which resulted in a household of unmarried men and women living together all their lives, with sisters or aunts assuming the role of house-workers.

If an unmarried woman chose to remain in Ireland, her risk of poverty decreased dramatically during the period. Older unmarried women were less liable to be residing in a workhouse on census day. More significantly, her risk of ending up in the workhouse declined faster than the risk of entering a workhouse faced by unmarried men (see Table 14.1).

Table 14.1 Percentage of all unmarried persons in Ireland residing in workhouses on census day, by sex and age, 1881–1911

Age and sex		*1881*	*1891*	*1901*	*1911*
15–19	Female	0.47	0.26	0.29	0.32
	Male	0.46	0.23	0.23	0.26
20–4	Female	0.74	0.57	0.48	0.54
	Male	0.38	0.28	0.27	0.29
25–34	Female	1.71	1.22	1.04	0.84
	Male	0.73	0.63	0.55	0.60
35–44	Female	3.91	2.39	1.81	1.50
	Male	2.01	1.53	1.44	1.36
45–54	Female	3.92	3.48	2.59	1.66
	Male	3.16	2.88	2.98	3.09
Over 55	Female	6.13	6.14	6.42	3.63
	Male	7.37	7.51	8.22	5.67

The move of women to full-time housework did not necessarily increase their risk (*vis-à-vis* men) of becoming a 'dependant' in the home of another person. Defining 'dependent' persons as men or women who were relatives (but not the 'head of the family') and over 40 years of age, then both men and women were more liable to be 'dependent' members of the households. In my sample from the census forms of eight district electoral divisions in 1911 compared with 1901, the percentage of women over the age of 40 who were 'dependent' increased from 14.8 per cent in 1901 to 16.6 per cent in 1911. However, the percentage of men who were 'dependent' members of households increased much faster, from 12.3 per cent in 1901 to 16.5 per cent in 1911. Both men and women over 40 years of age were liable to find themselves in households where they were under the headship of a person to whom they were not married, but the relative positions of men and women became almost identical. In other words, the chances of a man over the age of 40 establishing his own household decreased faster than the chances for a woman over the age of 40. Whether through emigration or marriage, women were more able to escape.[54]

The options outside of housework open to unmarried women were unattractive. Young unmarried women risked paying a high cost for engaging in paid employment: they risked celibacy. Paid work increased the time-costs of finding a husband. Employment lowered their status. Poverty is not simply a material concept: people are poor if they *feel* poor. If a particular culture frowns on female employment, and if a woman is employed, she may feel 'poorer' although her material lifestyle may be higher. Unmarried rural women preferred non-agricultural forms of employment – that is, employment which widened opportunities for marriage by providing them with male contacts outside the local parish, or by allowing more freedom than was permissible when a woman resided with her employers. Domestic service was particularly distasteful. Girls and women who, in previous decades, might have gone into service, increasingly regarded it as an inferior type of employment. Over and over again, contemporaries noted this change: 'Many an intelligent farmer's daughter considers it a great come-down in the world, a disgrace even, to become a domestic servant. A sense of slavery and servitude seems to have attached itself to the idea of domestic service.'[55] Servants recognized their subservience. Tenant farmers objected to marrying former domestic servants.[56]

> There is a great reluctance on the part not only of daughters of small farmers, but also the daughters of labourers to go out to service. This springs partially from pride such as deters farmers' sons from service, and partially from its becoming an obstacle to marriage.[57]

The unmarried woman deciding to take up paid employment would discover that she had few choices. Women were discriminated against, especially in the context of the newly reformed types of work catered for by the all-male agricultural colleges. Legislative changes restricted the employment of women. Economic reorganization and reform reduced the options for rural women in what had traditionally been female jobs.

Even for unmarried women, housework had certain benefits. In agricultural communities where work was physically demanding, monotonous and heavily dependent on factors such as the weather, women (and men) might have preferred working inside. The fact that domestic work was unpaid did not necessarily make it less satisfying than work that was paid. The move into the home allowed women to expand into other areas of life, outside the strictly economic realm:

> Marriage on a farm, as we understand it, is a contract based on quite other foundations than a salary. A woman wants something to love and look after, and wants somebody to love and look after her. She has her home and the affection of her husband and children, and these are her wages for long and tiresome labours, and if she is happy in her home, she counts herself well-paid.[58]

We cannot quantify the psychic benefits accruing to women able to devote their time to domestic work without any of the pressures peculiar to paid labour.

Once women were limited to work within the domestic labour markets, tension between reproduction and domestic production threatened women's welfare. This is especially true when the productive aspects of the home are removed, leaving women with only their *long-term* strategy for avoiding poverty (that is, reproduction). At least before the First World War, this did not happen in Ireland. Reproductive labour remained – as it had been – a crucial determinant of welfare: if anything, the value of women's reproductive labour increased as emigrant remittances became an established practice. But it was that hidden investment in the productive aspects of the household which was crucial. The coincidence of declining demand for female labour in jobs customarily reserved for women and the increasing potential for productive labour within the home, encouraged the movement of Irish women from paid employment (or work on the family farm) to unwaged production in the home. The changes occurring in rural Irish society between 1890 and 1914 led to the development of a non-market household sector which demanded skilled labour – this demand was met by women.

NOTES

1 *Irish Homestead*, 9 July 1898, p. 584.
2 For discussions of the problems of census statistics on female employment, see Edward Higgs, 'Domestic servants and households in Victorian England', *Social History*, 8, 1982; June Purvis, *Hard Lessons*, Minneapolis, Minn.: University of Minnesota Press 1989; and Elizabeth Roberts, *Women's Work, 1840–1940*, London: Macmillan 1988.
3 For further discussion of domestic service, as well as other sectors of paid employment, see my *Husbandry to Housewifery: Women, Economic Change and Housework in Ireland, 1890–1914*, Oxford: Clarendon Press 1993. For the comparative dimension, see my *Working-Class Cultures in Britain, 1890–1960: Gender, Class and Ethnicity*, London: Routledge 1994, esp. chapters 3 and 4.
4 For further detail, see my 'Women and poultry in Ireland, 1891–1914', *Irish Historical Studies*, May 1987, pp. 293–310, and 'Dairywomen and affectionate wives: Women in the Irish dairy industry, 1890–1914', *Agricultural History Review*, 38, 1990.

5 *Royal Commission on Labour, The Agricultural Labourer, Vol. iv, Ireland, Part iv, Reports by Mr. Arthur Wilson Fox (Assistant Commissioner), Upon Certain Districts in the Counties of Carlow, Mayo, Roscommon, and Westmeath, With Summary Report Prefixed* (C.–6894–xxi), House of Commons, 1893–4, xxxvii, part 1, report on Westport.

6 Evidence of Vere Foster, *Second Report from the Select Committee of the House of Lords on Land Law (Ireland); Together with the Proceedings of the Committee. Minutes of Evidence, and Appendix*, p. 241, House of Commons, 1882, xi, p. 801.

7 Horace Plunkett, *Ireland in the New Century*, London: John Murray 1904, p. 56.

8 Statistics from David Fitzpatrick, ' "A share of the honeycomb": Education, emigration and Irishwomen', *Continuity and Change*, 1, 1986, p. 233.

9 John Kenneth Galbraith, *Economics and the Public Purpose*, Boston, Mass.: Houghton Mifflin Co. 1973; Steffan Linder, *The Harried Leisure Class*, New York: Columbia University Press 1970; and Thorstein Veblen, *The Theory of the Leisure Class*, New York: New American Library 1953, all make the same point, but they ignore the fact that the maintenance of consumption goods is often done *not* by the consumer but by another person – the houseworker.

10 In this chapter, I can only provide a brief sketch of these changes. Many other aspects could be looked at to illustrate the increased labour requirements of the home (for instance, changes in clothing, fuel, care of the elderly, shopping and washing). Elsewhere I trace these rapid changes: ' "The health caravan": Female labour and domestic education in rural Ireland, 1890–1914', *Eire–Ireland*, 24, winter 1989, pp. 4–29, and 'Working women: The domestic labour market in Ireland, 1890–1914', *Journal of Interdisciplinary History*, 21, winter 1991, pp. 479–99.

11 For the best discussion of long-term changes in diet, see L.M. Cullen, *The Emergence of Modern Ireland 1600–1900*, New York: Holmes & Meier 1981, pp. 140–92.

12 Statistics from the annual trade returns in the British Parliamentary Papers.

13 *Vice-Regal Commission on Irish Milk Supply. Final Report* (Cd. 7134), House of Commons 1914, xxxvi, p. 80, evidence by James Stewart from Strabane; and 'Notes of the week. Poultry keeping more important now to Ireland than the butter industry', *Irish Homestead*, 11 February 1911, p. 105.

14 ibid.

15 Department of Agriculture and Technical Instruction for Ireland, *Sixth Annual General Report of the Department, for 1905–1906* (Cd. 3543), House of Commons 1907, xvii, p. 289; and *Abstract of Labour Statistics. Board of Trade (Department of Labour Statistics), Sixteenth Abstract of Labour Statistics of the United Kingdom* (Cd. 7131), House of Commons 1914, lxxx, p. 453.

16 Modern evidence shows that the average time spent on housework does not decrease with technological advance: summaries of this literature are given by Christine Bose, 'Technology and changes in the division of labour in the American home', *Women's Studies International Quarterly*, 2, 1979, pp. 295–304; A. Szalai, *The Use of Time*, The Hague: Mouton 1972; and Kathryn E. Walker and Margaret E. Woods, *Time Use: A Measure of Household Production of Family Goods and Services*, Washington DC: Centre for the Family of the American Home Economics Association 1976, p. 32.

17 Household goods include candles, lamps, electroplated ware, mats and matting, washboards, bedsteads, brushes and brooms, chinaware, clocks, ranges and ovens (including parts), pots, pans and buckets, cutlery, polishes, carpets, mattresses, picture frames and furniture.

18 Statistics kindly provided by David Fitzpatrick. His index of marital fertility

gives the ratio of births in each intercensal decade to the number expected from the same age distribution of married Hutterite women (1921–30), multiplied by 1,000. Births were estimated from censal survivors aged 2–9 years at the end of each decade, plus appropriate proportions of decadal deaths at ages 0, 1, 2, 3, 4 and 5–9 years, and also of quinquennial emigrants at ages 0, 1–5 and 5–9 years. He assumes that within each category the number of vital events was constant for each year of age and during each year of the period. The resulting estimates for births were converted to decadal estimates using the ratio of registered births for the decade to registered births for the first eight years. Demographers disagree about fertility trends: see Brendan M. Walsh, 'Marriage rates and population pressure: Ireland, 1871–1911', *Economic History Review*, second series, 13, 1970, pp. 148–62; and R.E. Kennedy, *The Irish. Emigration, Marriage and Fertility*, Berkeley, Calif.: University of California Press 1973, p. 176.

19 Statistics from the annual trade returns in the British Parliamentary Papers.
20 Fitzpatrick, ' ''A share of the honeycomb'' '.
21 For further discussion, see my article, ' ''The health caravan'' ', pp. 4–29.
22 Fitzpatrick, ' ''A share of the honeycomb'' ', p. 217. Also see Kennedy, *The Irish*, p. 84; Thomas G. Conway, 'Women's work in Ireland', *Eire–Ireland*, 7, 1972, p. 27; and J.J. Lee, 'Women and the church since the famine', in M. MacCurtain and D. O'Corrain (eds), *Women in Irish Society. The Historical Dimension*, Dublin: Arlen House, The Women's Press 1978, p. 37.
23 Charles A. Cameron, *Reminiscences of Sir Charles Cameron*, Dublin 1913, p. 169.
24 The diets of male and female paupers can be found in many reports and commissions of inquiry into the Poor Law. No comment was ever made which implied that the different diets were unacceptable. For instance, in an unnamed rural asylum which had 400 inmates in 1910, male paupers received 1.5 pounds more potatoes and 30 ounces more bread a week than female paupers. In another rural infirmary in 1910, men and women both received half a pound of meat and one egg daily, but men also received one bottle of porter. For these examples (and many others) see, *Royal Commission on the Poor Laws and Relief of Distress. Appendix Vol. xxviii. Reports of Visits to Poor Law and Charitable Institutions and to Meetings of Local Authorities in the United Kingdom*, pp. 357 and 355 (Cd. 4974), House of Commons 1910, liv, pp. 465 and 463.
25 'Is a woman a labourer?', *Kings' County Chronicle*, 17 February 1898, p. 1.
26 *United Irishman*, 12 July 1902, p. 5.
27 'Working overtime', National Library Australia, n.d. (music sheets).
28 Charlotte G. O'Brien, 'The Irish ''poor man'' ', *Nineteenth Century*, December 1880, p. 877.
29 In the same way that the dependency of a female householder on the services of a domestic servant increases the status of the female householder.
30 Quoted from the *Evening Mail*, probably 1901, by Michael J.F. McCarthy, *Priests and People in Ireland*, Dublin 1903, p. 300.
31 'Grania', 'Correspondence. Are mothers the ruin of Ireland?', *Irish Homestead*, 15 February 1913, p. 130. A similar sentiment is expressed by Mrs Frank Pentrill, 'Everyday thoughts. The teapot and kettles', *Irish Monthly*, 1882, p. 526; and Helen Hawthorn, 'The ideal girl', *Ireland's Own*, 26 November 1902, p. 8.
32 'Homely wrinkles', *Ark*, March 1913, p. 4.
33 T.B. Cronin, 'Systems of primary and secondary education relative to industrialisation', *United Irishman*, 18 November 1905, p. 7.
34 'Notes of the week. Feeling their way', *Irish Homestead*, 4 July 1914, p. 537.
35 'For wife and maid', *Irish Weekly Independent*, 14 December 1905, p. 10.

36 'Don'ts for mothers', *Irish Peasant*, 18 November 1905, p. 7.
37 P. Hickey, *The Irish Problem*, London 1906, p. 32.
38 'Letters to Nora', *Sinn Fein*, 19 May 1906, p. 6. For a discussion of Irish female exclusion from political movements, see Margaret Ward, 'Marginality and militancy: Cumann na mBanm 1914–1936', in Austen Morgan and Bob Purdie (eds), *Ireland. Divided Nation. Divided Class*, London: Ink Links 1980, pp. 96–110.
39 Workhouses of Glenties and Stranorlar in 1911 and Roscrea workhouse in 1901. From census manuscripts Donegal 149 and 56 and Tipperary 120, in the National Archive of Ireland. The statistics exclude females under the age of 18.
40 David Fitzpatrick, 'Retirement arrangements in rural Ireland: A study in family diplomacy', unpublished paper presented at Social History Workshop, Chicago, University of Chicago, November 1986, table 6.
41 'Women workers' column', *Irish Worker*, 19 August 1911, p. 2.
42 'For wife and maid', *Irish Weekly Independent*, 19 April 1906, p. 10.
43 'For wife and maid', *Irish Weekly Independent*, 27 October 1906, p. 10. Also see 'For wife and maid', *Irish Weekly Independent*, 3 September 1910, p. 9.
44 *United Irishman*, 12 November 1904, p. 3.
45 ibid.
46 'Women workers' column', *Irish Worker*, 19 August 1911, p. 2; and 'The country girl', *United Irishman*, 12 November 1904, p. 3.
47 For every 1,000 births in 1903, 6.5 women died, compared with 5.7 deaths by 1911: *Forty-Eighth Detailed Annual Report of the Register-General for Ireland Containing a General Abstract of the Numbers of Marriages, Births and Deaths Registered in Ireland During the Year 1911*, p. xxxv (Cd. 6313), House of Commons, 1912–13, xiv, p. 35.
48 Richard Breen, 'Dowry payments and the Irish case', *Comparative Studies in Society and History*, 26, 1984, p. 292.
49 David Fitzpatrick, 'The modernisation of the Irish female', in Patrick O'Flanagan, Paul Ferguson and Kevin Whelan (eds), *Rural Ireland, 1600–1900: Modernisation and Change*, Cork: Cork University Press 1987, p. 169.
50 Cormac Ó Gráda, *Ireland Before and After the Famine: Explorations in Economic History, 1800–1925*, Manchester: Manchester University Press 1988, pp. 167–8.
51 Fitzpatrick, 'Retirement arrangements in rural Ireland', table 6.
52 For example, the widowed mother (not the daughter-in-law) controlled the poultry.
53 Ned Buckley, 'The mother that didn't die', in Jack Lane and Brendan Clifford (eds), *Ned Buckley's Poems*, Aubane: Aubane Historical Society 1987, p. 23 (Ned Buckley was a Duhallow poet, 1880–1954).
54 The total numbers of women and men over the age of 40 who resided in households in the eight district electoral divisions were 728 and 697 (respectively) in 1901 and 716 and 747 (respectively) in 1911. 'Dependent' women were relatives such as daughters, sisters, in-laws, aunts, nieces, etc., who were not the 'head of the family' and who were over 40 years of age. The sample is taken from the census forms for eight district electoral divisions in both 1901 and 1911. The information on these forms was matched with data from the Valuation Office. It includes fifty-nine (1901) and sixty-two (1911) pieces of information on each individual in the 1,069 households in 1901 and 924 households in 1911. For further explanation of this sample of households, see my book, *Husbandry to Housewifery*.
55 Charlotte Dease. 'Domestic service as a profession', *New Ireland Review*, June 1903, p. 219. Also see the speech made by George Fletcher at the opening of a school for domestic servants, quoted in 'Northlands School of Housewifery, Londonderry (in connection with Victoria High School)', *Department of*

Agriculture and Technical Instruction for Ireland Journal, 9:4, July 1909, p. 713; and Kathaleen Roche, 'The lady teachers' own page', *Irish School Weekly*, 25 January 1913, p. 880.

56 'M.L.T.', 'Correspondence. Homelife in Ireland', *Irish Homestead*, 27 May 1899, p. 376.

57 *Royal Commission on Labour. The Agricultural Labourer, Vol. iv, Ireland, Part iii, Reports by Mr Roger C. Richards (Assistant Commissioner) Upon Certain Districts in the Counties of Cavan, Dublin, Galway and Tipperary, With Summary Report Prefixed*, p. 40 (C.–6894–xx), House of Commons, 1893–4, xxxvii, part 1, p. 304, report on the Poor Law Union of Roscrea (County Tipperary).

58 'Poor Economist', 'Notes of the week. The wages of the family', *Irish Homestead*, 23 March 1907, p. 225.

15 Some implications of the earnings, income and expenditure patterns of married women in populations in the past

Richard Wall

The position of the wife and mother in this and most other western countries according to theory and sentiment, according to law, and according to prevalent practice is a curious example of human inconsistency. Popular sentiment places her a little lower than the angels; the law a little higher than the serf. In life as it is lived in four households out of five or nine out of ten, her position is neither that of angel or serf, but of an extremely hard-worked but quite valued member of the family . . . in the fifth or tenth household – proportion is important but as it is unprovable I will not discuss it except to say that I incline myself to the more pessimistic view – the husband uses his power to make her position nearly or quite as bad as, or worse than, the law permits.

(Eleanor F. Rathbone, The Disinherited Family. A Plea for Direct Provision
for the Costs of Child Maintenance Through Family Allowances, London:
George Allen & Unwin 1924; 3rd edn 1927, p. 68)

EARNINGS AND STANDARD OF LIVING OF THE MARRIED AND NON-MARRIED

As Eleanor Rathbone, social investigator and campaigner for family allowances, observed in 1924, the many and varied inequalities that women can encounter within the family and the proportion who experience such inequalities in an extreme form are difficult to determine with any great degree of precision.[1] Despite the fact that the vast majority of women in historical populations were married throughout the greater part of their adult lives, it seems almost inevitable, as other chapters in the present volume testify, that the visible poverty of the single woman or the widow will be studied more often than are the hidden inequalities that affected the married woman. Yet some evidence survives from the eighteenth and nineteenth centuries on the role of married women in the family economy and on the variation in their earning power over the course of their life cycles. It is even possible to measure their value to their husbands (and, in certain circumstances, themselves) by calculating the amount expended on women's as opposed to men's clothing in different societies. The intention in this chapter is to review this evidence, while admitting that this is insufficient at present to permit a fully comprehensive account of the economic standing of married women in the past. We will draw on data from a variety of time periods and places and from sources that range from budgets of individual families collected from the middle decades of the nineteenth century by the French sociologist Frederic Le Play and his followers, to investigations of entire communities undertaken by those interested in social conditions.[2]

We may begin with a survey of the poor inhabitants of the East London parish of St George in the East in 1848. This particular population was selected by the Statistical Society of London as likely to represent 'the average condition of the poorer classes of the metropolis', but is also particularly revealing on differences in living standards within the working class.[3] As Table 15.1 makes clear, the earnings of single men were almost four times as great as those of single women, while the households of widows and children received only 40 per cent of the earnings available to the average married couple family. Not surprisingly, despite the fact that households of married couples contained a greater number of dependants,[4] there was a large difference in expenditure patterns. For example, as is again evident from a consideration of data set out in Table 15.1, widows spent a much greater proportion of their more meagre earnings on rent and economized both on food and on clothing. Around half of all widow-headed households had meat and dairy products only once a week compared with under a fifth of married couple households and just 2 per cent of the households consisting of single men.[5] Households of single women made comparable economies in the frequency with which they partook of meat and dairy products, but were no more likely to be deemed deficient in clothing than were members of married couple households. There was noticeably less of a difference in male- and female-headed households in regard to other types of expenditure, such as the furnishing of rooms or the possession of books, or in the standards of personal hygiene as established by the dirtiness of clothing. Such expenditure may have been influenced primarily by personal choice, and the needs of different families and individuals, rather than their level of income.[6]

The parish of St George in the East cannot, of course, be assumed to represent the situation throughout the rest of the country. Yet the analysis of the occupations, earnings and household patterns of the inhabitants of a small town and its rural hinterland half a century earlier does suggest a somewhat similar story. A local census of 1790 reports on some 1,239 persons in the parish of Corfe Castle, located a few miles inland of the Dorset coast.[7] The men were employed in a wide range of miscellaneous trades: in farming, dairy and fishing and as labourers and clay-cutters. Service, knitting and the spinning of flax were virtually the only employments for women. The census was completed in exceptional detail. Particularly useful for the present purposes are the estimates that were included of

Table 15.1 Expenditure patterns of different types of household within the working-class population of the parish of St George in the East, London, in 1848

Household type	Number of families	Weekly earnings (shillings and pence)[1]	Percentage of earnings devoted to rent (%)[2]	Percentage of households eating animal food[3] once a week, having insufficient or dirty clothing, badly furnished rooms and no books				
				Animal food once a week (%)	Insufficient clothing (%)	Dirty clothing (%)	Rooms badly furnished (%)	No books (%)
Married couples and widowers with child(ren)	1,651	24s 5d	15.4	14.4	44.6	10.8	15.4	25.6
Widows and child(ren)	151	9s 11d	31.1	49.3	64.4	13.4	27.9	23.2
Single women[4]	64	8s 2d	27.6	54.0	45.3	7.5	21.3	48.4
Single men	88	32s 4d	8.5	2.0	12.3	10.5	30.0	86.3

Notes: [1] Includes earnings of all household members.
[2] The number of households whose rent is known is somewhat less than is indicated in column 1: 1,619 married couples, 143 widows with children, 56 single women and 68 single men.
[3] For a definition of 'animal food' see note 5, p. 331.
[4] Includes childless widows.

Sources: 'Report of an investigation into the state of the poorer classes in St George's in the East', Quarterly Journal of the Statistical Society of London, August 1848, pp. 208, 213, 217, reprinted in Richard Wall, Slum Conditions in London and Dublin, Farnborough: Gregg International 1974.

the weekly earnings of the wage-earning population as these can be used, in conjunction with the information on other co-residents and their earnings (if any), to measure the variation in income according to age, gender and family circumstances. The list-maker also distinguished three broad economic statuses: persons who received constant support out of the proceeds of the poor rate, those who relied on wages and those who may be inferred to have been economically secure as no details of their income were deemed necessary. Table 15.2 provides an overview and shows that, as in the London parish of St George in the East, those men who remained unmarried were in a much stronger economic position than the women who had not married. For example, in Corfe Castle more than a quarter of all the unmarried women were on poor relief compared with only 2 per cent of the unmarried men, and fewer unmarried women than unmarried men were economically secure.[8] Widows, too, were more likely to experience poverty than were widowers,[9] while overall slightly more men than women were economically secure and a considerably greater proportion of women than of men were in receipt of poor relief. The economic advantage of marriage to women also seems abundantly clear in that married women were only rarely on poor relief and were more likely to be economically secure than were widows or unmarried women.

It could be argued that the earning patterns of the various marital status groups differ simply as a result of their different age distribution. Table 15.3 shows that independently of age, widows and unmarried women were more likely to be in receipt of poor relief on a permanent basis than were married women. The situation differs as regards the proportion deemed economically secure because after a certain age (mid-40s for the widows and the mid-50s for the unmarried) the proportion of economically secure single and widowed women exceeded the proportion of married women who were economically secure. However, almost certainly this is occasioned not so much by increases in the resources of older non-married women, for which there is very little evidence,[10] as by the marked decline in the proportions of older married women who were economically secure. This negative relationship between age and economic security implies that increasing age not only raised the proportions of the population receiving long-term assistance from the Poor Law, but also initiated for others in the population a social descent from more secure to less secure employments, from a position where dire poverty was unlikely or at least not imminent to a situation where such poverty was a distinct possibility.[11] Admittedly, other factors, either alone or in combination, cannot be entirely discounted on the basis of the present evidence. Among the possibilities that ought to be considered is that a greater number of the better-off had migrated to other communities in old age (or that a great number of poorer inhabitants had moved into Corfe Castle later in their lives). Economic disadvantage in old age could also have encouraged a higher proportion of poorer widows and widowers to remarry, thereby increasing the proportions who were economically

Table 15.2 Income sources of inhabitants of Corfe Castle aged 15+ in 1790 by sex and marital status

Income source	Males				Females			
	Marital status				Marital status			
	Never-married (%)	Widowed (%)	Married (%)	All (%)	Never-married (%)	Widowed (%)	Married (%)	All (%)
Poor relief	2	15	4	5	26	39	4	14
Wage-earning	54	46	53	52	45	26	53	46
Secure	43	39	43	43	29	35	43	40
N (=100%)	46	33	182	261	31	54	182	267

Table 15.3 Income sources of inhabitants of Corfe Castle in 1790 by age, sex and marital status

Age group	Married males				Married females			
	Poor relief (%)	Wage-earning (%)	Secure (%)	N (100%)	Poor relief (%)	Wage-earning (%)	Secure (%)	N (100%)
20–34	0	62	38	47	0	58	42	62
35–44	0	54	46	52	2	44	54	46
45–54	3	46	51	35	8	50	42	36
55–64	4	56	41	27	9	57	35	23
65+	29	38	33	21	13	60	27	15
	Widowed males				Widowed females			
20–34	0	100	0	1	20	60	20	5
35–44	0	60	40	5	57	29	14	7
45–54	25	25	50	4	36	18	46	11
55–64	0	50	50	8	46	18	36	11
65+	27	40	33	15	35	25	40	20
	Single males[1]				Single females[1]			
15–34	0	62	38	29	8	58	33	12
35–44	0	67	33	6	25	75	0	4
45–54	0	33	67	6	43	29	29	7
55–64	25	25	50	4	40	20	40	5
65+	0	0	100	1	33	33	33	3

Note: [1] Single persons living with relatives are excluded.

secure among the widowed but decreasing these proportions among the married population.

It is not surprising that the majority of married women in Corfe Castle, as in St George in the East, appear to have been in a much stronger economic position than were the majority of widowed and single women. In practice, however, any advantage might be undermined if the greater resources of the male-headed household were not shared out equally among all its members. Opinion on this issue is divided. One point of view is represented by the early twentieth-century social reformer, Helen Bosanquet, who stressed that it was the housewife who undertook all the budgeting responsibilities in the poorer households. Another perspective was offered by Eleanor Rathbone, who pointed to the unidentified, but large, proportion of husbands who passed to their wives as little as possible of their earnings.[12] Studies of household budgeting in present-day populations have drawn valuable distinctions between the management and control of household money. The former was likely to be shared or be the wife's responsibility, the latter that of the husband.[13] Fragmentary evidence from rural Ireland in the early nineteenth century indicates that in this very different society major decisions were also made by the husband, decisions which might affect the economy of the household, such as what products the household could afford to consume and what work might be undertaken by the housewife outside the household.[14] Another distinction that needs to be made is that between the management or control of the resources of the household and the purposes to which they were applied, whether by the housewife or her husband. Given that the well-being of so many families depended on the earning capability of the male breadwinner, it is only to be expected that it would be the latter who would receive the largest share and the best of whatever food was available. Numerous such instances can be documented, from both peasant and industrialized cultures, and from many parts of Europe.[15]

AN ECONOMIC MODEL OF INTRA-HOUSEHOLD INEQUALITIES

The present intention, though, is not to search out further documentation to supplement what is already available. Instead, the information provided by the census of Corfe Castle on the wage-earning population will be utilized in order to determine, first, whether a degree of inequality in the distribution of the resources of the household removes the apparent disparity between the income of married and non-married women and, second, to compare the variation over the course of the life cycle in the income available to men and women. The major difficulty is to determine what level of inequality best approaches the (unknown) reality.

For the purposes of estimating the impact of inequalities within the household it was decided to make the assumption that the husband would consume half as much again of the resources of the household as the wife, and that each adult son (aged 15 and over) would consume a quarter as much again.[16] The assumptions are arbitrary and could be varied to give the married woman a greater or lesser proportion of the household income, but they are not unreasonable. For example, although they assume a greater degree of inequality than a variety of commentators in the nineteenth and early twentieth centuries thought was justified on the basis of the dietary needs of men and women, the estimated inequality is lower than was enshrined in wage levels.[17] However, as is clear from a glance at Table 15.4, the degree of inequality between husband and wife would have to be seriously underestimated to compensate fully for the discrepancy in the income of married and non-married women that is evident in the estimates of income presented in the table. According to Table 15.4, if Poor Law payments are excluded, married women had something over twice the income of women who had never married or had been widowed. An entirely different pattern applies to men. Once allowance is made for the costs of their dependants, marriage apparently reduced the income of men by more than half against the income available to a man who had not married, and by almost a third as compared to the income available to a widower. The reason for this was that with males able to earn so much more than females,[18] a woman's income would rise as soon as she was able to supplement her own meagre earnings with an (albeit unequal) share of what a man could earn, whereas marriage and an increased number of dependants only served to depress male income. Nor does the position alter significantly if poor relief payments, principally directed at single and widowed women, are included. A notional amount of 2 shillings per week, added to the budgets of all receiving households, does lessen the differences between the estimated incomes of married, widowed and single women, but still suggests that married women had a standard of living that was between one-quarter and one-third better than that of widows or unmarried women.[19]

A further instructive comparison is that between the income of women over the age of 15 who were still resident in the parental household and the income of younger married women. This information is set out in Figure 15.1 in the form of a cumulative income distribution, in pence per week, for the two groups of women. Only slight differences are apparent between the income of women who were members of households which were in the later stages of development and the women who were members of newly-founded households. This implies that marriage and the creation of a new household independent of that of the parents had little immediate impact on income.[20] A fuller explanation of these findings would require a detailed examination of these households in terms of their size, composition and numbers of males and females present, both adults and children. Nevertheless, it seems very likely that the absence of any major difference in the level of income of younger and older households reflects the fact that the younger households were as yet not overburdened with dependants. In addition, the economic strength of some of the more mature households had been weakened by the

Table 15.4 Median income of wage-earning population of Corfe Castle aged 15 + in 1790

	Males			Females		
	Median income per week (pence)[1]			Median income per week (pence)[1]		
	Wages	Earnings and poor relief[2]	N	Wages	Earnings and poor relief[2]	N
Never-married	108	108	25	15	26	21
Widowed	70	72	20	14	24	14
Married	48	50	104	32	33	104

Notes: [1]For assumptions underlying calculations see text, p. 319.
[2]Estimated on the assumption that the Poor Law authorities provided 24d. in cash or kind to every household receiving assistance.

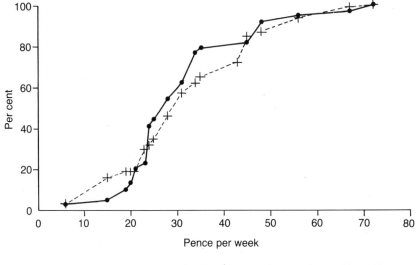

Figure 15.1 Cumulative distribution of the income in pence per week of younger women by family status, Corfe Castle, 1790

Source: Calculated from census of Corfe Castle 1790 in J. Hutchins, *The History and Antiquities of the County of Dorset*, edited by R. Gough and J. Nichols, London: J. Nichols 1796–1815, vol. 1, pp. xc–xciii.

departure of subsidiary earners and the fall in income of the male bread-winner, which the Corfe Castle census suggests was possible after the age of 60, and indeed probable for those who had passed the age of 70.

A broader perspective on the variation in income across the life cycle is provided by Table 15.5, which presents estimates of the median income of all males and females and married males and females in the wage-earning population. In considering the significance of these estimates, the assumptions that underlie them need to be kept in mind. The differences in the income ascribed to men and women are largely an artefact of the assumptions that have been made concerning the way in which income was distributed within the household, for persons who had reached the age of 10 and the age of 15.[21] By contrast, a variation in income with age does reflect the changes that occur in the composition of households as individuals age, and for older men and women the decline in men's earning capabilities after the age of 60. What is particularly interesting, therefore, about these estimates of income is that they identify a marked decline in male income in the late 30s and early 40s in addition to a final descent to lower levels of income in old age. This pattern of alternating periods of prosperity and poverty, it should be stressed, bears a close resemblance to the life cycle of poverty as it was delineated by Seebohm Rowntree for a different population, the working-class population of York at the beginning of the twentieth century.[22] The earlier dip in male earnings also encompasses a period in life, when men were aged between 35 and 40, that Bowley, a leading economist of the early twentieth century, identified as marking the height of privation in the families of married men resident in a number of towns in 1911. According to Bowley, it was when men were nearer to 40 than 35 that they would have had the largest number of dependants.[23] In more than a century, therefore, there would appear to have been no radical shifts in the profile of poverty across the life cycle.

Table 15.5 Median income in pence per week of wage-earning population of Corfe Castle in 1790[1]

Age group	All males	All females	Ratio	Married males	Married females	Ratio
1–4	12	12	100	—	—	—
5–9	14	13	108	—	—	—
10–14	26	20	130	—	—	—
15–19	50	35	143	—	—	—
20–4	65	34	191	68	41	166
25–9	55	25	220	42	28	150
30–4	51	24	212	49	24	204
35–44	45	24	188	38	27	141
45–54	58	28	207	52	35	149
55–64	54	32	169	54	43	126
65+	42	21	200	40	29	138

Note: [1] For assumptions underlying calculations see text, p. 319.

One of the weaknesses of Rowntree's original presentation of the poverty life cycle, that there was no separate representation of male and female experiences of poverty, can, however, now be rectified using the information that has been assembled on the estimated incomes of the inhabitants of Corfe Castle. Table 15.5 indicates, for example, a much steeper decline into poverty in old age for women than for men, no doubt a sign that women were more likely to be widowed and that more serious economic consequences were likely to follow for them when they were widowed. It is also implied by the estimates presented in Table 15.5 that the nadir of poverty for married women came somewhat earlier in life than it did for married men, for those aged 30–4 rather than for those aged 35–44. It is also noticeable that the income of married men exceeded that of married women to a considerably greater extent prior to the age of 35 than was the case at older ages. Since there is no evidence that wages were higher when men were in their 20s or 30s, it would appear that married men under the age of 35 must have had fewer dependants than had married women of the same age. Given that men married later, it is indeed to be expected that they would have somewhat fewer dependants earlier in their lives and more dependants in the later stages than would married women. Such indeed is the case in Corfe Castle.[24]

Another advantage of the data on Corfe Castle is that they make it possible to correct another of Rowntree's omissions and explore the variation in income levels within each age group. This issue is considered in Figure 15.2 which displays the inter-quartile range as well as the median income of the male and female populations, on the basis of the same assumptions as were used to create the earlier estimates of income. If these assumptions are justified, then the relative poverty of women is indeed striking. Throughout most of their adulthood, only a quarter of women had incomes that came near to matching those of the poorest 25 per cent of men.[25] It is also suggested that the income of women is much less likely to vary with age than is the income of men, which peaks twice, first when men were in their 20s and then when they were in their late 40s and early 50s. A minority of men in the former group, many of whom were clearly without any dependants, can be identified as having particularly high incomes. By contrast, much more modest income peaks are all that are evident for the wealthiest 25 per cent of women and for women with average incomes, and almost none at all for the poorest 25 per cent of women.

As a final commentary on all these estimates it is appropriate to reflect on the extent to which they might be dependent on the simplifying assumptions

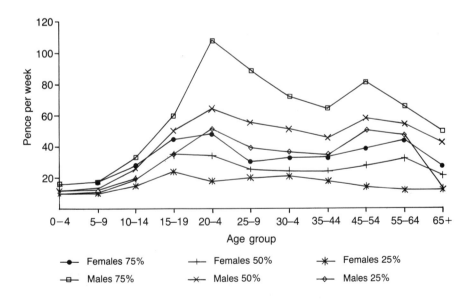

Figure 15.2 Income per head of 25, 50 and 75 per cent of males and females in Corfe Castle, 1790

Source: Calculated from census of Corfe Castle 1790 in J. Hutchins, *The History and Antiquities of the County of Dorset*, edited by R. Gough and J. Nichols, London: J. Nichols 1796–1815, vol. 1, pp. xc–xciii.

that had to be made in order to produce them, and on particular features of the social structure of the test population of Corfe Castle. No doubt the different incomes of men and women were affected by the extreme differential that existed between male and female earnings in this particular population, with men seldom earning less than 7 shillings per week and women only between 1 shilling and 2 shillings and 6 pence. In this context, the assumption introduced above that the male household head would consume 50 per cent more of the household resources than would his wife appears relatively modest. In a population where the earnings differential was somewhat less than in Corfe Castle or when husbands were less selfish than has been assumed, women would obviously have been better off than is implied by the above set of estimates. The apparent differences in the income of the husband and wife could also be reduced if certain deductions had been made from the income of the household, for rent and furnishing, for example, prior to estimating how the income might have been divided among the members of the household. On the other hand, as is proven by the *Report of the Statistical Society of London* into the condition of the working-class population of St George in the East in 1848,[26] it ought not to be assumed that rent would absorb a fixed proportion of household expenditure. If, following the hints in this survey, a greater proportion of income was allocated to rent by the poorest inhabitants of Corfe Castle, then a disparity in the disposable income of richer and poorer inhabitants, in particular between the incomes of widows or single women and the rest, would have been higher rather than lower than indicated above.

There are other ways, too, in which the estimates will need modification before they can be applied to another population, especially outside England. The nature of family life in Corfe Castle involved the majority of children leaving the parental household to set up an independent household when they married, if they had not already left to take up the position of servant in the household of an employer. In Corfe Castle, service for girls seems to have been possible from the age of 16 and for boys even a few years earlier.[27] Sending children into service relieved the parents of the cost of their maintenance, and servants might even remit a proportion of their earnings to the parents.[28].

The earlier, therefore, the departure of children from the parental home, the greater the economic benefit to both parents and children. This is to assume, of course, that the gains to the parental household resulting from the departure of children into service were not cancelled out by earnings lost because they no longer contributed all, or almost all, of their earnings to the communal 'pot'. It is conceivable that contributions were required from children who continued to live in the parental home, but in the event that they retained the bulk of their earnings for their own personal consumption it follows that it was to the advantage of the parents to encourage the early departure of their children. Prolonged co-residence of parents and adult children was only of economic benefit to the parents if children worked for the general benefit of the household. In such cases parents might be pre-pared to meet the additional costs of supporting adolescents in return for their continued co-operation as adults when the parents themselves would be old and less productive. The stem family system, where one son remains within the parental household, marries and eventually succeeds his father as household head, is a case in point.[29] Rowntree's implicit assumption, for York at the turn of the twentieth century, was that children did pass their earnings to their parents. Had they not done so, there would have been no peak in parental income in later middle age. The same assumption also underlies the estimates produced above of the income of the inhabitants of Corfe Castle in 1790. However, it is known that in some populations, older co-resident children, and in particular sons, paid their parents no more than they might have obtained from giving house room to a boarder or lodger.[30] If younger males were regularly allowed such latitude, the pattern of inequality within the household and family would differ from that suggested by the estimates of income already presented. In particular, there would be a greater differential in the incomes of males and females in early adulthood and a less deep descent into poverty in old age for both sexes.

A more general point is that measurement of income inequalities in the way that has been attempted here may also help to explain why in other populations large numbers of women from the lower classes chose not to marry. The wider the differential between male and female earnings, the greater were the economic pressures on women to marry. Conversely, higher earnings for women or the uncertainty of regular employment for men, reduced the pressure.[31]

THE CONTRIBUTION OF MARRIED WOMEN TO THE FAMILY ECONOMY

At this point it is appropriate to pause in order to assess, briefly, the role of married women within the family economy, using for this purpose not only the census of Corfe Castle, but, for a broader perspective, the budgets collected from many different parts of Europe by Frederic Le Play and his followers during the middle and later decades of the nineteenth century.[32] These budgets indicate the time spent by married women, measured in days per year, on both paid and unpaid work, and for their families as well as for others, and can be used to challenge two of the prevailing images of the nature of women's work in the past. The first is that following their marriage, women in the past would withdraw from the labour market to devote themselves exclusively to housework and child-rearing; the second, that work tasks performed for the family in and around the household were very likely to involve husband and wife working alongside each other.

In Corfe Castle in 1790 withdrawal of women from the labour market on marriage would appear to have been fairly general. Only 8 per cent of married women under the age of 40 were employed as compared with three-quarters of unmarried daughters over the age of 15 still living with their parents.[33] To leave the labour market was also the expectation of the woman who made all the wrong choices in Mary Leadbeater's fictitious account of the life histories of two Irish peasant women.[34] The potential 'lazy wife' of her tale was soon, however, disabused[35] and, elsewhere, the reality was certainly different. In the Bedfordshire parish of Cardington, for example, where many women were employed as lacemakers, women regularly continued to work after marriage,[36] while more generally Frederic Le Play's collection of family budgets indicates that four out of five married women from labouring, peasant and artisan milieux were employed by individuals who were not members of their families for at least a few days every year.[37]

The average experience, according to these budgets, was for a married woman to devote eighty-three days to work outside the family economy. In addition, she would spend a further eighty-seven days on average on a range of tasks for the family, tasks which might earn a payment in cash or kind or simply save the family the expense of buying in the service from elsewhere. Housework and the care of children necessitated an average of 141 days of work and the working year of the married woman was approximately the same length as the working year of the married man (314 days for the former and 317 for the latter).[38] There is, however, evidence of considerable variation in the work patterns of married women, associated in particular with the number and ages of their children. The information on the number of children which is set out in Table 15.6 indicates that the larger families required a greater investment of time in housework and child-rearing on the part of the housewife. This is precisely what one would have anticipated[39] and yields some credence to the data marshalled by Le Play. In addition, it would appear that a larger number of resident children may also have involved a married woman devoting more work time to the broader family economy. On the other hand, there is no sign that the number of children in the family influenced either the amount of work she undertook outside the family economy or the total number of days worked.

The research of Le Play and his colleagues can also provide some valuable detail on the division of labour within the household. Martine Segalen, using a variety of ethnographic evidence, principally collected after the end of the Second World War, in conjunction with the accounts of folklorists and an interpretation of proverbs in use among French peasants, has concluded that there was in practice an extensive intermingling of the work tasks of men and women. Certain types of work were reserved for women, but other work could be carried out, depending on the region, either by men or by women, while a third type of work, predominantly allocated to males, involved either intermittently or regularly the use of some female labour.[40] Le Play and his colleagues, however, were interviewing families in the middle of the nineteenth century, in both urban and rural areas, and their accounts were detailed, if perhaps not always to be trusted in regard to the contribution to the family economy from children under the age of 10.

Table 15.6 Work patterns of married women by number of children in family in mid-nineteenth-century Europe

		Median days worked per year			
Number of children	Families	Total	Housework and child-rearing	Family economy	Employment outside the family economy
1	4	261	115	52	44
2	7	326	113	65	100
3	7	326	120	96	40
4	10	313	138	78	63
5 +	8	324	186	92	40

Source: F. Le Play, *Les ouvriers Européens*, Tours: Alfred Mame et fils 1877–9, budgets of thirty-six families.

It is useful therefore to see how Le Play's findings compare with those of Segalen derived from very different sources, and, to some extent at least, from a different epoch.

Of the thirty-six married women whose work patterns were investigated by Le Play, twenty-one were solely responsible for housework, child-rearing and the repair and laundering of the family's clothes and linen. Fifteen women therefore had some assistance, with this assistance coming primarily from daughters who had reached the age of 13. Any other adult females present in the household (a mother, daughter-in-law or sister-in-law, for example) might also share in the work. Only rarely were any males reported as undertaking housework. All were sons, and in three out of the four families where they were involved there was either no daughter (when a son of 5 assisted with the housework) or the daughters were aged 10 or younger (sons aged 12–14 assisted). There is confirmation, therefore, of Segalen's description of the 'feminized' house based on the evidence of proverbs.[41] Unfortunately, there is insufficient detail in the budgets to enable one to determine whether, as Segalen claimed, cooking was the responsibility, indeed the privilege, of the wife of the household head.[42] Quite clearly the extent to which a married woman might have some help with housework in general would alter over the course of the family life cycle as her daughters reached an age where they could be a help but then left for service or marriage. The nature of the family system may also have had some effect as female relatives, if adult, generally seem to have helped with the housework and child-rearing, although without noticeably reducing the amount of time which the wife of the household head herself had to spend on such activities.

The intermingling of the work of men and women to which Segalen refers presumably took place within the broader family economy. There is very little sign of this, however, in the family budgets collected by Le Play. The only tasks which it was at all common for a husband and wife to share were gardening and the cultivation of potatoes, tasks which, ironically, Segalen reports respectively as 'highly feminized' and as shared work which the folklorists had ignored.[43] The activity of the husband within the family economy was by and large limited to the repair of the house and furniture and the provision of the household with both food and fuel. The responsibilities of the wife, on the other hand, were for the preparation of food, housework and the care of the children, the making, repair and laundering of the family's clothes and linen, the raising of poultry and gleaning. Where her tasks were shared it was more often with her daughters (twenty-six instances of task sharing) than with her sons (fourteen instances) or her husband (fourteen instances). The majority of her work activities, however (sixty-nine distinct tasks, 56 per cent of the total), were undertaken alone. Husbands, not surprisingly, were less active in the family economy. Nevertheless, it is possible to identify fifty-three separate tasks undertaken by husbands within the broader family economy. Just over half of these were also undertaken alone, a quarter in conjunction with wives and a little over a fifth with either sons or daughters (in equal proportions).

On the evidence of the budgets collected by Le Play and his associates it is therefore possible to establish that husbands and wives mostly worked separately even when they were working for what could be termed a joint enterprise, the family economy. It is also clear that many wives of artisans, peasants and labourers in the middle and late nineteenth century were also employed outside the family economy for at least part of the year. Both images of women's pattern of work in the past, that of participation in a closely integrated family work group, or of withdrawal from the labour market on marriage, can be refuted.

EXPENDITURE ON WOMEN'S AND MEN'S CLOTHING

This degree of segregation in male and female roles made women indispensable to the families and households to which they belonged. It did not, however, necessarily mean that women would receive an equal share of all available resources, or even of the product of their own work. The evidence cited by Shorter and discussed above[44] is clear on this point, but being essentially qualitative in nature does not enable one to determine whether at a particular time or in a particular population the degree of inequality in the allocation of resources was greater or less than was occurring elsewhere. For this purpose a more systematic measure is required, and among the many items of expenditure in the budgets documented by Le Play and his associates, there is one item which does provide at least a crude indication of how women were valued by their families: the amount expended on their clothing relative to the amount expended on men's clothing. As Table 15.7 makes clear, the families whose budgets were detailed by Le Play and others in the middle and latter part of the nineteenth century spent between 12 and

15 per cent more on the clothes of the head of the household than they did on those of his wife.[45] Comparisons with other surveys of a later date, covering a variety of English populations, reveal that this pattern was by no means unusual.

Table 15.7 Relative expenditure on the clothing of adult males and females in various European populations, 1842–1991

Area	Social characteristics	Date	Number of budgets	Relative expenditure[1]
Europe	Peasants, artisans and labourers	1842–53	24	112
Europe	Peasants, artisans and labourers	1856–81	37	115
York	Working class	1899	28	96
UK	Agricultural workers	1937–8	1,491	164
UK	Village households	1937–8	366	127
UK	Industrial workers	1937–8	8,903	115
UK	Recipients of clothing coupons	1941–2	4,739	97
UK	All households	1953–4	11,638	80
UK	All households	1961	3,486	77
UK	All households	1971	7,239	67
UK	All households	1981	7,525	61
UK	All households	1991	7,056	58

Notes: [1] Ratio of amounts expended on clothing of adult males and females over the course of a year (sixteen weeks in the case of the 1937–8 surveys). Ratios for Europe between 1842 and 1881 are based on the value of the clothing at the time of the investigation, but examination of the annual expenditure of thirty-one of the families investigated between 1856 and 1881 produces a similar ratio (113).

Sources: Europe 1842–53 – Frederic Le Play, *Les ouvriers Européens*, Paris: Imprimerie impériale 1855; Europe 1856–81 – *Ouvriers des deux mondes*, 1st series, 1–5, 1857–85, Société internationale des études pratiques d'économie sociale; York 1899 – B. Seebohn Rowntree, *Poverty: A Study of Town Life*, London: Nelson edition n.d., Appendix C, pp. 455–9; UK 1937–8 – Ministry of Labour, *Weekly Expenditure of Working Class Households in the United Kingdom in 1937–8*, London: HMSO 1941, p. 305, 1949, pp. 39, 52; UK 1941–2 – 'An enquiry into the clothing needs of 4,700 workers in 15 occupational groups made in March and April 1942 for the Board of Trade', *Wartime Social Survey*, new series, 14, 1942, p. 22; UK 1953–4 – Ministry of Labour and National Service, *Report of an Enquiry into Household Expenditure 1953–4*, London: HMSO 1957; UK 1961–91 – Ministry of Labour (later Department of Employment and then Central Statistical Office), *Family Expenditure Survey*, London: HMSO 1961, p. 8, 1971, pp. 14–15, 1981, pp. 15–16, 1991, pp. 18–19.

Rural populations in particular, even in the late 1930s, spent considerably greater sums on men's clothes than on those of women – in one instance almost two-thirds as much. Urban and industrial populations, on the other hand, appear to have spent slightly more on women's clothing.[46] However, it is evident that expenditure on women's clothing has only come to exceed expenditure on men's clothing to any significant extent during the course of the last few decades. In 1953–4, for example, families in the United Kingdom were still spending £80 on male clothing for every £100 spent on female clothing. By 1991 this had shrunk to £58.[47]

The greater physical nature of much of the work undertaken by men in past societies could explain the greater expenditure on their clothing. But the data collected by Le Play show that, in fact, greater sums were expended on not just men's work clothes but also on their 'best' clothes, worn only on Sundays and for holidays and festivals.[48] Nor can a change in the amount of physical effort required for men's work account for the fact that the ratios between the expenditure on men's and women's clothing move decisively in favour of women only after 1961. So recent an alteration in the balance of expenditure on clothing probably is a result of the growing power of women as consumers in a consumer economy reconstructed to take account of women's greater spending power. Such reasoning, however, also raises the issues as to whether improvements in the standard of living simply provided the necessary preconditions which allowed individuals within the family more latitude to spend on non-essentials, or whether economic growth itself could directly trigger the change in expenditure patterns. In this connection it is worth noting that neither urbanization nor industrialization, nor indeed improvements in the standard of living in the early part of the twentieth century, provoked a comparable response. Of itself this does not exclude the existence of an economic threshold above which expenditure patterns would change. More likely, however, is that the change in expenditure patterns is associated with the wide-ranging shift towards a greater stress on the rights of individuals, a cultural change of the 1960s identified by some as a second demographic transition.[49]

CONCLUSION

A variety of issues have been considered in this chapter: differences in the standard of living of single, widowed and married women, the impact of inequalities in the distribution of resources within the male-headed household on the standard of living of married women, the contribution of married women to the economic viability of their families and the significance of changes in the relative sums expended on the clothing of adult men and women. In the process a number of stereotypes have been rejected, to establish, for example, that women in the European past were employed regularly outside the immediate family economy, and that their tasks within the family economy were often performed alone or, at best, with the help of their daughters. It has also been possible to show that it is only very recently, in fact since the 1960s, that a greater proportion of the family budget has been devoted to the clothing of women than of men.

The methodology developed to explore the effect of inequalities within the household is clearly capable of further refinement and should be tested more fully on other populations where households are structured in a different way and the degree of inequalities in the earnings of men and women perhaps less sharply marked than was the case in Corfe Castle in 1790. A number of conclusions can, however, be advanced that are likely to have general applicability. The first is that women will encounter poverty at a different point in their life cycle than will men, reflecting the fact that they will be younger on average on marriage and more likely to be widowed. Widowhood, in conjunction with the greater earning capacity of men, ensured that women would experience a much sharper descent into extreme poverty in middle and old age. Another finding of general import is that the disparity in the incomes of married and non-married women was too large to be removed either by charitable payments from the community, whether through the Poor Law or by other means. Nor would they be affected by the presence of inequalities in the allocation of resources in male-headed households, unless the latter were considerably in excess of the 50 per cent additional allocations to the breadwinner, as was assumed above for the purposes of presenting estimates of the income distribution within households. Nevertheless, judged from the expenditure patterns on adult clothing, it is only in the last three decades of the twentieth century that women have had the opportunity to supplant men as the primary purchasers of products for personal consumption.

NOTES

1 In addition to the above quotation see also Eleanor F. Rathbone, *The Disinherited Family. A Plea for Direct Provision for the Costs of Child Maintenance Through Family Allowances*, London: George Allen & Unwin 1924; 3rd edn 1927, pp. 52–3.

2 Frederic Le Play, *Les ouvriers Européens*, 1st edn, Paris: Imprimerie impériale 1855; 2nd edn, Tours: Alfred Mame et fils 1877–9; and the journal *Les ouvriers des deux mondes*, 1st series, 1–5, 1857–85; 2nd series, 1–5, 1885–99, Société internationale des études pratiques d'économie sociale. For other surveys see below note 3 and the notes to Table 15.7.

3 'Report to the council of the Statistical Society of London from the committee of its fellows appointed to make an investigation into the state of the poorer classes in St George in the East', *Quarterly Journal of the Statistical Society of London*, August 1848, p. 193; reprinted in Richard Wall (ed.), *Slum Conditions in London and Dublin*, Farnborough: Gregg International 1974.

4 Married couple households contain an average 4.2 persons, households of widows and children 3.4 persons, households of single women and childless widows 1.2 persons and households of single men 1.4 persons.

5 The term used in the report of the Statistical Society is 'animal food'. No definition is provided but it seems likely that some dairy products such as eggs and cheese were included as well as meat, but probably not milk and butter. Both the latter appear in many of the budgets of the poor collected by Frederick Morton Eden at the end of the eighteenth century: see Frederick Morton Eden, *The State of the Poor*, vols 1–3, London: J. Davis 1797, *passim*.

6 Female-headed households may also have consumed less food as well as restricting themselves to a narrow range of products, but on this the survey is silent.

7 The census was first published in J. Hutchins, *The History and Antiquities of the County of Dorset*, edited by R. Gough and J. Nichols, London: J. Nichols 1796–1815, vol. 1, pp. xc–xciii. There is a photocopy of the census in the library of the ESRC Cambridge Group.

8 For the purposes of this comparison all children still resident in the household of their parents have been excluded, even if over the age of 15.

9 It may be noted, however, that just as widows were likely to be poorer than married women so too were widowers in general less economically secure than were married men. On the other hand, comparisons of widowers and married men of the same age, as in Table 15.3, remove many of the differences.

10 Only in the case of widows is there any sign of a rise with age in the proportion deemed economically secure and as there were very few younger widows, this particular association between age and economic standing cannot be held to be established with any degree of certainty.

11 The same association applies in the case of married men, although commencing for men at a slightly later age.

12 Compare for example Helen Bosanquet, *The Family*, London: Macmillan 1906, p. 199; cited in Elizabeth Roberts, *Woman's Place. An Oral History of Working Class Women*, Oxford: Basil Blackwell 1984, p. 111; with Rathbone, *The Disinherited Family*, p. 88. On Helen Bosanquet see also C.S. Nicholls (ed.), *Dictionary of National Biography. Missing Persons*, Oxford: Oxford University Press 1993.

13 See Jan Pahl, *Money and Marriage*, Basingstoke: Macmillan 1989, esp. pp. 78, 90.

14 Mary Leadbeater, *Dialogues Among the Irish Peasantry*, Dublin: J. and J. Carrick for John Cumming and William Watson 1812, pp. 48–50, 54–5, 58–9.

15 Shorter, for example, cites cases from Norway, England and Germany in the nineteenth or early twentieth centuries. See Edward Shorter, *A History of Women's Bodies*, Harmondsworth: Penguin 1984, pp. 21–2.

16 The full set of weights were as follows. All women over the age of 15, regardless of their relationship to the head of the household, were assumed to represent one consumption unit, male household heads 1.5 units, other adult males aged over 15, 1.25 units, children aged 10–14, 0.75 units and children aged 1–9, 0.5 units. Children under the age of 1 were ignored on the assumption that there was very little direct expenditure on children in their first year of life. These estimates could, of course, be made more flexible by varying the children's share according to age, gender and the level of their earnings. Lodgers were assessed separately and the rent they paid for their accommodation (not documented in the census) was ignored when estimating the budget of the principal household.

17 See Chapter 1 in this volume. It was argued that men required 25 per cent more food than women. Food, of course, constituted the major item in the household budget. The same commentators also attempted to estimate the caloric requirements of children at different ages. For wage differentials between men and women in Corfe Castle, see note 18.

18 All but one of the adult male wage-earners in Corfe Castle in 1790 earned at least 7 shillings a week and some earned as much as 16 shillings a week as clay-cutters. On the other hand, women, whatever their age, were limited to between 1 shilling and 1 shilling and 9 pence a week from knitting and up to 2 shillings and 6 pence a week if they spun flax.

19 One of the weaknesses of the Corfe Castle census is its failure to specify the actual amounts paid out in poor relief. The estimate of 2 shillings per week is advanced on the grounds that this represents the average payment made in the two Dorset parishes, Blandford and Durweston, as documented in Eden, *The State of the Poor*, vol. 2, pp. 146–51. In other parts of the country, payments could either be higher or considerably lower. See the reports on the parish of Colchester All Saints where a few adult poor received weekly sums of between 2 shillings and 5 shillings, and Bradford in Wiltshire, where payments of 1 shilling per week were commonplace, ibid.: p. 178; vol. 3, pp. 785–9.

20 The situation of women who went into service and then married may have been different. The census of Corfe Castle does not specify the wages of servants, but servants could and did put by some savings to cover the cost of marriage and a new home while in many cases enjoying a better diet than was possible at any other time in their lives. For specific examples, on England see Elizabeth Gaskell, *Cranford*, London: Odham edn n.d., pp. 156–7; and on Ireland Leadbeater, *Dialogues Among the Irish Peasantry*, pp. 19, 28, 46, 55; and for an overview of the problems and opportunities servants in England and France were likely to encounter in the early nineteenth century, Theresa McBride, *The Domestic Revolution*, London: Croom Helm 1976, esp. pp. 51, 56.

21 See above note 16.

22 B. Seebohm Rowntree, *Poverty. A Study of Town Life*, London: Nelson edn n.d., p. 171.

23 A.L. Bowley, 'Earners and dependants in English towns in 1911', *Economica*, 1921, pp. 109–10. The 'towns' were Bethnal Green, Shoreditch, Stepney, Bristol, Newcastle upon Tyne, Leeds, Bradford and Northampton.

24 For the purposes of this exercise, dependants were defined as children aged 1–14. There were 1.6 dependent children for every married man under the age of 35, but as many as 2.1 for every married woman under 35. Within the next age group (35–44) the position was reversed with married men having 3.5 dependants and married women only 2.9.

25 Compare the income distribution of the top 75 per cent of the female population with the bottom 25 per cent of the male population in Figure 15.2, p. 323.

26 See Table 15.1, p. 314.

27 This observation is based on the fact that there were only two girls under the age of 16 listed as servants in the census of Corfe Castle, whereas there were eight male servants under 16, one of them as young as 11.

28 Evidence on this point is scarce. For instances of servants who did and others who did not remit wages see Leadbeater, *Dialogues Among the Irish Peasantry*, p. 19. A more systematic inquiry into this issue by Charles Booth at the end of the nineteenth century was no more conclusive: see Charles Booth, *The Aged Poor in England and Wales*, London: Macmillan 1894 (reprinted New York: Garland 1980), p. 315.

29 The impact of the dependency burden on the viability of the stem family and patriarchal household (two or more married sons co-residing with their parents), and on the life course of individuals who passed through such households, has yet to be assessed in any detail. However, it is already clear that the more complex households did not altogether escape the problems of too many dependants: see Osamu Saito, 'Marriage, family labour and the stem family household: Traditional Japan in comparative perspective', in Richard Wall and Osamu Saito (eds), *The Economic and Social Aspects of the Family Life Cycle: Europe and Japan Traditional and Modern*, Cambridge: Cambridge University Press forthcoming 1995.

30 As, for example, in the working-class populations of New York at the beginning of the twentieth century: see Louise Bollard Moore, *Wage Earners' Budgets. A Study of the Standards and Cost of Living in New York City*, New York 1907, p. 87.

31 As indeed has been argued by Margareta Matovic to explain the frequency of consensual unions in nineteenth-century Stockholm: see Margareta Matovic, 'The Stockholm marriage: Extra legal family formation in Stockholm, 1860– 1890', *Continuity and Change*, 1:3, 1986, pp. 411–12. The proportions of men and women in a variety of European urban and rural populations who were still unmarried when they reached their 50s are set out in Richard Wall, 'European family and household systems', in Société Belge de Démographie Academia (ed.),

Historiens et populations. Liber Amicorum Etienne Hélin, Louvain-la-Neuve: Academia 1991, pp. 634–50.

32 These budgets despite or perhaps because of their detail have been unjustly neglected by historians. The budgets selected on the present occasion are those with the requisite detail in Le Play, *Les ouvriers Européens*, 2nd edn. Non-European families, together with those in Russia, have been excluded. For some of the interpretative problems that can arise in attempting to use these budgets see Richard Wall, 'The contribution of married women to the family economy under different family systems: Some examples from the mid-nineteenth century from the work of Frederic Le Play', unpublished paper presented to session 19 of IUSSP xxii General Conference, Montreal 1993.

33 See Osamu Saito, 'Who worked when. Life time profiles of labour force participation in Cardington and Corfe Castle in the late eighteenth and mid-nineteenth centuries', *Local Population Studies*, 22, spring 1979, pp. 22–3.

34 Leadbeater, *Dialogues Among the Irish Peasantry*, p. 51.

35 ibid.: p. 55.

36 Saito, 'Who worked when', p. 23, shows that 82 per cent of married women aged under 40 were employed in Cardington in 1782, representing almost no change in the percentage of daughters over 15 employed while still resident with their parents. Only in later life did the employment rate fall, for example, to 51 per cent for married women aged 40–59.

37 Inferred from Figure 3 of Wall 'Contribution of married women to the family economy'.

38 The figures given in the text and in Table 15.6 represent the mean amount of time devoted to each task. The median experience was 120 days on housework and child-rearing, eighty days on the broader family economy and sixty-five on work outside the family economy.

39 For the United States in the late twentieth century the presence of children, particularly young children, also increases the time spent on housework: see K. Warner Schaie and Sherry L. Willis, *Adult Development and Aging*, 2nd edn, Boston, Mass. and Toronto, p. 55, citing J. Bestion, 'Measuring household production for the GNP', *Family Economic Review*, 3, pp. 16–25.

40 Martine Segalen, *Love and Power in the Peasant Family. Rural France in the Nineteenth Century*, Oxford: Basil Blackwell 1983, pp. 78–111, esp. p. 82.

41 ibid.: p. 113.

42 ibid.: p. 88.

43 ibid.: pp. 93, 99. Leadbeater also identified gardening as a shared task among the peasantry: Leadbeater, *Dialogues Among the Irish Peasantry*, pp. 55–74.

44 See above note 15.

45 On this occasion sixty-one budgets have been analysed from Le Play, *Les ouvriers Européens*, 1st edn; and *Les ouvriers des deux mondes*, 1st series, 1–5, 1857–85.

46 Interpretation is made a little more difficult because those families who in 1937–8 recorded their expenditure over a full year spent relatively more on women's clothing: ratios of 122 as opposed to 164 for agricultural workers, 102 against 127 for village households and 89 as opposed to 115 for industrial workers. Budgets maintained for a full year were believed at the time to be more reliable, as they were less likely to include expenditure incurred before the start of the survey period, but for the purposes of calculating the ratio of expenditure on male and female clothing, preference has been given in Table 15.7 to the larger number of budgets which were maintained for sixteen weeks. See Ministry of Labour, *Weekly Expenditure of Working Class Households in the United Kingdom in 1937–8*, London: HMSO 1941, p. 305.

47 Alternative comparisons can be provided based on the expenditure patterns of

the median income group between 1961 and 1991 and of households of one male and one female adult and two children between 1961 and 1981. For these sub-populations the ratios in most years are close to those presented for all households in Table 15.7.

48 An analysis of the budgets of forty European families as presented by Le Play in *Les ouvriers Européens*, 1st edn; and *Les ouvriers des deux mondes*, indicates that for every 100 francs spent on the best clothes for women 109 francs was spent on those of men. Cf. the ratio of expenditure on all clothes in Table 15.7.

49 Dirk van de Kaa, 'Europe's second demographic transition', *Population Bulletin*, 42:1, March 1987. An important factor not taken into account in the argument developed in the text is the degree to which the price of women's clothing may have changed relative to the price of men's clothing or to other items of expenditure, essential or non-essential. These issues are complex and cannot be pursued further in the present chapter.

Index

166–8, 174–5, 185, 187–9, 197, 200–3, 205, 259, 263, 301–2, 303, 312, 315–17, 319–25; property owning 198, 233–5; refused admission to homes for elderly 25n, 202; social networks 15, 301; in workhouse 302, 305
Worcester 148
Wordsley 220
workers: agricultural 329; industrial 329; skilled 162–3, 164; unskilled

(*see also* labourers) 162–3, 199
workhouses 284, 285, 287, 289n, 290n, 299, 302, 304, 305, 309n
working class (*see also* labourers; framework knitting; mining) 5, 205, 221n, 248, 269, 271, 272, 290n, 313–14, 324, 329, 333n
Wycliffe, J. 143

York 2, 4, 7–8, 9, 34–5, 269, 322, 325